WITHDRAWN

44·4

Northern Ireland: the Orange State

Michael Farrell **Northern Ireland:**

the Orange State

Pluto Press

First published 1976
by Pluto Press Limited
Unit 10 Spencer Court, 7 Chalcot Road,
London NW1 8LH
Second Impression May 1976
Copyright © Pluto Press 1976
ISBN 0 902818 87 2

Maps by Ruth Tarling
Designed by Richard Hollis, GrR
Printed in Great Britain
by Unwin Brothers Limited
The Gresham Press, Old Woking, Surrey
A member of the Staples Printing Group

Contents

DA
990
.U46
F33

Preface / 11

Introduction / 13

1. **A Bloody Beginning: 1918–21** / 21
2. **Siege or Pogrom: 1921–24** / 39
3. **Consolidation** / 66
4. **A Protestant State** / 81
5. **The Opposition Enters . . . and Leaves: 1925–32** / 98
6. **The Violent Thirties** / 121
7. **The War Years: 1939–45** / 150
8. **The Anti-Partition League: 1945–51** / 177
9. **The Fifties Campaign** / 202
10. **The Rise and Fall of Terence O'Neill: 1960–69** / 227
11. **The Drift to Disaster: 1969–71** / 257
12. **The Day of Reckoning: 1971–75** / 285

Postscript: June 1975 / 322
Conclusions / 325
Individuals / 336
Organisations / 350
References / 366
Bibliography / 385
Index / 396

Maps:
Ireland / vii
Northern Ireland / vii
Belfast / viii
Derry City / ix
Derry March / ix

71788

Map 1:
Ireland, showing the six-county state of Northern Ireland, plus Cavan, Monaghan and Donegal, once part of the nine-county Province of Ulster

Map 2:
Northern Ireland, showing the predominantly Catholic areas of the six counties.
Over 55 per cent Catholic in shaded areas.
Note: within predominantly Catholic or Protestant areas there are many towns and districts of opposite complexion.

vii

Number and percentage of Catholics and Protestants in the six counties, Belfast and Derry City

| | 1911 | | | | 1961 | | | |
| | Protestant | | Catholic | | Protestant | | Catholic | |
	No.	%	No.	%	No.	%	No.	%
Belfast	293,704	75.9	93,243	24.1	301,520	72.5	114,336	27.5
Co.Antrim	154,113	79.5	39,751	20.5	206,976	75.6	66,929	24.4
Co.Armagh	65,765	54.7	54,526	45.3	61,977	52.7	55,617	47.3
Derry City	17,857	43.8	22,923	56.2	17,689	32.9	36,073	67.1
Derry County	58,367	58.5	41,478	41.5	64,027	57.4	47,509	42.6
Co.Down	139,818	68.4	64,485	31.6	190,676	71.4	76,263	28.6
Co.Fermanagh	27,096	43.8	34,740	56.2	24,109	46.8	27,422	53.2
Co.Tyrone	63,650	44.6	79,015	55.4	60,521	45.2	73,398	54.8

Sources: *Census of Ireland*, 1911, Vol. 3, *Ulster*, Cd. 6051–I, HMSO, London 1912, and General Register Office, *Northern Ireland, Census of Population* 1961, County volumes, Tables XVI, HMSO, Belfast 1964.

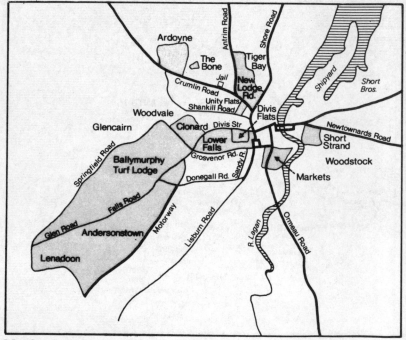

Map 3:

Belfast, showing Catholic ghettos and hard-line Protestant districts.

Over 70 per cent Catholic in shaded area.

Over 70 per cent Protestant: Donegall Road, Glencairn, Newtownards Road, Sandy Row, Shankill Road, Tiger Bay, Woodstock Road, Woodvale.

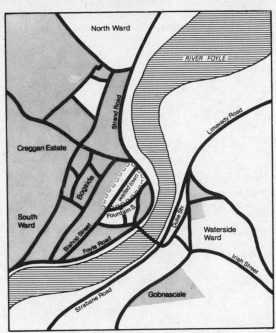

Map 4:
Derry City, showing Catholic and Protestant areas. Over 70 per cent Catholic in shaded area. Predominantly Protestant: the walled town, Fountain Street area and the Waterside.

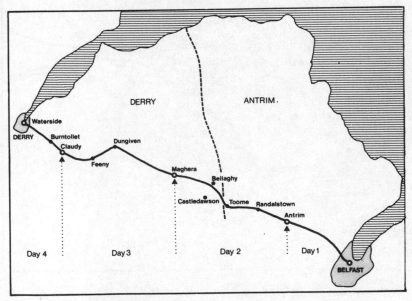

Map 5:
Route of Peoples Democracy march to Derry, 1–4 January 1969

Preface

The struggle in Ireland has produced a flood of books in the last few years, but almost all of them have focussed on events since 1968 with only the briefest glance at the origins of the conflict. There has been no attempt to record the history of the Northern Ireland state since its inception. The result has been great confusion and many failures of understanding in the thinking even of the socialist movement in Ireland itself. Most commentators have failed to grasp the extent of British government involvement in the establishment and underpinning of the Northern state; the degree of repression and violence maintained by that state; and the extent to which the Unionist Party and the state had become one. They have not given proper weight to the tradition of extreme para-military groups on the fringe of the Unionist Party, and their use – in tacit collaboration with the state forces – to crush any threat to the regime.

Most confusion of all has arisen over the relations between Protestant and Catholic workers in Northern Ireland, and the utter failure of the Labour movement there – even in so heavily industrialised a city as Belfast. This failure can only be understood against the background of religious discrimination in employment which divided the working-class, giving the Protestants a small but real advantage, and creating a Protestant 'aristocracy of labour', particularly in the Belfast engineering industry. Further, to put in proper perspective the recent emergence of 'working-class' Loyalist organisations such as the UDA and UVF, requires a full appreciation of the power of the Orange ideology, which was originally used by the Unionists to establish their own control over the Protestant population, and has now assumed a virulent life of its own.

The violence and determination of the revolt by the Nationalist/Catholic minority in the North, and the depth of their alienation from the Northern state, have surprised many who were unaware of the repeated rejection of all Catholic efforts at constitutional reform over the years, and the total frustration which this experience produced. In short, the extreme gravity of the current crisis in the North, and the impossibility of any lasting solution while the Northern state persists, can be fully evident only to those who view the current situation against the detailed background of fifty-four years of Orange rule.

This book attempts to fill the gap in the literature on Northern Ireland, by telling the story of the establishment of the Northern state and its subsequent history up to 1975. It is an attempt to supply a historical and political perspective to the current struggle which should remove much of the misunderstanding and confusion about what is happening here.

It is not an impartial book (I don't believe such a thing exists): it is written from an anti-imperialist and socialist stand-point. But as far as possible I have let events speak for themselves. I think they tell their own story, which is damning enough to Unionism, British imperialism and the Dublin government without any embroidery. It is not an academic book either. Books should be a guide to action. As a member of the Peoples Democracy I am actively involved in the struggle for a socialist republic in Ireland. If this book stirs a few more into action in Ireland or elsewhere I shall be well satisfied.

Introduction

In the United Irishmen's Insurrection in 1798 the backbone of the rebellion in the North of Ireland was provided not by Catholics but by Presbyterian merchants and tenant farmers. Yet 114 years later the Protestants of the North were preparing to fight to maintain their link with king and empire against the wishes of the majority of the Irish people. What had happened in the meantime?

The Protestant population in the North of Ireland has its origins in the plantation of Ulster[1] at the beginning of the seventeenth century. Ulster was then the most remote and troublesome of the Irish provinces, and after the defeat and flight of the last of the native Irish chieftains the British administration brought over English and Scottish planters and settled them on confiscated land in order to secure the area. The planters were Protestants, the native Irish whom they were displacing were Catholics. So Ulster became different from the rest of Ireland in that the Anglo-Irish Protestant group was not a handful of landlords and squires but a substantial tenant-farming class. Antagonism between settler and native was natural and was exacerbated by a major rebellion in 1641, the Williamite wars at the end of the seventeenth century, and the penal laws operated against the Catholics/native Irish by the victorious Loyalists.

By the end of the eighteenth century however, some of the descendants of the settlers were beginning to chafe under control from London. A thriving commercial and industrial class was developing in Ireland, especially in the North where the better terms on which the settlers held their land enabled them to accumulate some capital, and where the linen industry was taking root. But government restrictions designed to protect industry in Britain hindered the growth of industry in Ireland. Spurred on by the example of the American colonists, a movement developed which demanded and got a measure of legislative independence for the unrepresentative and exclusively Protestant parliament in Dublin. But efforts to reform the parliament failed and, influenced now by the French Revolution, the United Irishmen developed as a revolutionary movement demanding an independent democratic Republic with full equality for the Catholic majority of the population.

The United Irishmen found their greatest support in the growing commercial town of Belfast, among the prosperous tenant farmers of North Down and South and Mid-Antrim, and among Presbyterians who resented the privileges of the Anglican church – the church of the landlords and the aristocracy. But the United Irishmen never had the support of the majority of Ulster Protestants. Antagonism between Catholic and Protestant was still strong in many areas and was reinforced by competition for land tenancies. After a series of sectarian skirmishes in Armagh and Tyrone the Orange Order was formed in 1795 as a militant Protestant organisation dedicated to preserving Protestant supremacy, and it immediately began driving Catholics out of parts of North Armagh and South Tyrone. The Orangemen were loyal to the government as a bulwark of Protestant supremacy, and were quickly recruited into the yeomanry – a part-time force officered by the landlords. When the rebellion came in 1798 more Ulster Protestants served the king in the yeomanry than fought against him in the United Irishmen.

The crushing of the rebellion snuffed out the spirit of republicanism, but for some years the allegiance of Northern Protestants was divided between Orangeism and liberalism, with liberalism still strong among Belfast businessmen and Orangeism entrenched among the landlords and the most backward tenant farmers.

The British government had responded to the '98 Rebellion with the Act of Union, abolishing the Dublin parliament and integrating Ireland with the United Kingdom. The restrictions on industry and trade were lifted and Ulster, especially Belfast, prospered under the Union. Steam power revolutionised the linen industry, an engineering industry developed and eventually shipbuilding as well. The population of Belfast jumped from 20,000 in 1801 to 100,000 in 1851 and 350,000 in 1901. Belfast was becoming a major industrial city like Birmingham or Glasgow. Its industries depended on Britain for their markets and towards the end of the century they began to share in the benefits of the expanding Empire. The Belfast businessmen and merchants quickly forgot their former nationalism and republicanism and became strong supporters of the Union – after all they now had a vested interest in it.

'Instead of being the solitary Irish industrial city, Belfast, looked at this way, becomes an outpost of industrial Britain ... This in turn involved a withdrawal of industrial Belfast from the rest of Ireland and made its leaders singularly deaf to all appeals of economic nationalism.

This above all separated Ulster middle-class liberalism from nationalism'[2].

At the same time, in the rest of Ireland the Union had ruined the new and struggling industries established under the Dublin parliament, and free competition with industrialised Britain prevented others from developing. Meanwhile Catholic Emancipation gave the mass of the population a measure of political power for the first time. A powerful nationalist movement began to develop, expressing itself alternately in constitutional and physical force movements.

Ulster Protestants, whether liberals or Orangemen, were drawing apart from the rest of the Irish people. Ulster Catholics, concentrated in the South and West of the province, had little share in the commercial and industrial expansion and identified with the majority of the Irish population.

Things came to a head in 1885 when the Home Rule Party, led by Parnell, a Protestant land-owner but representing the growing Catholic middle class in the South, won 85 seats at Westminster including seventeen of the 33 seats in Ulster. Parnell held the balance of power in the House of Commons when in April 1886 Gladstone introduced his first Home Rule Bill. It provided for only the most limited form of self-government, but the Ulster businessmen still saw it as a threat to their prosperity. It was the moment of truth for them: the majority of the Ulster businessmen formed an alliance with the Conservative Party in England and the landlord-dominated local Tories.

But in their anxiety to preserve the Union and safeguard their profits many of them went even further. Colonel Saunderson, the former Liberal MP for Co.Cavan, joined the Orange Order as well, saying that 'the Orange Society is alone capable of dealing with the conditions of anarchy and rebellion which prevail in Ireland'[3]. He was followed by many ex-liberal businessmen and industrialists. The Orange Order was still a powerful if disreputable force in Ulster society. Virulently anti-Catholic, dedicated to maintaining Protestant privilege and supremacy, it had considerable influence over small farmers and Protestant workers demoralised and brutalised by life in the industrial slums. Its influence was increased by the growth of sectarian tension in Belfast.

Industrial expansion had brought religious strife to Belfast. In 1800 only 6 per cent of the town's population were Catholics and there was little religious tension, but as Belfast mushroomed, and especially after the famine, Catholics began to flood in, until in 1861 they made up a third of the population. Low wages and periodic depression made the established Protestant workers see the Catholic newcomers as a threat, and there were serious sectarian riots in 1857, 1864 and 1872. Sectarian feeling was exacerbated by the inflammatory anti-Catholic sermons of two Protestant fundamentalist preachers who wielded great influence in the city: Rev Thomas Drew and Rev Hugh (Roaring) Hanna. They were the first of a long line of extremist clerics in Ulster.

By joining the Orange Order and linking it to their party, by exploiting the tension between Protestant and Catholic slum-dwellers in Belfast, by stirring up memories of the ancient conflict between settler and native, and by claiming that Home Rule would mean domination by the Catholic Church, the Unionists – as the alliance of Tories and renegade Liberals was now called – were able to mobilise the mass of the Protestant population behind them. The bitterness of the feeling they aroused was shown in 1886 when Belfast experienced its worst rioting yet which lasted off and on from June to September.

The 1886 Home Rule Bill was defeated in the House of Commons by a revolt of the imperialist wing of the Liberal Party and Gladstone's government fell. But the Home Rule threat remained – Gladstone introduced another bill in 1893 and this time it passed the Commons and was defeated only in the Lords. The Ulster Unionists kept up their organisation, cemented the Orange link and secured the allegiance of the Protestant workers by a systematic policy of discrimination against Catholics which left the Protestants with a virtual monopoly of the well-paid skilled trades, especially in the shipbuilding and engineering industry. The shipyard workers were the aristocrats of Belfast labour, and as early as 1866 Harland and Wolff employed only 225 Catholics out of 3000 men (7·5 per cent)[4]. In 1911 things had not changed. In that year the census recorded that out of 6,809 shipbuilders and shipwrights in Belfast, only 518 or 7·6 per cent were Catholics. (Catholics made up 24 per cent of the population of Belfast in 1911). The shipyard workers were also intensely Loyalist. Recruitment was in the hands of the Orange foremen and one whole district of the Belfast Orange Lodge was made up of shipyard workers. The situation in the general engineering industry was little better. The 1911 Census showed that only 11·4 per cent of engineering workers were Catholics[5].

The Unionist bosses soon discovered that the policy of discrimination had an added advantage – it prevented any effective labour or trade union movement from developing in Belfast. Ramsay MacDonald, the British Labour leader described the situation succinctly in 1912:

'In Belfast you get labour conditions the like of which you get in no other town, no other city of equal commercial prosperity from John O'Groats to Land's End or from the Atlantic to the North Sea. It is maintained by an exceedingly simple device . . . Whenever there is an attempt to root out sweating in Belfast the Orange big drum is beaten . . .' [6].

By the beginning of the twentieth century the conflict between Orangeism and liberalism for the allegiance of the Ulster Protestants was over and Orangeism had won. And the Unionist bosses had ensured the loyalty of the Protestant masses. But it was at a price, the price of permanently maintaining discrimination and Protestant supremacy. Sixty years later, when some Unionist leaders were to contemplate dismantling some of the apparatus of the Orange state for the soundest of capitalist reasons, their followers would revolt. The Orange ideology with its combination of Protestant supremacism and evangelical religious fervour would assume a life of its own and defy its masters.

But the tide of Irish nationalism couldn't be stemmed forever. Early in the new century more extreme nationalist groups, notably Sinn Fein[7], began treading on the heels of the parliamentary Home Rule Party – now called the United Irish League (UIL) and led by John Redmond. The Irish people were getting impatient. When the 1910 Westminster election left the British Liberal government dependent on UIL votes, another Home Rule Bill was inevitable, and when the Parliament Act of 1911 removed the House of Lords veto, its success seemed guaranteed.

The Ulster problem remained however. Ulster, with 1,581,696 people, contained over a third (36·0 per cent) of the Irish population of 4,390,219. While Protestants were a minority (26·14 per cent) of the whole population of Ireland, they were in a small majority (56·3 per cent) in the nine counties of Ulster and in a much clearer majority (66 per cent) in the six north-eastern counties of Antrim, Armagh, Derry, Down, Fermanagh and Tyrone – though even then the last two counties had small Catholic majorities.

The economic gap between Ulster and the rest of Ireland had widened. Ulster, and especially the six-county area, was more heavily industrialised than the rest of the country. 21·5 per cent of the population of Ulster (339,878 people) and 25 per cent of the population of the six counties (312,585 people) were engaged in industry and commerce in 1911, compared with 13·9 per cent (384,662 people) in the rest of Ireland. Belfast, the Ulster capital, was both bigger, with a population of 386,947, and more industrialised, with 39·4 per cent of the population engaged in industry and commerce, than Dublin with a population of 304,802 and with 31·5 per cent of its people engaged in industry and commerce. Even in Derry City, the second town in Ulster, slightly more of the population, 13,919 out of 40,780 (34·7 per cent), were engaged in industry and commerce than in Dublin. In fact Ulster contained almost half (48 per cent) of all the industrial workers in Ireland and Belfast with only 8·8 per cent of the total population, contained 21 per cent of all industrial workers[8].

Belfast and its surrounding area had established its predominance in the linen industry by the middle of the nineteenth century, and had secured a near monopoly of the linen trade in the United Kingdom as well as a substantial export market by 1900. In 1910 there were more linen spindles in use in Belfast alone than in any other country[9]. Belfast's York Street Flax Spinning Mill was the largest linen mill in the world and Barbours of Lisburn was the biggest linen thread company in the world.

The linen industry gave rise to an engineering industry making textile machinery, and by 1910 two Belfast firms, Fairbairn, Lawson, Combe, Barbour Limited, and James Mackie's, monopolised the making of linen machinery in the United Kingdom, and had also developed a substantial export trade. Serious shipbuilding began in Belfast in 1858 and by 1911 Harland and Wolff's shipyard was the largest in the United Kingdom and had just opened the biggest dry dock in the world. Even Belfast's second shipyard, Workman, Clark Limited, was among the top half-dozen yards in the United Kingdom, and between them the two yards were to launch ships weighing 256,547 tons in 1914[10].

Belfast and Ulster's economic dominance was clearest of all in industrial output and exports. In 1907 industries centred in the Belfast region provided £19·1 million of the total of £20·9 millions' worth of manufactured goods (excluding food and drink) exported from Ireland[11]. 80 per cent of Ireland's total industrial output came from three product groups: linen; shipbuilding and engineering; and brewing, distilling and the production of aerated waters. The first two were centred in Ulster, while

Belfast also produced 60 per cent of all whiskey exported and dominated the aerated water trade as well.

The contrast was striking with the rest of Ireland, which was overwhelmingly agricultural, its industries being service-industries or agriculture-based. Belfast and its hinterland more than ever represented an outpost of industrial Britain in Ireland. Belfast was effectively one corner of a great industrial triangle which linked it with Clydeside and Merseyside – it was cheaper to transport goods by sea to Glasgow or Liverpool than to send them to Dublin by rail. Belfast was sharing to the full in the economic expansion of Britain and in its massive trade with the Empire. In the midst of this remarkable prosperity Ulster employers were more determined than ever to resist any move which might weaken or sever their links with Britain and the Empire – the more so as the home market in Ireland could never hope to absorb their greatly increased production – and they were supported by the bulk of the overwhelmingly Protestant workers in the shipyard and the engineering industry, anxious to hold on at all costs to their (relatively) secure and well-paid jobs.

As the Home Rule Bill loomed nearer and nearer the Unionists prepared to resist. Although they were opposed to Home Rule for any part of Ireland, in practice they now concentrated their preparations in Ulster. Already they had established a separate Ulster Unionist Council (UUC). In 1910 they selected Edward Carson MP, a Dublin lawyer and former Solicitor General in a Conservative government at Westminster, as their leader.

In 1911 Carson threatened to establish a Provisional government in Ulster if the Home Rule Bill was passed, and the Unionists began organising and drilling a private army recruited through the Orange Order. In 1912 400,000 people signed a 'Solemn League and Covenant' to resist Home Rule. In 1913 Sir George Richardson, a retired British general and veteran of many colonial wars, took command of the Unionist private army, now called the Ulster Volunteer Force (UVF) and in April 1914 they landed 25,000 rifles and two and a half million rounds of ammunition at Larne in Co.Antrim.

The Unionists had the fullest backing from the Conservative Party and the British military establishment. In July 1912 Bonar Law the Conservative leader said 'I can imagine no length of resistance to which Ulster will go in which I shall not be ready to support them . . .'[12] Sir Henry Wilson, the British Army's Director of Operations was an enthusiastic supporter and later became a Unionist MP. In March 1914 when the Westminster government finally summoned up courage enough to stage a precautionary move against the Unionists, a brigadier and fifty-four officers at the Curragh military camp mutinied rather than take part and the whole operation had to be called off.

The Liberals were granting a very limited measure of Home Rule to Ireland only under pressure from the Home Rule Party (UIL). Faced with resistance by the Unionists, mutiny by their own army, and the apparent danger of civil war throughout the United Kingdom, they were certainly not going to coerce the Ulster Loyalists. Negotiations were going on to exclude Ulster from the Home Rule Act when the First World War broke out and the whole question was suspended.

Meanwhile frustration had been growing in the South, as nationalists watched the Unionists openly arming to defy the British government while the government did nothing. At the end of 1913 recruiting began for a force of Irish National Volunteers to counter the UVF. Meanwhile James Connolly, the marxist revolutionary, had been recruiting a working-class Irish Citizen Army. The National Volunteers were controlled by an uneasy alliance of Sinn Fein supporters, members of the secret Irish Republican Brotherhood (IRB), and Redmond's United Irish League (UIL). Redmond had become involved only to exercise some control over the movement, and when the war began and Carson urged UVF members to join the British Army Redmond did the same with the Volunteers.

The Volunteers split, with a minority under Sinn Fein and IRB influence denouncing participation in the war. Connolly's Citizen Army took the same attitude, and on Easter Monday 1916 the Citizen Army and the Sinn Fein Volunteers proclaimed an Irish Republic and seized the centre of Dublin. The Rising was crushed after a week of fierce fighting and the leaders shot; but it changed the mood of the nationalist population. They would no longer be satisfied with limited Home Rule within the British Empire. They wanted an independent Republic, they had no more faith in British parliaments and they were prepared to support the use of force to get what they wanted.

The stage was set for confrontation.

A Bloody Beginning

The years from 1918 to 1923 were to be dramatic ones throughout Ireland. They were to see the ousting of the old Home Rule Party (UIL) by Sinn Fein, the establishment of an illegal Irish parliament in Dublin in defiance of Westminster, and the outbreak of a War of Independence against British rule in Ireland. In the North the violent confrontation between Unionist and Nationalist which had been looming for so long was finally to erupt. The outcome would be partial independence for the bulk of the country in the new Irish Free State, and partition leaving the six north-eastern counties under British rule in the United Kingdom – but with local self-government.

There was a general election in Britain and Ireland in December 1918, a month after the First World War ended. It was the first real opportunity to test feeling in Ireland since the dramatic events of 1916. The election results were almost as dramatic. There were 105 seats for Ireland at Westminster, and the parliamentary Nationalists of the United Irish League had held 80 of them in the old parliament. After the election Sinn Fein held 73 seats and the UIL six – four of them because Sinn Fein withdrew from the constituencies. John Dillon, the UIL leader, had been crushingly defeated by De Valera, the leader of Sinn Fein.

Sinn Fein members had campaigned for an independent Republic, and on a promise to refuse to take their seats at Westminster and to set up their own parliament in Ireland instead. They had got a massive endorsement for that policy.

But in Ulster the position was somewhat different. Of the 37 constituencies, the Unionists won 22. Even a rather sordid deal between Sinn Fein and the UIL to let the Catholic Cardinal allocate eight marginal seats[1] between them, couldn't win the combined Nationalist forces more than fifteen seats. In the whole of Ulster the Unionists won 265,111 votes to a combined Nationalist total of 177,557; while in the six counties of Antrim, Armagh, Derry, Down, Fermanagh and Tyrone they had a majority of slightly over two to one: 255,819 votes to 116,888.

For the Unionists it was a satisfactory result. In the negotiations over

Home Rule during the war, Redmond, the old UIL leader, had agreed in principle to the temporary exclusion of the six counties, and a convention of Ulster Nationalists in Belfast in June 1916 – after the Rising – had voted to accept this. The Unionist leaders themselves had privately decided to settle for six counties and abandon the other three Ulster counties, which had overwhelming Catholic majorities[2]. The election results strengthened their position and they were confident the British government had no intention of forcing them out of the United Kingdom. Their confidence grew when one of their leaders, Sir James Craig, and two other Unionist MPs became junior ministers. The Unionists felt they could safely await developments – they were in any case preoccupied with a virtual general strike in Belfast at the beginning of 1919.

The new Sinn Fein MPs lost no time in carrying out their pledges. They refused to go to Westminster, and on 21 January 1919 convened the first meeting of Dail Eireann in the Mansion House, Dublin. All the Irish MPs were invited to attend but both Unionists and UIL members refused. Of the 73 Sinn Fein MPs, 36 were in jail but the rest adopted a Declaration of Independence:

'... **We, the elected representatives of the ancient Irish people in National Parliament assembled, do, in the name of the Irish nation, ratify the establishment of the Irish Republic and pledge ourselves and our people to make this declaration effective by every means at our command ...'**

'**We ordain that the elected representatives of the Irish people alone have power to make laws binding on the people of Ireland and that the Irish parliament is the only parliament to which that people will give its allegiance;**

'**We solemnly declare foreign government in Ireland to be an invasion of our national right which we will never tolerate and we demand the evacuation of our country by the English garrison ...'**

The Dail appointed Cathal Brugha as Acting President in place of Eamon De Valera, who was in jail, and named several other ministers. Their intention was to attempt to take over most of the functions of the British administration in Ireland.

The Declaration of Independence was given force by the shooting dead the same day of two policemen at Soloheadbeg in Co. Tipperary. The attack was not authorised by the Dail and was an embarrassment to them. It was carried out by Dan Breen and Sean Treacy, local leaders of the Irish

Volunteers who were being re-formed and re-armed and would soon be known as the Irish Republican Army (IRA). Authorised or not, it was the first action in the War of Independence. The Dail soon sanctioned a policy of arms raids on the barracks of the Royal Irish Constabulary (RIC), a heavily-armed para-military force, and gun-battles between IRA units and the RIC became commonplace, together with counter-raids, reprisals and jailings. By the end of 1919 fifteen RIC men had been killed, though that was a small enough figure compared with the 418 RIC men and 146 British troops who would die before the Truce of 1921.

At first the violence was largely confined to the south and west of Ireland and Ulster enjoyed relative peace. One reason may have been the relative weakness of Sinn Fein and the IRA in the North: in a needle contest for the Falls constituency of Belfast Joe Devlin, the local UIL leader, had beaten De Valera even more convincingly – 8,488 to 3,245 – than De Valera had beaten Dillon[3].

The Unionists had not been wrong about the intentions of the British government. Lloyd George had given a virtual pledge to exclude them from Home Rule during the election campaign, and his Coalition government was returned with a massive majority. In October 1919 a Cabinet Committee was set up to review the Irish problem, and it produced the Government of Ireland Bill, introduced at Westminster in February 1920. The Bill proposed two Home Rule parliaments in Ireland, one for most of the country, the other for six of the nine Ulster counties. The local parliaments would have strictly limited powers and both areas would continue to be represented at Westminster. As a pious gesture to Nationalist feeling the Bill proposed a Council of Ireland between the two local administrations 'with a view to the eventual establishment of a parliament for the whole of Ireland and to bring about harmonious action between the parliaments and governments'.

The Bill caused some heart-searching by the Ulster Unionist Council. It proposed to give them Home Rule which they had never sought, but they soon concluded that a separate Northern administration would strengthen their position. As Craig's brother put it at Westminster, 'We profoundly distrust the Labour Party and we profoundly distrust the Rt.Hon Gentleman (Asquith). We believe that if either of those parties, or the two in combination, were once more in power our chances of remaining a part of the United Kingdom would be very small indeed.' With their own administration in Belfast they would be proof against any changes in British policy.

The size of the Northern area was a more serious problem. The Bill proposed to abandon the three Ulster counties of Cavan, Monaghan and Donegal with their 70,000 Protestants, to the Southern administration. But the Unionist Council was a nine-county body representing the Loyalists of these three counties as well. The Unionist leaders had already decided to accept the six counties arguing that a smaller area with a solid Protestant majority (66 per cent) was safer than the whole province with a small majority (56·3 per cent) which could be easily overturned. Moreover the other three counties had overwhelming Catholic majorities – Cavan 81·5 per cent, Donegal 78·9 per cent, and Monaghan 74·7 per cent – and the Unionists quailed at the prospect of trying to exercise authority over large areas which were completely Nationalist in sympathy, and where there often wasn't a Protestant or Loyalist for miles. Thomas Moles MP, later editor of the *Belfast Telegraph* (a Unionist evening paper in Belfast) put it bluntly: 'If a ship were sinking and there were only enough life boats for two thirds of the passengers, should they all drown rather than leave anyone behind?'

At successive meetings of the UUC in March and May 1920 it was formally decided, amidst considerable recrimination, to accept the six-county area. Meanwhile the Bill began its progress through parliament, becoming law in December.

But even the six-county area created problems. Though it had a Protestant majority of 820,000 to 430,000 this was not evenly distributed. Two whole counties, Fermanagh and Tyrone, had Catholic majorities of 56·2 per cent and 55·4 per cent respectively, and the second city of the area, Derry, had a Catholic majority of 56·2 per cent as well. There were also overwhelmingly Catholic areas in South Armagh and South Down, including the town of Newry, and even in Belfast there was a strongly Catholic enclave concentrated on the Falls Road in West Belfast. However, there was no question of the UUC jettisoning any more territory. A four-county state would have been physically, strategically and economically unviable, and would have involved abandoning another 90,000 Protestants to the South.

The results were seen in January and June 1920 when local elections were held throughout Ireland, using proportional representation (PR) for the first time. PR was introduced to reduce the power of Sinn Fein in the

South of Ireland; but in the North it had the effect of giving greater representation to non-Unionists. In the six-county area Nationalists (Sinn Fein and UIL supporters) won control of Derry City, Fermanagh and Tyrone County Councils, ten urban councils, including Armagh, Omagh, Enniskillen, Newry and Strabane, and thirteen rural councils. It was the first serious challenge to Unionist hegemony in the area.

The Derry City result was crucial. Derry held a central place in Orange mythology. Its walled town was built by the planters in 1614. It held out for the Protestant William of Orange in 1688-90 against the Catholic King James II. It was still very much a plantation town with its Protestant walled citadel perched on a hill overlooking the sprawling Catholic township of the Bogside which had grown up on the marshy ground outside the walls. The Corporation of Derry had been Protestant-controlled since the great siege in 1688 and careful gerrymandering had kept it that way despite a growing Catholic majority in the city. Now for the first time in 230 years the city had a Catholic and Nationalist corporation and mayor, who promptly voted their allegiance to the Dail and the Republican government.

The effect on the Loyalists of Derry was traumatic. The despised majority were at last in power and were using that power to back the Republican struggle. And the Nationalists themselves became more self-confident and assertive. For months after the election in January the city was tense. Rioting broke out in mid-April and May, with the RIC and British troops bayonet-charging and firing into Catholic crowds. The IRA returned fire in their first real action in Derry, and managed to kill the local head of the RIC Special Branch, the first RIC man to be killed in the six counties. The rioting saw a new and ominous development however. The UVF, which was still in existence, undumped their guns and began to fire from the walled city into the Catholic Bogside, and armed UVF men set up road-blocks on the only bridge across the river Foyle. The RIC did nothing to stop them.

Fighting erupted again on 18 June and lasted for a week. Catholic families were driven out of the Protestant Waterside and Prehen areas. The UVF poured a withering fire from the walls into the Bogside, and masked and armed UVF men occupied the Diamond and the city centre. Several Catholics were stopped, asked their religion, and shot dead.

The Catholics sealed off the Bogside and retaliated. Howard McKay, son of the Governor of the Apprentice Boys[4], was shot dead on the fringe of the Bogside and another Protestant was shot and thrown into the

Foyle. The IRA fought a fierce gun-battle to drive the UVF out of the grounds of St.Columb's College, a Catholic school which commanded most of the Bogside. Then British troops, who had stood aloof for almost a week, moved in in force. They concentrated their fire on the Catholics, using machine guns against the IRA in St.Columb's and killing six civilians. They cordoned the city off in sections, occupying it with a massive military force – 1,500 troops for a population of 40,780 – imposing a rigid curfew and disarming the Catholics. The UVF were left unmolested. The final death toll was eighteen: fourteen Catholics and four Protestants.

The alarmed Derry businessmen set up a mixed Catholic-Protestant Citizens' Conciliation Committee, which agreed to remove all flags and bunting in the city and ban all political or sectarian parades for three months. Between the Conciliation Committee and the military occupation force, Derry was quiet for some time.

Meanwhile the war in the South and West had begun to spread to the rest of the six counties. In April and May 1920, as part of a general campaign against the British civil administration in Ireland, IRA units attacked tax offices in Belfast and nine other Northern towns, and burnt a number of unoccupied RIC barracks – vacated as part of a general concentration of the RIC in larger more defensible centres. In June an RIC sergeant and a civilian were shot dead in an ambush in South Armagh, and on 16 June Patrick Loughran, an IRA man, was killed in an attack on an occupied barracks at Cookstown, Co.Tyrone: the first IRA man to be killed in action in the six counties.

The Loyalists were beginning to respond as well. UVF units were mobilised and guns undumped. Local magistrates, usually squires or prominent Unionists, turned a blind eye, if they weren't involved themselves. So did the RIC, now the target for IRA attacks. On 8 June an IRA raiding party entered the village of Lisbellaw in Fermanagh to burn the empty barracks and the local courthouse. They were surprised by armed Loyalists and driven off after a gun battle. A Unionist MP boasted at Westminster about this UVF action. When the British Army arrived the next day they allowed the Loyalists to keep their guns.

So far the violence in the North had been sporadic and mostly outside Belfast. But tension was growing in Belfast too. After the killing of McKay in Derry, Belfast shipyard workers had telegraphed Carson asking him to mobilise the UVF and take revenge. And a mob had attacked and tried to burn down a Catholic-owned[5] spirit grocery in the intensely loyalist

Sandy Row area. Now it was approaching 12 July, the Orangemen's annual festival and a time when sectarian passions ran very high. At Westminster, Asquith appealed to the government to take extra precautions to avoid trouble around the 12th.

The Unionist leaders had other ideas however. In the South the Republicans were having considerable success. Dail Eireann had secured the allegiance of almost all the local councils since the local elections, and had set up its own law courts and legal system which were supplanting those of the Crown. The British administration had virtually broken down over most of the country. Meanwhile the IRA were fighting a highly effective guerrilla war. It was evident that the Government of Ireland Bill would be a dead letter as far as most of Ireland was concerned, and that the British would have to make further concessions. But the Republicans would not accept partition. If they had many more successes the British might make concessions about the six counties as well, particularly now that the IRA campaign was spreading North.

The Unionist leadership also had a more localised problem. Industrial militancy was growing among Belfast workers. There had been a massive engineering strike at the beginning of 1919 which had brought Belfast industry to a halt for four weeks. Ominously for the Unionists the leader of the largely Protestant strikers had been a Catholic, Charles McKay. The workers' new class consciousness seemed to carry through to the local elections in January 1920, for twelve Labour councillors were elected to Belfast Corporation, one of them topping the poll in the Protestant stronghold of Shankill. The Unionists were desperately concerned that, in the poverty-stricken conditions of post-war Belfast, socialism might get a foothold among the workers, destroying the backbone of their Orange alliance. Worse still, class-conscious workers might throw in their lot with Sinn Fein. They were determined to nip this deadly growth in the bud.

Carson spoke at the main Orange rally at Finaghy, outside Belfast, and made a violently inflammatory speech:

'We must proclaim today clearly that, come what will and be the consequences what they may, we in Ulster will tolerate no Sinn Fein – no Sinn Fein organisation, no Sinn Fein methods ... But we tell you [the government] this – that if, having offered you our help, you are yourselves unable to protect us from the machinations of Sinn Fein, and you won't take our help; well then, we tell you that we will take the matter into our own hands. We will reorganise ... as we feel bound to do in our own defence, throughout the province, the Ulster Volunteers ... And those are not mere words. I hate words without action.'

He made a special attack on Labour:

'. . . these men who come forward posing as the friends of labour care no more about labour than does the man in the moon. Their real object, and the real insidious nature of their propaganda, is that they mislead and bring about disunity amongst our own people; and in the end, before we know where we are, we may find ourselves in the same bondage and slavery as is the rest of Ireland in the South and West.'

In the tense atmosphere of Belfast Carson's speech was virtually an incitement to riot. He didn't have long to wait for his action.

On 17 July Colonel Smyth, the Divisional Commissioner of the RIC for Munster, was shot dead in Cork. A month earlier he had made a blood-curdling speech to a group of RIC men in Listowel telling them: 'The more you shoot the better I will like you, and I assure you no policeman will get into trouble for shooting any man.'

Smyth came from Banbridge in Co. Down and his body was brought home to be buried. On the day of the funeral a meeting was held at the gate of Workman, Clark & Co's shipyard (the smaller of the two Belfast shipyards) by the Belfast Protestant Association, an extreme politico-religious group. There was a show of revolvers and it was decided to drive the 'Sinn Feiners'[6] out. Then, in the words of one of the expelled workers:

'Men armed with sledge-hammers and other weapons swooped down on Catholic workers in the shipyards and didn't even give them a chance for their lives ... The gates were smashed down with sledges, the vests and shirts of those at work were torn open to see if the men were wearing any Catholic emblems, and then woe betide the man who was. One man was set upon, thrown into the dock, had to swim the Musgrave Channel, and having been pelted with rivets, had to swim two or three miles, to emerge in streams of blood and rush to the police office in a nude state'[7].

The fiction that only Sinn Feiners were to be expelled was soon disposed of. All Catholics in the two yards were put out, together with a number of Protestants of radical or labour views, including James Baird, a Labour councillor, and John Hanna, ex-master of an Orange Lodge, who had worked with James Larkin in the Belfast dock strike of 1907 and who became chairman of a committee of the expelled workers. Charles McKay, the chairman of the engineering strike committee the previous year, went as well. Not for nothing had the men at the BPA meeting declared that 'As employees they would stand by the employers'[8]. Carson had no further need to worry about the Labour menace.

The expulsions soon spread to the other major firms in Belfast. Catholics were expelled from the four major engineering works: Mackie's; Musgrave's; Coome, Barbour, Fairbairn and Lawson's; and Davidson's Sirocco works. They were also put out of the main building firm, McLaughlin and Harvey's, and a number of the linen mills. A total of 10,000 men and 1,000 women workers were expelled according to the Catholic Protection Committee, a welfare agency established by Dr McRory, the Catholic Bishop of Down and Connor. Close on 9,000 of them remained unemployed for the next few years. The Catholic population of Belfast was about 93,000.

The expulsions were welcome to some people however. The postwar depression was setting in and redundancies were looming. By the following summer, unemployment in the six counties stood at 25·4 per cent or 70,000 workers. The wholesale expulsion of Catholic workers avoided the need for mass pay-offs. It also put a premium on loyalty and cemented the Orange alliance, since 'disloyal' Protestants were likely to be the next to go.

The disturbances were not confined to Belfast. In Banbridge, Smyth's funeral was followed by an onslaught on Catholic-owned businesses and homes in the town. Several shops were burnt and all Catholics driven from the local factories. The trouble spread to nearby Dromore and eventually all Catholic families fled the two towns. Even in the seaside resort of Bangor Catholics were attacked, and an attempt was made to burn down a holiday home for millgirls, because it was founded by Joe Devlin.

Meanwhile in Belfast, when news of the expulsions reached Catholic areas, Catholics stoned Loyalist shipyard men on their way home and widespread rioting broke out. Loyalist mobs burned down Catholic-owned shops and pubs in East Belfast and attacked the small Catholic enclave of Short Strand in the East, and the Clonard area between the Catholic Falls and Protestant Shankill Roads in West Belfast[9].

For the next two nights Catholic premises and isolated Catholic houses were burnt out in Protestant areas, and a 4,000-strong mob attacked St.Matthew's Catholic Church and the adjoining convent in the Short Strand, and the Catholic church and monastery in Clonard. British troops arrived belatedly and with fine impartiality fired into the crowd attacking the church in East Belfast killing several, and into the monastery in Clonard killing a brother and five civilians. The death toll for the three days was thirteen people, all civilians. Seven were Catholics and six Protestants.

There was a violent debate at Westminster over the riots, with Thompson Donald, a 'Labour'[10] Unionist defending the expulsions while Carson made an extraordinary speech asserting that the British were beaten in two-thirds of Ireland. He said Sinn Fein were trying to take over Ulster as well, but he hoped and knew the Ulster people would not take it lying down. The inference seemed clear. The Unionists knew the rest of Ireland was lost and the riots and expulsions were their way of holding on to the North. Devlin accused the government of deliberately fomenting, or at least tolerating, a religious war in the North to justify their proposed partition scheme.

At the same time the UVF was being openly re-organised on a six-county-wide basis. A notice in the *Newsletter*, Belfast's main Unionist paper, announced that Colonel Wilfred Spender[11] had been appointed chief of staff and called on all members to report for duty. Devlin and his colleagues protested but to no avail, since the divisional commissioner of the RIC in Ulster was General Sir William Hackett Pain, a former UVF chief of staff himself, and since Spender had been asked to re-activate the UVF by Craig who was still a junior minister in the government. Spender argued that the object of the UVF was to assist the military and police, and eventually prevailed on the Chief Secretary for Ireland to instruct both forces to co-operate with his men[12]. UVF men even went on joint patrols with British troops. The confidence of Northern Catholics in the British government or their future Unionist masters was not increased by the sight of British troops mounting joint patrols with a totally illegal Unionist and Protestant private army.

The North was quiet for the first few weeks of August but on Sunday 22 August District Inspector Swanzy of the RIC was shot dead in the centre of Lisburn on his way home from Church. Swanzy had been named by an inquest jury in Cork as one of the men responsible for the murder of Tomas McCurtain, the city's Lord Mayor, and he had immediately been transferred North.

A mob quickly gathered in Lisburn and began attacking all Catholic-owned premises in the centre of the town. A Catholic publican was shot and wounded as his pub was burnt down. In an orgy of destruction which lasted for three days, 60 business premises were burned or wrecked, together with the priest's house and several Catholic homes, and a man was burnt to death in the remains of a factory. Lisburn Council enrolled Special Constables, ostensibly to stop the violence, but they were all Loyalists and their calibre was shown when British troops had to arrest some of them for looting. When most of the town's Catholics had been evicted the remainder were told they would be safe if they signed a form saying 'I hereby declare that I am not a Sinn Feiner, nor have I any sympathy with Sinn Fein in any form and I also declare that I am loyal to king and country.' But the entire Catholic population fled, some going to Dundalk and some crowding into the Falls Road in Belfast.

Two days after Swanzy's death rioting broke out in Belfast again and lasted till the end of the month. St.Matthew's Church in the Short Strand was attacked again as well as the tiny enclave of the Marrowbone, or 'Bone' in North Belfast. There was also burning and looting on a massive scale. The London *Daily News* reported that there were 180 serious fires in six days, at a cost of nearly one million pounds and commented:

'Practically the whole of this damage has been done to the property of Catholics ... all but a very few of the business premises of Belfast Catholics except those in the very heart of the city, or in the Catholic stronghold known as the Falls, have now been destroyed.'

The paper summed up the period since the shipyard expulsions as

'five weeks of ruthless persecution by boycott, fire, plunder and assault, culminating in a week's wholesale violence, probably unmatched outside the area of Russian or Polish pogroms'[13].

There were also wholesale evictions of Catholics from Protestant areas, the *Daily Mail* putting the figure at 400 families, while 20 people were killed during the month of August, all of them civilians.

On 30 August the military authorities brought in a curfew from 10.30pm to 5.00am for the Belfast area. It was to last, with variations in the times, until 1924. On 2 September the government held a security conference in London attended by Craig. He demanded the establishment of a Special Constabulary, which effectively meant making the UVF an official government force and arming them. The next day the UUC backed the demand, and on 8 September the cabinet agreed to raise a Special Constabulary of 'loyal' citizens to operate only in the six counties. The limitation was significant. The Government of Ireland Act had not yet been passed. This was the first government measure which treated the six counties as a separate unit. It was prejudging both the establishment and the area of the Northern state.

The proposed establishment of the Specials was denounced as a capitulation to the Orange mobs and an intolerable provocation to the Catholics. The *Daily Mail* correspondent said:

'The official proposal to arm "well-disposed" citizens to "assist the authorities" in Belfast . . . raised serious questions of the sanity of the government. It seems to me the most outrageous thing which they have ever done in Ireland . . . A citizen of Belfast who is "well-disposed" to the British government is, almost from the nature of the case, an Orangeman, or at any rate, a vehement anti-Sinn Feiner. These are the very same people who have been looting Catholic shops and driving thousands of Catholic women and children from their homes[14].'

The expulsions and evictions in Belfast had their effect in Dublin. On 6 August Sean McEntee, a Belfast man and TD (Teachtaire Dail, member of the Dail) for South Monaghan, raised in the Dail a petition by four Sinn Fein members of Belfast Corporation and other prominent Catholics in the city. They appealed for help in 'the war of extermination being waged against us' and called for a boycott of goods from Belfast and a withdrawal of funds from Belfast-based banks by people in the rest of Ireland. But they added a caution: 'It should be strictly enjoined that Protestants in other parts of Ireland are not to be molested in any way on account of the actions of their co-religionists in Belfast'.

At first the Dail was divided on the issue; but when the riots were resumed at the end of August they agreed and from September a strict boycott of goods from Belfast, Lisburn and a couple of other Northern towns was begun. The Dail cabinet appointed a boycott director and voted £2,500 for the campaign in January 1921. The IRA attacked lorries and trains carrying Belfast-produced goods, and a special boycott patrol raided shops and warehouses in Dublin and other towns, seizing Belfast goods and taking reprisals against firms which handled them. The population were encouraged to boycott firms which dealt with Belfast. The boycott was effective and harmed the Belfast economy, but it failed to achieve its object – the re-instatement of the expelled workers. It was not sufficiently crippling, for though Belfast was the main distributing centre for large areas outside the six counties, the backbone of its economy was manufacturing industry, which exported the bulk of its products to Britain and the Empire.

Moreover the industries where most of the expulsions had taken place, shipbuilding and engineering, hardly traded with the rest of Ireland at all.

The trade union movement in Britain was also affected by the expulsions. The vast majority of industrial workers in Ireland, especially the skilled engineering workers of Belfast, were members of British trade unions which treated Ireland as a part of the United Kingdom for purposes of organisation. There was only one major Irish-based trade union active in Belfast, the Irish Transport and General Workers' Union (ITGWU)[15], founded by James Larkin in 1909, and its members were largely Catholic dockers. Most of the British unions were affiliated to the Irish Trade Union Congress (founded in 1894) as well as the British TUC, but the ITUC had no effective power. The British unions whose members were overwhelmingly Protestant had avoided the Home Rule or Republican issue and had acquiesced in religious discrimination over the years.

Nevertheless most of the expelled workers were members of British unions and, under pressure from the Expelled Workers' Committee, the British TUC discussed the question in September 1920. They decided to send a delegation to Belfast to investigate the situation, and then to call a meeting of the executives of the unions involved to decide upon action. The delegation didn't arrive until December. In the meantime the Amalgamated Society of Carpenters and Joiners (ASCJ) did take action. On 21 September they ordered their members in the seven major firms where Catholics had been expelled to walk out. Six hundred members obeyed the union, 2,000 stayed at work.

The ASCJ promptly expelled them. However, the TUC not only did not follow the ASCJ's example, but at the special meeting of union executives in January 1921 even tried to pressure the ASCJ into backing down from its tough stand. They stood firm but no further trade union action was taken. It was clear that the bulk of union members would resist efforts to reinstate the expelled Catholics. Holding onto the bulk of their members seemed more important to the trade union leaders than standing by their principles.

It was not as if they didn't know exactly what was going on in Belfast, and why. James Sexton MP, General Secretary of the British National Union of Dock Labourers, had seconded a motion by Devlin at Westminster on 26 July, saying:

'The spirit raised by these incidents [Carson's speech] **on 12 July is alone responsible for the dissension and division amongst the members of**

my own organisation ... We have had an organisation in Ireland for the last twenty-five years and every time we have made any attempt at any progress the same bitter feeling was introduced on 12 July to break down the organisation we have built up in Ireland.'

J.H.Thomas of the NUR echoed his views.

There was no major rioting in Belfast in September but on 25 September an RIC man was killed and another wounded on the Falls Road ... the first RIC man killed in Belfast. That night three politically uninvolved Catholic men were dragged from their homes and shot dead. Belfast had had its first taste of the reprisals policy now commonplace throughout the South and West. Murder squads of RIC, Black and Tans[16] and Auxiliaries[17] operated during curfew hours with the tacit consent of the authorities, taking reprisals for attacks on Crown forces by killing Catholic civilians. A yet more sinister note was sounded at Westminster on 4 November by the Labour Unionist MP Thompson Donald: 'If any more policemen or soldiers are murdered in Belfast there will be more than three Sinn Feiners shot.' It was no idle threat. Already the UVF and other Loyalist groups were shooting Catholics picked at random and sniping into Catholic areas. The IRA returned their fire and occasionally retaliated. So did local Catholic defence groups mostly composed of ex-servicemen. The death-toll for September was 23.

In the middle of October Craig made a remarkable speech at the unfurling of a massive Union Jack at the shipyards. He asked the shipyard men if they were still against Sinn Fein. Then, in the words of the *Northern Whig*, he said: 'Well, as they had answered those questions it was only fair that he should answer one that had not been put to him'. "Do I approve of the action you boys have taken in the past?" I say "Yes" '[18]. It was as clear an endorsement of the expulsions as they could get – and from a member of the British government.

Two days later, Loyalists returning from a football match attacked the Catholic enclave of the Bone on the Oldpark Road, but this time British troops intervened quickly and brutally. They ran down one of the Loyalist crowd with an armoured car and shot two more. Meanwhile the IRA had resumed activities in Co.Fermanagh. IRA men dressed in RIC uniforms captured Belleek RIC barracks and got away with guns and ammunition. Another unit attacked Tempo barracks killing an RIC sergeant but were driven off by the UVF, who then shot a local Catholic as a reprisal.

The reprisals policy however proved liable to backfire on its authors.

On 6 November two RIC men were shot in Derry. That night a number of Catholic-owned premises were set on fire. The fire brigade was called but was fired on as it arrived. The military escort fired back, hitting three men. Shortly afterwards three RIC men, members of a reprisal squad, were found wounded, and one died later.

But the most important event to mark the close of 1920 was the establishment of the Specials. There was an angry debate at Westminster in October with J.R.Clynes of the Labour Party saying that the government were arming the Orangemen, and Joe Devlin pointing out that 300 of the Special Constables recruited in Lisburn had resigned in protest when their colleagues were charged with looting. He declared '. . . the Protestants are to be armed . . . Their pogrom is to be made less difficult. Instead of paving stones and sticks they are to be given rifles.' But the protests were in vain.

Recruiting for the Specials began in November in Belfast. There were to be three classes or categories. The A Specials would be full-time, uniformed and paid. They were to be trained in a special depot at Newtownards, and would be used either to reinforce the RIC in manning barracks or as mobile units to go to trouble spots. The B Specials would be part-time but would be fully armed and would do patrol-duty in their own areas and back up the RIC. Initially they had no uniforms. The C Specials would be a reserve force with no specific duties but available for call-out in an emergency. They would get some arms and would be able to get gun licences – which most Catholics could not. In practice the C Specials were only a device for arming the Loyalist population.

Recruitment was based so closely on the UVF that whole UVF units formed Special platoons. The B Specials retained the hierarchical structure of the old UVF, based on the 'big house' or the local linen-mill, with the landlord or linen-boss as the commander and his tenants or workers making up the ranks. In the Upperlands area of Co.Derry the Clarke family, the local mill-owners, controlled both UVF and B men, while in Co.Fermanagh, Sir Basil Brooke took the initiative in re-forming the UVF and recruiting for the Specials[19]. The Specials were entirely Protestant and where there weren't enough UVF men they were recruited from the Orange Lodges. They also used Orange Halls extensively as bases and drill-halls. There were constant complaints about their indiscipline and sectarian behaviour. General Macready, the British Commander-in-Chief in Ireland, disapproved of them; even the RIC often disliked and distrusted them; while all shades of Catholic and Nationalist opinion hated and detested them.

By the beginning of 1921, 1,500 A Specials had already been enrolled – there were only about 1,000 RIC in the six counties – and 2,200 B Specials had been recruited in Co.Fermanagh alone. They had already seen some action and suffered some casualties. The first Special killed was hit in an IRA ambush in South Armagh early in January 1921. The second died in more dubious circumstances. On the evening of 23 January a platoon of fifteen A Specials from Newtownbutler in Co.Fermanagh drove to Clones in Co.Monaghan and broke into and looted a pub. The RIC were alerted and, thinking the culprits were civilians or IRA men, they opened fire, killing one of the Specials. The incident gravely embarrassed the government, and the platoon had to be disbanded.

1920 had ended relatively peacefully in Belfast with only six deaths in the last two months. The year's death-toll for the city stood at 74: five British soldiers, two RIC men, and 67 civilians, 35 of them Catholics and 32 Protestants. The fairly even casualty figures between the two communities, however, disguised the much greater hardship of the Catholics. Barely a quarter of the city's population, they had suffered over half the casualties, 11,000 of their number had been expelled from their jobs and several thousand driven out of their homes.

1921 began on the same low key 1920 had ended on. There were no serious riots in Belfast though there was a steady average of four deaths a month in the city. The IRA kept up a constant small-scale campaign of attacks on RIC barracks and RIC and Special patrols inside and outside Belfast, killing seventeen police and Specials in the first five months. On 23 April two Auxiliaries were shot dead in Donegall Place in the centre of Belfast. That night RIC men raided a Catholic home in the Clonard area, took out two brothers, Patrick and Daniel Duffin, and shot them dead. The murder squad was still in operation and claiming its steady toll as well.

Meanwhile the Government of Ireland Act had at last been passed and preparations were made to put it into effect. Elections were to be held in the six counties and in the rest of Ireland for the two separate Home Rule parliaments. Both elections would be under proportional representation and the Northern parliament would have 52 members. It was evident that Sinn Fein would sweep the board in the South and that the new parliament there would never operate. But in the North the Unionists would win and so the foundations of the new state had to be laid.

The Unionists were getting ready. Carson was sick and ageing. He didn't want the responsibility of running the new state, and he was never at home in the North anyway, he wanted to stay in England. On 4 February 1921 Sir James Craig took over as Unionist leader. On 21 March he resigned from the Westminster government. He was evidently going to be the new Northern Premier.

The election was held on 24 May amidst massive security and massive intimidation. The opposition candidates whether Sinn Fein, Nationalist (UIL) or even Labour were constantly harassed and intimidated by Loyalist supporters and by the Specials. There were three Labour candidates in Belfast. When they booked the Ulster Hall – a large Corporation-owned hall in the centre of Belfast – for a final rally it was taken over the night before by Loyalist shipyardmen and barricaded against them. The shipyardmen telegraphed Craig: 'Mass meeting of loyal shipyard workers who have captured Ulster Hall from the Bolsheviks Baird, Midgley and Hanna request that you address them for a few minutes tonight'. Craig replied that he had another engagement but said 'I am with them in spirit. Know they will do their part. I will do mine. Well done big and wee yards'[20]. The *Newsletter* reported the comments of one of the Labour candidates, James Baird, at the declaration of the count:

'During the election he had not been allowed to say a word. Since the day of his nomination he had been hunted and shadowed by Crown forces and he was unable to conduct his campaign. Intimidation reached the polling and many seeking to vote were brutally assaulted. He had been threatened and a threat made to wreck his house. Your election, he added, has been carried out under the worst intimidation and marked by wholesale impersonation'[21].

Sinn Fein workers were treated even worse. The *Manchester Guardian* reported

'No sooner has it been discovered that a man is a Sinn Fein election agent for a district than he has disappeared . . . At Martial Hill in Armagh the Sinn Fein director of elections for the district was taken out of his house by the Specials and made to go down upon his knees and promise he would take no further part in the elections . . .'[22]

There was an 89 per cent turn-out and the Unionists got their expected majority: 40 seats to six each for Sinn Fein and Nationalists. Craig was appointed Prime Minister and announced his cabinet on 31 May. On 7 June the new parliament met for the first time, minus the opposition, and Craig was officially sworn in. On 22 June amid even more massive security the king came to Belfast and formally opened the parliament. The new state had been established.

2

Siege or Pogrom

The king's speech, when he formally opened the new parliament in Belfast's City Hall on 22 June 1921, was very conciliatory and appealed for peace in the whole of Ireland. He said:

'I speak from a full heart when I pray that my coming to Ireland today may prove to be the first step towards the end of strife among her people, whatever their race or creed. In that hope I appeal to all Irishmen to pause, to stretch out the hand of forbearance and conciliation, to forgive and forget, and to join in making for the land they love a new era of peace, contentment and goodwill . . .

'The future lies in the hands of my Irish people themselves. May this historic gathering be the prelude of the day in which the Irish people, North and South, under one parliament or two, as those parliaments themselves may decide, shall work together in common love for Ireland upon the sure foundation of mutual justice and respect.'

It sounded like a prelude to negotiations and it was. British policy had collapsed dismally in most of Ireland. Sinn Fein had secured 124 of the 128 seats in the proposed Southern parliament unopposed. The parliament would never function. Meanwhile the IRA was active throughout the 26 counties and had just crippled the British civil administration by burning the Customs House in Dublin and destroying the records and files of nine government departments, including the tax and local government records. General Macready, the British Commander-in-Chief, informed the cabinet that only martial law and complete military dictatorship throughout the 26 counties could defeat the IRA[1]. A.W.Cope, the Assistant Under-Secretary for Ireland, argued that they couldn't be beaten[2].

Britain was going to have to come to terms with the Republicans. However, now that the Northern state had actually been established, the Ulster Unionists' hand was greatly strengthened. As Churchill, chairman of the cabinet committee on Irish affairs, put it succinctly: 'From that moment the position of Ulster became unassailable'[3].

On the day the king was in Belfast, De Valera, who had escaped from an English prison, was arrested in Dublin. He was hurriedly released. On 25

June he received a letter from Lloyd George inviting him and Craig to London to discuss a settlement, but he refused to attend any tripartite meeting because this would amount to recognition of the Northern state. After a fortnight of complex jockeying for position a truce was announced on 9 July between British forces in Ireland and the IRA. It came into force on 11 July and De Valera met Lloyd George on 14 July.

The Unionist leaders were alarmed however. The IRA had not been beaten, on the contrary, it remained intact and armed. The Republicans rejected partition, and now the British government was negotiating with them. Craig went to London on 6 July to seek reassurance. Some of his followers adopted more direct methods.

Already June had seen an escalation of violence. Two of the new MPs in the six-county parliament, both 'Labour' Unionists, had made violent speeches in the Shankill area on 6 June, the day the parliament first met. The *Newsletter* reported the words of Sam McGuffin MP:

'They would not tolerate this lawlessness and outrage in the six counties – and, if they could not achieve this through the instrumentality of the imperial parliament, they would assume control of affairs themselves, and by the organisation of a special force, they would drive Sinn Fein bag and baggage out of the six counties'[4]. William Grant, later to be Minister for Labour, was also quoted:

'They must have law and order before they could legislate. If the Sinn Feiners would not come under their law they would have to take steps to expel them from the six counties . . . . they would not tolerate Sinn Fein and Bolshevism in the six counties[5].

Four days later an RIC man was killed in Belfast. The following night three Catholics were dragged out and shot as a reprisal. On 12 June a Special was killed and two more Catholics shot in retaliation. At the same time intense rioting broke out in the York Street area. Loyalists threw a bomb into the Catholic Dock Lane, killing one man and injuring 20. There was heavy sniping and 150 Catholic families were driven out of mixed streets between the mainly Catholic New Lodge Road and the Protestant Tiger Bay area.

The reprisal policy was in operation outside Belfast as well. In Co. Derry the IRA killed an RIC man in Swatragh and a local Catholic was killed the same day. Near Newry a Special was killed on 8 June and the Specials raided a nearby house and shot dead two young Catholics called Magill and beat up their 78 year-old father. The Specials killed two more young Catholics at nearby Rathfriland later in the month. In the meantime the IRA had staged a spectacular attack, blowing up the train carrying the king's cavalry escort from Belfast back to Dublin on 23 June, killing four troopers and causing the destruction of 80 horses[6].

But it was the announcement of the truce that saw the worst single day's violence in Belfast throughout the Troubles. On the night of 9 July in a breach of the spirit, if not the letter, of the agreement a large force of police and Specials raided Raglan Street in the heart of the Lower Falls. They were driven off by a combination of IRA gun-fire and popular resistance – the women of the Catholic ghettos were by then well prepared for police raids and set up a wailing and banging of pots and dustbins to waken the whole neighbourhood to stone and harass the raiders. This time the RIC were driven off with one dead and two wounded.

There was terrible vengeance. The next day, 10 July, was to be known as Bloody Sunday. Specials and armed mobs attacked all the ghetto areas. 161 Catholic homes were burnt and fourteen people killed, ten of them Catholics. The violence went on for almost a week with a determined attack on the Short Strand on 14 July. The final figures for the week were 23 civilians dead – sixteen Catholics and seven Protestants; and 216 Catholic homes destroyed. An American delegation visiting Belfast found a thousand Catholics homeless and living in schools, halls and other makeshift accommodation[7]. One of the dead was a thirteen-year-old Catholic girl shot by Specials. At the inquest even the coroner's jury[8] said . . . 'We think that in the interests of peace the Special Constabulary should not be allowed into any locality occupied by people of an opposite denomination.'

Security in the North was still a British responsibility and British forces eventually asserted their control. The truce applied to all Ireland and under its terms both Crown forces and the IRA were to cease offensive action and the Crown forces to cease raids and harassment.

It brought a certain respite to the North. Patrols by the B Specials, now 16,000 strong, were discontinued, and the A Specials, who were still active, were kept out of Catholic areas. The IRA were able to exist openly but not obtrusively. General Eoin O'Duffy[9], a senior IRA staff officer, was sent North to act as truce liaison officer with the British, and the IRA also took the opportunity to send experienced commanders from the South into Belfast and the six counties to re-organise Northern units. The best known was Dan Breen who spent about six weeks in the North.

While the truce led to a temporary peace on the streets, however, the Anglo-Irish negotiations produced a bitter war of words between Craig, Lloyd George and De Valera. On 18 July, after seeing Lloyd George again, Craig issued a statement repudiating the demand for self-determination for the whole of Ireland and saying 'It now merely remains for Mr De Valera and the British people to come to terms regarding the area outside that of which I am Prime Minister'. De Valera immediately demanded clarification of whether the British government agreed with Craig, saying there was no point in further negotiations if they did. Lloyd George's reply was equivocal: 'I am responsible neither for Sir James Craig's statement to the press to which you refer, nor for your statement to which Sir James Craig's purports to be a reply.'

On 20 July the British proposals were given to De Valera. They offered a restricted form of dominion self government for the 26 counties, but required 'full recognition of the existing powers and privileges of the parliament of Northern Ireland, which cannot be abrogated except by their own consent'. The Dail cabinet rejected them stating 'We cannot admit the right of the British government to mutilate our country either in its own interest or at the call of any section of our population.' Lloyd George replied by saying that this was the most Britain would offer and that his government was resolved 'to resist any effort to coerce another part of Ireland to abandon its allegiance to the Crown'. The correspondence was published on 15 August.

In the meantime Sinn Fein had won, unopposed, 124 out of the 128 seats in the election for the new parliament of Southern Ireland provided for in the Government of Ireland Act. When the parliament was summoned only the four (Unionist) MPs for Trinity College, Dublin turned up and it was adjourned indefinitely. The 124 Sinn Fein members plus the Sinn Fein MPs elected in the North[10] constituted themselves the Second Dail instead. The new Dail met on 16 August and unanimously rejected the British terms on 23 August, though they also appointed plenipotentiaries to try to resume negotiations.

It was against this background that at the end of August Loyalists launched fierce attacks on Catholic streets in the York Street/North Queen Street/Dock area, leading to three days of intense rioting and gun-battles which left 20 people dead. The *Daily News* correspondent said the Catholics of the area were under siege and commented . . . 'The attack on the district is regarded as part of a Unionist plot to show the people of England and

Scotland that no settlement is possible in Ulster'[1]. The *Manchester Guardian* report said

> 'After a disinterested investigation, the conclusion one has been forced to is, that the blame for beginning the trouble lies at the door of the Orangemen, and that, for the desperate shooting of Monday and Tuesday, both sides must bear responsibility, with this point to be remembered in favour of the Catholics, that, as they were attacked and as there was no military protection available, the members of the IRA retaliated in kind and quite as effectively. Then came the call for the military'[12].

On 4 September Sinn Fein held a mass rally in Armagh. The speakers were Michael Collins, Minister for Finance in the Dail cabinet – and a member of the new six-county parliament – and General Eoin O'Duffy. They were officially welcomed by the chairman and members of Armagh Urban Council, which was Nationalist-controlled. Collins' attitude as reported in the *Newsletter* was firm towards Britain but conciliatory to the Unionists:

> 'The Sinn Fein proposal was that Ulster should come in. They [Sinn Fein] could afford to give the Ulster people even more than justice. They could afford to be generous. That was their message to the North and it was meant for those opposed to them rather than for those who were with them.'

O'Duffy on the other hand was threatening:

> 'if [the Unionists] were for Ireland then they [Sinn Fein] would extend the hand of welcome to them as they had done in the past, but if they decided they were against Ireland, and against their fellow countrymen they would have to take appropriate action. They would have to put on the screw – the boycott. They would have to tighten that screw and, if necessary, they would have to use the lead against them.'

For years afterwards O'Duffy was known to the Unionists as 'Give them the lead' O'Duffy. But Collins' approach was no more acceptable. The Unionists were having neither. And some sections of the Loyalist camp seemed determined to wreck the fragile peace in Belfast.

On 18 September Loyalists again attacked the Catholic area off York Street. This time the British troops replied quickly and indiscriminately. They fired into Loyalist crowds killing two women. On 23 September Catholic ex-servicemen working on an unemployment relief scheme on the Newtownards Road were attacked and beaten up. The next day the Short Strand was attacked again and a young Catholic shot dead as he left

St.Matthew's Church. The following day the attack was renewed and Catholics in Seaforde Street threw a bomb into the attacking crowd, killing two people. The same day Loyalists threw a bomb into the tiny Catholic enclave of Weaver Street/Milewater Street, off York Road. A man was killed and four young children under six seriously injured. A few days later a Protestant funeral was fired on and a man killed. For the rest of the month more Catholics were driven out of work in the docks and the GNR engine works. On 26 September the military authorities declared an assembly of three or more people illegal in the troubled areas of Belfast, while the IRA headquarters in Dublin announced that regardless of the cease-fire they would take action to defend the Northern Nationalists.

Meanwhile despite the Anglo-Irish negotiations in London the transfer of powers to the Belfast government went on apace. On 22 November Belfast was to assume the vital responsibility for law and order. The Unionists made no concession to Nationalist sensibilities. The new Minister for Home Affairs was to be Richard Dawson Bates, for 16 years secretary of the Ulster Unionist Council and closely connected with the organisation of the UVF.

The ministry's powers were limited by the fact that the only force it directly controlled was the Specials. The British Army and the RIC were still controlled by Westminster. But there was another force in the six counties. Even after the establishment of the Specials the UVF had continued organising and recruiting. Now run by Colonel F.H.Crawford, organiser of the Larne gun-running in 1914, the authorities reckoned its membership at 20,000. The British administration had tolerated its existence and involvement in the Northern violence, now Crawford hoped for official recognition and aimed at a membership of 150,000.

Outright legalisation of such a sectarian private army was impossible. It would be in breach of the truce, might force the South into an all-out war on the North and would alienate opinion in Britain. An ingenious solution was devised. On 9 November Colonel Charles Wickham[13], the divisional commissioner of the RIC in the North, sent out a secret circular to his officers:

'Owing to the number of reports which have been received as to the growth of unauthorised Loyalist defence forces, the government have under consideration the desirability of obtaining the services of the best elements of these organisations. They have decided that the scheme most likely to meet the situation would be to enrol all who volunteer and are

considered suitable into Class C [of the Special Constabulary] **and to form them into regular military units . . . There is no necessity to produce the maximum possible number of units; what is required is to ensure that every unit recommended for formation can be constituted from a reliable section of the population'**[14].

Since the circular was dated before the hand-over of security to Belfast, the British government was also involved in this attempt to legalise the UVF. Collins got hold of a copy of the circular and raised it at the Anglo-Irish negotiations on 23 November, while Sinn Fein published it in Ireland. It came at a crucial point in the negotiations and could well have jeopardised the chances of the Treaty being accepted there. Craig was summoned to London and telegraphed Bates to withdraw the circular. On his return to Belfast he authorised the recruitment of another 700 A Specials (full-time) and 5,000 B men.

The actual assumption of security powers by Bates was marked by further violence. After three days of assaults on the Short Strand, with the Sexton's house at St.Matthew's Church burnt down[15], another bomb was thrown among the attackers and the same day a bomb was thrown into a tram-load of Protestant shipyard workers. Two men were killed. The attacks on the Short Strand continued however and two days later another tram was bombed, killing two more. Craig was in London when he heard of the bomb attacks. He sent a telegram to the citizens of Belfast: 'I have learnt with the greatest horror of the dastardly outrages made against Loyalists in the city of Belfast. I am taking drastic action at once.' Seventeen Catholics had been killed as against ten Protestants in the previous few days. Craig's selective horror didn't give the Catholic population much confidence in the new security authorities.

The government did take drastic action. The Specials were allowed back into the Catholic ghettos and launched massive searches in the Short Strand, but the rest of the year was relatively quiet. On 6 December an agreement, commonly known as the Treaty, was signed by the Irish delegation in London. It provided for the establishment of an Irish Free State with dominion status. The six counties were nominally included but would have the right to opt out as a unit. If and when they did a commission would be established to review the boundary between the two states. The Irish delegates were led to believe that it would transfer large areas with Nationalist majorities to the South.

The Unionists were angry, they had wanted simple confirmation of their position. They certainly didn't want a Boundary Commission since, by any criterion, substantial areas of the six counties did not want to be ruled by them. But the Treaty was not universally welcomed in the South either and throughout December attention focussed on Dublin as De Valera and a minority of the Dail cabinet rejected the Treaty and the IRA leadership was sharply divided over it. The Treaty fell far short of the ideal of a sovereign independent Republic. The Free State government was to take an oath of allegiance to the king; the Free State was to be a member of the British Commonwealth; Britain was to retain naval bases and the use of ports in the South; and the North or a substantial part of it was to be abandoned. But the Treaty was signed under threat from Lloyd George of 'terrible and immediate war' if the negotiations broke down. Commercial and professional interests welcomed it immediately. They didn't want another long-drawn-out disruptive war, most of them had never supported the Republic anyway and they had no desire for a complete break with Britain and the Empire. The Catholic hierarchy welcomed it as well.

Within the Republican movement the Treaty was supported by a small majority of both the political leadership – the Dail cabinet and eventually the Dail – and the military leadership – the IRA general headquarters. A majority of the rank and file of Sinn Fein and of the IRA – 9 out of 15 divisions and 3 out of 5 independent brigades – opposed it. As for De Valera, his opposition was based mainly on the grounds that a better bargain could have been made with Britain. He tried unsuccessfully to propose a compromise solution in the Dail and only finally committed himself to the outright anti-Treaty group when the civil war began.

Initially the bulk of the population, confused about the issues involved and anxious for peace, welcomed the settlement. Later they were polarised roughly along class and regional lines. The middle and upper classes and the prosperous, commercial East and Midlands supported the Treaty; the workers and small farmers of the poorer Southern and Western areas opposed it[16].

The Dail debated the Treaty over Christmas amid considerable doubt about whether it would be accepted. The year ended uncertainly. The death toll in Belfast for 1921 was 128: thirteen members of the Crown forces and 115 civilians: 72 Catholics and 43 Protestants.

As the Dail resumed the debate on the Treaty at the beginning of January 1922, the Loyalists asserted themselves again in Belfast. In the first week of January five bombs were thrown into Catholic houses or streets and another assault was launched on the Catholic North Queen Street area. Eventually the whole York Street district was put under a tight 8pm curfew; but meanwhile the Short Strand was attacked again. By 13 January f fourteen civilians were dead.

On 7 January Dail Eireann accepted the Treaty by 64 votes to 57. De Valera resigned and Arthur Griffith was elected President, with Collins as Minister for Finance and effective leader of the pro-Treaty Party. A week later the Provisional parliament met and elected a Provisional government with Collins as chairman. The Provisional government set about establishing the institutions of the new Free State.

At the same time the British began concentrating their troops in the South in major barracks, preparatory to withdrawing them. The Black and Tans and Auxiliaries were to be disbanded and sent home on 18 February and the RIC were to be disbanded on 4 April. In the South security and law and order would be handed over to the IRA until a new police force could be formed. An amnesty led to the release of a thousand sentenced political prisoners, including 130 in the North, while all internees, including those held in Ballykinlar camp in Co.Down, had been released in December.

In the North, arrangements were made to strengthen security forces. British troops of course were to remain, while provision was made to replace the RIC with a new Belfast-controlled Royal Ulster Constabulary (RUC). In the interim, while the RIC, looking forward to their pensions, stayed in their barracks and avoided trouble, the Specials played a more and more active role and the British handed over 26,000 rifles and a consignment of First World War uniforms dyed black to equip them. Sir Neville Macready, the C-in-C, and Sir Henry Wilson[17], Chief of the Imperial General Staff and an Irish Unionist, visited Belfast to advise on security and defence.

For the new Provisional government the North was one of the outstanding problems. The escalation of violence against the Nationalist minority and the entrenchment of the Unionists throughout the six-county area threatened to inflame feeling in the South and discredit the Treaty. A quick settlement of the Northern problem would do a lot to consolidate the Provisional government's position. On 21 January Collins met Sir James Craig in London to discuss relations between the two governments. Since the ratification of the Treaty Collins seemed to accept partition as irrevocable, relying on the Boundary Commission to transfer the bulk of the North's Catholics to the South, and hoping to negotiate better conditions for the rest. The two men signed a five-point agreement. The first point provided for the tripartite London-Dublin-Belfast Boundary Commission to be replaced by a joint North-South body to report back to the Premiers, who would then reach an agreement. The second clause read . . . . 'Mr Collins undertakes that the Belfast boycott is to be discontinued immediately, and Sir James Craig undertakes to facilitate in every possible way the return of Catholic workmen to the shipyards, as and when trade revival enables the firms concerned to absorb the present unemployed'. The other clauses dealt with cross-border railways, the Council of Ireland and the holding of a further meeting to discuss the release of political prisoners arrested since the truce.

Northern Nationalists were aghast at the agreement and sent deputations to Dublin to protest. Craig was attacked in the Belfast parliament as well but assured his critics, 'I will never give in to any re-arrangement of the boundary that leaves our Ulster area less than it is under the Government of Ireland Act.' In fact he had conceded nothing except a vague promise about the expelled workers. By meeting him at all Collins had implicitly recognised the Northern state and he had specifically promised to end the boycott, a promise he carried out. Craig did see a deputation of shipyard workers about reinstating the expelled men, but on 30 January a meeting in the shipyard resolved that they would not work with any 'Papists'[18]. Craig took no further action. A further meeting between Craig and Collins on 2 February broke up over the boundary question.

Meanwhile tension was mounting in the border counties. The IRA had kept the truce, but the Specials had been raiding and harassing them and in mid-January Specials had arrested eleven Monaghan men, some of them Republicans, on their way to a football match in Derry. They had been carrying revolvers. The IRA replied by kidnapping three RIC men near Cookstown and holding them as hostages. The hostage idea caught on, and when the Craig-Collins talks broke down with no release of Republican prisoners the IRA staged a series of raids into Tyrone and Fermanagh in early February, capturing about 40 wealthy Loyalists and taking them across the border.

On 11 February there was an extraordinary incident. A platoon of sixteen armed A Specials left their depot at Newtownards for Enniskillen.

They took a train which travelled through Co.Monaghan in the 26 counties and at Clones station some of them got out. Their presence in the 26 counties was completely illegal and they were challenged by the local commandant of the IRA, which was now the security force in the South. The Specials shot him dead and then the IRA guard in the station opened fire on them killing four, wounding eight and taking another four prisoner. When the train arrived in Lisbellaw in Fermanagh carrying the bodies there was a riot in the village and all the Catholic families were put out.

The next day the Loyalists in Belfast took their revenge in a violent onslaught on the ghettos which went on for four days and then resumed again on 23 February. In one incident a bomb was thrown into a group of Catholic children in Weaver Street off the Shore Road killing six of them. Churchill, the pro-Unionist Colonial Secretary, described it as 'the worst thing that has happened in Ireland in the last three years'. The Catholics retaliated by bombing shipyard trams again. The death toll for February was 44, the highest monthly figure since the 'Troubles' began. Diarist in the London *Star* commented 'What is happening is a sort of a Protestant pogrom against the Catholic minority'[19], while Dr McRory the Catholic Bishop of Down and Connor protested at 'the butchery of my people'.

But moves were made to calm the situation. The British government ordered the release of the 'Monaghan footballers' and some other Republican prisoners and the IRA released most of the kidnapped Loyalists. A joint North-South-British Border Commission was set up to prevent cross-border clashes, though the Northern side never operated it fully, and a British officer claimed one of the Specials told him they had orders to fire on any vehicle flying the Commission's blue and white flag[20]. By the end of March the Commission was defunct.

At the end of February Craig toured the border inspecting his defences. Most minor roads across the border had now been blocked and the main ones were patrolled by Specials. The A Specials were now over 4,000 strong and had about 40 mobile platoons, many of them operating out of big houses they had commandeered as barracks in the border areas. Soon afterwards Craig invited Sir Henry Wilson to advise on security again. He recommended substantial increases in all the Crown forces and the appointment of a permanent military advisor. The British government agreed to his suggestions and by midsummer 1922 the British garrison had been increased to sixteen battalions backed by 5,500 A Specials, 19,000 B Specials and an unknown number of C Specials together with the infant

RUC[21]. There was also a new group, the CI Specials, which had been authorised at the start of 1922. They were a territorial-army-style force who were given full military training and used as a military reserve with their own command structure[22]. They were essentially what the Wickham circular had proposed in November 1921. By midsummer 1922 they had 7,500 men. The six counties were becoming an armed camp with close on one adult male Protestant in every five in the Specials.

The Unionist backbenchers were clamouring for martial law but Craig was not keen on the idea. 'I myself am dead against any suggestion of martial law . . . . If we have martial law our cause in England will suffer immediately and intensely. They will say one side is as bad as the other.' It would also of course have meant handing over security decisions to the British Army who might not have been so totally committed to the Loyalist cause.

Anyway it wasn't necessary. On 15 March Dawson Bates introduced the Civil Authorities (Special Powers) Bill in the Belfast parliament. It got a speedy passage. It was designed to replace the extremely harsh Restoration of Order in Ireland Act which the British had used in the South, but the Special Powers Act was even more draconian. It provided for search, arrest and detention without warrant; flogging and the death penalty for arms and explosives offences; and allowed for the total suspension of civil liberties. It seemed the prelude to a reign of terror in the North. The *Manchester Guardian* commented:

'Whilst envenomed politicians in the Ulster parliament are voting themselves power to use torture and capital punishment against citizens whom they forbid to defend themselves while they scarcely attempt to protect them from massacre, some of their own partisans in Belfast carry wholesale murder to refinements of barbarity hardly surpassed in Armenia and Constantinople[23]**.'**

The passing of the Special Powers Act and the build-up of the Crown forces led to a crescendo of violence in the North. As the Belfast government grew more repressive the IRA went on the offensive. The Northern authorities hit back with greater savagery still and tension rose sharply in the 26 counties. More people died in Belfast in the next three months than in either 1920 or 1921.

At the beginning of March Catholic ex-servicemen laying tram-lines on the Antrim Road were fired on and a Catholic workman was shot dead on top of a tram. Bombs were thrown into a crowd at the Catholic end of

Foundry Street in East Belfast and into the porch of St.Matthew's Church. The Catholics retaliated by bombing a tram going past the New Lodge Road. Sniping into Catholic areas was general. And there were some bizarre incidents: on one occasion a B man, Special Constable Vokes, was shot running away from a British Army patrol.

The IRA were hitting back, not only in defence of the ghettos, but at the government forces: three RIC men and three Specials were killed in March. But this increased activity led to a terrible reprisal. On 23 March two Specials were shot dead in the city. At 1.30 on the morning of 24 March armed Specials burst into the home of Owen McMahon, a Catholic publican, on the Antrim Road. They took the father, his five sons and a barman who lived with them into the sitting room, lined them against the wall and shot them all. Only two of the sons survived, both seriously wounded. At Westminster Joe Devlin burst out 'If Catholics have no revolvers to protect themselves they are murdered. If they have revolvers they are flogged and sentenced to death.'

The death toll in March was 61 in Belfast alone. Even the government were getting alarmed, for March saw the first condemnation of Loyalist violence by a government spokesman, when Lord Londonderry, the Minister for Education, said in the Senate on 14 March: 'A section of those who see eye to eye with us on the political situation are implicated in outrages as reprehensible as those committed by Sinn Fein.'

Outside Belfast the IRA took the initiative. In ten days in March they seized RIC barracks in Maghera, Co.Derry, Pomeroy, Co.Tyrone, and Belcoo in Co.Fermanagh, capturing sixteen RIC and Specials in Belcoo and an RIC sergeant in Maghera together with arms and ammunition. They also burnt a number of mills in Co.Derry and killed five Specials and an RIC man in different areas. Reprisals were now swift and vicious. Two of the Specials were killed at Trillick in Co.Tyrone. The next night three Catholics were taken out and shot in the surrounding area. In his book *Guns in Ulster* Wallace Clark, an ex-Special commander, gives an insight into the Specials' methods: 'The night after the RIC sergeant was captured at Maghera a note was received by three leading Sinn Feiners in the area telling them they could say their prayers if he was harmed.' And when the IRA blew up a bridge in South Derry and the Specials wanted it repaired, 'some twenty Fenians [Catholics] from the mountain were rounded up by No. 14 Platoon, Magherafelt, and forced to act as labourers for the job'[24].

The Belfast violence had its effect in the South. Hundreds of

Catholic refugees were streaming into Dublin. The IRA had now split sharply into pro-and anti-Treaty sections. To the anti-Treaty section the Belfast killings were the result of the abandonment of the six counties by the Provisional government. The anti-Treatyites re-started the Belfast boycott and seized the Fowler Hall, the headquarters of the Orange Order in Dublin, partly as a reprisal for the billeting of B Specials in St.Mary's Hall, the main Catholic hall in Belfast, and partly to accommodate the Northern refugees. On 28 March the Republican (anti-Treaty) TDs met and appealed to the Provisional government to cooperate with them in joint action to protect the Northern Catholics.

But Collins was proceeding in a different direction. On 30 March he and three of his ministers met Craig and representatives of the British government again and another more detailed pact was signed. It was headed 'Agreement between the Provisional Government and the Government of Northern Ireland', and so amounted to a formal recognition of the Northern state. It began:

'**1. Peace is today declared.**

'**2. From today the two Governments agree to co-operate in every way in their power with a view to the restoration of peaceful conditions in the unsettled area.**'

The Agreement had eleven clauses. The first provided for Catholics to join the Specials and an Advisory Committee of Catholics to be set up to assist in their selection. Catholic Specials were to patrol Catholic areas and mixed patrols mixed areas. All police were to wear uniforms and numbers, and all arms were to be held in barracks and issued only when police went on duty.

Juryless courts, consisting of the Lord Chief Justice and a local Justice of Appeal, were to be set up to try serious offences – Collins requested this because of the tendency of Northern juries to acquit Loyalists. A joint Protestant/Catholic conciliation committee was to be established to investigate cases of intimidation, outrages etc. and to pressurise newspapers into reporting only an agreed version of such incidents. All IRA activity was to cease in the six counties. Before the six counties opted out of the Free State the pact signatories were to meet to see:

'**A. Whether means can be devised to secure the unity of Ireland.**

'**B. Failing this, whether agreement can be arrived at on the boundary question otherwise than by recourse to the Boundary Commission under Article 12 of the Treaty**'.

People expelled from their homes were to be enabled to return and the Northern government was 'to use every effort to secure the restoration of the expelled workers' but 'wherever this proves impracticable at the moment owing to trade depression' they were to be employed on relief works. The British government agreed to supply £500,000 for relief schemes, two-thirds to go to Protestants and one-third to Catholics.

The two Irish governments were to agree to the release of political prisoners, but 'no offences committed after 31 March 1922 shall be open to consideration.'

Finally they appealed to all concerned to refrain from inflammatory speeches and to exercise restraint.

The pact was signed by Collins, Eamon Duggan, Kevin O'Higgins and Arthur Griffith for the Provisional government and Craig, Lord Londonderry and E.M.Archdale for the Belfast government. It was countersigned by Churchill and Sir Lamington Worthington-Evans for the British government[25].

The January agreement had brought a few weeks of peace. The 30 March pact brought none. On 31 March in a reprisal for the McMahon killing, a bomb was thrown into the Protestant Donnelly home in Brown Street in Belfast. Two young children were killed. The next day an RIC man was shot dead at Stanhope Street in the Catholic Carrick Hill area. A lorry-load of RIC and Specials immediately raided the area. They shot one man dead in Stanhope Street, another in Park Street. Then they came to Arnon Street. A grandfather was shot dead in bed beside his terrified grandson. At no.18 Arnon Street they broke down the door with a sledgehammer and ran upstairs to where Joseph Walsh was sleeping with his seven-year-old son and two-year-old daughter. The son was shot dead, the father killed with the sledgehammer and another son shot and wounded on the way out.

Perhaps the pact could have survived even the Arnon Street killings, but it couldn't survive the backlash in the Unionist Party. On 4 April it was debated in the Belfast parliament. It was criticised by Robert Lynn MP, editor of the *Northern Whig*, a Belfast Unionist paper, and denounced by William Coote and James Cooper, MPs for Fermanagh and Tyrone. With a fine disregard for the Catholic majority in both counties, Cooper declared that 99 per cent of the people of Tyrone and Fermanagh were opposed to the pact. Thompson Donald, the Labour Unionist, denounced the proposal to reinstate the expelled workers. Craig retreated before the onslaught and assured them 'If any person can be found in Ulster to lead the people into a Free State it will not be me.'

In fact the pact became a dead letter. No serious attempt was made to reinstate the Catholic workers. A twelve-man police advisory committee was eventually set up with Dr McRory the Catholic bishop as chairman but when it met two members were arrested and interned, and three others were put on the wanted list but got away. No Catholics joined the Specials. The conciliation committee never really functioned and the political prisoners were not released.

The breakdown of the pact was highly significant. The Free State government, representing the Southern business classes and anxious above all for stability, had offered recognition and acceptance of the Northern state in return for an end to the assault on the minority and a vague promise about the boundary issue. The Northern minority leaders had even agreed to support the police and Specials and to encourage Catholics to join them. Craig and his government had accepted the deal in the interests of stability; but their followers were having none of it. The Unionist leaders were finding that, having used discrimination and Protestant supremacism to establish their state, they could not dispense with them overnight. Orangeism and Loyalism had developed a dynamic of their own and Craig wasn't prepared to challenge them. It would not be the last time an Orange backlash would wreck attempts to stabilise the Northern state by concessions to the minority or to the South. Fifty years later a more elaborate version of the Craig-Collins pact, the Sunningdale agreement, would be brought down by a similar backlash.

Meanwhile the Northern government continued to strengthen its forces. On 4 April the RIC was disbanded and the new RUC took over. It was to be 3,000 strong, recruiting 1,000 A Specials and 2,000 ex-RIC men. Half of the RIC men were to be Catholics, giving Catholics a third of the places in the new force – though Catholic RIC men were quite unrepresentative of the Catholic population. At any rate less than half the requisite number of Catholics came forward and the balance was made up by more Specials, while the A Specials continued in existence as a separate force. On 7 April the Special Powers Act came into force and at the same time the Belfast government appointed Major General Solly Flood as military advisor – despite the fact that under the Government of Ireland Act they were prohibited from raising or controlling any military force.

And the violence continued. On 14 April a Catholic loco-man was shot dead at his work in York Road railway station. Three days later a Loyalist mob attacked the Bone, burning down two streets, Antigua Street and Saunderson Street. Fifty Catholic homes were destroyed and one Catholic and one Protestant killed. On the 23rd a bomb was thrown into the porch of St.Matthew's Church as people came out of Mass and one woman was killed. The death toll for the city in April was 36.

In the countryside the pact had no effect at all. At the beginning of the month 500 A Specials launched a massive comb-out of the remote valleys of the Sperrin mountains between Draperstown and Greencastle, rounding up 300 men – almost the entire male population – but holding only three. Elsewhere the IRA had the edge, killing two Specials, one in Fermanagh and one in South Armagh, and wounding five others and capturing their Crossley tender and arms at Wattle Bridge in Fermanagh.

As it happened the pact was about to be scrapped. On 22 April Collins telegraphed Craig to the effect that no further progress could be made unless prisoners on a list he had supplied were released and the joint conciliation committee was allowed to investigate the Arnon Str-eet/Stanhope Street killings. Craig replied on 25 April, sending a copy of his letter to the press. He complained of continued IRA action in the North, said the Belfast boycott had been more effective than ever since the pact[26], and accused Collins of failing to implement the agreement. He refused to release more than a handful of prisoners and said the conciliation committee should investigate only incidents which occurred after it was established.

Collins answered sharply, pointing out that he had secured the release of the B men captured in Clones and expected reciprocation, and that the Arnon Street killings had taken place after the pact was signed and published. As far as IRA action and the Belfast boycott were concerned he gave a damning list of attacks on Catholics and suggested that if they were stopped it would be easier to get the IRA to stop as well[27]. The correspondence put an end to the pact and to North-South negotiations, though, by signing it at all, especially the sections providing for a balanced police force, Collins had accepted both the legitimacy and permanence of the Northern state.

While these bitter letters were being exchanged incidents in Cork figured prominently in the press. The town and area of Bandon had a sizeable Protestant community. On 25 April the commandant of the IRA brigade in the area, now responsible for law and order, was shot dead when he called at a Protestant-owned house. Within a few days ten Protestant men had been killed in the district. Sinn Fein in Belfast immediately denounced the killings and the new brigade commandant called in all arms and announced that all citizens would be protected. There were no more killings.

The violence in Belfast reached its climax in May and June. There was constant heavy firing into the Catholic ghettos and Catholics were killed at random. The IRA didn't take direct sectarian reprisals though some Catholic defence groups did. But their efforts were puny compared with the Specials and the armed Loyalist groups, who operated murder squads designed to take immediate reprisals for all IRA action and generally to terrorise the Catholic population into a state of abject submission.

On 18 May two Catholics from Ligoniel, a village outside Belfast, were shot dead on their way to work and a third was shot on his way home. The next day three Protestants were shot at work as a reprisal. The day after five Catholics were shot at work and eight more at their homes, while 220 Catholic families were driven from their homes in a single parish in the York Street area. On 31 May a Special was killed in Belfast. His colleagues looted the nearest pub and careered through a nearby Catholic area shooting wildly. Loyalist mobs went on the rampage killing a Catholic mother and daughter in one house and an elderly Catholic and her Protestant lodger in another, and then burning the house around them. A whole Catholic street was burnt out and another 86 Catholic families made homeless. Sixty-six civilians died in May: 44 Catholics and 22 Protestants, and 400 Catholic families were evicted. Close on a thousand Catholic refugees fled to Glasgow at the end of the month.

The *Manchester Guardian* described 'the eviction from their homes by Orange mobs, led by Specials, of thousands of defenceless Catholics' and said:

'On these unfortunate beings the fury of Orange Specials and Orange mobs, unable to reach the Catholic gunman and fortified by sectarian animosity, falls daily and nightly. These people have committed no offence unless it be an offence to be born a Catholic . . . . On the simple charge of being Catholics hundreds of families are being continually driven from their houses . . . In these operations the Specials provide the petrol, fire-arms and immunity from prosecution'[28].

As the sectarian attacks mounted the IRA hit back with a new weapon: a campaign of burning businesses and factories and the homes of leading Unionists. *The Plain People*, one of the anti-Treaty Republican papers, outlined the reasons for the attacks:

'The one way to meet the Anglo-Orange extermination campaign as conducted by Generals Wilson and Solly Flood is the way the IRA are meeting it – consigning to the flames the manufactories and businesses of the powers behind the murders. Let that go on. The Orangeman will not be won until he is beaten to earth'.

'Every factory destroyed is a blow at the enemy. Collins' British-inspired ideas of conciliation by surrendering would not achieve that in a thousand years. The IRA, at whom he sneers as irresponsibles and irregulars, are already accomplishing it by their policy of hitting at the British Orange allies in their pockets and their stomachs. Therefore we say go on with the burnings'[29].

Between 10 May and 25 May there were 41 serious fires in Belfast and by the end of May the damage was put at half a million pounds. Outside Belfast IRA units burnt Shane's Castle, Randalstown, the home of the Speaker of the Northern Ireland parliament Colonel O'Neill[30] and six other country mansions as well as railway stations and local mills. But once again there were vicious reprisals. On 3 May three RIC men were killed in South Derry; a week later three Catholic brothers were taken out and shot in the same area. On 19 May the IRA burned a mill in Desertmartin, also in South Derry. That night two Catholic businesses and four houses were burnt in the tiny village and four Catholic men taken from their beds and shot[31]. All the Catholics fled the village and one of them was shot dead five weeks later when he returned.

The IRA had also decided to hit at those politicians who were urging more and more repression. On 17 May W.J.Twaddell, MP for West Belfast, declared that 'if the Loyalist population of Northern Ireland are pressed to any greater extent than they have been ... they will, irrespective of this House, defend and protect themselves.' On 22 May Twaddell, a shopkeeper, was shot dead in the centre of Belfast on his way to his shop.

The Belfast government used their new powers to impose a massive clampdown. They introduced a blanket curfew from 10pm to 6am in all areas of Belfast and later extended it to cover the six counties. Pubs were forced to close at 7pm and an order was introduced whereby everyone had either to spend the night in his own home or notify the police in advance where he would be. Ardoyne and the Bone were cordoned off and movement in and out restricted, while a District Inspector Nixon[32] and the Specials created a reign of terror there. Dawson Bates announced that firearms permits would be limited to the Specials i.e. no Catholic would get a gun licence. Craig said, 'In Ulster owing to the system of A, B and C Constabulary there is no reason why every Loyalist should not have arms to his hand, legally agreed to by the government.'

On 22 May the government outlawed the IRA and introduced internment. Over 200 men were arrested in the early hours of the morning and the number soon increased to 500. At first the internees were held in three centres: Crumlin Road jail in Belfast, Larne workhouse and a camp at Newtownards. In June the government bought an obsolete wooden ship called the *Argenta,* converted it and put most of the internees on it. At first the *Argenta* was moored in Belfast Lough but then it was moved to Larne harbour. Eventually some of the internees were moved to Derry jail.

Despite the widespread Loyalist violence the internees were all Republicans. They were by no means all IRA men. In Co.Fermanagh Cahir Healy, a local writer, county councillor and soon to be a Westminster MP, was 'lifted'. So were Sean Nethercott of Enniskillen Urban Council and Thomas Corrigan, the secretary of the County Council. In Derry, Eugene McGilligan, a county councillor and Sinn Fein candidate for North Derry in the 1918 election, was lifted. Many of the men interned were not to be released until the end of 1924.

The next day Craig announced that his government was introducing legislation to

'indemnify all officers of the Crown against all actions or legal proceedings whatsoever, whether civil or criminal, for or on account of any act, matter or thing done during the course of the present Troubles, if done in good faith, and done, or purported to be done, in the execution of their duty or for the defence of Northern Ireland, or the public safety, or for the enforcement of discipline, or otherwise in the public interest.'

As he said himself 'I do not suppose that officers in responsible positions have ever been given such powers before'[33].

In the South, the breakdown of the Craig-Collins pact and the reign of terror in Belfast had increased the pressure on the Provisional government, and it was forced to co-operate with the anti-Treatyites in supplying arms to the North. The Treatyites were getting arms from the British but they didn't want to send these North because they could be traced by their serial numbers, so they exchanged some consignments of British guns with the anti-Treaty units, for unmarked or captured ones[34].

The anti-Treaty IRA now launched a dramatic offensive. A triangular area of Co.Fermanagh, thirty to forty square miles in size and bounded by the villages of Belleek and Letter, was completely separated from the rest of the county and the six-county state by Lough Erne and a projecting part of Co.Donegal. The only roads to the area led through the 26 counties[35]. There were rumours that the IRA were going to attack the triangle, and on 27 May 50 Specials were sent by boat to garrison Magherameenagh Castle in the threatened area. The next day a patrol of Specials was ambushed in the border village of Belleek and driven back to the castle where the Specials were effectively besieged. A relief patrol from Garrison was also ambushed at Belleek and retreated, after losing one man killed and a Lancia armoured car captured. With the Belleek road closed the IRA moved in in force and the Specials in the Castle had to be evacuated in a pleasure steamer, while the IRA opened the sluices in an unsuccessful attempt to lower the level of the Lough and strand them. By 1 June the IRA was in full control of the area.

The Provisional government's co-operation with the anti-Treatyites over the North didn't go very far. Craig appealed to London over the occupation of the triangle. Churchill consulted Collins and was assured that the Free State was not involved. On 4 June a large force of British troops moved in equipped with artillery. They took the border village of Pettigo on the fringe of the triangle after a five-hour gun-battle in which they used their artillery. Four IRA men, a Special and a British soldier, were killed. The IRA made no effort to defend the open country of the triangle but there was a sharp battle at Belleek before they were driven out, and the British used their artillery again to shell an old fort on the 26-county side of the border.

Elsewhere in the countryside the fighting was bitter and sectarian. Early in the month the Specials took three Catholics out of their homes and shot them. Then on 18 June the IRA raided a number of Protestant homes near Dromintee in South Armagh and shot six men and a woman, who they claimed were Specials – only one of them was. Three Catholics were shot by the Specials in South Down in the next few days. On 21 June a tender-load of Specials drove into the mainly Catholic village of Cushendall in Co.Antrim and gunned down four Catholic youths – an enquiry was later held which condemned the Specials but the results were never published.

In Belfast the onslaught on the ghettos and isolated Catholic homes continued. 436 Catholic families were driven out in the first week of June alone. In the first few days a mob attacked a Catholic doctor's surgery in Donegall Pass, poured petrol over his housekeeper and tried to burn her alive. On 5 June the Specials even fired on the Catholic Mater Hospital in North Belfast. The IRA incendiary campaign continued. In the first three weeks of June another half a million pounds worth of damage was done and by the end of the month there had been 82 serious fires in Belfast in May and June.

On 22 June Sir Henry Wilson was shot dead in London – two men were caught and later hanged for the shooting. And this death, together with the burnings, was a profound shock to the authorities. At a special meeting of Belfast Corporation held to condemn the killing, the Lord Mayor appealed for a ten-day truce in the city. In fact the businessmen of Belfast had been alarmed at the increasing violence for some time. In March a deputation of Catholic and Protestant businessmen had appealed to Craig to try to end it. On 4 April over 2,000 business and professional men had met in Belfast under the chairmanship of the president of the Chamber of Commerce, and the Stock Exchange had closed early to facilitate the meeting. They were addressed by Craig and were clearly Unionist. They assured Craig of their 'unwavering support in the determined stand which he, as head of the Ulster government is making against the attacks which are being made . . . . upon the integrity of the constitution.' But the president of the Chamber of Commerce proposed another motion expressing their 'strongest condemnation of the appalling atrocities and outrages perpetrated in our midst, from whatever quarter inspired' and strongly supporting the Craig-Collins pact. It was carried unanimously. Violence was endangering trade and perhaps even undermining the state it was designed to uphold.

The small Catholic business class were even more alarmed. They were prepared to accept the six-county state if the anti-Catholic violence was stopped. Two prominent Catholic businessmen had gone to see Craig in April, and a Nationalist councillor attended the special Corporation meeting in June – for the first time in two years, since Sinn Fein and the Nationalists were boycotting Corporation meetings – and supported the Lord Mayor's appeal for a Truce.

Suddenly events in Dublin took a hand. Tension had been building up in Dublin since April, when the anti-Treaty forces had seized the Four Courts building near the centre of the city and established it as a military headquarters. It was a direct challenge to the authority of the Provisional government. At the same time the British government was demanding that Collins suppress the anti-Treaty IRA. In a heated Westminster debate after the shooting of Sir Henry Wilson, Churchill demanded that the Free State Army move against the Four Courts or the British would do so themselves, using the troops still stationed in the South.

That very day, 26 June, Leo Henderson, director of the Belfast boycott, and a party of anti-Treaty IRA men seized sixteen motor cars imported from Belfast – they intended to use them for an attack on the North. Henderson was arrested by Free State forces and jailed. The IRA (from this point on IRA is used to describe only the anti-Treaty forces) kidnapped the deputy chief of staff of the Free State forces in retaliation. The next morning Free State troops began shelling the Four Courts with artillery borrowed from the British. The civil war had begun[36]. The Provisional government's official account of events stated that their action was aimed at stamping out the Belfast boycott and the lawlessness associated with it: their forces also attacked and captured the Fowler Hall, the Orange Order building used to direct the boycott. Thus the immediate cause of the South's bloody civil war was the Provisional government's determination, under British pressure, to stamp out attacks on the North.

The civil war had a devastating effect on the IRA in the North. It stopped an offensive planned for the next few days, it cut them off from their source of arms and supplies. It split their forces which had hitherto avoided the Treaty division. Many who were in the South took up opposite sides. Others went South to join in and those left in the North were demoralised. The commanders of two of the four Northern divisions were to be executed by Free State troops – Joe McKelvey from Belfast in December 1922, Charlie Daly from Tyrone in March 1923, while Sean Larkin, the local IRA commander in South Derry, was executed with Daly in Drumboe Castle in Co.Donegal.

This depleted and demoralised force was left to face sixteen battalions of British troops and nearly 50,000 police and Specials. At the wildest estimate the IRA's pre-civil war strength in the six counties was 8,500. Nearly 500 were interned and the courts were busy jailing as many as possible. In April there had been 470 prisoners in Northern jails, and even then many of these were political. By October, there were 870. The increase was almost entirely political. The odds were impossible and IRA activities petered out until by the autumn they were virtually inactive.

Even if the IRA had been able to fight on, the Catholic population had no stomach for continuing. The Catholic establishment slavishly supported the Free State government. The Catholic Protection Committee, the mouthpiece of the bishop, said on 4 July: 'This Committee, grateful for the work of the Provisional government for the Catholics of Belfast, congratulates the government on the success of its labours for the restoration of peace and good order in Dublin and the country, and wishes it god-speed in its efforts.' The mass of the Catholic population, who had looked to the South for protection were confused and disheartened to find the Dublin government suppressing the people who had defended them.

If there was peace it was the peace of the vanquished however. It was not because the minority had been reconciled to the state. Between July 1920 and July 1922, 453 people had been killed in Belfast, 37 members of the Crown forces and 416 civilians: 257 Catholics, 157 Protestants and two of unknown religion. Of the city's 93,000 Catholics, a quarter of its population, nearly 11,000, had been put out of their jobs and 23,000 driven from their homes. Over 500 Catholic-owned shops and businesses had been burned, looted and wrecked. Outside Belfast at least 104 people had died, 45 Crown forces and 61 civilians; 46 Catholics and fifteen Protestants. The Catholic population had been beaten into submission.

The violence wasn't over however. It spluttered on in July and August and then flared up in September with several shootings and bombings, almost all directed at Catholics. By October another twelve Catholics had been killed, most of them in East Belfast. Up to this, Craig's government had turned a blind or at least a tolerant eye towards Protestant violence. In the countryside reprisals had become commonplace – for every RIC man or Special killed one or more Catholic civilians, usually with no connection with the IRA, were taken out and killed by the UVF or Specials. In Belfast the same policy was supplemented by assaults on Catholic ghettos, bomb-throwing, sniping and random murders, sometimes as part of a deliberate and calculated terror campaign, sometimes as a result of sheer sectarian hatred. Yet searches and raids were concentrated in Catholic areas, internment was reserved for Catholics and the military fired mainly into Catholic districts. It was logical enough. Protestant violence supplemented the work of the Crown forces and terrified the minority into submission. That was the government's priority.

But already in March and April the businessmen had begun complaining. Now with the IRA quiescent the Loyalist gangs were continuing. The city was still in a state of fear and the IRA might be forced into action again to defend the minority.

The main culprits were the Ulster Protestant Association. The UPA had existed as a secret terrorist group since 1920 alongside the open UVF and Specials. A remarkable picture of its organisation and police action against it is given in a memorandum from District Inspector Spears of the RUC in East Belfast to Dawson Bates in February 1923[37]. Spears describes the UPA as having been formed in the autumn of 1920 'by well-disposed citizens for the protection of Protestants and Loyalists from Sinn Fein aggression'. There were branches in North, South, East and West Belfast and it speedily became dominated by what he calls 'the Protestant hooligan element' whose 'whole aim and object was simply the extermination of Catholics by any and every means'.

They first became really active in July 1921 when they 'entered thoroughly into the disturbances, met murder with murder and adopted in many respects the tactics of the rebel gunmen.' The police didn't move against them until the end of March 1922 when they seized a large arms dump and the chairman of the East Belfast UPA, Robert Simpson, was jailed for eleven months. There was no further police action until October. In the meantime IRA activity ceased in June and Spears reported:

'from then until October six deliberate and cold-blooded murders of harmless Catholics took place in this district together with an attempt to murder a Protestant constable of the RUC ... These murders were accompanied by numerous attempts to murder Catholics, shooting into Catholic houses and areas and throwing bombs into the houses of Catholics, both police and civilians.'

On 5 October a Catholic woman, Mary Sherlock, was shot dead on the Newtownards Road. Spears got authority to arrest and intern two UPA leaders, Joseph Arthurs and Frederick Pollock, and two more were arrested elsewhere in Belfast. But the government was still not prepared to use the full rigour of the Special Powers Act against Loyalists. Arthurs and Pollock were held for a month and then deported to England on condition they stay away from the six counties for two years.

In a series of raids Spears acquired a lot of information about the

East Belfast UPA. They had about fifty hard-core and a hundred floating members and met each week in a pub on the Newtownards Road. They got their money by collections backed by intimidation and the club's officers took a fair percentage for themselves. They had a brutal system of internal discipline and had a 'flogging horse' set up in their club-rooms where vicious beatings were handed out.

Since violence continued in East Belfast Spears had a further four UPA men interned in November, while four more were arrested on fire-arms charges and two of the principal murderers and gunmen joined the British Army. Finally in a series of raids the police seized almost all the UPA's arms and in February Spears could report: 'As matters at present stand the UPA is entirely broken up and peace has since been restored to this district.'

Altogether between ten and twenty Loyalists were interned but the policy was not popular in some sections of the Unionist Party. As soon as the first Loyalists were interned in October Sam McGuffin and Thompson Donald, two of the MPs who had been loudest in their demands for law and order and tough measures, began criticising internment and demanding the release of Loyalists. Dr Morrison, MP for Queen's University, put the professional classes' point of view. He said he had only recently learned that 'there is a set of men who deliberately plotted and deliberately carried out the murder of unoffending Roman Catholics. I say that if such men exist it is the duty of the government to put a stop to it. I will never raise my voice to have them protected'[38]. He was a little late: the UPA had been active for over a year. Craig himself made clear that now that things were relatively peaceful the government would act firmly against Loyalist violence. At last he was prepared to take on the extreme fringe of Loyalism – but only when Protestant supremacy had been securely established and all but a handful of Loyalists were satisfied.'

The internment of Loyalists created some anomalies. Two B Specials, Samuel Ditty and James Mulgrew, were interned for about six months. Mulgrew, who was an ex-serviceman and old UVF man, reported back to his Special platoon when he was released and was re-engaged and served as a Special for another thirteen years. When Ditty was released he was the guest of honour in his B man's uniform, at a welcoming function on the Shankill Road which was attended by a government MP.

By the end of 1922 the six-county state was peaceful. The government was taking no chances and continued its precautions. But peace continued in 1923 and 1924, and at the end of 1924 internment was ended and the curfew finally lifted. The new state had survived.

3

Consolidation

While the War of Independence had been going on in the rest of the country and intense sectarian violence had been raging in Belfast the institutions of the new Northern statelet were steadily being established. The elections for the six county parliament in May 1921 were held under proportional representation as provided for in the Government of Ireland Act. There were 52 seats to be filled: four each for North, South, East and West Belfast and Co.Armagh, five for Co.Derry, seven for Co.Antrim, and eight each for Co.Down and the combined counties of Fermanagh and Tyrone. Graduates of Queen's University, Belfast, also elected four MPs. There were 77 candidates: 40 Unionists, nineteen Sinn Fein, thirteen Nationalists (as the UIL members were now called), three Candidates from the Independent Labour Party (ILP), and two un-affiliated Labour candidates.

The Nationalists had been in disarray since the 1918 election and the old UIL organisation was falling apart, so they summoned a special six-county conference on 4 April to decide on policy towards the election. Attendance was over 800 and the *Irish News*, the Belfast nationalist newspaper, described the meeting as very representative of the clergy and the members of the public boards, together with the UIL, the AOH and the Irish National Foresters[1]. The Nationalists were then and for a long time afterwards very much the mouthpiece of the Catholic clergy in the North, and in the absence of any real party organisation the clergy, who after all had a province-wide organisation with full-time men in every parish, exerted considerable influence on them. Sinn Fein, though by no means secularist, were not so closely identified with the Catholic Church and after the outbreak of the civil war were frowned upon and condemned.

Joe Devlin took the chair and a resolution proposed by a Canon Crolly was passed:

'That we enter our solemn protest against the imposition on any part of Ireland of a constitution conceived by a foreign legislature for British political purposes ... believing this so-called Northern parliament is a danger to our liberties and a barrier to the permanent solution of

the Irish problem, we can neither give it recognition nor lend it support, and we call on all those who are opposed to the partition of Ireland to support at the forthcoming elections for the North-east Ulster parliament only candidates who will unreservedly pledge themselves neither to recognise nor enter into it[2].

They also decided to call on the six-county and 26-county parliaments to meet together as a Constituent Assembly for Ireland.

Sinn Fein of course were pledged to abstentionism as well, and three days later Devlin made a pact with De Valera providing for an agreed number of candidates in each constituency and for the transfer of preferences between Sinn Fein and Nationalist candidates. He confided to John Dillon, the former leader of the UIL, that without a pact the Nationalists would have got no seats at all outside Belfast.

The three ILP candidates were Councillor James Baird and John Hanna, who had been expelled from the shipyards, and Harry Midgley[3]. They were all Protestants but their manifesto stated 'We are completely against partition. It is an unworkable stupidity as the inner circle of political wire-pullers well know, but it is considered good enough to fight an election on ... the interests of the workers of Ireland are politically and economically one'[4]. They made no electoral alliances.

All the churches intervened in the campaign. The heads of the main Protestant churches backed the Unionists, while the Orange Order provided their electoral machine. Dr McRory, the Catholic Bishop of Down and Connor, in a letter read in all churches urged his flock to vote against partition. The Unionist candidates were all Protestants, the Nationalists and Sinn Feiners all Catholics.

The results were predictable, though the Unionists got more seats than expected. With 341,622 first preferences, all 40 Unionist candidates were elected. Sinn Fein and the Nationalists got six seats each[5] with 104,716 and 60,577 first preferences respectively. The three ILP candidates fared disastrously compared with their showing in the 1920 local elections, getting a joint total of 1,877 votes. They were obviously swept aside in the basic conflict over partition.

The new parliament met formally on 7 June to be sworn in and elect a Speaker and a government. The Sinn Feiners and Nationalists didn't attend – and never did during the life of that parliament. Colonel William Hugh O'Neill, a Co.Antrim landowner, was elected Speaker and Sir James

Craig became Prime Minister and announced his government. The list read like an executive committee of Northern industry and commerce:

Prime Minister: Sir James Craig, landowner and shareholder in the family whisky business, Dunvilles' Distillery.

Minister of Finance: Hugh McDowell Pollock, Managing Director of Shaw, Pollock and Co. Ltd, flour importers, Director of the Belfast Ropeworks and former President of the Belfast Chamber of Commerce.

Minister for Education: Marquis of Londonderry, landowner, and one of the biggest coal-owners in Co.Durham in England. (He later left Northern Ireland politics and became Leader of the British House of Lords.)

Minister for Agriculture and Commerce: Edward Mervyn Archdale, a Co.Fermanagh landowner.

Minister for Labour: John Millar Andrews, chairman of J. Andrews & Co. Ltd, Linen Manufacturers, and Director of the Belfast Ropeworks and the Belfast and Co.Down Railway Company.

Minister for Home Affairs: Richard Dawson Bates, solicitor, and Secretary of the Ulster Unionist Council since 1906.

The Parliamentary Secretaries were of the same ilk:

Prime Minister's Department: Viscount Massereene and Ferrard, landowner and Chairman of the LMS Railway Company.

Finance: John Milne Barbour, Director of William Barbour & Sons (linen manufacturers), the Linen Thread Co. and Great Northern Railways Ltd, and former President, Belfast Chamber of Commerce.

Chief Whip: Capt. Herbert Dixon, Chairman of the Commercial Insurance Company of Ireland and Director of Thomas Dixon & Sons, timber merchants and ship-owners.

Education and Commerce: Robert John McKeown, Managing Director of the Milfort Weaving Company.

Home Affairs: Robert Dick Megaw, barrister and Law Professor.

Finally, to maintain the Unionist Alliance, two posts went to working-class members of the Unionist Labour Association:

Parliamentary Secretary to the Ministry of Labour: John Fawcett Gordon, linen worker.

Assistant Whip: Thomas Henry Burn, former typesetter and Westminster MP.

Under the Government of Ireland Act the elected MPs formed the six-county House of Commons. There was also a Senate of 26 members, 24 of them elected by the Commons and two ex-officio members, the Mayors of Belfast and Derry.

The Senate was elected on 11 June. Since the Nationalists and Sinn Fein members didn't attend, it was entirely Unionist with the single exception of Hugh O'Doherty, the Mayor of Derry, who didn't attend either. It was also entirely Protestant, as were the government and the 40 sitting members of the House of Commons.

The social composition of both bodies was similar to that of the government. Of the 40 Unionist MPs 20 were company directors or merchants, three landowners, ten members of the professional classes, and only four were working-class. In the Senate there were five lords, two baronets and three workers among the 25 Unionist members. It was fairly clear what social classes the Unionist Party represented.

Sinn Fein had nominated some of its leading figures in the contest and the Sinn Fein MPs included De Valera, Michael Collins and Arthur Griffith. Five of their six MPs had also been elected in the South, and sat in the Dail in two capacities. The odd man out was Sean O'Mahony, elected for Fermanagh and South Tyrone. The Nationalists included two of the old UIL MPs at Westminster, Devlin and T.J.S.Harbinson, and J.D.Nugent, the general secretary of the AOH and formerly an important figure in the UIL. They represented the small Catholic middle class: two were hotel-owners, two solicitors, one was an insurance agent and Devlin himself, a former barman, held shares in a liquor wholesaler's.

The new parliament was formally opened by the king on 22 June and then, with little conviction of its own importance, adjourned until September. Its first few meetings were held in the City Hall in Belfast, then it leased the Presbyterian Assembly's training college near Queen's University and met there until 1932, when it moved to a grandiose new building at Stormont, outside Belfast.

Meanwhile a new threat to its existence had arisen. The Treaty negotiations had begun. Craig went to London on 6 July 1921, returned to Belfast for the 12 July parade and back again to London on 14 July, demanding assurances that there be no change in the position of the North. He had some success. De Valera himself conceded the principle of separate treatment and autonomy for the North. He said:

'Ireland, so far from disregarding the special position of the minority in North-East Ulster . . . [the Protestants, who were a minority in all Ireland] **would be willing to sanction any measure of local autonomy**

which they might desire, provided that it were just and consistent with the unity and integrity of our island.'

Lloyd George's proposals, however, insisted on maintaining partition, with the result that the negotiations broke down[6]. Craig was still not satisfied, though, and wrote an open letter to Lloyd George making clear he would not meet De Valera until he accepted 'the sanctity of the powers and privileges of the Northern Ireland parliament'.

Negotiations were resumed in October, and the Dail cabinet's proposals now suggested that while the six counties should come under the jurisdiction of an all-Ireland parliament, the Belfast parliament should continue and keep all the existing powers allotted to it under the Government of Ireland Act – presumably including security and control of the police. The Dail cabinet was weakening, and already deputations of Northern anti-partitionists were going to Dublin to reiterate their refusal to submit to any partition parliament.

Lloyd George began to bargain. The British government recognised that a substantial measure of independence would have to be given to the South. Their concern was to limit it as far as possible, keep Ireland within the Empire, and retain certain naval and military rights there. Lloyd George offered control over the North in exchange for concessions by the Dail. On 27 October Arthur Griffith reported to De Valera, who had stayed in Dublin, that the British would insist on the North going under an all-Ireland parliament if the South accepted the sovereignty of the king. Lloyd George managed to get him to give a personal assurance in writing that he would recommend to the cabinet acceptance of the king, 'free partnership within the Empire' and the granting of naval facilities to Britain – if the British put pressure on the North[7].

Of course the weakness of that bargain was that, even if Britain did put pressure on the North, the Unionists might still refuse to give way, especially if the pressure were to be less than whole-hearted. But by now the will of the Sinn Fein/IRA leadership, or a section of it, was weakening. The War of Independence and especially the policy of reprisals – the Black and Tans had burnt down the commercial centre of Cork in December 1920 causing two to three million pounds' damage – had devastated much of the country, ruined trade, and created massive unemployment. The business classes wanted peace and they wanted it quickly. Though IRA/Sinn Fein members were largely workers or small farmers, the leadership were petty bourgeois, interested mainly in the development of a strong industrial and commercial economy, with themselves in control. They were receptive to the businessmen's pleas and the North was not central to their plans anyway. Half the cabinet were now for compromise and had no intention of renewing the war over the issue of the North. And, as we have seen, when the Treaty was signed the middle and upper classes backed it solidly.

On 5 November Lloyd George saw Craig in London and suggested that the six counties agree to what were effectively the Dail proposals if Ireland stayed in the Empire and owed allegiance to the king. Craig refused and Lloyd George threatened to resign – a threat of which no more was heard. On 10 November he invited the Belfast government to talks and outlined his proposals in writing, pointing out the disadvantages partition would bring to the North, and mentioning the possibility of a commission to review the boundary of the partitioned area if the Unionists would not give way. Craig replied for his cabinet the next day, rejecting the proposals out of hand. The Unionists would not tolerate a united Ireland of any kind and would not even talk to Lloyd George unless the idea were ruled out. They would not consider any review of their boundaries and resented even the assurance that their powers would not be curtailed.

Lloyd George now secured another concession from Griffith, arguing that he was under attack from the Conservative Party in Britain. The six counties would have to join the 26, but the Dail would agree that they should have the right to opt out after twelve months, in which case a Boundary Commission would be set up. If the Unionists would not agree the Prime Minister promised he would try to get Westminster to pass an act establishing an all-Ireland parliament; and if he failed he would call a general election. Griffith agreed[8].

There was now intense argument in the Dail cabinet. Members were distinctly uneasy about the concessions they were making. On 1 December they were given the British proposals, which provided for roughly dominion status within the Empire, an oath of allegiance to the king for members of the Southern parliament, and reserved naval facilities to Britain. The status of the North would remain unchanged for twelve months. At the end of that time the six-county area would become part of the Irish Free State, with the same relationship with Dublin as it had with Westminster – unless, within the twelve months' both houses of the Northern Ireland parliament requested that they should not be included in the Free State. In that case a Boundary Commission would be set up by the British government[9].

Three cabinet members, Griffith, Eamon Duggan and, to a lesser extent, Michael Collins, favoured acceptance of the proposals. The majority were against, but the negotiators were sent back to London. De Valera refused to go himself. Lloyd George – by breaking off the negotiations, holding a private meeting with Collins, and threatening war within three days – exploited the divisions in the Irish delegation. If he did not promise that the Boundary Commission would dismember the North, he also did not contradict Collins when he said it should give Tyrone, Fermanagh and parts of Derry, Armagh and Down to the South. The delegation signed the British proposals with a few minor amendments. They were to become known as the Treaty.

As far as the North was concerned there were three changes. The time within which the Belfast parliament could vote itself out of the Free State was shortened to one month after the passing of the British Act of Parliament to ratify the Treaty. The Boundary Commission was to consist of three members, one nominated by each government with the British representative being chairman. Its terms of reference were unchanged. They were: 'to determine in accordance with the wishes of the inhabitants, so far as may be compatible with economic and geographic conditions, the boundaries between Northern Ireland and the rest of Ireland.' A new article was included to prevent either Irish government giving privileges to or imposing disabilities on anyone because of religion[10]. In retrospect the Boundary Commission, because of its built-in British and Unionist majority and its circumscribed terms of reference, was unlikely to make much change.

On 5 December Lloyd George sent Craig a copy of the Treaty, pointing out that Northern Ireland must now either enter the Free State or submit to a Boundary Commission. On 9 December he saw Craig in London and assured him that any changes made would be minor ones[11] and would transfer as many Unionists to the six counties as Nationalists to the 26 counties. But Craig was adamant. On 14 December he wrote to Lloyd George rejecting the whole idea of the Boundary Commission.

At Westminster Lloyd George defended the Treaty and argued that only the establishment of the Northern state – financed and armed by Britain of course – had made it possible:

'That accomplished fact – by legislation, by the setting up of the government, by the operation of the government – it was there to deal

with, not in the abstract, not in an agreement, not in contention, across tables, but in an actual living government.'

He maintained, despite his private assurances, that Fermanagh and Tyrone might be lost to the North:

'There is no doubt, certainly since the Act of 1920, that the majority of the people of the two counties prefer being with their Southern neighbours to being in the Northern parliament. Take it either by constituency or by poor law union, or, if you like, by counting heads, and you will find that the majority in these two counties prefer to be with their Southern neighbours .... if Ulster is to remain a separate community, you can only by means of coercion keep them there and, although I am against the coercion of Ulster, I do not believe in Ulster coercing other units'[12].

The Unionists were outraged. Craig's brother said in the same debate:

'Our Northern area will be so cut up and mutilated that we shall no longer be masters in our own house. The decision of that Commission may be a matter of life and death to us. I submit to the Prime Minister that he had no right to do that and that he was in honour bound not to allow such a Commission to appear in this document by the promise he had given to the Prime Minister of Northern Ireland.'

Lord Londonderry, Northern Ireland Minister for Education and after Craig the most influential member of the Northern cabinet, spoke threateningly in the House of Lords:

'All that I would say now is that it may be necessary for the government of Northern Ireland to refuse to nominate a representative on the proposed Boundary Commission and that, if by its findings any part of the territory transferred to us under the Act of 1920 is placed under the Free State, we may have to consider very carefully and very anxiously the measures which we shall have to adopt, as a government, for the purpose of assisting Loyalists whom your Commission may propose to transfer to the Free State but who may wish to remain with us, with Great Britain and the Empire'[13].

In the meantime the Provisional government had been established in the South. When Craig met Collins on 20 January 1922 – for the pact discussions – and again on 2 February – the duplicity of Lloyd George became clear. The 2 February meeting broke up with total disagreement over the boundary question. At a subsequent press conference Craig said he had been assured by Lloyd George and other British ministers that the Commission would deal only with minor rectifications of the boundary, while Collins had been promised 'almost half of Northern Ireland including the counties of Fermanagh and Tyrone, large parts of Antrim and Down, Derry City, Enniskillen and Newry'. Craig threatened again: if the Commission were 'to make anything more than the very minutest change in our boundary, the inevitable result of that would be bloodshed and chaos of the worst description'[14]. He needn't have worried. With the Provisional government established the British government was back-pedalling fast on the boundary question. Only two months after Lloyd George's statement about Fermanagh and Tyrone, Churchill, the Colonial Secretary, described the possibility of the Commission reducing Northern Ireland 'to its preponderatingly Orange areas' as an 'extreme and absurd supposition, far beyond what those who signed the Treaty meant'[15], while Austen Chamberlain reminded the Unionists that the Commission would have an 'impartial' chairman, appointed by Britain.

Despite all the signs Collins still seemed to believe the boundary could be changed by negotiation. Or else he found it necessary to maintain this as a polite fiction to keep his political support in the South. The second Craig-Collins pact of 30 March again provided for discussion of the boundary. Yet five days later Craig was telling his parliament: 'There shall be no tampering with our boundaries without the agreement of my government and myself[16].' The pact collapsed in a few weeks anyway.

Elections were to be held in the South in June 1922. On 20 May Collins and De Valera announced that they had made an agreement to nominate a joint panel of candidates[17]. There was uproar at Westminster at the idea of the Provisional government co-operating with the anti-Treatyites, and the British government made clear its basic commitment to the six county regime. On 29 May Churchill announced that British forces in the North had been increased to nineteen battalions and more would be sent if necessary, while a destroyer and gunboats had been sent to Belfast Lough. The evacuation of British forces from the South had also been stopped. In June he revealed that the Belfast government had been supplied with 50,000 guns for the Specials.

The election crisis passed. Collins himself broke the pact and the pro-Treaty groups secured a bigger majority while the anti-Treatyites boycotted the new parliament[18]. Within a few weeks the civil war had broken out and Craig and his cabinet could relax. For the next year the

Provisional government was to be far too busy suppressing the IRA to do anything about the Boundary Commission.

Meanwhile a number of events occurred to strengthen the Northern position. On 12 August 1922 Arthur Griffith died. Ten days later Collins was killed in an ambush. William T. Cosgrave took over as head of the Provisional government, with Kevin O'Higgins as Minister for Home Affairs and effective strong man of the cabinet. They represented much more clearly than Collins and Griffith the professional middle class and the wealthy commercial class, who threw all their weight behind the Provisional government in the civil war. Their primary concern was stability and law and order, and they had no intention of plunging the country into another war over the boundary. On 10 November 1922, Craig met Cosgrave in London. In general Craig recorded that his relations with the South improved greatly when Cosgrave took over[19].

Changes were also taking place in Westminster. On 19 October Lloyd George resigned. The new British Prime Minister was Bonar Law, whose father was an Ulster-born Presbyterian minister, and who had long been one of the Northern Unionists' strongest supporters in parliament. There would be no concessions on the boundary from him, and when he was succeeded by Baldwin in May 1923 Craig's brother became a junior minister in the government, giving the six counties a voice at the highest level.

On 6 December 1922 the Irish Free State was formally established. The following day both houses of the Northern parliament passed addresses to the king requesting their exclusion from the Free State. Craig declared that since his government had not been a party to the Treaty it would not nominate a member to the Boundary Commission. The day afterwards — 8 December — the Free State government shot four IRA prisoners as a reprisal for the killing of one of their TDs. One of the four was Joe McKelvey, former commander of the 3rd Northern Division of the IRA, covering Belfast, Antrim and North Down. McKelvey's funeral provoked the last flicker of the Belfast riots when Loyalists attacked the procession as it left Great Victoria Street station in Belfast, and the RUC seized the Irish tricolour from the coffin outside St.Mary's Church in Chapel Lane.

The civil war in the South ended with complete defeat for the IRA on 24 May 1923. There was a general election in August and the government party promised to demand the implementation of Article 12 of the Treaty providing for the Boundary Commission. They named

Professor Eoin McNeill, Minister of Education in the Free State government and the man who, as nominal head of the Irish Volunteers, had tried to countermand the Easter Rising in 1916, as their representative on the Commission. He was, ironically, MP for Derry in the Northern parliament.

In December 1923 another British election brought in the first Labour government under Ramsay MacDonald. The Free State government and the Northern Nationalist minority were encouraged. The British Labour Party had no love for the Unionists. The Free State pressed the issue of the Boundary Commission again. Cosgrave met Craig in February and April of 1924 to try to find an amicable solution. There was none. On 26 April the Free State government formally requested Westminster to establish the Commission.

The British government requested Craig to nominate his Commissioner. He refused. The British refused to go ahead without a Northern representative and referred the question to the Judicial Committee of the Privy Council. They ruled on 31 July that 'if no appointment is made, the Commission cannot go on.'

Eventually the British government decided to amend the Treaty to allow themselves to appoint a representative for the North, highlighting the fact that the Commission was weighted against the Free State anyway. The amendment was passed on 9 October 1924 and on 24 October the British government appointed J.R.Fisher, former editor of the *Northern Whig* and a well-known Unionist, as the Northern representative. They appointed Justice Feetham, a South African judge, as British representative and chairman. On 6 November 1924, almost three years after the Treaty was signed, the Commission held its first meeting in London.

The Northern minority were delighted. They had little reason to be. On 7 October Craig had declared in the Northern parliament that if the Boundary Commission was unfavourable to the North he would resign as Prime Minister and take any steps necessary to defend their territory. To do that he still had 40,000 armed Specials paid for by the British government.

There was little chance of the Commission's report being unfavourable anyway. A series of British spokesmen had given their opinions on the subject. Sir Lamington Worthington-Evans, one of the signatories of the Treaty, said:

'It was not intended that there should be large transfers of territory . . . If by any chance the Commissioners felt themselves at liberty to order the transfer of one of these counties nothing would induce the

Ulster people to accept such a decision and no British government would be guilty of the supreme folly of trying to enforce such a decision.'

Lloyd George himself said the same, and the House of Lords passed a resolution declaring that the Treaty 'contemplated nothing more than a re-adjustment of boundaries . . . no other interpretation is acceptable or could be enforced'[20].

Meanwhile on 29 October a general election brought in another Tory government sympathetic to the Unionists. It would have been a brave British Commissioner who flew in the face of all this opinion. However the Commissioners went ahead with their work. They toured the North and met deputations from Nationalist districts who demanded a plebiscite in the disputed areas, only to be told the Commission itself had no power to hold a plebiscite and the British government had no intention of holding one. In March 1925 the Commissioners moved back to London.

Craig was taking no chances however. In January 1925 he had a meeting with the British GOC Northern Ireland to discuss co-operation between the Army and the Specials in the defence of the six counties, and informed the British government – who was paying for them – that he couldn't begin to disband the Specials until September 1926[21], well after the Commission would have reported. He also called a general election on 3 April to strengthen his hand and show that the Unionists still commanded overwhelming support in the North. In fact the result was not as satisfactory as Craig had hoped. The Unionists' total of first preferences dropped to 211,662 compared with 91,452 for the Nationalists and 20,615 for Sinn Fein. Nationalists topped the poll in three constituencies – West Belfast, Co.Derry and Counties Fermanagh and Tyrone; Independent Unionists in two – South and North Belfast; Labour in one – East Belfast; and the Unionists only in two, neither of them in Belfast[22]. The Unionist Party held only 32 seats in the new parliament compared with 40 in the old one. The Nationalists held ten, Independent Unionists four, Labour three, Sinn Fein two and there was one Tenants Representative. If anything the election strengthened the Nationalist case, as the combined Nationalist/Sinn Fein vote in Counties Fermanagh and Tyrone was 42,270 compared with 40,465 for the Unionists, and in Co.Armagh the Unionists had a majority of only 493 over the Nationalists and Sinn Fein.

During the summer of 1925 the Commission continued meeting. In the autumn they began drafting their report. On 7 November the London *Morning Post* carried an amazing story: it reported that not only would the

Commission not recommend the transfer of Counties Fermanagh and Tyrone, Derry City or any major town to the South, but they would in fact recommend the transfer of a prosperous part of East Donegal and possibly part of the Inishowen peninsula in North Donegal to the North. In return the South would get unimportant strips of territory in South Fermanagh and South Armagh.

The *Morning Post* story was an accurate leak. It caused consternation in the South. The population of the threatened area of Donegal demanded protection. The Labour Party, now the opposition in the Dail, demanded a statement from the government. On 11 November Cosgrave said the government would not agree to the transfer of any territory from the South and cast doubt on whether the Commission could have agreed to any such report. On 21 November McNeill resigned from the Commission but the other two Commissioners claimed that he had agreed to the proposals in October. On 24 November McNeill resigned from the Free State government as well.

In the midst of the furore Craig's government arrested 50 Republicans under the Special Powers Act (many of them not long released), moved large numbers of Specials into Derry and other border areas and put the rest on stand-by.

The Judicial Committee of the Privy Council had ruled in 1924 that once the Commission was set up it could carry on its work with only two members. Feetham and Fisher said they were going to go ahead and present their report. The British government could then argue that this was binding, while Cosgrave had pledged himself in September 1924 to accept the Commission's findings whatever they might be.

The Free State government seems to have panicked. Cosgrave and O'Higgins went to London on 25 November. At Chequers they negotiated with Craig and Baldwin and on 3 December they signed an agreement confirming the existing boundary. They also agreed to scrap the Treaty provision for a Council of Ireland – an inter-parliamentary body to organise certain joint functions, which had never been set up because the Southern government had not wanted to collaborate with or formally recognise the Belfast regime. And they agreed to recompense Britain for compensation the British had paid out for damage done by British forces in the War of Independence. In retrospect the Commission's recommendation that Southern territory be transferred to the North seems to have been a transparent stratagem to have the whole thing dropped. It is highly improbable that Britain would have attempted to seize part of the South.

Craig returned to Belfast to be welcomed by a large and enthusiastic crowd. He had got all he wanted. The Free State had abandoned all serious claim to his territory and the British government was now committed to defending its frontiers. The crucial factors were: first, the fact that the six-county state had been in existence for four and a half years, enabling Feetham and Fisher to ignore the incontrovertible evidence of the wishes of the population in the border areas; and second, the presence of the Specials to resist any attempt at transfers. The British government, though it pleaded neutrality on the issue, had been responsible for setting up the state in the first place and had armed and paid for the upkeep of the Specials as well. They had contributed £6,780,000 of the seven and a half million pounds which the Specials had cost up to then. Churchill put it plainly at Westminster a few days after the agreement was signed:

'While the Boundary question was in suspense Sir James Craig and his government felt it necessary to maintain between 30,000 and 40,000 armed Special Constables in various degrees of mobilisation . . . On the basis of there being no settlement they were proposing to me that we should provide for the maintenance of all the Special Constables in their present state of efficiency up to at least September 1926 . . . but as soon as this settlement was reached Sir James Craig informed me that he would be able to proceed immediately with the winding up of the Special Constabulary[23].

In the South the Free State parliament – without the 48 Republican Deputies – ratified the agreement by 71 votes to 20, the Labour Party voting against. Even if the Republicans had been present it would have been passed. Cosgrave later commented frankly that the business classes liked the agreement[24]. Relations between the Free State and the six counties became quite cordial. Craig's biographer, St.John Ervine, tells how during the Chequers talks Craig's car broke down and the Southerners gave him a lift in theirs and they became quite friendly. He quotes a letter from Cosgrave:

'Lord Craigavon improved on acquaintance. It is but just and fair to say that we found him honourable and straightforward. I never knew him to finesse and he never sought to break a conference to his own advantage when he had the opportunity. He was, in my opinion, a loss to

that greater Ireland which the statesmanship of his time had been unable to bring into being'[25].

While this friendship was maturing the Northern Nationalists were despairing. They felt they had been betrayed into permanent subjection to a hostile regime which had given them every reason to fear its rule.

The boundary agreement had one embarrassing sequel. There was no longer any justification for the huge army of Specials. The British government agreed to make a final payment of £1,200,000 for them, but most of them were going to have to go. The most expensive part of the force were the 3,553 full-time A Specials and on 10 December 1925 Craig announced that they and the part-time CI force would be disbanded immediately. They would get two months' pay as a gratuity. It was a poor reward for nearly five years of service. Unemployment at the time was over 20 per cent and it was coming up to Christmas. Most of the Specials faced the prospect of a long time on the dole. Discontent grew, meetings were held and on 14 December the A Specials at Derry and Ballycastle mutinied and arrested their officers. The mutiny quickly spread to other units and on 16 December a representative meeting demanded a £200 tax-free bonus for each man. On the 18th Dawson Bates announced that there would be no increase in the bonus and any Special who refused to obey orders after his announcement would be dismissed immediately and lose even the paltry two months' gratuity. The A Specials, so long the enforcers of a particularly tough form of law and order, were unlikely rebels and the mutiny collapsed the next day. By Christmas the whole force had been disbanded.

4

A Protestant State

The Unionist government had survived the boundary crisis with their territory intact, and even with the goodwill of the Free State administration. But their very success brought problems, for they now had to contend with a minority of one-third of the population who had been beaten and terrorised into submission and were deeply suspicious and resentful.

It was a crucial moment. Whatever policy the Belfast government adopted now would determine the minority's attitude to the state and the future history of the state itself. The obvious policy would have been to exert every effort to rule fairly and impartially in order to win the confidence of the minority and reconcile them to the new six-county state. But the Unionist leaders were not free agents: they had mobilised the Protestant masses to resist Home Rule and inclusion in the Free State, through the policy of discrimination and the ideology of Protestant supremacy. Now their followers were seeking their reward. If a lasting loyalty to the new state was to develop among the Protestant masses, they had to be given a privileged position within it. Moreover a government of industrialists and businessmen was no doubt not unmindful of the fact that a policy of discrimination and Protestant privilege would effectively prevent the emergence of any working-class solidarity.

So the Unionists set about constructing an Orange and Protestant state with almost all political power and patronage in their own hands – right down to the humblest rural council – and operated an elaborate and comprehensive system of discrimination in housing and jobs which kept the minority in a position of permanent and hopeless inferiority.

The Northern state, born in bloodshed, inherited ready-made huge para-military and sectarian forces and an array of repressive legislation formidable enough to crush any foreseeable resistance. Both were clearly aimed at the Nationalist minority. In the quieter years after 1922, and especially after 1925, the obvious policy would again have been to dismantle this intimidatory machine in the interests of conciliation. But the Unionist leaders chose instead to keep their followers in a permanent state of siege, and maintain a rigorous system of repression against all but the most innocuous opposition.

The practical result of the creation of this Protestant police state was to be the permanent disaffection of the Nationalist minority and the alienation of the Southern population, preventing even the Cosgrave government from establishing closer links with the Belfast regime.

The 1920 local elections had left 25 local councils in the six counties in Nationalist hands, and many of them had already voted their allegiance to Dail Eireann. This was embarrassing to the Northern government, and in November 1921 when the question of a Boundary Commission was first mooted, it became a serious danger. Nationalist-controlled county councils in Fermanagh and Tyrone and local councils in other border areas were an almost irrefutable argument for the transfer of those areas to the South.

Control of local government was to be handed over from Dublin Castle to the Belfast government on 21 December 1921, so in November the Northern Ministry of Home Affairs sent out circulars to all local authorities requesting their co-operation. Tyrone County Council replied refusing to recognise the Northern government and re-affirming its support for Dail Eireann. The RIC promptly seized the council offices, records and documents. On 6 December a Local Government (Emergency Powers) Bill was rushed through the parliament in Belfast. Dawson Bates explained that under it

'**the Ministry, in the event of any of the local authorities refusing to function or refusing to carry out the duties imposed on them under the Local Government Acts, can dissolve such authority and in its place appoint a Commission to carry on the duties of such authority**'[1].

On 21 December, the day that power was transferred to Belfast, Fermanagh County Council passed the following resolution:

'**We, the County Council of Fermanagh, in view of the expressed desire of a large majority of people in this county, do not recognise the partition parliament in Belfast and do hereby direct our secretary to hold no further communications with either Belfast or British local government departments, and we pledge our allegiance to Dail Eireann.**'

Again the council offices were seized by the RIC, the council officials expelled and the county council dissolved.

By April 1922 Armagh, Keady and Newry Urban Councils, Downpatrick Town Commissioners, Cookstown, Downpatrick, Kilkeel, Lisnaskea, Strabane, Magherafelt, and Newry No.1 and No.2 Rural

Councils, and a number of Boards of Poor Law Guardians, had all been dissolved and Commissioners appointed to carry out their functions. Derry Corporation alone escaped. The Commissioners appointed were not chosen to placate local opinion. The Commissioner for Armagh and Keady Urban Councils was Colonel Waring, later to become a County Commandant of the B Specials.

With the problem temporarily dealt with the government set about producing a permanent solution. In July 1922 another Local Government Bill was introduced to abolish proportional representation (PR) in local elections and make a declaration of allegiance to the Crown and government obligatory on all councillors. It was rushed through parliament because further elections were due in 1923, and with the Boundary Commission looming over them the government couldn't afford another round of Nationalist victories. However the British government was embarrassed at such a prompt attempt to remove one of the safeguards they had introduced for minorities North and South, and for the first – and last – time the Royal Assent to the Bill was withheld for a few months.

When the Bill became law the job was only half done. The local boundaries had still to be redrawn and the elections had to be postponed till 1924[2]. The Minister of Home Affairs, Dawson Bates – who as former secretary of the Ulster Unionist Council had an intimate knowledge of Unionist organisation throughout the six counties – appointed Sir John Leech KC, as a one-man Judicial Commission to fix the new boundaries.

Normally electoral commissions work slowly, inviting submissions, putting forward proposals, holding public enquiries and concluding with a right of appeal. Leech was not concerned with such democratic niceties. He worked with speed, giving a week or a fortnight's notice for proposals to be submitted to him for each council. The Nationalists mostly boycotted the proceedings, partly in protest at the abolition of PR and Leech's dubious procedure, and partly because they were so confident of the outcome of the Boundary Commission that they thought it was all irrelevant. The Unionists on the other hand had a scheme for every area. Invariably Leech accepted it. William Miller, Unionist MP for Fermanagh and Tyrone, was able to boast on the following 12 July (1923):

'When the government of Northern Ireland decided to do away with proportional representation the chance that they had been waiting for for so long arrived and they took advantage of it . . . they divided the country in the way they thought best[3].'

The immediate result was devastating. After the elections in 1924 Nationalists controlled only two out of nearly 80 local councils in the North, compared with 25 in 1920. The 1924 result was exaggerated because in many areas the Nationalists had boycotted the elections in protest against the new boundaries and the oath of allegiance; but when the dust settled and elections began to be contested again it was clear that Leech had accomplished a massive gerrymander. In the two Catholic-majority counties of Fermanagh and Tyrone the Nationalists had lost the county councils and every single rural council. In Fermanagh they controlled nothing; in Tyrone only Strabane and Omagh Urban Councils. Some of the results were bizarre. In the Omagh Rural Council area, with a 61·5 per cent Catholic majority, the Nationalists had won the council in 1920 with 26 seats to 13. After Leech's endeavours the Unionists held it with 21 seats to 18. Magherafelt Rural Council had had a Nationalist majority of 17 to 11. After 1924 it had a Unionist majority of 18 to 11. And the gerrymandering didn't stop in 1924. It was a continuous process.

Leech's brief had not included corporations and urban councils, but the abolition of PR and a slight boundary re-adjustment secured Derry City and Enniskillen Urban Council. In March 1934 the Nationalist Armagh Urban Council was dissolved again, this time for corruption, but the dissolution lasted twelve years. When the council was restored in 1946 it had new wards and a Unionist majority. In 1936 Derry had to be gerry-mandered again – the Catholic majority kept increasing – and Omagh Urban Council was re-organised and got a Unionist majority.

The technique involved in all this was simple but effective. In areas with a Nationalist majority the wards were so drawn that Nationalist seats were won with huge majorities, thus 'wasting' Nationalist votes, while Unionist majorities were small but adequate. The process was aided by the restricted franchise – limited to rate-payers and their wives – which discriminated against the poorer Catholic population; by the virtually complete identification of religion and political views; and by the high degree of religious segregation even in rural areas.

Probably the clearest example of gerrymandering at work was Derry City. In 1966 the adult population of Derry was 30,376 – 20,102 Catholics and 10,274 Protestants – yet the Corporation was still Unionist-controlled. First the restricted franchise reduced the Catholic majority substantially, to 14,429 Catholics to 8,781 Protestants. Second, after constant boundary revisions the city was divided into three wards as follows[4]:

South ward	*North ward*	*Waterside ward*
11,185 voters	6,476 voters	5,549 voters
10,047 Catholics	2,530 Catholics	1,852 Catholics
1,138 Protestants	3,946 Protestants	3,697 Protestants
8 (Nationalist) Councillors	8 (Unionist) Councillors	4 (Unionist) Councillors

Eventually the Nationalists were left in control only of those areas where the Catholic majority was so large that no gerrymander could do away with it. They included only two towns of any importance: Newry and Strabane. The effects of the gerrymander were also permanent. No council which became Unionist as a result of it was ever re-captured by the Nationalists, and they soon gave up trying[5]. Local elections became foregone conclusions and the bulk of seats were left uncontested. The average of uncontested seats between 1923 and 1955 was: rural councils 96 per cent, county councils 94 per cent, and urban and borough councils 60 per cent[6].

There was a threat to this elaborate set-up in 1945 when the Labour government at Westminster abolished the restricted franchise for local government in Britain and introduced universal suffrage. The Stormont government ensured that Northern Ireland was excluded from the scope of the Act and introduced their own Representation of the People Bill in 1946 which not only confirmed the restricted franchise but restricted it further by taking votes away from lodgers who were not ratepayers. Some 10,000 young married couples lost the vote in Belfast. The Bill also retained the extraordinary principle of company voting, whereby limited companies received up to six votes according to their rateable valuation, the votes to be exercised by the company directors. Company votes were also brought in for elections to the Northern Ireland parliament. The number of company votes was never large but with their built-in Unionist bias they could have tipped the scale in closely contested wards and they certainly showed where the Unionist Party's loyalties lay.

The Bill was bitterly opposed by the entire opposition at Stormont, the Labour Party protesting at its class bias. The government Chief Whip, Major L.E.Curran[7], was frank about its objectives. It was to prevent 'Nationalists getting control of the three border counties and Derry City'. He went on to say 'The best way to prevent the overthrow of the government by people who had no stake in the country and had not the welfare of the people of Ulster at heart was to disenfranchise them'[8]. This extraordinary statement had an extraordinary sequel. Curran evidently realised he had gone too far. His statement was reported in the press the next day, but the Stormont *Hansard* was edited to leave it out. It was inexpertly done and the opposition's outraged reaction to a statement which isn't there is still recorded. The whole thing caused something of a parliamentary storm with Curran back-pedalling and denying he ever made the statement and the opposition maintaining that he did.

The gerrymandering process went on right up to 1967. In that year the Stormont government re-organised local government in Co.Fermanagh, replacing the existing five councils with a single county council. The population of Fermanagh was then 51,613: 27,291 Catholics and 24,322 Protestants. This small Catholic majority in the county was turned into a 36 to seventeen Unionist majority on the county council.

The effects of the local government gerrymandering were far-reaching. Immediately it strengthened the Northern government's position before the Boundary Commission. As far as the Catholic minority were concerned it sharpened their sense of grievance. They were paying the price of defeat. And it deprived them of power even in the areas where they were in a majority, most notably in Derry. It seemed there was no place for them in the new state.

But control of local government was of more than symbolic significance. Local councils controlled the building and allocating of public housing and appointment to hundreds – later thousands – of jobs which were vitally important in an area of high unemployment, bad housing, and emigration. Unionist control of local government even in Nationalist areas, could deprive Catholics of jobs and houses and give local Unionist or Orange bosses a powerful source of patronage to use to keep their Protestant supporters loyal.

And that is what happened. In 1951 after 30 years of Unionist control the figures were incontrovertible. Frank Gallagher cites some for local government employment in his book *The Indivisible Island*[9]:

The relatively high number of Catholics employed in Co.Down is due to the fact that there were five non-Unionist councils in the county, four of them clustered around Newry. Discrimination was at its most intense in the rural councils and the 28 Unionist-controlled rural councils in 1951 employed 218 non-manual workers of whom only eleven, or five per cent

	No. of non-manual government employees	No. of Catholics	Catholics as % of employees	Catholics as % of population
Antrim	257	19	7·8%	22%
Armagh	129	16	12·5%	46·5%
Derry	206	16	7·8%	43%
Down	294	56	19%	30%
Fermanagh	53	5	9·4%	55·4%
Tyrone	156	18	11·5%	55·3%
Total	1095	130	11·9%	34%

were Catholics. The figures for the less well-paid manual workers were somewhat, but not greatly, better.

Sometimes discrimination went to ludicrous extremes. In January 1942 W.L.Allen, Town Clerk of Barrow-in-Furness in England, was chosen by a selection committee of Belfast Corporation and appointed as Town Clerk of Belfast. He was of course a Protestant. Before he took up the post it was discovered his wife was a Catholic. The Ministry refused to sanction his appointment and he didn't get the job[10].

It also continued right up to 1969. One example was quite striking. In that year Co.Fermanagh Education Committee employed 77 school bus drivers[11]. In a county with a small Catholic majority only three of the 77 were Catholics.

Discrimination also affected housing and housing standards were grossly inadequate. In 1944 a Northern Ireland government survey showed that 30 per cent of all houses in the state were in urgent need of replacement. Co.Fermanagh was the area worst affected, with a figure of 43·7 per cent for Enniskillen and over 50 per cent for most of the rural districts. The unusually high figures were explained by the fact that no houses at all were built by any of the three Fermanagh Rural Councils between 1921 and 1945. After 1945 however, they bestirred themselves and between 1945 and 1967 the local authorities in Fermanagh built 1,048 houses, of which 195 or eighteen per cent were allocated to Catholics and 853 or 82 per cent to Protestants[12], despite the fact that the Catholics, being the poorer section of the population, were more in need of rehousing. It is hardly surprising that the Catholic majority in Fermanagh has been steadily declining since 1921.

An added reason for discrimination in housing was that with the restricted local government franchise the tenancy of a local authority house brought with it votes; so that the allocation of quite a small number of houses could swing the balance in a finely gerrymandered ward and eventually in a council. Unionist councils in Catholic majority areas faced a dilemma. They had either to allocate almost all houses to Protestants or to build no houses at all. The ruling Unionist members of Omagh Rural Council (62 per cent Catholic) summed it up in June 1936 when they wrote to the Unionist whip at Stormont seeking a way of allocating houses only to Unionists:

'We would point out that in certain districts cottages are required by Unionist workers but we hesitate to invite representations as we know there would be a flood of representations from the Nationalist side and our political opponents are only waiting the opportunity to use this means to outvote us in divisions where majorities are close'[13].

The Omagh RDC, like the Fermanagh councils, solved the problem by not building any houses for years.

Ultimately the councils were forced to build some houses as the Protestant population were suffering as well, but then the solution adopted was to give Catholics houses only in Catholic wards where they would merely reinforce the existing Catholic majority. Councillor George Elliot, a Unionist member of Enniskillen Borough Council, said in 1963: 'We are not going to build houses in the South Ward [Unionist held] and cut a rod to beat ourselves later on. We are going to see that the right people are put into these houses and we are not making any apology for it'[14]. On some councils eventually a deal was done – known as the 'gentleman's agreement' – with the Nationalist councillors, whereby they were given the right personally to allocate the houses in the Catholic wards in return for keeping quiet about the general set-up.

In general however the Unionists were remarkably frank about their policies. In April 1948 E.C. Ferguson MP told the annual Unionist convention in Enniskillen

'The Nationalist majority in the county Fermanagh, **notwithstanding a reduction of 336 in the year, stands at 3,604. This county, I think it can safely be said, is a Unionist county. The atmosphere is Unionist. The Boards and properties are nearly all controlled by Unionists. But there is still this millstone around our necks. I would ask the meeting to authorise**

their executive to adopt whatever plans and take whatever steps, however drastic, to wipe out this Nationalist majority'[15].

And this preoccupation wasn't confined to areas where they were in a minority. Tom Teevan, chairman of Limavady Rural Council and a few months later MP for West Belfast, said in 1950:

'In Londonderry City and County, where we should have been on our guard, our majority has dropped from 12,000 to a perilously low figure. How did that come about? Through the ruinous and treacherous policy, pursued unwittingly perhaps, of handing over houses owned by Protestants to Roman Catholics. It is also caused by the great employers of labour in the North of Ireland employing Roman Catholic labour'[16].

At the same meeting J.C.Drennan, chairman of North Derry Unionist Association and later a Senator, said: 'They should return members to the local authorities who would not be afraid to support the Unionist cause when houses became vacant. Then let them get down to the employers of labour.'

The evidence of both gerrymandering and discrimination was overwhelming. The Cameron Commission[17], appointed by the Northern Ireland government in 1969 to investigate the causes of the Civil Rights Movement, commented:

'In certain areas ... namely Dungannon, Armagh, and in particular, Londonderry, the arrangement of ward boundaries for local government purposes has produced in the local authority a permanent Unionist majority which bears little or no resemblance to the relative numerical strength of Unionists and non-Unionists in the area. As we show later we have to record that there is very good reason to believe the allegation that these arrangements were deliberately made and maintained with the consequence that the Unionists used and have continued to use the electoral majority thus created to favour Protestant or Unionist supporters in making public appointments – particularly those of senior officials – and in manipulating housing allocations for political and sectarian ends'[18].

The Central government began by making one or two well-publicised Catholic appointments. The first Lord Chief Justice of Northern Ireland was a Catholic, Sir Denis Henry, and so was the Permanent Secretary of the Department of Education, Bonaparte Wyse. They were untypical however. Sir Denis Henry had been MP for South Derry at

Westminster – the only Catholic Unionist MP ever – and Attorney General for Ireland in the British administration during the War of Independence. He was decidedly unrepresentative of Ulster Catholics. Bonaparte Wyse was one of a number of Catholic civil servants in the Dublin Castle administration who were transferred to the North after partition. They were not universally welcomed by Unionist ministers. Sir Edward Archdale was reported by the *Northern Whig* as saying in 1925

:   **'A man in Fintona asked him how it was that he had over 50 per cent Roman Catholics in his ministry. He thought that was too funny. He had 109 on his staff and so far as he knew there were four Roman Catholics. Three of these were civil servants turned over to him, whom he had to take when he began'[19].**

A senior Stormont civil servant later commented that Dawson Bates 'had such a prejudice against Catholics that he made it clear to his Permanent Secretary that he did not want his most juvenile clerk or typist, if a Papist, assigned for duty to his ministry'[20].

Soon discrimination had become admitted government policy. Craig, now Lord Craigavon, said at Stormont on 21 November 1934: 'The appointments made by the government are made, as far as we can possibly manage it, of loyal men and women . . .' But the definitive statement of Unionist policy came from Sir Basil Brooke MP[21] speaking on 12 July 1933 when he was a Parliamentary Secretary in the Stormont government. Brooke was reported in the *Fermanagh Times*:

'There were a great number of Protestants and Orangemen who employed Roman Catholics. He felt he could speak freely on this subject as he had not a Roman Catholic about his own place. He appreciated the great difficulty experienced by some of them in procuring suitable Protestant labour but he would point out that Roman Catholics were endeavouring to get in everywhere. He would appeal to Loyalists therefore, wherever possible, to employ good Protestant lads and lassies'[22].

Brooke's speech caused considerable controversy, but by the end of the year he had been appointed Minister of Agriculture. Then in March 1934 he returned to the theme. He assured the Derry Unionist Association that he hadn't lost any sleep over all the criticism and went on

'I recommended those people who are Loyalists not to employ Roman Catholics, 99 per cent of whom are disloyal; I want you to remember one point in regard to the employment of people who are

disloyal . . . You are disfranchising yourselves in that way . . . You people who are employers have the ball at your feet. If you don't act properly now, before we know where we are we shall find ourselves in the minority instead of the majority. I want you to realise that, having done your bit, you have got your Prime Minister behind you'[23].

The reference to the Prime Minister's support caused uproar. Craigavon was asked at Stormont the next day to repudiate the statement. He replied: 'There is not one of my colleagues who does not entirely agree with him and I would not ask him to withdraw one word he said'[24].

A pattern of discrimination in government employment and public appointments was established which persisted until the last days of the Unionist administration. As late as 1969, out of 209 people employed in the technical and professional grades of the Northern Ireland civil service, only thirteen were Catholics, and of the 319 employed in the higher administrative grades 23 were Catholics. Of 115 people nominated by the government to serve on nine public boards only sixteen were Catholics[25].

Brooke's speech had advocated discrimination in private employment as well. It was periodically encouraged by Unionist spokesmen. A Mr H.McLaughlin speaking at a Unionist meeting in Derry in 1946 said that for the past 48 years since the foundation of his firm there had been only one Roman Catholic employed – and that was a case of mistaken identity[26]. And as late as 1964 Senator J.Barnhill said: 'Charity begins at home. If we are going to employ people we should give preference to Unionists[27].'

Discrimination was already common in Belfast and had been strongly reinforced by the expulsions in 1920. The shipyards and the heavy engineering industry remained a Protestant preserve. Even in 1970 there were only about 400 Catholics among the 10,000 workers in Harland and Wolff's[28]. While Catholics were also in a tiny minority among the workers in Mackie's and there were only a handful out of 3,000 workers in the Sirocco Engineering Works, both of them situated in Catholic ghettos. In general there was a disproportionate number of semi-skilled and unskilled workers among the Catholic population even in the smaller country towns. A survey in Portadown, Co.Armagh, in 1961 showed that 55 per cent of Catholics fell into these two categories compared with 26 per cent of Presbyterians, 33 per cent of Church of Ireland members and 21 per cent of Methodists[29].

In July 1961, when the average unemployment figure for Northern Ireland was 7 per cent, the five unemployment exchange areas with the highest figures were: Newry 17·2 per cent, Newcastle 16·4 per cent, Strabane 14·4 per cent, Derry 13·8 per cent and Limavady 13·0 per cent, all with large Catholic majorities. The five lowest figures were Ballyclare 2·2 per cent, Bangor 2·7 per cent, Lisburn 3·3 per cent, Carrickfergus 3·5 per cent and Newtownards 4·2 per cent, all solidly Protestant areas.

This disproportion was also found in the Belfast area. A survey in January 1972 of the Belfast urban area – including Newtownabbey, Lisburn and Holywood – divided the area into 97 sub-districts of about 6,000 people each. It found the average figure for male unemployment in the area to be 8·2 per cent. The ten sub-districts with the highest figures were Ballymurphy-New Barnsly 33·3 per cent, Dock 23·7 per cent, Whiterock 20·4 per cent, Lower Falls 19·7 per cent, Glenravel 19·1 per cent, Milltown-Turf Lodge 18·8. per cent, St Pauls 16·8 per cent, Glenard 13·9 per cent, Markets 13·8 per cent, Broadway-St James 13·6 per cent. All had Catholic majorities. Altogether there were fourteen Catholic majority districts in the 97. The average male unemployment figure for the fourteen districts was 16·9 per cent, or twice the overall average[30].

Not surprisingly, Catholics, though only one third of the population, also provided the bulk of those on the emigrant boat – 90,000 out of the 159,000 who emigrated between 1937 and 1961[31].

All this took place in a state where the government and the government party were entirely Protestant and remained so for fifty years, and where almost all Unionist MPs and all but one Minister until 1966-67 were members of the fiercely anti-Catholic Orange Order and paraded and spoke constantly at Orange parades. The ethos of the state was summed up by Craigavon himself in April 1934 when he said:

'I have always said that I am an Orangeman first and a politician and a member of this parliament afterwards . . . All I boast is that we have a Protestant parliament and a Protestant state'[32].

The overall effect on the Catholic population was to make them despair. Many of them had been attacked, terrorised and driven from their homes. They had been cut off from the rest of Ireland and forced into a state run by their enemies. Now they were deprived of political power, discriminated against and driven on to the dole or the emigrant boat. They were soon to find that if they put their trust in politicians their representatives met with no response. It was inevitable that some would turn to violence.

But the Unionists were ready for that too.

The Civil Authorities (Special Powers) Act had been rushed through the Northern parliament in April 1922 at the height of the Belfast violence as an emergency measure intended to last for only one year. It was an extraordinary Act. The first sentence read:

'**The Civil Authority** [the Minister of Home Affairs] **shall have power, in respect of persons, matters and things within the jurisdiction of the Government of Northern Ireland to take all such steps and issue all such orders as may be necessary for preserving the peace and maintaining order.**'

It expressly provided for the introduction of the death penalty for some firearms and explosives offences, and flogging as well as imprisonment for others, for the prohibition of inquests and for arrest without warrant. It also gave the minister power to make further regulations, each with the force of a new law, without consulting parliament, and to delegate his powers to any policeman. And in case there was anything the minister had overlooked it provided that

'**If any person does any act of such a nature as to be calculated to be prejudicial to the preservation of the peace or maintenance of order in Northern Ireland and not specifically provided for in the regulations, he shall be deemed to be guilty of an offence against the regulations**'.

Even the Northern parliament was a little disturbed by the Bill and one Unionist MP, G.B.Hanna, summed it up as providing that 'the Home Secretary shall have power to do whatever he likes or let someone else do what he likes for him'[33]. Within a few weeks Dawson Bates had introduced a number of other regulations empowering him to outlaw organisations, to detain or 'intern' people indefinitely without charge or trial, making it an offence to refuse to answer questions put by a policeman, Special Constable, or soldier, and taking power to block roads and bridges and evacuate or destroy houses and buildings. He already had the power to impose a curfew and he took the power to make exclusion orders – orders barring named persons from all but a small and remote area of the six counties and thereby effectively excluding them from the whole area. In 1923 he made a further regulation empowering the government to examine bank accounts and seize money deposited in banks.

It was little wonder that Mr Vorster, then South African Minister for Justice, introducing a new Coercion Bill in the South African parliament in April 1963, commented that he 'would be willing to exchange all the legislation of that sort for one clause of the Northern Ireland Special Powers Act.'

The ending of violence in the North after 1922 didn't see the ending of the Special Powers Act. It was renewed every year until 1928, then renewed for five years and in 1933 it was made permanent. Nor was it let fall easily into disuse. If in doubt the Northern government always erred on the side of repression. Both internment and the Belfast curfew were maintained until the end of 1924 despite two years of almost complete peace, and the detention powers were used again in 1925 when the Boundary Commission broke down.

During the thirties more organisations were banned and powers taken to prohibit meetings and processions. The effect of the power to make new regulations was dramatically illustrated in 1933. In October of that year the government rounded up and detained between forty and fifty Republicans, but as there was no violence going on at the time it was reluctant actually to intern them. Accordingly the minister issued a regulation making it an offence to refuse to answer incriminating questions in a private examination by a magistrate. The men were examined, refused to answer and were duly convicted of an offence created subsequent to their arrest[34].

New regulations indeed continued to be made right up to the suspension of Stormont, and though old ones were sometimes allowed to lapse they could be renewed at a moment's notice. The regulations also gave power to ban newspapers, books and films. Republican publications were constantly banned and in 1940 and 1941 *The Red Hand* and the *Irish Workers Weekly*, two Communist papers, were banned. In 1943 when a Catholic religious journal, the *Capuchin Annual*, published a strongly anti-Unionist supplement called 'Orange Terror', it was banned as well. In June 1940 a six-months' ban was even placed on the *Derry Journal*, the main local newspaper in Derry, but it was lifted again after only a fortnight because of widespread protest.

The most effective single power of the Act was internment, enabling the government to jail indefinitely anyone who might be a threat to it militarily or politically, and it was used lavishly. Internment was re-introduced in December 1938 and lasted until 1946. It was introduced again in December 1956 and lasted until 1961. And it was introduced finally and on the largest scale ever in August 1971, eventually bringing down the government which introduced it. It is still in operation (April 1975) over three and a half years later.

As if the Special Powers Act were not enough, the Northern government later reinforced it with the Public Order Act (1951) and the Flags and Emblems Act (1954), giving itself further control over purely political opposition to the regime; and further amended and strengthened the Public Order Act as late as 1969.

To enforce these draconian laws the government had the Specials and the RUC. From the beginning the Specials were a Protestant and Loyalist force. As soon as they were formed the Ulster Unionist Council passed a resolution 'strongly recommending all Loyalists to join and give the new force their support in every way possible'[35]. In May 1922 Sir Henry Wilson noted in his diary: 'The Specials are now all Protestants'[36]. While Craig, speaking on 12 July 1922, said 'It is also from the ranks of the Loyal Orange Institution that our splendid Specials have come.'

As we have seen they were largely recruited from the ranks of the UVF, and the *Manchester Guardian* described their role in the Troubles thus:

'The Unionists have an important ally   they have a coercive police force of their own ... They [the Specials] **have become what everybody who knows Ulster perceived they would become – the instruments of a religious tyranny ... some of them, the A Class, became regular RIC, the rest, the B and C classes parade their districts at night with arms, harassing, threatening, beating and occasionally killing their Catholic neighbours and burning their homes'[37].**

The A and C Specials were disbanded when the boundary question was settled at the end of 1925, but the B Specials were kept on with an average membership of between 11,000 and 12,000, reduced to 8,500 after an economy drive in 1968. They were eventually disbanded only in October 1969. They retained their peculiar characteristics throughout. William Grant MP said at Stormont in 1936: 'I would like to point out that the Special Constabulary are composed entirely of loyal Protestant working men ... there are no Roman Catholics among the Special Constabulary'[38]. And in 1969 the Hunt Committee on the Reorganisation of the Police in Northern Ireland commented: 'while there is no law or official rule that precludes any person, whatever his religion, from joining the Ulster Special Constabulary the fact remains that, for a variety of reasons, no Roman Catholic is a member'[39]. They recommended the disbandment of the USC.

The Specials were a formidable force. Even in quiet periods they did regular drills and weapon training. They were armed with rifles, revolvers, bayonets and later sub-machine guns which they kept in their homes, and in the 1950s and 1960s they had access to Bren-guns and Shorland armoured cars. They could be mobilised for full-time duty at very short notice, providing the government with an almost inexhaustible para-military reserve. Most of the time they were used for part-time work such as manning road-blocks and patrols, and with their intimate knowledge of local geography and the politics of their Catholic neighbours they were extremely effective in suppressing all resistance to Unionist rule. They were also of course a constant irritant to the Catholic population and with their weapons at home they represented a constant threat of sectarian attack.

The regular police, the RUC, were to have been one third Catholic, but in 1922 Catholics were unlikely to join a force so much identified with the new state. Less than one sixth of the new force was Catholic, and the balance was made up by recruitment from the Specials. Entrance standards were waived for members of the Specials and at any given time about one third of the force were ex-Specials. The Catholic proportion never increased and the Hunt Committee found that in 1969 only about eleven per cent of the force was Catholic[40].

The RUC was also a para-military force. They were always armed and were trained with and had access to rifles, sub-machine guns and machine guns and armoured cars. From 1950 on the RUC included a special Commando or reserve force whose functions were almost entirely para-military. The strength of the RUC was about 3,000 and in times of emergency it was quickly reinforced by fully-mobilised B Specials. Catholic confidence in it was not increased by the fact that for 23 years it was headed by Colonel Sir Charles Wickham, who had commanded the RIC and RUC in 1921-22 and had organised the formation of the Specials[41].

The tone of the force was set early, when in August 1922 Dawson Bates gave permission for a special RUC Orange Lodge to be formed and in April 1923 spoke at its first reunion. Open involvement in politics was later discouraged, and District Inspector John Nixon was dismissed, after widespread complaints, for making a fiercely Unionist speech at an Orange function in 1924. But the force's character had been fixed. The minister in charge was an Orangeman, there was a police Orange Lodge: the RUC could hardly be impartial where the Orange Order or the Unionist Party was concerned. An enquiry by a commission of the British National Council for Civil Liberties commented in 1936: 'It is difficult to escape the conclusion that the attitude of the government renders the police chary of interference with the activities of the Orange Order and its sympathisers'[42].

Moreover the RUC were constantly identified with the use of the Special Powers Act: raids on houses, internment swoops, the enforcement of bans on meetings and publications. They were seen by most Catholics as merely the coercive arm of the Unionist Party.

The Catholic minority was deprived of political and economic power through gerrymandering and discrimination. If they turned to extra-parliamentary agitation for redress, they were prevented or inhibited under sections of the Special Powers Act and later the Public Order Act. The Unionist government, by its maintenance of the Special Powers Act and the Specials and by keeping the RUC as a para-military force, evidently expected the minority to turn to violence. When they did so they were ruthlessly suppressed. The NCCL commission commented that the Unionists had created 'under the shadow of the British constitution a permanent machine of dictatorship'[43]. They compared Northern Ireland with the fascist dictatorships then current in Europe. In so far as the total identification of party and state was one of the hallmarks of European fascism, the comparison was apt.

5

The Opposition Enters . . . and Leaves

After the violence of the early 1920s and before the consolidation of Craigavon's Protestant state, however, the six counties were to experience a brief interlude when the Nationalist minority began to work through the Belfast parliament, when a Labour opposition emerged and 'normal' politics seemed to be developing in the new state.

In a revulsion against violence and anything which might bring the wrath of the Loyalists on their heads again, the minority turned solidly to Joe Devlin and his constitutional Nationalists, while at the same time the Church and the Catholic business class were urging the Nationalists to enter the Northern parliament and uphold their interests. Slowly, in ones and twos, they did so. Meanwhile rising unemployment, appalling living conditions, and the removal of the threat to the state – at least as far as Belfast workers were concerned – rekindled something of the spirit of 1919 when the whole city had been brought to a standstill by a massive engineering strike. Three Labour candidates, carefully avoiding the partition issue, were elected to the parliament in 1925. The Nationalists, Labour and a few Independent MPs combined in opposition and for a time the Belfast parliament took on an air of normality. But it was to be short-lived. The abolition of proportional representation (PR) for Northern elections drove a wedge between Labour and the Nationalists, and the utter intransigence of the Unionist regime disillusioned the Nationalists and drove them back to abstentionism. The pattern was set for the future.

The six Nationalist MPs elected to the Northern Ireland parliament in 1921 never took their seats there. They also refused to sit in the second Dail to which all elected representatives in Ireland were invited.

As the remnant of the UIL, the Nationalists, were bitterly anti-Republican. Joe Devlin, their unofficial leader, believed in the British Empire and had wanted to join the British Army when the First World War began. He had been, with John Redmond, one of the leaders of the British recruitment campaign. The Nationalists had been against the 1916 Rising and the War of Independence, not least because these events had deprived them of their chance of power in a Home Rule parliament and government. They were not going to associate with revolutionaries by sitting in the Dail nor take part in an assembly dominated by the men who had ousted them.

On the other hand five of the six Sinn Fein MPs elected in the six counties already held Southern seats while the sixth, Sean O'Mahony, was a Dubliner, and since he opposed the Treaty, boycotted the Dail after January 1922. The result was that the only political platform left to the Northern minority was Westminster.

Of the five UIL MPs elected for Ulster – four of them from the six counties – in 1918 only two, Joe Devlin and T.J.S.Harbinson, remained active. But when the new state was established in 1921 its representation at Westminster was cut from thirty to thirteen and the boundaries were redrawn. One of the casualties was Devlin's constituency of Falls which was merged into a larger West Belfast seat with a Unionist majority.

There was a Westminster election in October 1922. By then the old United Irish League had fallen apart. Devlin and his supporters didn't contest West Belfast which went unopposed[1]. There was a Catholic majority in the two-seat Fermanagh and Tyrone constituency however and there a local convention nominated Harbinson and an ex-Sinn Fein Fermanagh County Councillor, Cahir Healy, who was at the time interned under the Special Powers Act. A Protestant, Capt. Macnaghten, a cousin of the Unionist candidate, also stood in Co.Derry as an Independent Nationalist. Macnaghten was heavily defeated but Harbinson and Healy were elected.

A Liberal MP, W.M.R.Pringle, raised the question of Healy's internment when the parliament assembled, but no action was taken and the Northern Nationalists' only voice was now Harbinson, an elderly and not very articulate country solicitor. There was another election in December 1923 and Harbinson and Healy were elected again. Healy was still interned and it was only after Pringle had put down a motion calling for an enquiry into the case, and the new Labour government had put pressure on Craig, that he was released in February 1924. He took his seat in March but his tenure didn't last long because there was another election in October.

This time Sinn Fein, now re-organising itself after the civil war in the South, decided to contest the Northern seats, and nominated candidates for all but two of the nine constituencies, including Fermanagh and Tyrone. The Nationalists were enraged. Without PR a three-cornered Unionist-Nationalist-Sinn Fein contest would inevitably mean a Unionist victory.

They decided not to stand and as a measure of their bitterness urged their supporters not to vote.

The Republicans mounted an intensive campaign, bringing North prominent figures like Mary McSwiney, sister of the Lord Mayor of Cork who had died on hunger strike in 1920, and Mrs Sheehy Skeffington whose husband had been murdered by a British officer in 1916. De Valera himself, who was banned from the North under an exclusion order, tried to speak at a rally in Derry but was arrested and jailed for a month for contravening the order. He had also tried to speak in Newry but had been deported back across the border by the Specials. It was an ironic situation. De Valera was still an MP for Co.Down in the Belfast parliament yet the Belfast government had barred him from entering his constituency[2].

The results were a disaster for Sinn Fein however. The Nationalist boycott was extremely effective in Fermanagh and Tyrone, and the Unionists won the seats with massive majorities of 38,026 and 37,904. Even more humiliating was the result in West Belfast where the Unionist won as expected, but the Sinn Fein candidate trailed far behind a Labour man and lost his deposit[3]. Elsewhere the figures weren't as bad, but the eight Sinn Fein candidates won only 46,257 votes compared with 104,716 in 1921, or 165,293 for Sinn Fein and Nationalist together.

The explanation seemed to lie in a reaction against the violence of 1920-22. The Catholic minority had been defeated and cowed. They had no stomach for another round of violence and the vengeance it would bring upon them, and most of them were not prepared even to vote for people associated with violence. They were prepared to give parliamentary politics a try instead. Moreover Sinn Fein in 1924 were no longer the victors of the War of Independence. They were now the defeated side in a bloody civil war and had incurred the antagonism not only of the Redmondite Nationalists, but of the supporters of the Free State government: and perhaps most important of all they had been denounced and excommunicated by the Catholic hierarchy.

The most remarkable result had been in West Belfast. Harry Midgley, the labour candidate, had stood there before, in December 1923, and had done slightly better, winning 22,255 votes and being defeated only by 2,720. But then there had been no Nationalist or Sinn Fein candidate. It had looked as if he had just collected all the Nationalist votes[4]. His massive victory over Sinn Fein in 1924 seemed to indicate a major swing to Labour by the Catholics of the Falls Road – or at least to the concept of working for reforms within the structure of the new state and putting more emphasis on social and economic issues than on Irish unity.

The Nationalists, and especially Devlin, sensed this. West Belfast was his constituency and it was intensely working-class. Devlin had always been careful to cultivate the workers through welfare work: he started a holiday home for mill-girls in Bangor, and strongly supported social reforms such as the introduction of an old-age pension. Now the Labour Party was eating into his support among a population stricken by chronic unemployment (there were 48,000, or 24 per cent, out of work in the six counties in 1925), low wages and terrible living conditions, and which had been effectively disenfranchised for six years. In January 1925 Labour fought the Nationalists in the two Catholic wards of Smithfield and Falls in the Corporation elections, beating them in Smithfield. In another general election, if the Nationalists were still tied to an abstentionist policy, Labour could oust them in all the Catholic areas of Belfast. Devlin did not want to see his party wiped out for the second time in seven years.

The Nationalists were also under pressure from other directions. The one area where Craig's government had acted with a fair degree of impartiality had been education. Under the British administration education in Ireland had been under denominational control. Now Craig established a committee under Robert Lynn MP to consider the organisation of education in the new Northern state. The Lynn committee recommended the establishment of a system of state schools where there would be no religious instruction and no account would be taken of religion in appointing staff. They hoped by financial inducements to get the churches to transfer their schools to the state. An Education Bill containing these proposals was passed in May 1923.

The Catholic Church, which had always insisted on religious segregation in schools and its own complete control of the education – and hopefully the attitudes – of its members, was alarmed. The new proposals threatened its power. The Northern bishops contacted Devlin and the Nationalists, and in October 1923 called on them to take their seats in the Northern parliament to defend Catholic interests. If the bishops had to choose between accepting the Northern state and losing their schools then they were going to keep their schools.

They need not have worried. The Protestant churches were just as keen on denominational education and had more power over the government. The General Assembly of the Presbyterian Church unanimously condemned sections of the Act on 26 June 1923, and they, the Church of Ireland, and the Methodist Church sent a joint letter to Craig on 31 July, demanding changes. Later a committee of the Grand Orange Lodge of Ireland was set up to join in the campaign and a long and bitter battle ensued, with the churches and the Orange Order demanding Bible instruction in the schools, denominational management, and 'the right to appoint Protestant teachers for Protestant children'.

Eventually in 1930 they got their way. Bible instruction became part of the curriculum in state schools, and churches who transferred their schools to local education authorities were given a permanent voice on the management committees. The state schools became effectively Protestant schools.

The Catholic Church was given added incentive to stay out of the state system and did, with their main grievance now that the Protestant schools got more in state grants than they did.

As well as the bishops, the Catholic businessmen and the Catholic middle class in general were pressing the Nationalists to take their seats and come to terms with the new state. Business after all had to go on.

They were pushing an open door. When Craig announced the 1925 election an ad hoc Convention met in Belfast on 21 March composed of the six outgoing MPs in the Belfast parliament, Cahir Healy the ex-Westminster MP, and a large collection of local councillors, priests and Catholic business and professional men. They decided unanimously (1) to contest the election; (2) that, since the Boundary Commission was currently sitting, MPs in areas likely to be affected by its recommendations should make no decision on attendance until after it reported; and (3) MPs who represented areas which couldn't possibly be affected by the Commission (e.g. Belfast and Co. Antrim) would take their seats.

Devlin gave his reasons for urging the change in an open letter to the *Irish News* three days later:

'I have felt very keenly the complete disfranchisement, during the last four years, of the Nationalists in the partitioned area; but that was due to circumstances over which none of us had any control and was part of a definite policy, decided on at that time, to meet an exceptional situation. Since then the Treaty was negotiated and the Boundary Commission set up. We were convinced that that Commission would have been set up in 1922 and would have long since finished its deliberations and left to those in Ulster who are, under any circumstances to be included in the partitioned area, an opportunity of defending interests which are vital and causes which are dear to them . . . I have decided that as soon as its deliberations are concluded and its decisions arrived at, it shall be my duty, if elected, to enter the Northern parliament and apply myself to the task of fighting for those National and democratic interests to which I have given a lifelong devotion . . . Permanent abstention means permanent disfranchisement and to any such policy, leading as it inevitably would to helplessness, confusion and failure, I could not give the slightest countenance'[5].

The election was on 3 April. The Nationalists only nominated eleven candidates – Devlin was the only candidate in Belfast. Sinn Fein, after their defeat in the Westminster election, had only six candidates. There was no pact: Sinn Fein was committed to abstention, the Nationalists more or less to attendance – and in any case great bitterness remained over the loss of the Fermanagh and Tyrone seats in 1924. The Nationalists were emerging as a Catholic party: eight of the eleven candidates were proposed by priests; and the same issue of the *Irish News* which carried Devlin's open letter also carried an open letter from Archdeacon Convery of Belfast, saying; 'I hope to see the Catholic voters united like a bar of steel all over the six counties.' The Unionists of course were an avowedly Protestant party, and one of their Westminster MPs since 1922 had been Dr J.M.Simms, a Church of Ireland minister – only the first of some five Protestant ministers to become official Unionist MPs, and two of them government ministers.

The Nationalists did well. They topped the poll in three constituencies, West Belfast – where Devlin got a massive 17,559 first preferences – Co.Derry, and Fermanagh and Tyrone. They won ten seats with 91,452 votes compared with six seats and 60,577 votes in 1921. Sinn Fein repeated their Westminster election debacle, winning only two seats – one of them unopposed – with 20,615 votes, less than half their 1924 Westminster vote and only a fifth of their 1921 vote. There was no doubt that the Catholic population had swung back to constitutional politics.

But the most striking result of all was the Labour vote. The Labour Party had nominated only three candidates: one each in East, West and North Belfast[6]. Despite a government campaign based on the boundary issue, Jack Beattie the Labour candidate topped the poll in East Belfast with 9,330 votes and was elected, ousting the Labour Unionist, Thompson Donald. Sam Kyle was elected in North Belfast and William McMullen got in in West Belfast on the transfer of Devlin's massive surplus. More of Devlin's surplus votes went to McMullen than to the Sinn Fein candidate McConville, showing the depth of the antagonism between the Nationalists and Sinn Fein, and confounding Archdeacon Convery since McMullen was a Protestant and McConville a Catholic.

The Labour victories were alarming to the Unionists since they had obviously won a substantial Protestant working-class vote. Their alarm was increased by the fact that George Henderson, a Protestant tenant farmers' candidate, had been elected in Co.Antrim – with the help of Nationalist transfers — ousting a government Parliamentary Secretary, and Independent Unionists had topped the poll in North and South Belfast. In the calmer conditions of 1925 and under the pressure of mounting unemployment the Unionist alliance seemed to be breaking up and the Unionist Party losing its grip on the Protestant working class.

This was the result of tensions which had been there since before 1921. On 14 January 1919 over 20,000 shipyard and engineering workers had marched to the City Hall in Belfast to demand a 44-hour week, and then voted by 20,225 to 558 to strike for it. Throughout the First World War they had worked a 54-hour week, leaving home before dawn and returning after dark most of the year round and having to work for several hours before breakfast. They had put up with it grudgingly during the war, but once peace came they were determined to end these conditions. It was part of a UK-wide movement, for there were strikes in British cities as well, especially in Glasgow.

The strike began on 25 January, a Saturday, but didn't begin to bite until the Monday. The shipyards and engineering factories were closed down by pickets and even the bosses had to get permission from the strike committee to go into their works. The gas supply was shut off and electricity limited to the hospitals and essential services, and shops using electric light were stoned. The trams were stopped and by the end of the week there were nearly 40,000 workers on strike and another 20,000 laid off because of it.

The strike was unofficial and hardly any of the men got strike pay so the strike committee began collecting and distributing food. The *Belfast Newsletter* called the strikers 'Bolsheviks, Anarchists and the hirelings of Germany'[7] and the Belfast Grand Orange Lodge condemned them, but they remained remarkably solid for three weeks. However they had only succeeded in shutting down industry; commerce continued without interruption and, facing a trade recession, many of the employers were not sorry to shut down for a couple of weeks. The struggle turned into an endurance test and the workers, with empty stomachs, were suffering most.

The strike committee had promises of support from dockers, carters and railwaymen. They could have turned it into a general strike but their nerve failed them. One of the organisers explained 'the transport workers would come out at any time but they hadn't called on them as the strike committee wasn't sure it could run the city'[8]. Once they decided not to extend the strike they were effectively beaten because the men couldn't hold out much longer.

To add to their trouble the authorities had managed to crush the Glasgow strike, by arresting several members of the strike committee, repeatedly baton-charging crowds of strikers and bringing in troops to occupy the city centre. After two weeks the Belfast strike committee was ready to negotiate. Even then, after three weeks on strike and two days after the Glasgow strike had collapsed, the workers rejected a compromise settlement by 11,963 votes to 8,774. But already the government had made it illegal under the Defence of the Realm Act (DORA) to deprive the community of electricity, and after appeals from city businessmen, the Lord Mayor of Belfast had met the British Army Commander-in-Chief for Ireland. On the night after the ballot, 14 February, British troops, fully armed and in battle gear, moved into the power stations. Three extra magistrates were brought into the city to deal with the expected arrests.

But there were only two arrests – of shop stewards who tried to prevent a return to work. The strike committee took its pickets off the power stations and, though workers attacked the trams when they re-appeared and fought a running battle with the RIC in Royal Avenue, the strike was almost over. The strike committee recommended a return to work on 20 February and the workers, voting union by union, accepted it. They had gained little tangible after four weeks on strike – a 47-hour week, which had been promised in negotiations anyway – but they had given the employers and the Unionist leaders a severe shock[9].

The industrial militancy of the engineering strike seemed to be reflected in politics. A few months later nearly 100,000 workers took part in a May Day march from the City Hall to the Ormeau Park, where the speakers called for more Labour representation in the city; and in January 1920 in the Belfast Corporation elections, Labour candidates who held no seats on the old Corporation, suddenly won twelve seats out of 60 with a total of 16,913 votes[10]. The Labour upsurge wasn't confined to Belfast either. In all the urban district elections in Ulster in 1920 they got 27,504 votes – a fifth of the total[11]. As late as May Day 1920 there was another massive demonstration with a resolution supporting the Bolshevik government in Russia.

It was this sudden Labour challenge which had prompted Carson's violent anti-Labour outburst on 12 July 1920 and led to the peculiar virulence of the shipyard pogromists against Labour Party members and trade union militants. The Unionist leaders – understandably because of their business interests – had a greatly exaggerated fear of the socialist menace.

In fact the 1919 strike and its aftermath had shown the weakness as well as the strength of Labour in Belfast. The strike committee had reflected the consciousness of the shipyard and engineering workers, and was an extraordinary coalition of militant trade unionists who were generally mildly anti-partitionist members of the ILP, such as Charles McKay, the chairman of the strike committee, James Baird and Sam Kyle; and members of the Unionist Labour Association such as Robert Weir, D.Clarke and William Grant – later to become a Unionist MP and cabinet minister. The Labour Unionists opposed militant action in the strike – years later Grant explained that he had voted against the strike himself and only joined the strike committee to oppose the socialists on it[12]; while Clarke boasted that the committee 'had never once said a harsh or unkind word about the employers.' And they vigorously opposed attempts to use the strike to spread socialist politics among the strikers. To preserve the unity of the strike committee the ILP members almost fell over themselves to say that 'politics have nothing to do with the hours of labour'[13].

The result was a massive industrial struggle fought with kid gloves and leaving only the shallowest, most superficial impression on the politics of the men involved. Above all the strike committee avoided like the plague any reference to Home Rule or the momentous events taking place in the South. The Labour candidates in the 1920 elections – some of them ILP members, others nominees of trade unions – took the same ambivalent stance. Some were pro-Home Rule, some against, and they had no official attitude to it. As a result the impressive Labour vote had little permanent significance and when the national question forced itself sharply to the fore later in 1920 most of it evaporated almost overnight. In the 1921 election, when the three ILP candidates opposed partition, their vote was minimal.

After 1922 as the urgency of the partition issue receded and unemployment remained constant at between 40,000 and 50,000, the working class began to turn to Labour again. Labour picked up seats in ones and twos on the Corporation, and the 1925 election was fought in the middle of a major campaign for unemployment relief. But again the Labour candidates were ambiguous on partition. Even in the 1923 Westminster election Midgley had told a Protestant audience on the Shankill Road that he was as loyal as Craig on the boundary issue, while letting the Catholics of the Falls believe he was still as anti-partitionist as two years before. The Labour support was fragile and might evaporate again if the partition issue returned to the fore.

The Independent Unionists, with one exception, James Gyle, were at least as Loyalist and Protestant as the official party. They represented either local grievances or a milder form of working-class discontent with the stoutly employer-dominated official party. They were an irritant but not a threat to the party leadership. On the ultimate question – the existence of the state – there was no doubt what side they were on. Later on in fact Independent Unionists came to represent working-class Protestant frustration at the official party's occasional restraints on their sectarian exuberance.

Still, Craig and his colleagues were worried by the 1925 election.

The new parliament met on 14 April. The Nationalists didn't attend but the Labour MPs did and took up the role of official opposition. Sam Kyle the Labour leader concentrated on the 48,000 unemployed, bad housing, and social conditions in the North. Despite Craig's attempt to focus the election on the boundary issue he said, 'the people, at least in Belfast, conceived the issue to be the boundary line that divides the poor who have no bread from the rich who have a surplus'[14]. Jack Beattie called for old age pensions to be paid at the age of sixty not seventy, and William McMullen demanded urgent action on unemployment. Two weeks later, on 28 April, Joe Devlin and T.S.McAllister, the Nationalist MP for Co.Antrim, took their seats. They had agreed to wait till the Boundary Commission reported but they couldn't let the Labour Party steal the show. They supported a motion by George Henderson, the tenant farmers' representative, on land annuities.

There was no great welcome for them even though Craig had been urging the Nationalists for two years to take their seats and accept the state. He clashed with Devlin almost immediately so that even Tommy

Henderson, an Independent Unionist, complained: 'After the appeals that have been made for the last two years by our PM for an opposition, I thought he would have had his arms wrapped round the hon. member for West Belfast but today, I see they are in opposition to one another'[15].

Devlin quickly made clear his attitude to the parliament and his intention to concentrate on social reform in co-operation with the rest of the opposition:

'This Ulster parliament is a parliament of rich men. Those who are not rich are representatives of the rich and therefore it is our business, this small minority, let it come from the ranks of Labour or Independent or those I represent, it is our business to come here in face of the powerful body behind the Prime Minister and his friends to see that justice is done to these people [old-age pensioners].'

He described himself and his colleagues as 'the representatives of the poorest and the lowliest and the most defenceless of the community'[16].

This was the new state's honeymoon period. It had been born in bloodshed and pogrom and for five years it had been an armed camp, its jails filled with political prisoners. Now the tension was relaxing. The Southern government had accepted its existence and now the leaders of the Catholic minority had done so as well. Soon its frontiers were to be confirmed. Meanwhile the advent of an opposition lent an air of normality to the tiny one-party parliament. The presence of Devlin, a fine speaker who had been a major figure at Westminster, even lent it a touch of class.

When the Boundary Agreement was signed in December 1925 the remaining Nationalists considered their position. On 10 March 1926 George Leeke and Basil McGuckin, MPs for Derry, and Patrick O'Neill, MP for Co.Down, took their seats. O'Neill explained his position:

'I have been a member of this House for five years but this is the first occasion on which I have had the pleasure of addressing it, due to the fact that I represent a section of the people of Down, a large majority of whom did not expect to be more than temporarily under the jurisdiction of this House, and consequently did not desire to be represented in it. But, with a decision on the boundary question having been arrived at . . . they have now decided to accept the situation as it is and to endeavour to make the best of it'[17].

He warned however that if the government was unresponsive to the opposition . . . 'then I am afraid it may be said that I can serve no useful purpose by being here.' The other five Nationalists, four of them from

Fermanagh and Tyrone, stayed out. They had confidently expected their counties to be transferred to the South and were extremely bitter about the Boundary Agreement.

Already the honeymoon was turning slightly sour. The Unionists were inflexible in the extreme. They made no concessions. As early as July 1925 a row flared up over the Senate elections. Half the Senate membership retired every four years and this was the Nationalists' first chance to win a Senate seat. Devlin, McAllister and Henderson voted for Vincent Devoto, a Catholic businessman. Their postal votes, though sent in time, were delayed by the 12 July holiday and disregarded. Craig rejected a call by the three MPs, the Labour Party, and one of the Independent Unionists for a recount. The incident was trivial but it made an inauspicious beginning. At the start of the 1926 session Devlin said: 'We [Catholics] claim that there never was a community so badly treated as we have been in all that concerns our public life. We have not a single Catholic in the Senate; we have not a Catholic on the judicial bench'[18]. A few weeks later he added: 'We have no place in the administration of the Province whose laws we are supposed to accept, and do accept. I do not think that the representations we make have the slightest possible effect'[19]. McAllister in the same debate argued that the other five Nationalists hadn't taken their seats because they didn't believe they would get justice in the parliament. 'Can we', he asked 'after our own experience here on other occasions, prove to them any act to show that we are justified in coming here'[20]?

A year later, in March 1927, Devlin put it more strongly:

'I came into this parliament for the purpose of representing the minority who were not represented before . . . at the end of two years I am more profoundly dissatisfied than ever I was about the conduct of the government towards the minority.'

He complained that over the door of every government department seemed to be written 'Jew, Turk or atheist may enter here but no Papist', and concluded:

'I did not come to this House as the representative of a crawling minority, begging for their rights . . . Therefore I say that if this is to go on I, for my part, will have to reconsider, much to your delight, whether I should remain in this House'[21].

Nonetheless the other Nationalists came in. On 19 October 1927 a meeting of MPs, councillors, Catholic businessmen and clergy in Fermanagh and Tyrone decided they should take their seats and a week later they did. Two factors influenced them strongly. In August 1927 Eamon De Valera and his newly-formed Fianna Fail party in the South had entered the Dail, finally acknowledging the Treaty settlement and partition 'and agreeing to work within it. Abstentionism was now the policy only of the small remnant of Sinn Fein. And on 12 July Craig had told an Orange rally that he intended to abolish PR for parliamentary elections in Northern Ireland. This would involve re-organising the constituencies as well, and the Nationalists, fearing another gerrymander like the local government one, were determined to fight it.

Though the government rarely listened to them the Nationalists had formed a fairly cohesive alliance with the rest of the opposition. When the government introduced a Trades Disputes Bill similar to the one passed in England after the General Strike – there had been no strike in Northern Ireland – they opposed it as well as Labour. Devlin expressed his sympathy with the strike and attacked William Grant, the Labour Unionist, for slandering his own class and his fellow workmen for the benefit of the capitalists. With impeccable social democratic logic he said that he was no revolutionist and was against class warfare, but that laws like the Trades Disputes Act would lead to class war.

When Labour, Nationalists and Independent Unionists combined to propose a censure motion on the government in 1927, Craig – now Lord Craigavon – denounced the Independent Unionists and said they should call themselves Independent Nationalists, they voted with the Nationalists so often.

Early in 1929 Devlin, attacking the proposal to abolish PR, outlined the way he wanted politics to develop in the North. Politics should be about social and economic issues, not religion.

'There should be Tories – despite their limited intelligence – and democrats . . . for the next four years . . . you are going to perpetuate the old party divisions of Protestant and Catholic, Orange and Green . . . .

'For my own part I would rather see the whole Nationalist Party disappear and form themselves with other elements into what would be called a Progressive party – a party that would be progressive because it would be opposed to the government – and try to wipe out religious differences altogether, and instead of having Protestant and Catholic have democrat and Tory'[22].

His populist views, born of the needs of a working-class city constituency, didn't always sit too well on the shoulders of some of his rural colleagues though. Cahir Healy had chided the Unionists in 1927 for their treatment of the Nationalists because they would soon need the Nationalists' help 'against the socialists of Belfast who will have gone with the red flag'[23].

But Craig was out to eliminate the Labour and Independent threat to the Unionist hold over the Protestant masses, and the developing opposition alliance in parliament made him more determined. He spelt it out:

'What I want to get in this House and what I believe we will get very much better in this House under the old-fashioned plain and simple system, are men who are for the Union on the one hand, or who are against it and want to go into a Dublin parliament on the other'[24].

The entire opposition fought the abolition of PR and the associated re-drawing of constituencies, introduction of extra votes for company directors, and three-year residential qualifications for the franchise; and fourteen MPs – nine Nationalists, three Labour, George Henderson, the tenant farmers' representative, and one Independent Unionist, James Gyle – issued a joint manifesto opposing these moves in January 1928. But they were passed all the same and so was a measure to renew the Special Powers Act for five years despite the continuance of peace in the area. By the end of the parliament tempers were flaring, and in November 1928 when the government tried to railroad parliamentary business Devlin denounced them as 'villains, bullies, conspirators and ruffians' and was promptly suspended and removed by the RUC. Then one by one all the Nationalists, the three Labour MPs, and two of the Independent Unionists protested and were suspended as well.

Meanwhile the Nationalists, now at full strength in parliament and united at last on the policy of working within the Northern state, were organising themselves. On 28 May 1928 a conference was held in St.Marys' Hall, Belfast, summoned by nine of the ten MPs[25]. Devlin gave the reasons:

'After waiting for seven years – years of justice denied, disabilities imposed, and religious and political inferiority branded on our people – we have decided to start this organisation. The demand came, not from the leaders, but from the people themselves. They revolted against the system of which they are the victims and they felt the helplessness of their position – over one third of the population reduced to impotence and with no machinery even to make vocal their protest against the wrongs they are enduring'[26].

The Northern Nationalists had been deeply divided after 1918 between the Redmondite Home Rulers such as Devlin, McAllister and Harbinson, and the supporters of Sinn Fein. The Sinn Feiners had been further divided by the Treaty split and even those who had supported the Republicans during the civil war had split again over the formation of Fianna Fail. But by 1928 they had all, except the Republicans, recognised they would get no help from the South, accepted the Northern state, and agreed to work within it. There was now a basis for unity and their action would be more effective backed by a party organisation. The Church was interested too – the education dispute hadn't been settled and they had other interests to protect. And the Catholic middle-class, publicans, lawyers and businessmen, all wanted a share in power and patronage. The MPs were sensitive to their wishes. Of the ten MPs elected in 1925, five were lawyers, two hotel-owners, and one involved in the drink trade; the other two were a large farmer and a journalist.

The conference was attended by the MPs and 200 'delegates': local councillors, the editors of the *Irish News* and several local Nationalist papers, and nine priests. The Republicans were not invited, nor, despite Devlin's populist ideas, were any of the trade unions or the Labour Party – even its anti-partitionist members. It was a conference of middle-class Catholic, constitutional Nationalists. The memory of previous divisions was still fresh. Devlin took the chair only after some hesitation lest he antagonise some of his past opponents. However the *Irish News* reported that he assured the attendance:

'the Nationalist members of the Northern parliament were absolutely united in aims and policy . . . They had no means other than the Northern parliament for making their voices heard. Before setting out they had consulted the Northern bishops and secured their approval . . . . They wanted to bury old differences. Things were changing. There was a fresher atmosphere in Belfast; the masses of the people were now friendly; politics were no longer a cause for men hating each other'[27].

The conference voted to set up a new political organisation called the National League of the North, with local branches, an annual conference and an elected central council. The Catholic emphasis in the organisation was stressed when the motion was proposed by Father Coyle, parish priest of Belleek. Devlin was elected president, Archdeacon Tierney of Enniskillen vice-president, and Cahir Healy MP and Patrick O'Neill MP joint secretaries. A temporary central council was elected consisting of the nine MPs and 44 others representing Belfast and each of the six counties.

There were five priests on the council while the rest were mainly councillors and local election workers.

The new organisation set to work. It was very active for the next few months establishing local branches and on 24 July 1928 they held a mass rally in Belfast. Between 10,000 and 15,000 people marched up the Falls Road to a meeting in McRory Park, a Gaelic football stadium. It was the largest Nationalist demonstration in the North for many years and Devlin was accusing yet confident when he addressed the crowd:

'We have still the means to expose before the world the meanness and the malignity with which 420,000 of our people are defrauded of their rights, swindled out of their proper share of representation in the Senate, in the courts of justice, in the magistracy, in the grand jury, in the county councils and corporations and municipal councils and every other public body. We can put up a fight, not only for our own people, but for the Protestant working-class who are living on the dole (some of them even denied that miserable pittance) . . .'

He went on with more enthusiasm than accuracy:

'A few of us, single-handed, without organisation, without resources and faced by a government with well-equipped official machinery ready at hand, went into the parliament and we made our mark on the character of its legislative output. We fought for the poor, for the aged, for the feeble, for the bereaved widow and the friendless orphan, and we did not fight in vain. . . . With a vigorous organisation, a determined spirit amongst our people and a large number of representatives acting in unison in the Northern parliament, still more effective work can be accomplished'[28].

T.S.McAllister reinforced the message: 'Parliamentary representation, to be able to pull its full weight, to be complete in its effectiveness, must have an organisation behind it.'

The National League could do nothing to save PR but when Craigavon called a general election in May 1929 the League organised conventions in each county, except Antrim, to choose candidates for the new single-member constituencies. And they drafted an election manifesto. It called for a united Ireland but opposed the use of force to achieve it. Within the North they demanded an end to unemployment, raising the school-leaving age to thirteen (and paying parents a maintenance allowance as compensation for the children's earnings), old age pensions of £1 a week at 60, town planning, slum clearance and public utility works to help relieve unemployment.

It was quite a radical programme for the times and seemed to be aimed at the Protestant worker as much as the Catholic Nationalist, but the League promptly belied that by nominating only eleven candidates in the eleven constituencies they were fairly sure had Catholic majorities.

With PR abolished there were 48 single-seat constituencies – graduates of Queen's University could still elect another four MPs by PR. There was not, as feared by the Nationalists, a massive gerrymander. Fermanagh County was so arranged as to return two Unionists for three seats. Derry City had a grotesquely shaped Loyalist area grafted on so that it would return one Unionist out of two seats. But where Nationalists and Sinn Fein had won twelve seats in 1921 and 1925 they seemed likely to hold eleven. They were already somewhat under-represented. The difference was marginal. As Craigavon had made clear, the object of the exercise was to secure a straight Unionist/Nationalist – and in practice, Protestant/Catholic – confrontation and to eliminate the Labour and Independent Unionist menace.

It certainly did that. Labour didn't make a big effort in the election, putting up only five candidates, four in Belfast and one in Newtownards, but there were six Liberals, two town tenants' candidates and ten Independent Unionists. There was also a campaign being waged by extreme temperance groups at the time for 'local option' – a system where local government wards could vote to outlaw completely the sale of drink in their areas. There were three local option candidates, all Unionists, who were more extreme on this issue than the official party. Out of these 26 candidates only three were elected, one Labour and two Independent Unionists.

Sinn Fein had put up no candidates and the Nationalists won their expected eleven seats, two in Belfast, three in Tyrone, two in Derry, two in Down and one each in South Fermanagh and South Armagh. Six of them were unopposed and there were no election contests at all in Fermanagh or Derry and only one in Tyrone. Of the Labour candidates only Beattie, who had topped the poll in East Belfast in 1925, was elected. He won in Pottinger with a majority of just one thousand[29]. Sam Kyle was defeated by only 189 votes in Oldpark and the Unionist in Dock was elected with less than the combined total of the Labour candidate and James Gyle, a liberal

Independent Unionist. The four Labour men in Belfast had polled 20,516 votes, a respectable total, but not enough under the straight vote system.

The two Independent Unionists elected were Tommy Henderson, who had topped the poll in North Belfast in 1925 and now scraped home with a majority of 281 in Shankill, and J.W.Nixon in Woodvale. They were no threat to Craig: Henderson had only stood as Independent Unionist in the first place because he didn't get an official Unionist nomination, and Nixon was an ultra-Unionist District Inspector who had been sacked from the RUC. Most of the Independents and the Liberals saved their deposits but they didn't seriously threaten their Unionist opponents.

Craig was well satisfied. He held 38 seats in the parliament now instead of 32 and faced a potential opposition of 14 instead of 20. He had defeated the Labour threat and had disciplined the Protestant population into backing the official Unionist party. He had been helped by a steadily improving economic situation and unemployment which had dropped to 35,000 or fifteen per cent. But a major factor had been the abolition of PR. And it had brought an added bonus. It had driven a serious wedge between Labour and the Nationalists.

The Nationalists and Labour had worked together in the previous parliament and Devlin had advocated an alliance between them. But Devlin's idea seemed to be that the Nationalists would represent the Catholics – of all social classes – and Labour would win the support of Protestant workers. Then they could combine against the Unionists. The alliance could work alright, so long as Labour didn't challenge the Nationalists' leadership of the Catholic masses or try to split the Catholic population on class lines.

Under PR there was no problem, there was no confrontation. Under the straight vote there was. Billy McMullen, outgoing Labour MP for West Belfast and a Protestant, stood for election in the new constituency of Falls in the heart of the Catholic ghetto. The National League put up Richard Byrne, a conservative Catholic publican and slum landlord. This put Devlin's radicalism to the test: a straight choice between a radical and a reactionary, or between a 'democrat' and a 'Tory' in Devlin's own words. Devlin chose the Tory. He met a Labour deputation including McMullen and appealed to him to stand down, offering him a seat in the Senate instead. He made no secret of his own contempt for Byrne, calling him an 'old pisspot'[30] but made it clear he would back him fully in an election.

It was a dirty fight. The Nationalists made as much capital as they could out of McMullen's religion. Byrne was proposed and seconded by priests, and a body called the Catholic Union called on all its members to work and vote for Byrne 'because Catholic representation is required to defend Catholic interests especially on the education question'[31]. The *Irish News* carried a long article by a priest a few days before the election on the incompatibility of socialism and Catholicism, and T.J.Campbell, the editor of the *Irish News*, summed up the Nationalist approach: 'Mr Byrne's nominator was their Venerable Archdeacon (a high-ranking Catholic cleric). His seconder was Fr Fullerton. Could they have better guides?'[32]

During the contest the National League was defining its own position. It was not, despite its manifesto, a socialist or even a radical party – Byrne was a Tory. It was not really a Nationalist party – McMullen was more of a Nationalist than Byrne. In effect it was a Catholic party claiming to represent the Catholic population without distinction of class or politics but therefore in practice representing the Catholic Church and the Catholic middle class.

McMullen hit back hard. He brought out a broadsheet called the *Northern Worker* attacking Byrne as a slum landlord and describing slum property owned by him in the docks area. Byrne took out a court injunction to stop its distribution two days before polling day.

Byrne won by 6,941 votes to 5,509. McMullen had done fairly well. His vote was up by nearly 3,000 on his 1925 total in a much smaller constituency, but it wasn't enough. McMullen had been the toughest and most radical of the 1925 opposition and the Unionists were glad to see him replaced by the safe and ponderous Byrne; but the real significance of the result was that the abolition of PR had smashed the Labour-Nationalist alliance, stopped dead any trend towards secular radicalism in the Nationalists and forced them back into narrow Catholic sectarianism.

There was a Westminster election three days after the one for the Northern parliament. The Nationalists nominated Devlin and T.J.S.Harbinson, who had not stood for the local parliament, for Fermanagh and Tyrone. They also put up Frank McDermott, an ex-major in the British Army and a partner in an international banking firm, for West Belfast. He was an old UIL associate of Devlin's and his nomination showed the increasing dominance of the UIL tradition in the National League. There were six Liberal candidates and a couple of Independent Unionists.

They were all easily defeated, except Devlin and Harbinson who were unopposed.

The Nationalists returned to the Northern parliament in full strength except for Devlin, who was ill. Labour was no longer the official opposition but the Nationalists refused to take up the position. Nonetheless Craigavon wrote to his wife: 'The new Nationalist members are really rather a kindly lot'[33].

It was clearer than ever that they were basically a Catholic party. Byrne declared 'It is our duty in this parliament . . . to look after the interests of the faith to which I am proud to belong'[34]; and they devoted most of their attention to the 1930 Education Amendment Act which finally met the demands of the Orange Order and the Protestant churches and made state schools effectively Protestant schools. J.J.McCarroll, editor of the *Derry Journal* and MP for Foyle, described even these schools as 'Godless'. The debates were heated and increasingly sectarian and dissatisfaction was growing again. George Leeke warned in March 1930 that if the government didn't make some concessions 'the whole question of Catholic representation in the six counties will have to be reconsidered and their future policy defined at some public meeting'[35].

As unemployment rose drastically with the depression, from 35,000 in 1929 to 72,000 in 1930 and 76,000 in 1932, the Nationalists were forced to concentrate on social issues once more. Devlin was active again by now and took a radical attitude to the depression. Sitting with the remnant of the Labour Party at Westminster after the formation of the National government in England, he denounced his old friend Ramsay MacDonald for cutting unemployment benefit, and advocated public investment and public works instead of cuts in public expenditure. At home he and his colleagues opposed a local cut in unemployment benefit.

The frustration at Unionist unresponsiveness which was normal by now was aggravated by the crisis and by the sharp pressure of thousands of starving workers in Belfast. The government, ultra-conservative in politics, and made up of industrialists and landowners, reacted with stolid unconcern. Unemployment didn't affect them and, with the abolition of PR, it wasn't even likely to affect their majority in elections. They brashly went ahead with plans for a gala state opening of their grandiose and extravagant new parliament building at Stormont, while local Boards of Guardians were cutting off men's benefit to save public money.

Devlin spoke bitterly on the king's speech in March 1932:

'The fundamental principle of citizenship and of all Christian or humane law is either work or maintenance for the people . . . The people are not responsible for unemployment. Their masters are responsible for it. The conditions of industry today are due to causes over which the working people have no control whatsoever'[36].

Earlier he had condemned the government's inaction on the depression, their use of sectarianism and the border issue to stifle all political development, and their treatment of the opposition. In a sweeping finale he summed up the frustration of seven years of parliamentary opposition:

'I only want to say in conclusion that I believe this is the last time we shall meet in this House. Well thank God for that. My colleagues and I who represent democracy have no reason to rejoice at the years we have been here . . . You had opponents willing to co-operate. We did not seek office. We sought service. We were willing to help. But you rejected all friendly offers. You refused to accept co-operation . . . You went on on the old political lines, fostering hatreds, keeping one third of the population as if they were pariahs in the community, refusing to accept support from any class but your own and relying on those religious differences and difficulties so that you could remain in office for ever'[37].

It was to be his last major speech in the Northern parliament. The frustration had reached breaking point. On 11 May Cahir Healy was speaking on the Northern budget when the Speaker ruled that he could not discuss the services reserved to Westminster, which accounted for £10 million out of the £11½ million budget. Devlin burst out,

'It is obviously a sham and a farce being members of parliament elected by the people to discuss public expenditure . . . if our rights and liberties are to be so circumscribed that we are not permitted to discuss them. I, for one, will take no part in this sham discussion.'

All the Nationalist MPs then walked out.

The next day the three newly elected Nationalist Senators walked out as well and all fourteen issued a joint manifesto refusing 'to take any further part in the farcical procedure'. The *Irish News* backed their action in its editorial. The immediate cause of the walk-out was trivial but the discontent and sense of impotence which inspired it had been steadily building up. It was accentuated by the appalling misery of the depression, soon to explode in violence. And the Nationalists were encouraged to adopt a more militant attitude by the election in February 1932 of the first Fianna

Fail government in the South. De Valera had campaigned under the slogan 'On to the Republic'. Perhaps he could achieve more by pressure on England than they could in a parliament where they were daily spurned and humiliated.

Meanwhile the parliament was left with a three-man opposition. It didn't sit much longer anyway and, blithely insensitive to the starving workers in Belfast, adjourned for a six-month-long summer holiday. It met for one day on 30 September for a formal sitting and the Speaker refused to let Jack Beattie (Labour) and Tommy Henderson (Independent Unionist) raise the question of unemployment. Beattie lifted the mace and threw it at the Speaker saying 'I absolutely refuse to sit in this House and indulge in hypocrisy while the people are starving outside.' Then he walked out, followed by Henderson. The government was left with an opposition of one – the ultra-Unionist ex-District Inspector J.W.Nixon.

There was violent rioting by the unemployed in Belfast in October but the government went ahead with plans for the gala opening of Stormont by the Prince of Wales on 16 November.

The Nationalist MPs and Senators issued another manifesto on 6 November 1932. They placed more stress on partition than for a long time and appealed to the South for support. They announced that they would boycott the Stormont ceremony and continue their boycott of the parliament and they denounced the government as responsible for provoking the recent riots.

'The government that not only fails to deal with such an evil as unemployment but even ostentatiously refuses to listen in parliament to the people's representatives when they seek to expound grievances and suggest a remedy, is itself responsible if desperate men are driven to apply desperate remedies and to lend attentive ears to those who preach a propaganda of destruction ... When we voiced the grievances of the workers of Northern Ireland our representations were treated with contempt with the result that the government were responsible for transferring the exposition of the people's grievances from the parliamentary arena to the public streets and for substituting for constitutional means the violent methods of men grown desperate through lack of food and want of work.'

The Nationalists, the statement went on, had hoped for a change of heart but 'relying on their majority the government derided the opposition, scoffed at their offers of co-operation and rejected every suggestion they made'[38].

Devlin's hand was clear in the manifesto. It was imbued with his belief that social reform was the only safeguard against social revolution and it gave his verdict on the years in the Northern parliament. It was the lament of parliamentarians forced out of parliament. That they had no desire to be abstentionists was shown by the fact that Devlin and Healy had been elected to Westminster in 1931 and had continued to attend regularly. These 'nice kindly men' were appalled by the prospect of street politics, but parliament for them had held nothing but frustration.

The *Irish News* summed up the parliamentary experience:

'Whenever they rose to address the House the Prime Minister and other Ministers and many of their followers retired ostentatiously and deliberately to the smoke-room. This wilful rudeness to the minority's representatives was repeated in their dealings with the people who comprised that minority. They were denied every possible right: the stamp of scorned inferiority was stamped on the brows of one third of the area's population, and they were allowed no say whatever in guiding the destinies of the country in which they lived and for whose welfare their regard was at least as sincere and deep as that of those who had placed them in subjection'[39].

The honeymoon was over. The Catholic middle class had offered their co-operation in the running of the state in return for some share in power and patronage. Their offer had been spurned.

6

The Violent Thirties

Though the Unionist leaders had constructed a system which divided the Northern working class and bound the Protestant workers to them by links of ideology and material advantage, and though they had checked the advance of the Labour Party, the system was not invulnerable. It was not proof against an economic disaster which, for thousands of Protestant workers, could wipe out their marginal advantage over their Catholic fellow-workers and underline the real gulf between them and their leaders. And so, for a time during the great depression, the Orange system was to teeter on the brink of collapse as Protestant and Catholic unemployed united in a great struggle for survival. Even then the solidarity and determination of the Outdoor Relief (ODR) strike in 1932 was not created overnight: it only came after years of smaller struggles against unemployment and a cruel and heartless relief system which had changed little since the time of Dickens.

The Northern state had been dogged by chronic unemployment from the beginning. There were 103,000 people out of work when the state was established in June 1921. That was an exceptional figure due to a post-war trade depression and the virtual civil war raging in the six counties at the time; but, though the figures dropped over the next few years, they began to climb again in 1925 due partly to a recession in the textile industry. There were 48,000 out of work in April 1925 when the election to the local parliament was held and the growing unemployment helped to elect the three Labour MPs.

The numbers out of work continued to climb during the summer and by September 1925 there were 56,000 wholly unemployed and 6,000 on short time, according to the official figures. 38,000 of the wholly unemployed were in Belfast. In fact the government had to recall parliament in September specially to vote extra money for the unemployment fund, which had run out. Meanwhile however the government had also introduced tough new regulations governing who could get unemployment benefit. Under the regulations workers were only eligible for benefit if they had been in work and paid contributions in the past two years, if they passed a stringent means test, and if they were 'genuinely seeking work'.

In an area with chronic unemployment many people had been out of work for two years or more and so were refused benefit; and, since a worker on the dole could be, and often was, offered a job in England which he wasn't prepared to take, others were struck off as not 'genuinely seeking work'. Jack Beattie MP claimed in November 1925, when the official figure had gone up to 64,000 out of work, that another 13,000 to 14,000 had been struck off the register and refused benefits under the regulations.

In Britain those struck off got Outdoor Relief (ODR) – a sort of supplementary benefit – from the local Poor Law Guardians, but the Belfast Board of Guardians refused to give ODR to all but a handful of applicants, and when they did it was in kind, not in cash. The only alternative to ODR was to enter the workhouse, where families were still split up and the inmates forced to wear workhouse clothes and obey prison-like rules. Most of the unemployed chose semi-starvation outside. On 5 November 1925 an unemployed ex-seaman committed suicide in Belfast in despair at his predicament[1].

In this situation, with thousands on the verge of starvation, an Unemployed Workers' Committee was set up and a special trade union conference in August 1925 denounced the new regulations and launched a campaign against them. When parliament met specially in September the three Labour MPs denounced the government and William McMullen said:

'I warn the government very seriously that they have a very direct and definite responsibility. If they are not prepared to accept that responsibility and do something for the large number of people unemployed at the present time – the large number of people who are starving and whose wives and families are starving through no fault of their own – then there will be a day of reckoning as far as the government is concerned . . . and in a way they will not like'[2].

The new session of parliament was to open on 6 October. The Unemployed Workers' Committee, the Belfast Trades Council and the Labour Party planned a mass march from the City Hall to the parliament building in Botanic Avenue. All through September local meetings were held all over Belfast and feelings ran high. Hugh Gemmell of the ILP threatened that they would make Craig's knees knock 'like the bones in a jazz band' and that they would dissolve the Belfast parliament the way

Cromwell had dissolved the English one[3]. Others were more vehement still. Richard McConnell warned that the revolution was coming.

Three days before the opening of parliament, Dawson Bates banned the demonstration under the Special Powers Act and on 6 October he had a massive force of police on hand to prevent any attempt to march. The organisers protested loudly. Even the moderate, respectable Sam Kyle MP said:

'I accuse the Home Secretary of trying to provoke disorder so that he may divert the attention of the people of Belfast from the things that really matter – from the unemployment situation – so that he may get the Catholics and Protestants at each other's throats'[4].

But they called the demonstration off.

Agitation didn't end however and the government continued to use a very heavy hand to put it down. On 25 November Sam Patterson, a Labour Party member, was sentenced to six months' hard labour for making a seditious speech. He had said:

'While the people of Belfast are starving we have rogues, vagabonds, thieves and murderers in Sir James Craig and his government ... by the aid of the rifle, revolver and bomb we can blow the government to hell, their proper country. By constitutional means and the ballot box this would take about fifty years: but by banding ourselves together and using the forces I mentioned we can free ourselves in twelve months'[5].

In fact the Unionists had become extremely alarmed at the Labour threat and in a by-election for South Belfast early in November their campaign was run by the Unionist Labour Association in an effort to keep the support of Protestant workers, while Babington, the Unionist candidate, said 'This election is being fought on the issue – Constitutional Government, Communism or Socialism'[6].

Babington won fairly easily however,[7] partly because the Boundary Commission was about to report and the constitutional issue was again to the fore. The boundary crisis dominated the close of the year, cementing the Unionist alliance again and undermining the fragile and temporary support the Labour Party had won among the Protestant masses.

But the depression didn't end and in the calmer atmosphere of 1926, with 61,000 still officially out of work, agitation revived. Men were still being struck off – between October 1925 and October 1926, 48,960 applications for benefit were turned down[8] – and then refused Outdoor Relief. In May, during the General Strike in Britain – which didn't really apply in the North, though the British government sent a destroyer to Belfast Lough just in case – there was a mass march of unemployed from the City Hall to the workhouse where the guardians saw a deputation from the Trades Council and the Unemployed Workers' Committee. They got no satisfaction however.

On 15 June 1926 when the guardians were meeting again several thousand marched to the workhouse. This time the guardians refused to see their spokesmen and Beattie and McMullen, who were members of the Board, tried to obstruct the meeting. They and two other Labour members were forcibly removed by the RUC and Beattie was punched and manhandled down the stairs. Outside, the crowd, some of them armed, were angry and about to riot but the MPs got them to disperse.

It was the last big demonstration. The government and the guardians would not give way and would tolerate no challenge. The Labour leaders, basically constitutionalists and parliamentarians, were unwilling to risk a clash with the police. Their natural inclinations were reinforced by the knowledge that their hold over the unemployed was tenuous and a violent clash with the government would only send the bulk of their supporters back into the arms of the Unionists. But they had reached an impasse and could get no further with constitutional means.

An improvement in trade leading to the relative boom of the late 1920s and reducing unemployment to 34,000 in 1927, together with a major concession by the guardians who eventually agreed to give Outdoor Relief to heads of families, resolved the crisis. A continuing improvement and the abolition of PR removed the immediate threat to Unionist hegemony. But a serious clash was only postponed, not averted.

The Northern state was hard hit by the world depression. Unemployment soared again to 76,000 or 28 per cent in 1932. (The real figure was probably closer to 100,000 because of the numbers struck off the register.) And it was concentrated among the urban industrial workers – 45,000 of the unemployed were in Belfast alone – while agricultural workers were not so badly affected. There had been 20,000 men employed in the two Belfast shipyards in 1924 but Harland and Wolff didn't launch a single ship in 1932 or 1933, and there were only 2,000 men in the two yards in 1933. Workman Clark's yard closed down for good in 1934. The Protestant skilled engineering workers, the backbone of Unionist support in Belfast, were as hard hit as the Catholic labourers.

Conditions for the unemployed were grim. A married couple with no children got eight shillings a week; with one child, twelve shillings; with two children, sixteen shillings; with four or more children a maximum of twenty-four shillings a week. To qualify for this miserable pittance the husband had to do two and a half days 'task work' per week on the Outdoor Relief schemes, mostly mending roads and laying pavements. Even then there was not enough work to go round and men had to take their turn getting on the schemes. Husbands who didn't do the task work in any week were paid in kind, meaning they couldn't pay their rent or gas bills, buy clothes or even cigarettes or a drink. Single men got nothing unless they got work on the task-schemes. Then they got 3/6d a week. Single men who got no work, single girls, widows and orphans had either to live off their relations or to go into the workhouse.

The Belfast relief rates were lower than any British city, in most of which a married couple with one child could get twenty-six or twenty-seven shillings a week with the possibility of a rent allowance as well; but the Belfast Board of Guardians were deaf to all pleas. A Methodist minister, Rev J.N.Spence, gave the explanation in a letter to the papers:

'In seventeen large British cities chosen at random the average rate (local government tax, levied on property owners or occupiers) per head is £4.3s.0d. and in Belfast rather less than £2.10s.0d. per head, whilst the Poor Rate is also greatly lower . . . it is only true to say that Belfast has a smaller rate per head of population than any British city of comparable size'[9].

The Corporation and the guardians, elected by the ratepayers and dominated by businessmen, were looking after their own interests.

At the beginning of the 1930s a number of Revolutionary Workers' Groups – loose marxist organisations – had been established in Ireland. They had taken the lead in resisting the dole cuts in 1931 and early in 1932 Tommy Geehan, one of their activists, called, at a trades council conference, for a strike by the men on the ODR schemes. The trades council and the Labour Party turned the idea down but the RWG went ahead, with the support of left-wing Labour branches, and spent the summer organising an Outdoor Relief Workers' Committee. They held a series of mass meetings and rallies during August and September while anger and frustration grew among the workers, faced with the prospect of winter on the dole or in the workhouse. On 20 September the Board of Guardians even rejected a proposal by a Nationalist, Councillor James Collins, to supplement all relief grants for the winter with a grant of ten shillings a week for rent and coal.

On 29 September the ODR Workers' Committee voted to strike on 4 October. It was on the next day that Jack Beattie MP, responding to the mood of the workers, threw the parliamentary mace at the Speaker. 4 October was a Monday and 600 men were due to start on the task work. Pickets marched from site to site closing them down and the strike was 100 per cent solid. That evening the strikers and their supporters marched from the Labour Exchange in Frederick Street to the Customs House steps, demanding 'work and wages, not charity'. The crowd was huge. Estimates ranged from 15,000 (the anti-strike *Newsletter*) to 60,000 by the organisers. The speakers were Jack Beattie, two Nationalist councillors – James Collins and Harry Diamond – an Independent Unionist, Alderman Pierce, and Geehan and Betty Sinclair of the Revolutionary Workers' Groups (RWG). Geehan called for a rent strike and 'tick'[10] strike. Murtagh Morgan, one of the organisers, recalls that there was an air of tremendous enthusiasm and excitement. He thought an insurrection was quite possible[11].

The next day 7,000 unemployed marched to the workhouse on the Lisburn Road – now the City Hospital – where the Guardians were meeting. Outside the workhouse thousands lay on the tram-lines to block the traffic while a meeting was held. The committee outlined their demands for a minimum of 15/3d for a single man and 13/6d for a single woman, all payment to be in cash; the abolition of the means test, and an end to task work. One speaker warned that if they didn't get their demands 700 single men would enter the workhouse where it cost 16/1d a week to keep one person.

Already the Unionist leaders were getting worried. The *Newsletter* editorial commented:

'An admittedly serious state of affairs is being seized on by socialist and Nationalist orators, not so much with the hope of discovering a practical remedy as in the hope of discrediting the authorities, state and local, and of paving the way to revolutionary changes'[12].

On the Wednesday the RUC banned another march to the workhouse and lined the route with police and cage cars[13], but the demonstrators walked there and 300 men were admitted to the workhouse. That night a vast crowd filled the road down to Bradbury Place and serious rioting broke out after the meeting when the RUC repeatedly baton-charged the crowd. A tram was hijacked and wrecked in Gt Victoria Street and others were pulled away from the overhead cables. Shop windows were smashed in Sandy Row and shops looted in Divis Street.

Inside the workhouse there were stormy scenes when the men danced, shouted and sang and refused to go to bed at 8pm. The RUC were called in and arrested the two organisers. In the morning the rest were expelled when they demanded eggs for their breakfast.

By Friday the government and the corporation had agreed to provide more money for relief schemes and the guardians had decided to increase relief rates by 50 per cent and make all payments in cash. But it was too late for that. Even the leaders of the Protestant churches were calling for substantial increases – though the Catholic church kept remarkably quiet because the bishops were alarmed at the 'Communist Menace'. The Trades Council was considering a call for a general strike and at an unemployed meeting William Boyd, an RWG member, said:

'We can paralyse this city. We can stop the trams, the gas, the electricity and bring the city to stagnation if we only have solidarity. The very threat of a general strike will be sufficient to bring these people to their knees'[14].

The ODR men totally rejected the increased rates, and called for mass meetings and bonfires on Monday, 10 October and a monster demonstration starting from four different points on Tuesday 11th.

The level of destitution they were fighting against was illustrated dramatically over the weekend when a man was arrested for breaking the windows of Anderson and Macauley's department store in the city centre. He told the court: 'I broke the window because I was hungry. Jail is the only place where I can get food'[15]. Meanwhile the strike committee had set up a food distribution centre in Corporation Street. Through collections and contributions from shops they had acquired 4,927 loaves, 800 stone of potatoes, 727lbs of sugar, 170lbs of tea, 91lbs of butter, 131 pots of jam, and 10 stone of flour. The Belfast Co-op gave them 500 gallons of milk. None of it lasted long.

On Monday Sir Charles Wickham, head of the RUC, banned meetings and bonfires for that night and Tuesday's marches – all under the Special Powers Act – and drafted another 700 police into the city. Geehan outwitted them by speaking at a rally of women and girls in St Mary's Hall, saying:

'For many years the workers of Belfast had been divided by artificial barriers of religion and politics but the past two months had witnessed a wonderful spectacle because the workers were now united on a common platform demanding the right to live.

'Tomorrow you will see the mightiest demonstration of unity that has ever been seen in Belfast ... The authorities have banned the demonstration tomorrow but the workers of Belfast are going out ... to the guardians to show them that the mass of workers organised and unorganised, employed and unemployed, are determined that we will no longer live under rotten conditions of poverty'[16].

The RUC broke up meetings at Cromac Square and on the Shankill Road and arrested Maurice Watters, an RWG member, and charged him with incitement to murder John Wilson and Lily Colemen, two prominent Unionist members of the Board of Guardians. He was bound over for twelve months.

On Tuesday morning crowds began to gather at the four main assembly points: Clonard Street on the Falls Road, Tennent Street on the Shankill, Templemore Avenue in East Belfast and Canning Street on York Road. They were to march to the Labour Exchange and thence to the workhouse again. At Templemore Avenue, the RUC baton-charged as the march was forming up. There was some fighting but they managed to clear the area. In York Street they arrested William Boyd of the RWG and again broke up the crowd with baton charges.

On the Falls Road, the RUC moved in in massive strength, armed with rifles and backed up with cage cars and armoured whippet cars mounted with machine guns. They attacked the crowd at Clonard Street, rioting began immediately, and soon the whole Lower Falls was in turmoil. The RUC began to use their guns and shot one man dead and wounded fourteen others – one of them died the next day. Side streets were trenched or barricaded and the RUC nearly lost a Lancia armoured car which fell into a trench at Raglan Street and was crippled. When news of the fighting reached the Shankill area rioting broke out there as well and back streets were barricaded, shops looted and the RUC attacked. The RUC fired over the heads of a crowd in Agnes Street but there were no casualties.

Rioting became general in all the assembly areas. Streets were barricaded in the Short Strand, North Queen Street and Ardoyne as well. Troops were put on stand-by in Holywood Military Barracks and a curfew from 11pm to 5am was imposed.

Disturbances continued on the Wednesday with barricades still up and hijackings in East Belfast, the Falls and Shankill. But by now the RUC were concentrating their attention on the Falls where they opened fire again in Leeson Street. By the third day the remaining violence was concentrated in the Catholic ghettos and the RUC were beginning to get the upper hand and take their revenge. They stopped food deliveries to the Falls Road and then smashed their way into the area with armoured cars, rounding up and arresting dozens of workers. Local men were forced at bayonet-point to dismantle the barricades. After curfew on Tuesday night (13 October) armed police broke into the Short Strand home of Councillor James Collins who had supported the strike, and forced him and his son at gun-point to work all night in the rain taking down barricades.

Channelling the rioting into the Catholic ghettos seemed to be deliberate policy: to portray the outburst as an IRA plot and split the impressive unity the workers had displayed on Tuesday. The *Belfast Telegraph* voiced considerable alarm at the non-sectarian nature of the rioting. John Campbell, the secretary of the Labour Party, claimed:

'Lord Craigavon's solution was to divide the workers into different religious camps and it was noteworthy that although the recent trouble was spread all over the city only in a Roman Catholic area did the police use their guns'[17].

In fact the IRA, influenced a bit by a strong leftward trend in its Southern membership[18], and more by the fact that its own members were on the dole and the ODR schemes, had given considerable local support to the strike. They also mobilised their volunteers when the RUC started shooting, and two IRA men were caught with guns near the Short Strand on the night of 11 October. But the IRA had had no real influence on the organisation or course of the strike.

Yet the Unionist politicians lost no time in stirring up sectarian feeling and representing the whole thing as a Republican/Communist plot. The *Newsletter* reported the chairman of Pottinger Unionist Association as saying:

'It was a shame to see their own Protestant people being driven by hirelings from Dublin, Glasgow, and from Moscow if they liked – for where was the money coming from? They did not want such people here. They had had enough troubles in the past, but, thank God, they had surmounted those troubles and would surmount the present troubles, for they had Ulster forces able to deal with these people – whether in the Short Strand, Falls Road, or anywhere else – who had no love for the Union Jack. That was their flag and it would always be the flag of the six counties'[19].

Craigavon himself, who had said nothing about the conditions of the unemployed, broke his silence and addressed himself to 'those mischief-makers who have come into our midst', telling them:

'**If they have any designs by the trouble they have created in our city, if they have it at the back of their minds that this is one step towards securing a Republic for all Ireland . . . . Then I say they are doomed to bitter disappointment'**[20].

By now two of the strike leaders had been arrested and nearly a hundred men were in jail on rioting charges. Most of the rest of the strike leaders were in hiding because of police harassment. The official trade union leaders, who had resented the influence of the militants in the strike, took advantage of the confusion to negotiate with the government and the guardians. Craigavon was glad to get off the hook and said,

'**I publicly thank them for coming to meet the ministry because I am a great believer in the trade unions if they are properly led, and if the leaders will meet the government it is infinitely preferable, because we shall then have some responsible persons with whom to negotiate rather than having a rabble run the town'**[21].

On Friday 14 October the guardians offered new relief rates. A married couple with no children would get 20/-a week, a couple with one or two children 24/-, with three or four children 28/-and with over four children 32/-. All payments would be in cash, the means test would be modified and single persons living on their own would get benefit. The strike committee was not completely satisfied – all single people weren't entitled to benefit – but they had managed to double the rates and they recommended an end to the strike. Tommy Geehan waxed a little lyrical when he commented:

'**What we have achieved is in direct contradiction to those who said that the workers could not unite and could not fight, and the past fortnight will be recorded as a glorious two weeks in the history of the working-class struggle. We saw Roman Catholic and Protestant workers marching together and on Tuesday last we saw them fighting together. As a result poverty and destitution have been swept away and homes will be made brighter for many of the unfortunate workers'**[22].

The strikers returned to work on Monday 17 October, but in the meantime there had been a curious incident.

Tom Mann, the veteran British communist and organiser of the unemployed, came to Belfast on Saturday 15 October for the funeral of Samuel Baxter, one of the men shot dead by the RUC. He was to speak at a mass rally at the Customs House the next day. He helped to carry Baxter's coffin, and as he left the cemetery he was arrested and served with a banning order under the Special Powers Act restricting him to Clogher in Co. Tyrone. He commented defiantly: 'I had come here to bring revolutionary greetings from my English comrades to their Irish friends who are fighting against aggression . . . . Our Communist organisation is growing and we will bear opression no longer.' The RUC deported him back to England the next day.

The curfew was lifted after eight days and the man-hunt against 'subversives' was called off, but there were still a lot of men in jail and much of the militants' energy for the next few months was to go into a campaign for their release.

The ODR strike, like the 1919 engineering strike, was an example of how Belfast workers could show great solidarity and militancy on a single economic issue. The marches and rallies were completely united and Geehan's leadership readily accepted even though he was a Catholic. The government and the Unionist Party were terrified, as the statements of the politicians and the hysterical outbursts of the *Newsletter* showed. The recently formed Ulster Protestant League summed up Unionist attitudes. They,

'deplored that these unfortunate conditions were used as a cloak by the communist Sinn Fein element to attempt to start a revolution in our province. We also greatly deplore that some few of our loyal Protestant unemployed were misled to such an extent that they associated themselves with the enemies of their faith and principles. We congratulate the government of Northern Ireland on the firm steps they have taken to preserve law and order in our city'[23].

But, as in 1919, this working-class unity was fragile and would soon be shattered by the clever use of sectarianism. Dramatic though it was the struggle had been too short and too quickly forced back into the Catholic ghettos for it seriously to shake the Orange ideology or to change the political consciousness of the Protestant workers. In fact this time the strike didn't even carry its impact on into the next elections for the Corporation in January 1933 and the Poor Law Guardians in May. In the Corporation elections the Labour vote was only slightly up on the previous year. Labour gained no new seats and actually lost their last seat in Dock. Geehan himself beat a Labour candidate into third place in Court ward but the combined vote was nowhere near the Unionists'. Even in the Poor Law elections

Labour won only one seat and the Unemployed Workers none, leaving the Unionists with 29 seats to four Nationalist and one Labour.

In fact the most lasting result of the ODR strike was to bring many of the most active and militant workers into contact with revolutionary ideas for the first time, and provide the basis of the membership of the Communist Party, the left wing of the Labour Party and the leftist Republican groups for the next twenty or thirty years.

The working class held the centre of the stage for a while longer however. In November 1932 the Irish railway companies applied to the Railway Wages Board for a fifteen per cent cut in railwaymen's wages, and the Board recommended a cut of ten per cent. The Unions rejected this immediately and in the South the government stepped in with a temporary subsidy to avoid wage cuts. The Northern government refused to follow suit, and on 31 January 1933 railwaymen employed by five of the six companies operating in the North went on strike – the sixth company, the Bangor and Co.Down Railway Company, had a separate agreement. The strike was official, and strongly backed by the two railway unions, the NUR and ASLEF, both British-based, because they thought the companies were trying to force wage-cuts in Ireland as a precedent for doing it in Britain.

This time the strike was led not by unofficial militants but by the official union leadership from London, who had no desire to broaden it into a general clash with the state and the whole capitalist system. Yet it was to become the most violent strike in the North's history. From the beginning the companies used blacklegs on a massive scale. Railway office staff who weren't on strike scabbed on the manual workers, and students from Queen's University in Belfast queued up to do their bit for their country and their class. The wage-cuts would have brought the railwaymen's wages down to below £2 a week, yet the companies paid their blacklegs £4.10s.0d. a week and put some of them up in the posh LMS-owned[24] Midland Hotel in Belfast.

The workers hit back quickly. On the first day of the strike a Dublin/Belfast train manned by blacklegging office staff was de-railed at Dromiskin, Co.Louth, and two of the blacklegs killed. The line had been tampered with but the railwaymen claimed that experienced men could have stopped the train. Elsewhere trains which did run were stoned and railway lorries stopped and the drivers threatened. The unions decided to stop GNR[25] buses as well, and this extended the strike to the South where the GNR ran services in Co.Louth and Dublin. From the beginning the RUC in armoured cars escorted lorries driven by blacklegs in the North, while the Gardai and the Irish Army were used to escort buses in the South and Army lorries replaced buses in Dublin. Stoning of railway lorries and buses became commonplace even in the smallest towns, and railway lines were constantly interfered with even in remote areas.

Both sides saw the conflict as a major one and huge solidarity demonstrations were held at the Customs House steps in Belfast. On Sunday 12 February 1933 even the cautious William Dobbie, president of the NUR, declared,

'We are determined to put up the greatest and fiercest industrial struggle that has been seen in this country for some time and to the transport men and the dockers we say that the owning and controlling classes are concentrating on this struggle. If the railway workers go down, wages of workers in every other industry will be subjected to an attack'[26].

By now the RUC in the North were blacklegging themselves, operating signal boxes and working as porters. They had also stepped up their security and a 100-strong flying-squad armed with rifles was patrolling the Belfast railway lines. In the South the Irish Army was using armoured cars to escort buses while Gardai rode beside the drivers, though it had been decided to withdraw the army lorries in Dublin. The level of violence was steadily increasing. The first GNR bus to reach Dublin for a fortnight was burnt by a crowd at Eden Quay, and a full-scale riot followed with Gardai baton-charging in Gardiner Street. Meanwhile bombs were going off under bridges and grenades being thrown at railway property in Belfast and outside.

The Revolutionary Workers' Groups had backed the strike from the beginning, trying to broaden it into a general political conflict. By now the leftist sections of the IRA were involved as well. On 28 February an IRA unit fired warning shots at scab lorry-drivers leaving the GNR goods depot at the Grosvenor Road in Belfast. They were chased and fired on by an RUC patrol and two IRA men were cornered in a cul-de-sac off Durham Street. They shot one RUC man dead and escaped. Three days later a train was derailed coming into Omagh and thirteen people injured, one seriously. Again the unions argued that the train was going far too fast and the companies were ignoring safety regulations.

The Unionist establishment were getting alarmed again, the more so as two cabinet ministers, J.M.Andrews and J.M.Barbour, were directors of railway companies and many other Unionists had important railway interests. The *Newsletter* ranted about Republican involvement in the strike and Sir Edward Archdale, the Minister for Agriculture, told the Grand Orange Lodge of Belfast that undoubtedly communists were at the bottom of the present outrages. He was perfectly certain the outrages were due to people who came from other countries[27]. Some weeks later Craigavon denounced the 'insidious attempt by Nationalists, Communists, and Socialists to betray Ulster into an all-Ireland Republic'[28].

In an ironic alliance with the Unionists, several of the Catholic bishops took the opportunity to issue Lenten pastorals denouncing communism and, around the same time, inspired by their urgings, hymn-singing mobs attacked Connolly Hall, the headquarters of the Revolutionary Workers' Groups in Dublin.

Attrition was telling on the union leaders and by mid-March they were anxious for a settlement; while both the government and the companies, alarmed at the solidarity of the strike, the increasing violence and the damage to trade, were now willing to talk. Negotiations began and quickly broke down but not before the union leaders had accepted the principle of a wage-cut.

The workers were uneasy at the negotiations and determined to stay out. On 16 March a bomb was thrown into a bus-load of blacklegs with a Garda escort in Dundalk and a Guard seriously injured. There were more mass meetings and on 24 March a torch-light procession 5,000 strong marched from the City Hall in Belfast to the Customs House. William McMullen of the ITGWU said his dockers had already taken sympathetic action and warned, 'We don't care about governments. The industrial army and the working class have only to remain passive and the wheels of industry will cease'[29]. Another speaker estimated that the strike had cost the Northern economy four or five million pounds and demanded the nationalisation of the railways.

Negotiations began again though, and the employers were more forthcoming when 800 carters and dockers in Belfast struck because of the use of blacklegs under armed RUC guard to load blacked goods. Finally on 6 April a settlement was reached. NUR and ASLEF members were to take a cut of seven and a half per cent on the 1931 wages, including a cut of four and three eighths per cent already in operation. They would get no holiday pay in 1933 and could make no wage claims for two years. There would be no victimisation and all railwaymen would be reinstated, but after four weeks the companies could dismiss men if there was overstaffing. Blacklegs would be kept on.

It was a partial defeat for the railwaymen and the strikers didn't like it. In the South, where the government subsidy had stopped, Great Southern Railway (GSR) employees went on unofficial strike for a few days but within a week the strike was over. The defeat was only partial however, because the final wage-cut was only half what the companies wanted, and because if the railway wage-cut had been easily enforced it would have been the prelude to a general round of cuts. As it was, the railwaymen had put up such a tough fight that the employers didn't dare launch a general offensive.

Though the strike had little impact at the polls, either at the Poor Law Guardians (PLG) election in May or at a Stormont election in December, it was significant. The railwaymen were mainly Protestant and Loyalist yet they had accepted the intervention of the RWG, the IRA, and Southern workers without alarm. In fact much of the sabotage had been done by the railwaymen themselves. A few more of the most militant and radical Protestant workers even joined the RWG or the left of the Labour Party and became actively involved in Republican and leftist politics[30]. In June 1933 most of the membership of the Revolutionary Workers' Groups came together to form the Communist Party of Ireland whose first secretary, Sean Murray, was a Co.Antrim man living in Dublin.

The Northern government's paranoia about communism was clearly demonstrated in October 1933 when Sean Murray and Harry Pollitt of the British Communist Party were due to speak at a CP rally in the Labour Hall in York Street. Banning orders were made against both of them. Pollitt was arrested coming off the boat, held all day and put on the return boat that night. Murray was arrested at gunpoint in the hall and put on the next train to Dublin.

Meanwhile, in an interesting example of the employing classes' complacency about violence during strikes, Lord Justice Best opening the city commission, commented on the shooting of the RUC man:

'One may speculate as to who the people were who fired on the police . . . . They may have been railway servants, although it is very hard to believe that they were. They may have been "Bolshies" who took advantage of the strike to create trouble, they may have been strangers not from our part of the world ... It was unfortunate that these cases of bomb-throwing and of shooting at policemen should have arisen out of

the strike, but when one considered how long the strike had been going on, now about ten weeks, one was amazed, certainly pleased at the fact that so little disturbance from a criminal point of view had arisen out of it'[31].

Despite the mass solidarity of the ODR and railway strikes there had been a steadily growing undercurrent of militant sectarianism since the beginning of the 1930s. The Ulster Protestant League (UPL) was formed in 1931. It was typical of many hysterical politico-religious bodies in Belfast and its platforms were graced with the usual quota of unfrocked priests and ranting anti-Catholic bigots. But there was one important difference. Unemployment was soaring and one of the objects of the UPL was 'to safeguard the employment of Protestants'. From the beginning there were those who were trying to turn the anger of the Protestant workers at their poverty and destitution against their Catholic fellow-workers.

In March 1932 an AOH St Patrick's Day parade was fired on in South Derry and two Hibernians wounded. In June there was a Eucharistic Congress – an international Catholic religious festival – in Dublin. Special trains and buses went from Catholic areas all over the North and were attacked or stoned in Lisburn, Loughbrickland, Lurgan, Portadown, Banbridge, Kilkeel and other areas, while pilgrims arriving from England and Scotland were attacked in Larne. In this inflammatory atmosphere Craigavon had declared at a 12 July rally at Poyntzpass, 'Ours is a Protestant government and I am an Orangeman'[32]. On 27 August a mob wrecked a number of Catholic pubs in Dungannon after an Orange rally.

Sectarianism retreated during the great strikes but it reappeared in the summer of 1933. And this time it was openly stirred up by government ministers, thoroughly frightened at the prospect of working-class unity. On 12 July 1933 Sir Basil Brooke made his famous 'I have not a Roman Catholic about my own place' speech, while J.M.Andrews, the Minister for Labour, indignantly defended the government against a foul smear:

'Another allegation made against the government, which is untrue, is that of 31 porters at Stormont 28 are Roman Catholic. I have investigated the matter and I have found that there are 30 Protestants and only one Roman Catholic, there only temporarily'[33].

On 27 August Senator Sir Joseph Davison, Grand Master of the Orange Order, made the most blatant effort yet to divide the working class:

'When will the Protestant employers of Northern Ireland recognise their duty to their Protestant brothers and sisters and employ

them to the exclusion of Roman Catholics? It is time Protestant employers realised that whenever a Roman Catholic is brought into their employment it means one Protestant vote less. It is our duty to pass the word along from this great demonstration and I suggest the slogan should be: Protestants employ Protestants'[34].

Brooke repeated his statement several times in the winter of 1933 and early in 1934, and when the Nationalists at Stormont proposed a motion of censure on him Craigavon moved an amendment saying, 'the employment of disloyalists . . . is prejudicial to the state and takes jobs away from Loyalists'[35].

Between the violent propaganda of the UPL and the open incitement of government ministers, sectarian feeling was growing fast. In November 1933 Dan O'Boyle, a Catholic publican, was shot dead in York Street, the first sectarian killing since 1922. In May 1934 the UPL, now backed by Major J.H.McCormick, an official Unionist MP, held a rally in the Ulster Hall (owned by Belfast Corporation) to protest against an application by the Catholic Church to use it for a missionary exhibition.

The speeches were particularly violent. Mrs Dorothy Harnett told her listeners to 'get training in firing', and resolutions were carried calling for a ban on the exhibition anywhere in the North and for counter-demonstrations against it[36]. A mob returning from the meeting attacked Catholic homes in the York Street area. Mrs Harnett and the Rev Samuel Hanna, a Presbyterian minister and a leader of the UPL, were later convicted of incitement to disorder, but Mrs Harnett was bound over and the Rev Hanna got off under the Probation Act. The Catholic authorities withdrew their application.

Violence was now increasing and most of it centred on the York Street area. In July 1934 shots were fired into the Catholic North Thomas Street but no one was injured. On 16 September a mob invaded New Dock Street and Marine Street, wrecking 40 Catholic homes and injuring a crippled youth who died soon after.

On 13 April 1935 another Catholic publican was shot in York Street. May 1935 was the Silver Jubilee of King George V and was treated in Belfast as a Loyalist festival. Tension escalated sharply during the celebrations and shots were fired into Catholic streets and Catholics were beaten up on their way to work. On 6 May, the actual day of the Jubilee, two Catholics were shot and wounded and two bombs were thrown into a Catholic street – all in the

York Street area. By 9 May the government had to bring in a curfew for that area.

The curfew and the end of the Jubilee celebrations brought a fortnight's peace but the UPL held a big rally on 31 May which was followed by shooting into New Dock Street, and another on 12 June followed by mobs attacking Catholic streets and shops. On 16 June a fifteen-year-old girl was shot and wounded on her way to mass. Two days later Dawson Bates made an order banning all parades, including 12 July, because of the violence they would provoke.

On 23 June an Orange parade was held in York Street in defiance of the ban and the RUC took no action. The same day Sir Joseph Davison, the Orange Grand Master, said:

'You may be perfectly certain that on the 12 July the Orangemen will be marching throughout Northern Ireland . . . . I do not acknowledge the right of any government, Northern or imperial, to impose conditions as to the celebration'[37].

The government was in direct conflict with its main supporters. On 27 June Bates capitulated and lifted the ban. The 12th would go ahead with no restrictions. From then on almost nightly shooting and attacks took place on Catholic areas.

To the Catholics the 12th parade was the triumphalist conclusion to a sustained campaign against them. There was trouble at three places as the parade passed Catholic areas accompanied by a Loyalist mob. There was fighting at Stewart Street in the Markets area and three Catholics were shot and wounded, another Catholic was badly beaten up at North Street, but the most serious trouble was at Lancaster Street, a Catholic area off York Street, as the local Lodges, notorious even in Belfast, returned home. The start of the trouble was disputed. Catholics claimed that parade followers broke into the street and started wrecking houses, and only then did Catholic vigilantes fire at them, killing one Protestant youth, Edward Withers, and wounding another. The RUC then fired down Lancaster Street, killing one Catholic, John McKay, and wounding nine others. The Orangemen claimed that the Catholics fired into the parade first.

There was immediate retaliation. A Catholic housewife, Mrs Peggy Broderick, was shot dead in nearby Marine Street, and another was wounded in Fleet Street. Another Protestant died in confused fighting in the warren of narrow streets around the docks. The next morning the Unionist press ran inflammatory headlines about the parade being attacked, and an armed mob attacked the Catholic area of the Docks burning or wrecking 56 Catholic homes. The RUC stood by and refused to intervene, but the fighting was so fierce that the government had to call in British troops. Eventually they fired into a Loyalist crowd attacking New Dock Street and killed two men.

By now the rioting had spread. Mobs attacked the Short Strand ghetto in East Belfast and Catholic homes and property in the Sandy Row and Peter's Hill areas. A Catholic youth called Edward Brady was walking home with his girlfriend up the Shankill Road when he was caught by a mob and so badly beaten that he died a few weeks later. Another curfew was introduced in the York Street area, but nightly burnings and evictions went on. The trouble spread to Portadown where Loyalist gangs went on the rampage attacking Catholic homes and property and a Catholic was shot dead when the RUC invaded the Catholic ghetto of the Tunnel.

When the factories and mills re-opened after the 12 July holiday, the Catholics were expelled from the shipyard – there were 200 out of 4,000 workers there – and Catholic girls were put out of the linen-mills round York Street and the Crumlin Road.

There was also another flare-up after the funerals of some of the Protestants killed when mobs beat up Catholic passers-by, and fired into and tried to invade Catholic streets. There was constant sniping into Catholic streets in the docks and some of the residents knocked holes in their back-yard walls so that they could move about without making targets of themselves.

The riots spent themselves after three weeks or so. But the British troops erected corrugated iron barricades at the ends of the Catholic streets along York Street and the inhabitants lived in a virtual state of siege for months. There was another outbreak in September when a Protestant youth was killed in a riot at the small Catholic enclave of Greencastle on the Shore Road. In the next few days a Catholic publican called J.J.McKiernan was shot dead in his bar in York Street and a Catholic woman was shot and wounded in Little Ship Street. At the trial of the men accused of killing McKiernan the Attorney-General, A.B.Babington MP, made the remarkable comment that 'The man was a publican and a Roman Catholic and was therefore liable to assassination'[38]. When the two accused, both Orangemen, were acquitted a crowd of thousands outside the courthouse cheered and sang 'God Save the King' and bonfires were lit in York Street to celebrate.

The barricades weren't taken down until March 1936. By then the great working-class solidarity of 1932 and 1933 had been thoroughly dissipated. One of the early casualties in the rioting was the Labour Hall in York Street, scene of many strike meetings, which was burnt down by a Loyalist mob.

The Catholic population had suffered another onslaught. Catholics who had begun to move out of the ghettos into 'mixed' or Protestant areas, even Catholics who lived in vulnerable ghettos, had been driven out of their homes again, to crowd into refugee huts on the Falls Road or half-built houses at Ardoyne. 514 Catholic families, totalling some 2,241 people, had been driven out of their homes[39]. Only about a score of Protestant families had been evicted. Hundreds of Catholics had lost their jobs, many of them permanently – a serious matter with nearly 70,000 unemployed. For many of them it was the second time in fourteen years. The death toll for the riots had been somewhat deceptive: five Catholics and eight Protestants. The Loyalists as the aggressors had suffered more fatalities. Catholics predominated among the wounded.

And the sectarian incitement didn't end even when it had achieved its effect. In August 1935 the Orange Order began an official boycott of Catholic pubs, while an unofficial boycott of Catholic shops and businesses had been going on for some time. The UPL announced its policy as:

'Neither to talk with, nor walk with, neither to buy nor sell, borrow nor lend, take nor give, or to have any dealings at all with them [Catholics], **nor for employers to employ them nor employees to work with them'**[40].

At an ultra-Loyalist rally in the Ulster Hall in August, one speaker, referring to the cost of the riots, said, 'If it cost a million a week to get rid of the Fenians [Catholics], it would be worth it'[41].

The British National Council for Civil Liberties was investigating the Special Powers Act at the time, and Ronald Kidd, their secretary, was in Belfast throughout the riots. He wrote to Baldwin, the British Premier,

'Long before the 12th it was freely prophesied that there was going to be trouble on that day and it was believed that the anti-Catholic speeches of ministers heralded a so-called pogrom on the Catholic population'.

He complained of cases of Orange mobs attacking Catholic homes while the RUC stood by and of Dawson Bates' capitulation to the Orange Order; he ended by demanding, 'a strictly impartial enquiry to be set up by the imperial parliament to investigate these and other responsible allegations of misrule and abuse of authority by the Northern Ireland government'[42].

The *Manchester Guardian* had commented in a trenchant editorial on 13 July:

'Craigavon's government has been continuously in power since 1921. The circumstances in which it came into power explain why it then adopted the theory and technique of the "one party state", regarding its political opponents as intending rebels and basing its power on the Orange Order. That may have been necessary in 1921. If so it was at best an ugly necessity . . .

'There was thus the temptation to presume that every Catholic was disloyal until the contrary was proved, to base the state on the old principle of a Protestant ascendancy and to strengthen the position of the government and its "one party state" by stimulating the anti-Catholic bigotry of all sections of the population, especially the least enlightened.

'. . . It was possible to hope that . . . the Northern Cabinet . . . would shake themselves free of sectarianism . . . The Northern government has chosen the opposite course, either influenced by the Nazi example, or because it finds itself too weak to oppose the Orange Order . . .

'There had been too much talk of a Protestant government for a Protestant people. The ban on processions imposed last month because of recurrent riots was withdrawn when an Orange Grand Master threatened defiance . . .

'What followed after the Orange demonstrations of 12 July is what might have been foreseen. Craigavon's government is now in a difficult position. All see it for what it is – a government which has chosen to seek support for a new state from the strength of ignorance, sectarian prejudice and the passions of faction'[43].

Craigavon was impervious to such strictures however. His government was secure again. On 12 July 1936 he announced, 'Orangeism, Protestantism, and the Loyalist cause are more strongly entrenched than ever and equally so is the government at Stormont'[44].

The 1935 riots had a sequel at Westminster. The Northern government refused to hold an enquiry, and the Nationalists and the Catholic Bishop of Down and Connor turned their attention to Westminster. On 24 June 1936 thirteen MPs, three Tory, three Liberal and seven Labour, including Jimmy Maxton of the ILP, organised a private meeting of a hundred or so British – not Northern Ireland – MPs to hear Dr Arthur Ryan, a Catholic priest, T.J.Campbell, a Stormont Nationalist MP, Ronald Kidd of the NCCL, John Campbell, secretary of the Belfast Trades Council, and Samuel Geddes another Belfast trade unionist, give their accounts of the riots. By 59 votes to 25 they passed a resolution stating, 'This meeting recognises the necessity for a full and extensive enquiry into the Belfast riots of 1935 and calls upon His Majesty's Government to take the necessary steps for that purpose'[45]. On 7 July Baldwin wrote to J.R.Clynes, MP, the chairman of the meeting, saying, 'This matter is entirely within the discretion and responsibility of the government of Northern Ireland, and for fundamental constitutional reasons the possibility of holding an enquiry by the imperial government is completely ruled out'[46].

The Westminster government would brook no interference with their subordinates in Belfast though they had been quick enough to supply them with troops when things got out of hand.

For a time during all this turmoil and violence on the streets the Nationalist parliamentarians, who were still boycotting the Stormont parliament, had become quite militant in response to the general mood. There were a number of Republicans in jail at the beginning of 1933 and on 15 January Joe Stewart, the MP for East Tyrone, a leading member of the AOH and an old Redmondite, had spoken at a rally for them with Sean McBride, a member of the army council of the IRA. Sensing the depth of feeling against the Northern parliament, Joe Devlin had talks early in 1933 both with his old opponent De Valera and even with the Republicans, suggesting the idea of a united party with himself as leader and an abstentionist policy.

The talks came to nothing and the pull of parliament proved too strong. After more pressure from the hierarchy about Catholic schools and with an election pending, the Nationalists returned to Stormont in October 1933. But Republican feeling was growing. The Republicans had been active in the South in a campaign against land annuities and had played an important part in De Valera's election victory in 1932. In the North they had intervened effectively in the railway strike. Their support was growing. And the government was stepping up its activities against them – partly to alarm the Protestant masses. It was in October 1933 that between thirty and forty Republicans were detained under the Special Powers Act and then convicted of refusing to answer questions under a new 'Cat and Mouse' regulation introduced to deal with them. Demonstrations were organised against this procedure and they were then banned and the organisers jailed as well.

The Nationalists' decision to go back to Stormont was not popular. The election was in November and the Republicans nominated four candidates as abstentionists, including one against Devlin himself in Belfast Central. One of their speakers in the campaign for Central put their position succinctly. The *Irish News* reported:

'**Republicans were contesting this election to repudiate partition and the puppet parliament where the so-called Nationalists represented – or misrepresented them . . . Referring to the abstention policy he asked what the Nationalists ever did in Stormont. The only time ever concessions had been obtained was when the Catholics and Protestants of Belfast stood shoulder to shoulder in the street together'.** [A reference to the Outdoor Relief strike of 1932][47].

The Nationalists themselves made no effort to capitalise on the discontent among the Protestant masses. They put up only eleven candidates in the eleven safe Catholic seats they had won in 1929. One of the candidates was a little unusual however. He was Eamon De Valera. The South Down Nationalist Convention decided to nominate him on the grounds that it would strengthen his position in raising the Northern question at the League of Nations or with Britain if he was elected by a Northern constituency.

Labour, demoralised by their failure to make any impact in the 1933 Corporation and PLG elections, nominated only three candidates.

The results demonstrated the continuing frustration of the Catholic population with the Northern parliament. A Republican, P.J.McLogan, won easily in South Armagh, while Patrick Thornbury got 4,650 votes to Devlin's 7,411 in Central. The only Republican to do badly was the one who stood against De Valera in South Down. Harry Midgley won an extra seat for Labour in Dock, but it was one where the Unionist had got in on a minority vote in 1929; and Jack Beattie's Labour majority was down in Pottinger. There were seven Independent Unionist candidates but all except the sitting two, Tommy Henderson and District Inspector Nixon (now associated with the UPL), were easily defeated. The government's effective majority had increased by one.

Joe Devlin died in January 1934. He was a constitutionalist, a parliamentarian and a believer in the British Empire. In the Catholic community he was the main proponent of participation in the Northern state and a social reforming, populist policy. He was strongly opposed to violence and believed in Irish unity only by consent. He had offered the government the prospect of co-operation from the Catholic middle class. They had rejected it and chosen to base themselves on the Orange Order and anti-Catholic prejudice. They chose temporary security at the price of permanent instability. The mass of the Catholic population soon turned to more militant voices than Devlin's.

Even in death the Unionists were ungenerous. James Gyle, the liberal Independent Unionist MP, now a Senator, visited Devlin's death-bed while prayers were being said and was suspended from the Orange Order for seven years for doing so. There was no protest from Craigavon or other leading members of the Order.

Without Devlin the eight remaining Nationalists had no policy or strategy. They raised the question of Catholic schools immediately and complained about discrimination, but got no response. Within a few months of their return Cahir Healy, now the effective leader, was saying,

'I warn you now that you are moulding a policy that may soon drive the Nationalists out of this House altogether. At the moment they see little use in playing politics with people who do not possess even the most elementary notion of justice or fair play. They are indeed beginning to ask themselves if it is worth while keeping representatives here'[48].

The Unionists' reaction was to bring in a Bill requiring candidates for Stormont elections to give an undertaking to take their seats. But allegiance to the state cannot be legislated.

As government speeches became more sectarian and violence escalated up to the riots of 1935, the Nationalist party fell apart and creeping abstentionism set in. A.E.Donnelly, MP for West Tyrone, didn't go to Stormont after April 1934, and Hugh K. McAleer, (Mid-Tyrone) stayed away after October 1935. Patrick Maxwell[49] was elected in a by-election for Foyle in May 1937 and attended only the one day necessary to qualify for his salary. By the end of 1937 only the two Belfast members – Richard Byrne and T.J.Campbell, editor of the *Irish News*, who had succeeded Devlin, still attended regularly. They were the MPs most closely in touch with the Catholic business and professional classes and the hierarchy, who still had interests to be protected. All the MPs were anxious to keep their seats – and salaries – however, and when Edward VIII abdicated in December 1936 and MPs had to take an oath of allegiance to the new king all the Nationalists did so.

Abstentionism spread to Westminster as well. There was a Westminster election in November 1935 and the Republicans, still on the offensive, said they'd stand. Under pressure the Nationalist Convention for Fermanagh and Tyrone decided by 128 votes to 68 to nominate the outgoing MPs, Healy and Joe Stewart (who had succeeded Devlin at Westminster), as abstentionists. The Republicans wouldn't give way and eventually on the morning of nomination day they reached a compromise. Two non-party candidates, Anthony Mulvey and Patrick Cunningham, would go forward as abstentionists, Cunningham declaring 'I'm a farmer, being an MP doesn't interest me'[50]. They were elected, and for the ten years the war-time Westminster parliament lasted they never attended. The Republicans also contested West Belfast, Armagh and Co.Down and the growing militancy of the Catholic population was shown by the 56,833 votes their three candidates got, as well as over 50,000 for Mulvey and Cunningham.

By the time of the next Stormont election in February 1938, abstentionism had nearly won the day. There were no Republican candidates because of the new regulation requiring a declaration of intent to sit in parliament, but the South Down Nationalist Convention voted unanimously not to contest the South Down seat: 'We affirm that attendance at the parliament by loyal Irishmen is harmful to the cause of Irish unity since it bolsters up this alien institution and misrepresents the state of Northern opinion'[51]. South Armagh, where the sitting MP was a Republican, followed suit, and so did Mourne. In Tyrone it was decided to contest the election but a number of delegates were opposed and walked out. In Fermanagh Cahir Healy said he was glad the Convention did not tie his hands by asking him to make regular appearances at Stormont as he would have found it necessary to refuse in those circumstances[52]. In Derry, Maxwell condemned both attendance at Stormont and the boycott.

When the parliament met, only the two Belfast Nationalists attended, and when George Leeke, MP for Mid-Derry, died in March 1939, the writ for a by-election was never moved and the seat remained vacant until 1945. Leeke himself, though boycotting the Commons, had regularly attended the Public Accounts Committee for which there was an attendance allowance.

The Nationalist boycott was a gesture of apathy and despair rather than a political tactic however. The Nationalist MPs made no effort to set up an alternative assembly, to lead extra-parliamentary agitation, or even to build up a strong political organisation. They just stayed at home and looked after their businesses, meeting occasionally to discuss important topics and issue infrequent press statements. The National League, set up with such enthusiasm in 1928, rapidly fell apart and there was no Nationalist party with a conference or individual membership. Local constituency groups or Catholic registration committees met once a year, to review the electoral register and ensure that as many Catholics as possible were included, or at election times.

The Labour Party fared poorly after 1933. Though Jack Beattie, the sole Labour MP from 1929 to 1933, was joined at Stormont by Harry Midgley, the party's chairman and one of its leading figures, the partnership soon broke up. The party was anxious to contest the Belfast Central by-election when Devlin died. Beattie was ordered to move the writ when the Nationalists stalled. But Beattie had worked closely with the Nationalists for ten years and had got their support in the 1933 election – his Pottinger constituency contained a large Catholic electorate in the Short Strand. He refused and was expelled from the party. Meanwhile relations with the Nationalists had got sharply worse.

Without Devlin the Nationalists had degenerated even further into reactionary clericalism and when the Spanish Civil War broke out in 1936 their organs, such as the *Irish News* and the *Derry Journal* took a wildly pro-Franco stand. Most of the left – and the Republicans – supported the Spanish Republic and Midgley engaged in a bitter controversy with the Nationalists, writing a pamphlet in reply to them called, *Spain, the Press, the Pulpit and the Truth*. Anti-communist hysteria reached fever-pitch and a Catholic priest in Newry urged Catholic workers in the town to leave the Amalgamated Transport Union because it sent money to the 'Reds'[53]. In the 1938 election, the Nationalists put up a candidate against Midgley in Dock – where he was dependent on the Catholic vote – and, partly because of his stand on Spain, partly because he had refused to defend the Catholics of the area when they were being driven out in 1935, he was pushed into third place and easily defeated[54].

Beattie was re-elected however, and in South Armagh a Labour candidate, Paddy Agnew, stepped in unopposed because of the Nationalist boycott, to give Labour its first Catholic MP. These two became virtually the sole opposition at Stormont.

There had been a new challenge to Craigavon at the election – the Progressive Unionist – but it met with little success. By 1938 unemployment in the North had reached 90,000. Craigavon's government had changed little since 1921 and was still run on a part-time basis by industrialists and landowners. It showed no sign of urgency in dealing with the problem. There was discontent within the Unionist party, not so much from the working class whose loyalty had been secured by the sectarian speeches and the riots of the mid-thirties, as from more enterprising elements of the middle class. W.J.Stewart, a businessman and Westminster Unionist MP for South Belfast, had formed a group firmly committed to the link with Britain but calling for action to end unemployment, more house building, and for reforms in agriculture. This group also avoided the open sectarianism of the party leadership.

Craigavon responded with the traditional Unionist rallying cry – the border. In December 1937 De Valera's new constitution came into operation in the South. It claimed the whole island of Ireland – including the six counties – as the national territory, though specifically excluding the North from the jurisdiction of the Dublin government, 'pending the re-integration of the national territory'. It was an example of De Valera's masterly word-juggling. While seeming to claim the North it actually gave formal recognition to partition. In January De Valera's government began negotiations with Britain to end his 'economic war'[55] with them and settle their outstanding differences. The papers reported that the question of partition would be raised. It gave Craigavon an excellent opportunity. The election was called to answer De Valera's claim to the North. A historian of the Unionist Party commented.

'Just as the sensational novelists of the early nineteenth century introduced apparitions to deter their characters from rash or criminal enterprises, so the invocation of political phantoms was expected to deter Protestant voters from supporting Unionist dissidents'[56].
It worked.

Craigavon denounced the Progressive Unionists as 'wreckers' and they were easily defeated. Stewart himself was beaten by 3,500 votes in Cromac, in his own South Belfast constituency, by a political newcomer. The twelve Progressive Unionists collected 47,888 votes, but only one came within a thousand votes of his official Unionist opponent. After the election they disappeared.

Lurking in the background throughout the thirties were the Republicans and the IRA. Recovering from their disastrous slump in the late twenties they had built up considerable support in the North through their involvement in the great strikes, and because of the evident failure of the parliamentary Nationalists. They made efforts to win Protestant support as well. In July 1933 the IRA issued a long, well-meaning but confused manifesto to the Orangemen, appealing to them to join in a joint campaign for the Republic. They referred to the common struggle of their ancestors in 1798, forgetting that it was the Orange Order which formed the basis of the yeomen then and which represented the most extreme pro-imperialist tradition in the Protestant population. Not surprisingly, they got no response.

In 1934 a James Connolly Club was formed for unemployed Protestant and Catholic workers, and in June that year a number of Northern Protestants went to the annual Republican commemoration at Wolfe Tone's grave at Bodenstown. At the same time, however, a split had been developing in the IRA as the leftward trend accelerated and leftist IRA men like Michael Price and Peadar O'Donnell tried to form a broad alliance of the IRA, the Communist Party and the left of both Northern and Southern Labour Parties, called the Republican Congress. O'Donnell and Price were expelled from the IRA and there was a scuffle at Bodenstown between their Republican Congress Group and the mainstream IRA. The Northerners were with the Congress group and had an unfortunate introduction to Republicanism when they were attacked by IRA men from Tipperary.

When the Republican Congress finally met in September 1934 it had a fair sprinkling of Northern delegates, mostly from the Communist Party, but it split as well and was never very effective. Its last major action was to send some two hundred volunteers, some ex-IRA, some Communist Party, to fight in Spain, in the James Connolly battalion of the International Brigade. 42 were killed and twelve captured, several of them Belfast Protestants.

The 1935 riots put an effective stop to the tentative alliance of radical Protestants and the IRA. The IRA was forced to defend the Catholic ghettos and turned its mind to more traditional activities. After the Republican Congress division there was a swing to the right among Republicans, while the utter frustration which had driven the Nationalists out of Stormont was driving the more militant sections of the Catholic community to the use of force.

In December 1935 the Belfast IRA staged a raid on the Officer Training Corps Hall at Campbell College, one of the North's poshest

Protestant schools. It ended in a gun-fight with police and one IRA man was sentenced to ten years. In April 1936 the RUC swooped on an IRA court martial in Crown Entry in Belfast, capturing the adjutant-general of the IRA, Jim Killeen, and ten others, including Jimmy Steele and most of the Northern leadership. They were charged with the archaic offence of treason felony, and sentenced to a total of 48 years in jail. But the arrests didn't stop the re-organisation of a growing IRA and from the increased activity it was evident they were preparing for something.

Craigavon's intransigent Unionism was leading to its inevitable conclusion.

The War Years

   So by the close of the 1930s politics in both parts of Ireland had reached a state of utter impasse. In the North the early hopes of working-class solidarity had been shattered, the Unionists seemed more entrenched than ever and the Nationalists had abandoned parliamentary politics without adopting any other method of remedying the minority's grievances. In the South, Republican attempts to involve the masses in social agitation had petered out and the Fianna Fail government, after the initial confrontation over the land annuities, had made its peace with Britain and was busy suppressing anyone who didn't accept it.

   But Republican feeling was still strong in parts of the South and among the Northern minority and had focussed on the issue of partition. Politics had failed to remove it. It was inevitable that force would be tried again.

   The IRA was still in existence in the South but it had been going through a period of depression and demoralisation. The opening to the left and the intense political activity of the early thirties had borne no obvious fruit: in fact the organisation had lost some of its best men to the Republican Congress and the Spanish Civil War. De Valera, whom the IRA had helped to put into power, had turned on them and his Special Branch police, mostly ex-IRA men, were hounding Republicans. Many were jailed and held in conditions so bad that one man, Sean Glynn, committed suicide in September 1936. Another was shot dead in a Dublin street by the Special Branch in June 1937.

   Frustration and anger at their lack of progress led the Southern IRA to turn to the advocates of physical force, pure and simple. This coincided neatly with the growing and equal frustration of the Northern IRA. Already there had been some activity in the North. In the summer of 1936 a raid had been planned on Armagh military barracks but had been called off at the last moment because information had leaked out. In December 1936 and January 1937 two Belfast officers of the IRA were killed as informers and in the summer of 1937 a number of customs huts on the border were blown up as a protest against the visit of the new king and queen of England. On 11

July 1938 IRA men and Republican supporters from the surrounding Sperrin mountains took over the town of Maghera, tore down the Orange bunting and decorations put up for the 12th, and attacked the RUC station, besieging and wounding several RUC men until RUC and B Special reinforcements arrived from Magherafelt and Upperlands.

Meanwhile the IRA had elected a new chief of staff, Sean Russell, who was committed to a bombing campaign in England; and preparations for it were going ahead. It was to be accompanied by attacks in the North as well and on 28 November 1938 three IRA men, J.J.Reynolds, J.J.Kelly and Charles McCaffrey, were killed while making a bomb in a house in Donegal, just across the border. McCaffrey was from Tyrone, the other two from the 26 counties. They were preparing to bomb a customs post. That night and the following night a number of customs huts were successfully demolished. The RUC immediately stepped up their activity, the B Specials were put out on patrols again and on 22 December Dawson Bates announced the re-introduction of internment, saying 'The government decided there was no alternative other than to arrest and intern well-known leaders and prominent members of this illegal organisation.'

Only 34 men were arrested in the first swoop and some of the Northern leaders escaped, but it was enough to prevent any serious campaign getting off the ground in the North. It was to have no real effect on the English campaign however. But there were certain preliminaries to be completed before the campaign in England could begin.

Most guerrilla organisations base their moral right to use force on the simple argument that their opponents use it to keep themselves in power. In particular, marxists believe that in a capitalist society the government, even a democratically elected one, is merely an instrument of the capitalist class who manipulate the mass media to get themselves elected, and who will use the army and police to suppress any threat to themselves. The traditionalist and Catholic section of the IRA, then in the ascendant, could not accept such an argument, yet were extremely concerned about the moral justification for their actions. They recognised the remaining handful of Republican members of the Second Dail Eireann elected in 1921 – i.e. those who rejected the Treaty and didn't join Fianna Fail – as the legitimate government of Ireland. On 8 December 1938 Sean Russell announced that the members of the Second Dail had signed over their authority to the army council of the IRA, making it the *de jure* government of the Republic, and thereby giving the IRA the right to use force and levy war.

Having completed the legal niceties, on 12 January the IRA sent a grandiose ultimatum to the British government, with copies to Stormont and the governments of various European countries. It began,

'I have the honour to inform you that the government of the Irish Republic, having as its first duty towards the people, the establishment and maintenance of peace and order, herewith demand the withdrawal of all British armed forces stationed in Ireland . . .

'The government of the Irish Republic believe that a period of four days is sufficient for your government to signify its intention in the matter of the military evacuation and for the issue of your declaration of abdication in respect of our country. Our government reserve the right of appropriate action without further notice if, on the expiration of the period of grace these conditions remain unfulfilled'.[1]

When the four days were up they issued a manifesto declaring war on Britain, which was posted up around the country. On 16 January 1939 there were seven explosions in three centres, London, Birmingham and Manchester. There were more the following day. The object was sabotage of basic installations, such as electricity, water and train services. Civilians were not to be harmed but in fact a Manchester fish porter was killed in the first series of blasts.

Tactically the start of the campaign was well planned. There were no more blasts for three weeks, to keep the British police guessing, and then another series on 4, 5 and 6 February. This time two civilians were seriously injured in a London Underground station. The campaign continued, building up momentum in May and June. By July there had been 127 explosions, and anger was growing in Britain. On 24 July the Westminster government introduced the Prevention of Violence Bill, assuming sweeping powers to demand the registration of all Irish people in Britain, and to deport Irish citizens at will. Two days later a bomb at King's Cross station in London killed one man and injured fifteen others. The Bill was passed in five days. Within a week 48 people had been expelled and five prohibited from entering Britain. On 25 August a bomb went off in a Coventry shopping centre, killing five people and injuring over fifty.

The Coventry deaths and England's entry into the war on 3 September 1939 effectively finished the IRA campaign. Far from irritating and frightening the British public into wanting to get out of Ireland, it had merely succeeded in alienating them, ensuring their support for harsh measures against the IRA and inducing them to inform on suspicious Irishmen. Without any real strategy, the IRA targets had been picked at random and they had done no serious damage to the British economy or essential services. After nine months of police harassment and without a sympathetic population to swallow them up, the IRA volunteers, many fresh from Ireland, were finding it impossible to exist.

The campaign stumbled on and the British police arrested two Irishmen, Peter Barnes and James McCormack, for the Coventry bombing. It later emerged that Barnes had had no part in the bombing at all and McCormack had had no part in the panic dumping of the bomb in a busy street which had caused the casualties. But hysteria had set in in England and neither the British public nor the courts were interested in such technicalities. The two men were sentenced to death in December 1939 and hanged on 7 February 1940. The IRA responded with another series of bombs aimed especially at the postal services, but it was a dying kick. By the end of March 1940 the English campaign was over. It had been the IRA's biggest military effort since the civil war but it was a total failure. Based on a misapprehension – that any guerrilla campaign could be carried on, much less succeed, in a foreign country where there was no popular support – it made no impact on the British or Stormont governments, and only brought the wrath of three governments down on the IRA's head, leaving them with men in prison in Britain and both parts of Ireland.

Even before the English campaign De Valera had shown all the vigour of the reformed revolutionary in suppressing his former colleagues, but now harassment was sharply increased. War between Britain and Germany was imminent. De Valera was intent on keeping the South neutral despite its membership of the British Commonwealth. His decision would not be popular in Britain, especially as Britain had just evacuated the Irish Treaty ports and handed them back to Dublin under the Anglo-Irish Agreement of April 1938. The ports were of great strategic value and already there were voices in Britain deploring the handover. When the war began there would be considerable pressure on the South to join in, failing which, it was at least possible that Britain would try to invade and take over the ports or whole 26 counties. In the event there was constant and intense pressure over the ports, especially from Churchill. It reached a climax at the end of 1940 when the British Dominions Secretary, Lord Cranbourne, was advocating economic sanctions against the South, and early in 1941 when

Churchill refused to give an assurance that Britain wouldn't invade the South[2]. In fact Britain had plans drawn up for an invasion, either to seize the ports or as a pre-emptive strike to prevent a German invasion. The German High Command had plans for an invasion as well.

The bombing campaign in England had of course done nothing to improve relations with Britain and when the IRA made contact with Germany the Dublin government, fearing that this might provide the excuse for an invasion, cracked down even harder. On the IRA side contact had been made with Germany on the simple basis that England's enemy must be their friend and the Germans might supply much needed money and arms. The IRA leadership were not pro-Nazi; but they were advocates of 'physical force', and impatient with the niceties of politics. They saw no difference between taking arms from Germany in 1916 and 1939-40, and they could see little moral difference between Britain – to them the imperialist oppressor of their country – and Germany. They were uninterested in any global struggle against fascism, but if they were successful they had no intention of letting the Germans dictate to them either.

An agent of the German Abwehr (Military Intelligence) visited Ireland early in 1939 and made contact with the IRA, and an IRA representative visited Germany to arrange supply routes. Early in 1940 Sean Russell, the IRA chief of staff who had been in America and was ordered out when the war began, arrived in Germany. The Abwehr gave him training in espionage and agreed to send him back to Ireland by U-boat, but he died on the way and was buried at sea. After that a series of spies were landed in Ireland, but all were quickly picked up by the Gardai. German interests in Ireland were always divided. The Abwehr naturally wanted to encourage the IRA to attack the British in the North, but the German Foreign Office thought little of the IRA's capabilities and was more concerned to preserve Irish neutrality and not to antagonise Dublin by interfering in Irish internal affairs or backing De Valera's enemies. In practical terms German aid to the IRA never amounted to more than a few thousand pounds and some radio transmitters, and it ended effectively by 1942. It certainly didn't make up for the Fianna Fail government's determined repression. On 14 June 1939 the Offences Against the State Act became law in the South. It was a toned-down Special Powers Act, giving power to intern without trial and to set up military 'courts' for certain offences. Over fifty IRA men were quickly interned, but on 1 December a high court judge held that the section of the Act providing for internment was unconstitutional and they had to be released.

Two days before Christmas 1939 however, the IRA successfully raided the Irish Army's main ammunition dump in the magazine fort in the Phoenix Park in Dublin. They got away with over a million rounds of ammunition in thirteen lorry loads – almost the whole of the Army's reserve supply. But it was an expensive exploit, because the government hit back hard. All but one of the lorry-loads of ammunition were quickly recovered and on 5 January 1940 the Dail passed the Emergency Powers (Amendment) Act, again giving the government power to intern without trial. The cabinet's resolution had been further strengthened when an IRA man in Cork had shot dead a civic guard on 3 January. This time there was no legal redress, as the Dail had already declared a state of emergency because of the war.

There was further expression of the government's extreme hard line in April 1940. Nine Republican prisoners went on hunger strike on 25 February to demand treatment as political prisoners. Prior to this the government had given in to several hunger strikes, but this time no concessions were made and two men, Tony D'Arcy and Jack McNeela, died on 16 April and 19 April. The others ended their strike without concessions.

Hard-hit in England and the South the IRA now turned its attention back to the North, where another 45 Republicans had been interned when war was declared and Craigavon had said they would be held until the war was over. The 65 Republicans interned in Derry jail staged a revolt on Christmas Day 1939 and the RUC had to be brought in to help the warders to suppress it. Eventually the prisoners were subdued with fire-hoses and some were very badly beaten-up afterwards; but the incidents won them a good deal of public sympathy.

On 11 February 1940 the IRA raided the British Army camp at Ballykinlar and got away with a hundred rifles. Around the same time they set up a pirate radio station in Belfast. In April and May there were thirteen bomb attacks, seven of them in Belfast, and in July three successful raids on Belfast banks. Around the same time four IRA men were captured after a gun-battle in Carrickmore, Co. Tyrone. Then in September another two banks and a number of post offices were raided in Belfast, and in November five more IRA men were arrested after a gun-battle with the RUC at Cullyhanna in South Armagh. They each got twelve years in jail and ten lashes of the 'cat' – a common punishment in the war years and one which did much to increase bitterness among Republicans.

But the Stormont government had been stepping up its activities in the meantime. In July, regulations were brought in under the Special Powers Act requiring everyone over fourteen years of age to carry an identity card, and requiring Southerners entering the North to prove that their purpose was peaceful. Internment continued and, as the numbers were increasing, the government bought an old merchant-ship, the *Al Rawdah*, transferred most of the internees to it and moored it in Strangford Lough. Conditions were terrible however and it caused such controversy that they had to abandon it in November. Meanwhile as the IRA ranks in the South were depleted more Northerners became involved there, and in September a Lurgan man, Thomas Harte, was sentenced to death by the South's military tribunal and executed in Dublin together with a veteran of the War of Independence, Patrick McGrath.

The Northern action in 1940 had been of little real effect, however, and by the end of the year, under the constant weight of repression on both sides of the border, the IRA was quiescent again.

As war became imminent Westminster had introduced conscription in Britain in April 1939, but left out Northern Ireland. In May 1940, the Stormont government requested that it apply there as well, but there was a storm of protest from the Nationalists, the Catholic hierarchy and the Irish Trade Union Congress. The British decided that trying to force conscription on an unwilling Catholic population would be more trouble than it was worth.

There was indeed little support for the war among Northern Catholics. Few were enthusiastic about fighting to defend a government which had brought them nothing but discrimination and humiliation, and a state whose existence they opposed. Further, to Nationalists it seemed hypocrisy for Britain to pose as the champion of democracy and the freedom of small nations when it was Britain that maintained and supported the Northern state. Many were influenced as well by the attitude of the South in staying neutral, and some were even quite pleased that the traditional enemy, England, was under attack – at this stage the full horror of life under the Nazis was not widely known. Moreover even Catholics who supported the war opposed conscription, on the grounds that neither Stormont nor Westminster had the right to demand military service from people who had never wanted to live under their rule. This attitude did change eventually however, after the bombing of Belfast and America's entry into the war; and as many Northern Catholics and Southerners joined the British forces, the minority became more identified with the conflict.

Initially the war in any case made little impact on the North. But slowly Northern Ireland was drawn into war-time measures. In February 1940 Craigavon broadcast to the Commonwealth countries, pledging his government's full support for the war effort and declaring, 'We are King's men.' In May 1940 all adult male Germans and Austrians were rounded up and interned for the duration of the war – they were kept separate from the 76 Republican internees. When Italy entered the war in June Italians were rounded up as well. The Southern government also officially interned military personnel from the belligerent countries who strayed on to Southern territory. But they operated double standards. RAF men who crash-landed in the South were discreetly sent to the North and it was only the Germans who were actually interned.

In May 1940 a press censor was set up in Belfast and a body of Local Defence Volunteers established. There was a lot of haggling over this body, which was trained and armed like the English Home Guard. The Unionists were alarmed at the prospect of an armed volunteer force which might have a high proportion of Catholics in it. The Stormont government wanted to control this force itself and Craigavon spelt out his reasons: 'There is a fifth column and we require to go very carefully along the road of arming people in Northern Ireland', he said[3].

But the Northern Ireland government was prohibited under the Government of Ireland Act from raising any military force.

In the end the Local Defence Volunteers (LDV) were attached to and trained by the B Specials, wore black uniforms and khaki coats, and were technically an auxiliary police force; but, since police were supposed to remain non-combatants in an invasion, arrangements were made that in an emergency they and the Specials would come under the command of the GOC Northern Ireland and become a military force. At any rate this subterfuge served its purpose. Because of the LDV's close connection with the B Specials hardly any Catholics joined it, and it became effectively an extension of the Specials. By November 1940 their combined strength reached 40,000 but it declined after that. It became something of a white elephant as it never saw any action but was somewhat accident-prone, and in July 1942 Lieut. Col. Hammond Smith, the Tyrone Co. commandant of the Specials, was shot dead at an LDV training exercise[4].

Around the same time a form of economic conscription was introduced whereby the unemployed in the North could be forced to go to England to do war work. Anyone who refused had his unemployment benefit stopped for six weeks. Eventually about 60,000 workers went to Britain, helping to reduce the North's unemployment total from a massive 91,000 in 1938 to 16,000 in 1944. The balance of the reduction was due to enlistment in the army, increased production in factories and compulsory tillage on farms.

The war inevitably began to affect the lives of everybody with the introduction of rationing, the black-out, and a ban on all but essential journeys between Ireland, North and South, and Britain. But Craigavon's cabinet, all veterans of the first parliament in 1921, were slow to react to the war situation. They showed no urgency in taking security precautions or stepping up production, and for a long time unemployment remained very high – it was still 77,000 in 1940.

There was growing back-bench discontent in the Unionist Party and in May 1940 Edward Warnock, Parliamentary Secretary to the Ministry of Home Affairs, resigned in protest at the government's lack of vigour in the war effort, saying: 'I am no longer a member of the government. I have heard speeches about Ulster pulling her weight but they have never carried conviction'[5]. He was followed in June by another Parliamentary Secretary, Lieut. Col. A.R.Gordon, and Craigavon was forced to create a new post of Minister for Public Security, responsible for civil defence, air-raid precautions and, for a time, general security, and to appoint a new MP, J.C.McDermott, to it. A Home Defence Executive Committee was also set up consisting of the British Army GOC Northern Ireland and the Stormont Ministers of Public Security, Home Affairs, and Finance. The idea was to co-ordinate security and make preparations for resisting an invasion.

Still the government remained lethargic and the population apathetic. In July 1940 the government made arrangements to evacuate 17,000 Belfast children to the countryside, but only 7,000 turned up on the day and in August when they planned to evacuate another 5,000 only 1,800 turned up. By September Warnock was proposing a vote of censure on the government, demanding a re-shuffle of the cabinet and the appointment of younger men. He commented, 'No limpet clings to a rock with the tenacity with which members of the government have clung to their posts'[6]. No other Unionist supported him but he was evidently articulating the feelings of some of his colleagues.

Craigavon died suddenly on 24 November 1940. Though he himself had wanted Sir Basil Brooke to succeed him[7] in fact it was J.M.Andrews, his Minister for Finance, one of the 'Old Guard', who had been a minister in the first government of 1921, who took over. Andrews re-appointed the entire cabinet and retained the Ministry of Finance himself. In January 1941 he was confirmed in office by the Unionist Council, when he re-shuffled his government with the minimum of change, bringing in one new cabinet minister and two parliamentary secretaries. Of the eight members of Andrews' cabinet, five had been in the 1921 government. Party and public discontent continued and this time it had a potential focus in Brooke who had been passed over for the leadership.

In March 1941 the government lost the by-election for Craigavon's seat of North Down to an Independent Unionist; but even this didn't instil any sense of urgency into them. By March for instance only fifteen per cent of houses in Belfast were provided with air-raid shelters, when government plans required all houses to have them.

What is more, almost all the anti-aircraft guns in the North had been sent to Britain. The results were seen in April. On the night of 7-8 April 1941 a small force of German planes bombed Belfast. Thirteen people were killed but little other damage was done. It was only a probing exercise. On 15 April 180 German planes staged a major raid which left 745 people dead in Belfast, fifteen in Derry and five in Bangor. It was the heaviest death toll in a single raid on any city in the British Isles, and large parts of Central Belfast around High Street, Donegall Street and York Street were devastated as well as whole streets in the densely-packed docks area. On the night of 4 May there was another major raid by 200 planes, which concentrated on the industrial areas of East Belfast, killing 150 people and doing extensive damage to the shipyard and to Short and Harland's aircraft factory. The final raid came the following night but it was a minor affair, killing fourteen people and doing little damage.

The total devastation was terrible. Apart from the 942 dead, the damage to the city centre and to the war industries, 56,000 houses were badly damaged: 3,200 of them totally destroyed. A hundred thousand people were temporarily homeless, and 49,000 officially evacuated. For weeks afterwards up to a hundred thousand left their homes in the city at night and spent the night in halls in the suburbs or even in the fields at Hannahstown. The government had to set up ten camps of Nissen huts around the outskirts of Belfast and another sixteen elsewhere to cope with the homeless and refugees. Some of them continued in use until the end of the war. Eventually all available open space, including parts of the public parks, was taken over to build prefabricated houses as temporary homes. A few were still occupied in 1974.

The government had been totally unprepared for such a disaster. Even the fire service was inadequate and the Southern government had to send fire engines from Dundalk, Dublin and Dun Laoghaire to Belfast to help out. Tommy Henderson, the Independent Unionist MP for Shankill, was speaking for many of the Unionists' traditional supporters when he attacked the government at Stormont.

'The Catholics and Protestants are going up there [Hannahstown] **mixed and they are talking to one another. They are sleeping in the same sheugh, below the same tree or in the same barn. They all say the same thing, that the government is no good'**[8].

The government blundered on. Andrews again requested Westminster to introduce conscription for Northern Ireland and this time the British government said they were considering it. There was another storm of protest from the Nationalists, the Catholic hierarchy, the trade unions and the Labour Party, who called for a plebiscite on the issue. De Valera also intervened and protested strongly at the proposal. On 25 May 1941 several big protest demonstrations were held and two days later Westminster dropped the idea – to the great relief, it was rumoured, of many Unionists as well as Nationalists. The government was floundering and the Unionist leadership becoming more and more discredited. In June an enquiry into the running of Whiteabbey Sanatorium outside Belfast, which implicated leading Unionists in serious irregularities and compromised Belfast Corporation, lost the authorities still more respect, the more so as they took no action over it. It was not until over a year later in October 1942 that they suspended the Corporation.

In December 1941 the Unionists lost a by-election in Willowfield in East Belfast to Harry Midgley[9] of the Labour Party. This was a major blow. It was the first time the Unionists had lost a safe, staunchly-Protestant seat to Labour. The two seats Labour had won up to this, Pottinger and Dock, had substantial Catholic minorities. After Willowfield no seat seemed safe.

The Willowfield result led to something of a backbench Unionist revolt and at a meeting of backbenchers in January 1942 there were calls for Andrews' resignation. He weathered the storm. But meanwhile Sir Basil Brooke had been strengthening his position. He had become Minister for

Commerce in the Andrews government and this was becoming a key ministry. Under war-time conditions more and more areas of life had come under direct Westminster control, by-passing Stormont. The growing powerlessness of Stormont was shown by the fact that the parliament met for only 25 days in 1941. However Brooke's ministry became the agent for many Westminster departments, so that as main overseer of war production in Northern Ireland he was able to accumulate a great deal of power in his own hands.

1942 also saw a renewal of IRA activity in the North and a number of serious strikes which harmed production. The government came in for more criticism. Then on 10 February 1943 there was a by-election in West Belfast and Jack Beattie was elected[10], the first time a non-Unionist had won West Belfast since 1922. Already the Labour Party was calling for a general election. It looked as if the Unionists would lose half their seats if there was one. Criticism of Andrews was immediate and widespread. He replied in Derry on 12 February: 'At such a time captious and carping criticism is indefensible. Its only effect is to impair Loyalist unity and to weaken the effectiveness of our war effort'[11].

But the criticism persisted and he had to refer to it several times more in the next few months. Early in March, Brooke and three junior ministers threatened to resign and a meeting of the parliamentary Unionist Party demanded changes in the cabinet. On 16 April the Ulster Unionist Council met and Andrews got a vote of confidence after a stormy discussion. It was not unanimous however. Andrews himself spoke strongly:

'A considerable number of statements have been made in public of late which have been damaging to our party and unkind to me. Fully two years ago you elected me as Ulster's Unionist leader ... and you have done so again today. I am only the servant of the people, whom I have endeavoured to serve.'

'The political waves may be ruffled but I am not going to lay down my task and run away so long as I enjoy your confidence and the support of the people generally ... When changes in the personnel of the government are necessary they will be made ... but so long as I remain I must be left free to choose my colleagues as every Prime Minister in the world is free to do. I will not, simply for the sake of change, replace men who have given and are still giving valuable service to Ulster ... If I may say so, it is fortunate for Ulster, however, that some of the "Old Guard" are still on the active list'[12].

The *Newsletter* backed him and suggested that the critics were 'disappointed aspirants to office'[13].

A week later, on 24 April, the government was bitterly attacked at a meeting of the parliamentary party and Brooke, McDermott the Attorney General[14] and four Parliamentary Secretaries, Mrs Dehra Parker, William Lowry KC, Maynard Sinclair and W.B.Maginess openly threatened to resign unless there were changes. Andrews appealed to Brooke to stay on, but he refused and on 30 April 1943 Andrews resigned. On Monday, 3 May, Brooke became Prime Minister.

The new cabinet was remarkable. The discontent with the Andrews government, though persistent and widespread, had been neither coherent nor fundamental. It had been based partly on frustration at bad social conditions and lack of government action to improve them – that explained the Labour victories. And it had also been based partly on jingoism and chauvinism as expressed by the government's main critic, Warnock, who complained about lack of energy in the war effort and about immigration of Southern workers into the North. Brooke's cabinet was designed to stop the rot among the Unionist Party's traditional supporters.

The new cabinet contained only one senior member of Andrews' government apart from Brooke himself – the Attorney General, J.C.McDermott. But it did contain Harry Midgley, who had recently left the Labour Party to form a more pro-Unionist Labour group, as Minister for Public Security, and William Grant, the ex-shipwright, as Minister for Labour. They could be expected to allay working-class Protestant discontent. To satisfy the jingoist element and to make amends for bringing a non-member of the Unionist Party into the government, the Orange Grand Master, Sir Joseph Davison, became Leader of the Senate and two Presbyterian ministers joined the cabinet – the Rev Robert Moore as Minister for Agriculture, and Rev Professor Corkey as Minister for Education. It was an extraordinary feat of balancing.

The ruthless axing of the 'Old Guard' caused considerable bitterness in the Unionist Party. When the parliamentary party met to endorse the new cabinet the ex-ministers and their supporters stayed away and only 20 out of 36 MPs turned up. The Unionist Council continued to elect Andrews as leader of the party until 1946.

The opposition were not any better pleased. The inclusion of Midgley was obviously designed to ward off calls for the formation of a national government like the war-time government in Britain – the latest call had come from the Communist Party the day Andrews resigned. But Jack Beattie denounced the new cabinet at Stormont, calling Midgley a traitor and a Quisling to the Labour movement, and saying that his inclusion in the cabinet didn't broaden its base of support at all. The Nationalists and the Catholic minority on the other hand could hardly have been expected to welcome a government led by Brooke, the arch-sectarian of the 1930s, and including two Protestant ministers. The new government satisfied the disgruntled Unionist voters however, which was what it was intended to do, and Brooke survived the rest of the war with no serious threat to his position.

In the meantime a new dimension had been added to Northern affairs. In December 1941 the USA entered the war and on 26 January 1942, 4,000 US troops landed in Belfast. They were only the advance guard of what was to become a sizeable force, and in fact preparations for the establishment of US bases in the North had been going on secretly since March 1941. The Southern government made a formal protest to the US government about sending troops to Ireland without seeking permission from Dublin, and the IRA denounced the landing and warned the US forces not to become tools of the British government. The Americans went to some lengths to deal with this problem and the US Commander contacted the IRA through his head Catholic chaplain to let them know he had no wish to clash with them[15].

By May 1942 there were 38,000 US troops in the North and in August a huge new air-base was opened at Langford Lodge on Lough Neagh. It was to become the headquarters of the Eighth US Army Air Force in the UK for the next two years. By October 1942 it was decided to withdraw all US ground forces from the North again for use in the North African campaign, but a year later the Fifteenth US Army Corps arrived for preliminary training prior to the Normandy landings. In February 1944 the US forces strength had reached a peak of 120,000, though most of them were gone again by June and in September even the big US Navy base at Derry was handed back to the British. Yet this massive US force – one soldier to every twelve or thirteen people in the North in early 1944 – had little lasting impact on Northern Ireland; though their presence there and close co-operation with the British (at one stage they replaced British troops as the garrison for most of the North) undoubtedly made the US government more sympathetic to the Unionist and British position on Northern Ireland.

The US entry into the war led to one peculiar incident. The British

Premier, Churchill, had a virtual obsession with the question of the Irish ports, and in the light of the traditional friendship between Ireland and the United States he hoped the Southern government might be more willing to abandon its neutrality now. So the day after Pearl Harbour he sent De Valera an extraordinary secret telegram saying 'Now is your chance. Now or Never, "a Nation Once Again." Am ready to meet you any time'[16]. It seemed to offer a united Ireland in return for the South's entering the war but De Valera was suspicious and didn't take up Churchill's offer of a meeting. When he did meet the Dominions Secretary ten days later the British proposal had been reduced to a suggestion that Irish entry to the war would create a climate which would facilitate unification. It is doubtful if Churchill's offer was at all serious. If it was it would have involved an utterly cynical abandonment of the Ulster Unionists who had not even been consulted.

Meanwhile IRA offensive action had virtually ceased in the North by the end of 1940 but the IRA was by no means dead. It had been very hard hit in the South however, by the De Valera government's policy of internment and executions – two more men were executed in 1941. The well-organised Northerners, only too used to coping with state repression, had to take over and reconstruct the faltering leadership. In June 1941, in an internal coup, the chief of staff, Stephen Hayes, was arrested as a suspected informer and replaced by the Northern commander Sean McCaughey. IRA chiefs of staff didn't last very long at the time due to the efficiency of the Dublin Special Branch but McCaughey was succeeded by a series of Northerners until the organisation was firmly in Northern hands. Attention, naturally enough, began to focus on the idea of a campaign in the North.

In January 1942 the Civil Defence Headquarters in Belfast was raided and £5,000 taken. In February an IRA convention was held and agreed to a Northern campaign. The Northern structure was re-vamped with Hugh McAteer from Derry as commander and John Graham as intelligence officer, director of publicity, and editor of the IRA's paper, *Republican News.* Graham was a Protestant and one of a small but significant group of radical Protestants who had joined the IRA about this time. Most of them had been members of the Ulster Union Club, a loose propagandist organisation of Protestant nationalists led by Capt. Denis Ireland. Their Ulster Union colleagues were shocked when they learnt of their activities, but Graham and his associates helped to stop the IRA from becoming a purely Catholic defence force, a tendency which was strong after 1935.

The Belfast IRA was fairly strong at the time. It had three hundred volunteers grouped in four companies plus auxiliaries and members of Cumann na mBan, the women's section. The Ulster Union men formed a Special Operations Group which was very effective in gathering information, as it lay outside the normal Republican channels which were watched by the Special Branch. On 25 March 1942 the IRA Northern Command resolved:

'That military action be taken against the enemy forces in the six-county area by Oglaigh na hEireann, (the IRA) reinforced by the entire resources and equipment of the army in the 26-county area, by sabotage of war industries and enemy military objectives by a semi-military force'[17].

The campaign wasn't due to begin for some time but the new aggressive IRA attitude soon precipitated them into action. On 3 April in Dungannon two IRA men opened fire on RUC men about to stage a raid. One RUC man was killed and another wounded and the IRA men got away. On Easter Sunday, 5 April, a group of IRA men fired on an RUC patrol car in the Kashmir Road in Belfast. It was intended only as a diversion to draw police away from another part of the Falls Road where a banned commemoration of the 1916 Rising was being held, but the diversion turned into a serious gun-battle as the RUC pursued the IRA men into a house in Cawnpore Street. An RUC man was killed and the leader of the IRA unit, Tom Williams, wounded before the group surrendered. A violent Easter was rounded off when another IRA man shot and seriously wounded an RUC man at Strabane.

Meanwhile the six men involved in the Kashmir Road/Cawnpore Street gun-battle were convicted of murdering an RUC man and sentenced to death. No Republican had ever been executed in the North before despite the violence of the twenties and thirties. So most of the Catholic community were appalled at the prospect of a mass hanging, and many others were alarmed at its likely repercussions. A reprieve committee of members of the Labour Party, trade unions, Communist Party and the Ulster Union Club was set up in the North and another, headed by Sean McBride, in the South. 200,000 people from all over Ireland signed a petition for a reprieve and mass meetings were held all over the South. Dublin Corporation sent its Lord Mayor to Belfast to plead for the men. The Irish Trade Union Congress, a Church of Ireland bishop, and a group of Northern Protestant clergy all joined in the appeals. De Valera, despite his own government's executions in the South, put pressure on Britain, and even the US Secretary of State appealed to Westminster for clemency.

Stormont seemed adamant. The men's appeal was heard on 19-20 August 1942; but despite evidence of irregularities and brutality in taking statements from the men the convictions and sentences were upheld. The Attorney General, J.C.McDermott, refused leave to appeal to the House of Lords and the Minister of Home Affairs, William Lowry, refused to see a deputation of Nationalist MPs and Senators about the case. Finally, four days before the execution date, five of the men were reprieved. The sixth, Tom Williams, would still be hanged, though he had not fired the fatal shots. Last-minute appeals were unsuccessful. Williams was hanged on 2 September 1942 in Crumlin Road jail.

Hundreds of police guarded the jail all night and the area around it was cordoned off in the morning. Even so, women knelt and prayed in the streets nearby and there were some ugly incidents. The *Newsletter* reported:

'Police had to intervene at the corner of the Old Lodge Road and Florence Place which runs alongside the county court house. Here on the stroke of eight [the time of the hanging] **a crowd of about 200 women and girls burst into "God Save the King" while on the other side of the street a score of women were kneeling. Cheers followed the national anthem and then the crowd sang "Land of Hope and Glory" and "There'll always be an England", the praying women meanwhile remaining on their knees'[18].**

The hanging was bitterly resented and black flags were flown and sullen crowds gathered in the Catholic ghettos, while the RUC patrolled constantly in cage cars; but there was no violence. In Dublin and other parts of the South, shops, factories and trams stopped for an hour in mourning and ITGWU dockers staged token strikes in Belfast, Newry and Derry.

On 15 August the army council of the IRA had met and finalised their plans. They had collected twelve tons of arms and ammunition. Some was to be moved into the North, some left on the border for flying columns who would strike into the North. On 30 August three tons of arms and ammunition were left at a farmhouse at Hannahstown, outside Belfast. The next day the RUC surprised two IRA men at the dump and shot one of them, Gerard O'Callaghan, dead. The circumstances were suspicious. Republicans claimed O'Callaghan had offered no resistance and was shot out of hand. The government used the Special Powers Act to prohibit any inquest.

On the day Tom Williams was hanged a flying column crossed the border to attack Crossmaglen RUC barracks. They ran into an RUC patrol at Culloville in South Armagh and opened fire, wounding one RUC man and capturing another, whom they soon released. The next day Randalstown RUC barracks was bombed and a sergeant injured, and the day after RUC patrols were fired on in the Lower Falls and Belleek RUC station in Co.Fermanagh was attacked. All IRA units had been ordered to take offensive action if Williams died. On 6 September a B Special and an RUC man were shot dead in Clady, Co.Tyrone and an RUC man and a young IRA man wounded in a gun-battle in Belfast. The situation was serious enough for the Catholic clergy to warn young men against joining the IRA in many churches in Belfast.

But the RUC were hitting back too. Early in September they launched a massive round-up in the Belfast ghettos, 'lifting' over 120 men and interning 90 of them under the Special Powers Act. Outside Belfast they picked up nearly two hundred men, mostly in border areas. The number of internees trebled overnight. On 10 September the RUC raided a house on the Crumlin Road and fought a dramatic gun battle with John Graham and David Fleming, a Kerryman, before they surrendered. Inside they found a secret room containing six revolvers, a radio transmitter, duplicators, typewriters, copies of IRA manifestoes and posters, and 5,000 copies of *Republican News*. The IRA had lost their publicity headquarters as well as one of their best men.

On 6 October Hugh McAteer and his director of intelligence were caught and four days later a curfew from 8.30pm to 6.30am was imposed on the Lower Falls. By now there were constant B Special or RUC road blocks, patrols and raids. Donegall Pass police barracks in Belfast was bombed and a B man shot dead outside it on the first night of the curfew, but repression was having its effect. By mid-October there were 477 men interned in the South and over 400 men and a few women in the North. IRA activity tailed off again.

But it was not quite over yet. In January 1943 four leading Republicans including Hugh McAteer and Jimmy Steele made a dramatic escape from Crumlin Road jail. The tottering Andrews government was seriously embarrassed and put a price of £3,000 on McAteer's head. On 21 March 21 internees tunnelled out of Derry jail and got across the border to Donegal. Most of them were promptly captured by the Free State Army and transferred to the Curragh internment camp but the two escapes were a big boost to IRA morale. Then on Easter Sunday, 25 April, armed men seized the Clonard cinema on the Falls Road, stopped the film and McAteer and Steele went on stage and read the 1916 Proclamation of the Republic and a statement by the army council of the IRA. It was a considerable propaganda coup, as commemorations of 1916 were still banned and the Unionists were particularly annoyed when the incident was reported on German radio.

The seizure of the Clonard cinema was the IRA's last real success however. Steele was re-captured in May 1943 and McAteer in October. Another RUC man was shot dead in October during a wages-snatch but the short-lived campaign was effectively over. Any encouragement to be gained from the prospect of a British defeat in the war had also faded, as the tide turned in favour of the Allies. The last acts came in February and April 1944. On 11 February a wanted IRA man, Seamus 'Rocky' Burns, was shot dead by the RUC in the centre of Belfast. And on 11 April a 16-year-old boy, a member of the junior IRA from the Upper Falls, died in a training accident. By December 1944 the Northern government felt secure enough to stand down the Ulster Home Guard, reducing the B Specials to their pre-war strength. The Southern government released most of its internees in November 1944 though Stormont kept theirs till the war ended, and on both sides of the border convicted prisoners were held for several years more.

The Northern campaign had thus been as ineffective as the English one. The Catholic ghettos had provided the IRA with some base from which to operate, but the support of the Catholic population was passive rather than active. The bulk of the minority had become disillusioned with Stormont but didn't automatically support a military campaign. In fact most people looked for direction to the Southern government, with whom the IRA was in deadly conflict. The Northern campaign also did not develop out of any campaign of agitation which might have mobilised the Catholic masses, brought them into direct conflict with the state and developed some form of popular resistance to the forces of the state. And the IRA themselves had no clear strategy or plan. They had a generalised policy of attacking the RUC and Specials, but with the forces and weapons at their disposal they weren't capable of inflicting more than token losses on them. They made no attempt to attack commercial or industrial targets or vital installations. As a result they had never posed a serious threat to the Northern government.

The militant activities of the IRA tended to push the Nationalists into the background during the war, while the Nationalists' own activities did little to keep them in the public eye. All but the two Belfast MPs Richard Byrne and T.J.Campbell were boycotting Stormont, and the two Westminster MPs were abstaining as well. As in the 1930s the abstentionists mounted no campaign, led no agitations. They did protest in 1940 when a joint London-Dublin-Belfast defence agreement was mooted, fearing it would involve some recognition of partition, but this came to nothing anyway. They supported the anti-conscription protests in May 1941 and the campaign to reprieve Tom Williams and his colleagues in August 1942, but they were not a major force in either campaign. They didn't even mount a protest when one of their number, Cahir Healy, was interned in July 1941 by the Westminster government under the Defence of the Realm Act; though in this case they may have found themselves somewhat embarrassed, for Healy was a fervent anti-communist, an admirer of Sir Oswald Mosley, the British Fascist who was also interned at the time, and a friend of General O'Duffy, the leader of the fascist-style Blueshirts in the South. He was believed to be sympathetic to the Germans and to have been in correspondence with them. At any rate he was held in Brixton prison for a year and a half.

The two Nationalists who did go to Stormont were not very active either. They protested about internment, police harassment and the Special Powers Act, with support from the Labour MPs Beattie and Agnew. They complained about discrimination, which was now so blatant that in 1941 the Catholic bishops of the North issued a lengthy statement beginning, 'our people suffer grievances and disabilities which extend to every phase of their life, ranging from indignities which bitterly afflict all sensitive minds to discrimination in employment'[19] and pointing out, among other examples, that of the 123 most senior posts in the Northern Ireland civil service and legal system only two were held by Catholics.

They also raised the perennial question of Catholic schools, but as usual their complaints met with no response. In 1941 they were joined by an Independent Nationalist, Michael McGurk, who got in in a by-election for Mid-Tyrone and took his seat, but after three years McGurk too was disillusioned with Stormont:

'I hope my suggestions will bear fruit in this session, that my attendance will be of some good to the people whom I represent and that I will not have to consider whether it is any use attending this parliament,

or if I should take my place with some of my fellow members of parliament and abstain'[20].

Meanwhile an attempt was being made to unite several strands of Nationalist opinion on a policy of boycotting Stormont and Westminster, and instead focussing attention on the partition issue by a publicity campaign in Britain, the United States and other countries. The boycott was advocated not just as a gesture of frustration and despair but as a symbol of the minority's rejection of the Northern state and its institutions. The policy brought together the abstentionist Nationalists and some ex-Republicans and had the tacit support of Fianna Fail in the South. So when Richard Byrne MP died in 1942 the abstentionist group seized the opportunity to test their policy at the polls. The writ for the by-election in Byrne's Falls constituency was moved, not by T.J.Campbell his colleague at Stormont, but by Joe Stewart, MP for East Tyrone, in what was to be his only appearance at Stormont for seven years. The abstentionist group nominated Eamon Donnelly who had been successively a Sinn Fein MP in the North and a Fianna Fail TD in the South. He had also been secretary of the Tom Williams reprieve committee and was currently secretary of the Green Cross Fund for the relief of the dependants of internees and political prisoners. He was backed by all the Nationalist MPs except Campbell and by four of the five Nationalist Senators as well as a number of Fianna Fail TDs and old former Republicans. Only the IRA stayed aloof.

Campbell and the remaining Senator – T.S.McAllister, an old UIL member – nominated a Belfast doctor, George McGouran, who promised to take his seat if elected. The contest summed up well the political dilemma of the Catholic middle class: whether to go to Stormont at least to voice their grievances, remedy individual complaints and secure minor concessions by day-to-day representations, but thereby run the risk of recognising and perhaps propping up a system they opposed; or whether to oppose the system outright but thereby forgo short-term remedies and concessions with no guarantee of ultimate success. It is a dilemma they have never resolved. Campbell stated clearly the case for attendance, as reported in the *Irish News:*

'Like Dr McGouran, he had never been a Republican. He had been a Nationalist all through life. A Nationalist he remained.

'Absenteeism to his mind was never a policy, seldom a remedy and at best a risky experiment. The Nationalist MPs tried it 20 years back and abandoned it. They tried it again eleven years ago. Nine years ago after seeking very wise and disinterested counsel [from the Catholic hierarchy] they abandoned it again and Joseph Devlin concurring, resolved after full deliberation to take their seats, and do whatever the circumstances permitted for their people . . .

'It was no joy at times to go to Stormont when necessity demanded someone's voice – an almost solitary voice – to expose the grievances and portray the wrongs of our people. He went from duty and not from desire. They had no representative at Westminster or Dublin. Were they to be the only community of white ones with no representation anywhere and were the 430,000 free people of the North to be worse off than their ancestors of pre-emancipation times'[21].

The election was in November. Feelings were bitter after the hanging of Tom Williams and the shooting of Gerard O'Callaghan, and with a curfew in the constituency. Donnelly won easily. McGouran barely pushed a Labour candidate into third place[22]. The Catholic population had decisively rejected Campbell's and McGouran's old-style Redmondite parliamentarianism. But they hadn't completely endorsed abstentionism. Four months later in the by-election for the West Belfast seat at Westminster, the group which had backed Donnelly nominated Hugh Corvin as an abstentionist candidate but Jack Beattie won by 19,936 votes to Corvin's 1,250. It seemed the minority wanted more vigour and action than they'd got from the old Nationalists: they didn't necessarily want abstentionism. And they also wanted to win West Belfast for the first time in 20 years. Beattie could do that by getting some Protestant votes: Corvin was unlikely to.

While the Nationalists failed at any time during the war to grasp the initiative in opposition, the Labour opposition had a rather chequered career. The Labour Party started the war with only one official MP, Agnew, who had got in by the back door and made little impact. But the Unionist government's bungling and the formation of a National government in Britain which included the Labour Party brought an upsurge of support and boosted their morale. Harry Midgley won the Willowfield seat for Labour in December 1941 and Beattie re-joined the party early in 1942. But the old strains were not easily mended. Midgley had been moving steadily to the right and towards a pro-Unionist position all through the 1930s. His defeat in Dock had embittered him against Nationalists and Catholics and when the war began he became as jingoistic as Churchill: he was out to purge the party of anti-partitionists and Communist sympathisers. At the

Labour Party Conference in October 1942 he denounced the IRA as 'Quislings in our midst'; in November he made a strongly Unionist speech in his Willowfield constituency, and early in December he called for a special conference of the party to endorse Northern Ireland's constitutional position.

Thus when Beattie was appointed leader of the three-man parliamentary party, Midgley denounced the move as the culmination of an anti-partitionist trend and resigned from the party on 15 December 1942. A week later he set up the Commonwealth Labour Party, with himself as chairman and leader, committed to maintaining the link with Britain and to mildly social democratic policies. Four months later he was providing the working-class flavour in Brooke's new cabinet, though he kept the Commonwealth Labour tag.

Meanwhile Beattie won the West Belfast by-election in February 1943, giving Labour its first ever seat at Westminster, and the Labour Party discussed a request to affiliate by the Communist Party. The CP's fortunes had improved considerably. When the war began they had opposed it, and in October 1940 their paper *Red Hand* was banned under the Special Powers Act and two prominent party members – Betty Sinclair and W.H.McCullough – were jailed for two and four months respectively. But when Hitler invaded Russia the Party reversed its attitude, became a vehement supporter of the war effort and won considerable popularity. The affiliation request got the support of most of the constituency parties and was only defeated by the block vote of the big unions. Ironically however on one major issue the Labour Party was to find itself to the left of the Communist Party: during the Andrews crisis the CP constantly called for a coalition government, led by the Unionists, and even gave the Brooke government a qualified welcome, while the Labour Party rejected the idea of any coalition and called for a general election – in which the Unionists would probably have lost several seats.

Labour ended the war period with the same strength as it began, because Beattie was expelled again in 1944 for refusing to press for a Senate by-election when one of the Nationalists died and his colleagues refused to move the writ. Once again he was reluctant to antagonise his parliamentary allies.

The war also inevitably produced a great deal of industrial unrest. All strikes were banned under the Defence of the Realm Act (DORA) and all industrial disputes had to be referred to a slow-moving National Arbitration Tribunal which operated against the workers and held wages down. By the middle of 1942 there had already been several short strikes and some 1,563 workers had been convicted of offences under DORA and fined a total of £4,025.

Sectarian tension had still been strong at the start of the war and the day after war was declared, Monday 4 September, the Catholic workers had been driven out of the shipyard again. But as unemployment went down sectarianism decreased and the workers became more self-assertive. A Belfast shop stewards' committee was set up, determined to fight the war-time system of long hours and low wages and the DORA regulations.

In October 1942 the management at Short and Harland's aircraft factory[23] in Belfast sacked two shop stewards and all their engineering workers walked out. A strike of electricians broke out simultaneously in Mackie's engineering works. Both firms were doing important war work and the strikers were denounced from all the usual quarters – the government, the *Newsletter* – and from some unusual ones. Harry Midgley, still in the Labour Party, said 'the extension of the strike plays right into the hand of the subversive elements and influences in the community . . . at this time no stoppage is justified'[24]. And W.H.McCullough of the Communist Party declared:

'Today the streets of Stalingrad, the Volga river and the country between it and the Don are drenched in blood and yet in Belfast, during the greatest crisis in the history of humanity, aid to our Russian comrades is being held up because of strikes. An hour lost in the factories of Northern Ireland is an hour gained for Hitler'[25].

Nonetheless the Belfast Shop Stewards' Committee called sympathetic strikes in other factories, the Belfast Trades Council backed the men and at the end of October electricians in the shipyard and most other engineering works came out as well. That really threatened the war effort and both firms gave in immediately. It was an impressive demonstration of the power of the Shop Stewards' Committee and of the new-found militancy of Belfast workers.

Early in 1943 there was a further series of short but serious stoppages by trolley-bus operators, dockers and carters – who were paid £3.12.6d for a 48-hour week including working on Sunday cleaning out their stables – in all of which the government used troops to strike-break and large numbers of strikers were fined under DORA regulations.

But the most serious dispute of the war broke out in February 1944. On 25 February several hundred AEU members in the shipyard went on strike demanding a minimum wage of 3/-per hour or £7 per week. They were getting an average of £4.10.0d for a 47-hour week, and they were particularly angry because engineers in smaller Belfast firms, including those doing subcontracting work in the shipyard, were getting up to 23/3d a week more than they were. A meeting of Belfast shop stewards backed the strike on 5 March, and warned that if the government didn't force the management to settle the claim, 'The shop stewards' movement will place the full strength of the workers of Belfast behind the men on strike'[26].

Both the AEU executive and the local Confederation of Shipbuilding and Engineering Unions urged a return to work, but 3,000 men in the shipyard stayed out. On 15 March a mass meeting of Confederation members voted their support and the next day between 2,000 and 3,000 men in Short's came out. Within a few days the numbers of Short's workers involved had risen to 6,000 as the strike spread to its outlying branches – dispersed as a precaution against air-raids. On 21 March the management of Mackie's rejected the 3/-an hour demand as well, and 2,000 of their workers came out.

The government was getting alarmed and Brooke denounced the stoppage as 'an act of sabotage against the war effort and a betrayal of the men who fight'[27]. By 24 March there were 20,000 workers idle, between strikers and those laid off because of the dispute. The strike was illegal, it had been denounced by the government, the AEU executive, the Confederation, the Church of Ireland Dean of Belfast, and the *Newsletter*. But it went on.

On 31 March the government acted. Summonses were issued against five of the strike leaders. On 3 April the five – Jimmy Morrow, Bob McBrinn, Billy Baxter, Tommy Telford and Alex McAteer – were all sentenced to three months' hard labour. The magistrate said, 'The law has been broken deliberately, callously and calculatedly . . . imprisonment is the only cure for such deliberate sabotage.' The men refused to appeal and went straight to jail[28].

The Shop Stewards' Committee reacted sharply. They threatened to shut down the shipyard completely if the men weren't released. The Minister of Home Affairs, Lowry, replied curtly: 'Demand contained in your telegram is refused.' All 20,000 men in the shipyard stopped work and thousands more in Short's and in the docks. While the Confederation, as ever, urged a return to work, the Shop Stewards' Committee held a mass meeting in High Street and told the men to stay out till the five were released. The dockers returned the next day but the shipyard and Short's remained deserted.

Meanwhile the employers made an improved offer and Andrews, the ex-Prime Minister, the Confederation, and the AEU executive all pleaded with the jailed men to appeal their sentences. A deputation from the AEU and the Belfast Trades Council, accompanied by Jack Beattie MP, saw them in prison and finally prevailed on them. They were released on 7 April and on 8 April the shipyard engineers accepted the employers' terms – a basic increase of eight shillings a week, a better bonus system and the introduction of piece work rates. The released stewards addressed a mass meeting on the Sunday and hailed the agreement as a victory for the shop stewards' movement, especially a clause promising freedom of operation for the shop stewards. Their jail sentences were dropped on appeal.

The 1944 strike was the last major clash between government, employers and labour during the war. It was the high point of the shop stewards' movement, which had shown that it could defy the bosses, the government, the press and even the official trade union leadership and yet retain mass support. It also frightened the Unionist government members, with their obsessional fear of leftist influence on the Protestant working class. But they needn't have worried too much: the strike was much less political than those of the early 1930s. The shop stewards themselves were no revolutionaries, they were mostly orthodox Labour Party members concerned only to get better wages and conditions within the existing system. They made no effort to broaden the strike into a political conflict, much less to link it up with the other serious challenge to the state at the time coming from the Republicans. The Communist Party, who did claim to be revolutionaries, who had had contact with Republicans, and whose theory demanded the linking of industrial and political struggles, refused to support the strike because it was hindering the war effort. It had been vehemently denouncing the IRA for the same reason.

The Northern state had thus been challenged from a number of directions during the war. The Unionist government's own alienation of the Catholic minority produced the IRA campaign; the complacency and incompetence of the 'Old Guard' during Craigavon's last years and Andrews' ministry produced the widespread frustration among Unionist voters which lost them several by-elections and ultimately led to Brooke's palace revolution; and grasping employers and the government's determination to back them up produced the series of war-time strikes.

But the regime weathered the storm. The IRA's English campaign had been doomed to failure from the start, their campaign in the North started when half their organisation was already in jail and when they had only the sympathy, not the active support, of the Catholic population. The frustration at the Unionist 'Old Guard' on the other hand was not deep-seated and didn't lead to any large-scale rejection of Unionism; it was easily dealt with by the Brooke administration. And the 1944 strike came when the other two challenges had already been met and Brooke's government was firmly in the saddle and able to weather it. In the meantime, as the IRA moved away from politics and social agitation towards pure physical force, and the Communist Party towards reformism and working within the state, the tenuous links between Republicanism and working-class discontent were broken.

Moreover the very fact that the Northern state had been involved in the war while the South remained neutral widened the gap between the Northern majority and the South, while it served to strengthen the commitment of the British government to Stormont. Churchill, speaking in 1943 of Britain's difficulties in getting food and supplies in the early years of the war, said:

'Only one great channel remained open. That channel remained open because loyal Ulster gave us the full use of the Northern Irish ports and waters and thus ensured the free working of the Clyde and Mersey'[29].

Indeed Churchill was so indignant at the loss of the Southern ports that he returned to the theme even in his victory broadcast on 13 May 1945:

'Owing to the action of the Dublin government . . . the approaches which the southern Irish ports and airfields could so easily have guarded were closed by hostile aircraft and U-boats.

'This was indeed a deadly moment in our life, and if it had not been for the loyalty and friendship of Northern Ireland, we should have been forced to come to close quarters with Mr De Valera, or perish forever from the earth'[30].

In the long run, then, by forging tighter the links with Britain and further straining those with the South, the effect of the war was to sharpen rather than resolve the conflicts in the North.

The Anti-Partition League

The end of the war was a natural moment for the Northern Nationalists to re-open the question of partition. Attempts to remedy their grievances within the Northern state had led only to frustration and abstentionism. They wanted to go to the root of the problem – the existence of the state itself – and the time seemed ideal. The Allies had just fought the war in the name of democracy and new governments were being established all over Europe. For the first time ever there was to be a Labour government with a clear majority in Britain which might be sympathetic to their cause.

The life of the Stormont parliament had been extended during the war and when Germany surrendered in May 1945 an election was two years overdue. It was held on 15 June.

The war-time IRA campaign had petered out in 1944 and was formally ended by a cease-fire declaration on 10 March 1945. Anti-partitionist opposition was back in the hands of the Nationalists. Seven years of abstention from Stormont and Westminster had achieved nothing and Nationalist opinion was swinging back towards attendance, coupled with the new emphasis on ending partition, which had emerged in the Falls by-election in 1942. No doubt they were influenced towards attendance by the prospect of a flood of legislation which would flow through Stormont in the wake of the Beveridge Report and the Butler Education Act in Britain to set up a welfare state and re-shape the educational system: the interests of the Church and the Catholic middle class would have to be defended again.

The three seats abandoned in 1938 were contested again and the Nationalist convention in South Fermanagh, Healy's seat, decided in favour of attendance at Stormont. The Co. Tyrone convention, covering three Nationalist-held seats, decided to refer the question of abstention or attendance to a general conference of Nationalists after the election. It was also hoped that this conference would heal the division between Campbell and the other MPs.

The Nationalists put up eleven candidates for the eleven seats they held in 1933. Ten were elected. They lost Falls to an ex-Nationalist Harry

Diamond, standing as Socialist Republican, while their candidate came third, after the Labour man[1]. (Eamon Donnelly MP had died in 1944). Evidently the working-class Catholics of the Falls were no longer content to be represented by wealthy conservative publicans. However they won back South Armagh from Paddy Agnew, the Labour candidate[2]. And a Catholic doctor was elected as an Independent Nationalist for one of the university seats.

A Westminster election followed in July. Mulvey and Cunningham, the outgoing MPs for Fermanagh and Tyrone, were re-selected and the question of attendance referred to the general convention, together with a recommendation for the 'establishment of a united organisation for the entire partitioned area and the framing of an effective policy to undo partition'[3]. Mulvey and Cunningham were elected together with Beattie in West Belfast while a Labour government got in with a big majority in Britain.

The election of the first majority Labour government clinched the matter for the Nationalists. Labour had supported Irish self-determination in the 1920s. Many Labour MPs were of Irish extraction, tens of thousands of Labour voters were Irish. With a sympathetic government in Westminster, parliamentary politics might bring some results. Stormont re-assembled on 17 July. The Nationalist MPs and Senators met the day before and decided to take their seats as a body. On 11 August a convention for Fermanagh and Tyrone decided by 113 votes to 23 to instruct their MPs to attend Westminster. On 22 August Mulvey and Cunningham, who had been MPs for ten years, took their seats for the first time. The *Irish News* reported their comment:

'They came to Westminster at the request of the people of their constituency with the object of doing everything in their power to forward the claims of the Irish people for the unity and sovereignty of the Irish nation, unnaturally divided twenty years ago by the British government ... We believe in the present changed political circumstances in Britain our policy can best be served by attendance'[4].

But to be effective the Nationalists needed a strong united organisation, inside and outside parliament. Early in November 1945 two of the new Stormont MPs, Eddie McAteer – a brother of Hugh McAteer, the former IRA chief of staff – and Malachy Conlon (South Armagh), invited all 'nationally minded' groups and public representatives to a conference in Dungannon on 15 November. Harry Diamond refused to go because they hadn't invited the Socialist Republican Party and the Ulster Union Club – both of which had had a substantial Protestant membership – and denounced the convention as a 'sectarian manoeuvre'.

It went ahead however, attended by all the Nationalist MPs and Senators, including McGurk the former Independent Nationalist in Mid-Tyrone, and by about 500 delegates and local councillors. The chair was taken by James McSparran, a prominent Catholic barrister with interests in the *Irish News*, who had been elected MP for Mourne. The Catholic emphasis was underlined, not only by the absence of the Ulster Union Club and the Socialist Republicans, but by the presence of a large number of priests and by messages of support from the bishops of Derry and Dromore.

The convention decided unanimously to set up 'a new organisation called the Irish Anti-Partition League with the object of uniting all those opposed to partition into a solid block'[5]. McSparran was elected chairman and Malachy Conlon MP as full-time secretary. An executive was elected, consisting of all the MPs and Senators and three representatives of each county plus Belfast and Derry City. Resolutions were passed condemning gerrymandering and demanding the release of all internees and political prisoners.

The new organisation represented the Catholic small businessmen, farmers and professional classes, and its support was predominantly rural. Of the fifteen MPs and Senators five were lawyers; four were publicans, insurance agents or similar; three were farmers; and two were editors of Nationalist newspapers. There was one company director and no industrial or manual workers. The composition of the convention delegates was much the same. A collection at the conference brought in £1,000.

The Anti-Partition League got down to business quickly, trying to establish the first real Nationalist Party organisation since Devlin's National League. They opened an office in Belfast and began to establish branches round the North. The combination of a united movement with some sense of direction for the first time in nearly twenty years, and the hope that the Labour government in Britain would mean a change of policy towards the North, generated quite a high level of enthusiasm. Meetings and rallies were held throughout the six counties; an Anti-Partition Association was set up among the Irish in England to influence the Westminster government on its own doorstep; and interest was reawakened in the United States. A series of meetings was held in the South as well, and the Nationalist MPs and Senators were kept busy speaking in Ireland, England and America.

But the League, or APL, had its teething troubles. After the frustrations of the war years it was a considerable triumph in itself to unite the different sections of the (Catholic) Nationalist movement: the old Redmondites such as T.J.Campbell and T.S.McAllister; the more militant Fianna Fail supporters such as Healy, McAteer and Conlon; and even some former Republicans such as Jack McNally, who had been interned during the war and was to become an APL Senator. But this was a superficial unity without basic agreement on tactics. A fortnight after the Dungannon convention, T.J.Campbell MP was appointed a county court judge. He didn't consult the APL about accepting. To many Nationalists to accept such a post at all was to condone and collaborate with the Northern state; and to accept it at a time when there were still Republicans interned and large numbers of political prisoners serving sentences was tantamount to treason. Most APL members were indignant, but the executive took no action. They were not prepared to enforce a unified policy – an unwillingness that would create problems later on. Peter Murney, the MP for South Down, withdrew from the parliamentary party in protest at their lack of action.

The Campbell case subsequently brought out into the open a further weakness in the APL. Campbell resigned his Stormont seat of Belfast Central, but it was seven months before his colleagues moved the writ for the by-election, and even then they didn't contest it. For the APL was a rural, clergy-dominated organisation which, while verbally militant about partition, was intensely conservative about social issues. They had no appeal to the Belfast working class and after the Falls result in 1945 they didn't want another humiliation. So the Nationalists abandoned their last seat in Belfast without a fight. Ironically the contest for it was between a constitutionalist Catholic member of the Labour Party, Frank Hanna, and a Protestant Socialist Republican, Victor Halley. Hanna won[6].

Inside Stormont the Nationalists were fairly active however and had the support of Diamond, Beattie and two official Labour MPs for protests about internment, political prisoners and the Special Powers Act. They also raised the question of Catholic schools, of course, and McSparran made absolutely clear who they spoke for: 'We have a different concept of education probably from those who differ from us in religion ... our concept of education has been expressed by the Pope in an encyclical'[7].

They had as little success as before the war. When the Labour government brought in 'one man one vote' for local elections in Britain – a measure which would seriously have upset the delicate gerrymandering of Derry City and other local authorities in the border areas – the Unionist government actually restricted the franchise further in Northern Ireland, and the Chief Whip Major L.E.Curran, made his remark about disenfranchising the government's[8] opponents. Almost the entire Stormont opposition fought the Local Government Bill early in 1946, and the Labour Party sent a delegation to Westminster to protest, but to no avail.

Sir Basil Brooke, the Prime Minister, made no conciliatory gestures. In February 1947, speaking at a meeting of the City of Derry and Foyle Unionist Association, he praised a fund set up by them to prevent Catholics buying Protestant-owned property. The *Newsletter* reported:

'The Prime Minister said that there was for the past ten years a similar fund in Fermanagh which had worked well and had saved many Loyalist farms. They in Londonderry could do similar work by their trust fund'[9].

Questioned at Stormont he refused to retract in any way. A couple of months later an extremist Church of Ireland rector, Rev Godfrey McManaway, was selected as the official Unionist candidate for a by-election in Derry City and elected, while other backbenchers continued to make virulently sectarian speeches.

Inevitably disillusion with attendance at Stormont began to set in again. Maxwell, MP for Foyle, didn't attend after 1946, while his colleagues became much less active. They were also growing disillusioned with the Labour government for refusing to intervene in Northern affairs, and in September 1947 the APL denounced the Westminster government after Chuter Ede, the British Home Secretary, had refused to discuss the Special Powers Act, gerrymandering and local grievances with an opposition deputation when he visited Belfast.

Two factors however encouraged the APL and kept them at least a little hopeful. One was the formation in 1945 of a group of thirty or so Labour MPs called the 'Friends of Ireland'. One of the most prominent was Geoffrey Bing, a Protestant lawyer from Northern Ireland who had been elected MP for Hornchurch. Most were of Irish extraction and committed to ending the minority's grievances in Northern Ireland and to supporting Irish unity. Ironically, since they were in alliance with the conservative and devoutly Catholic APL, most of the Friends of Ireland were left-wingers and they had the support of the Communist MPs Willie Gallacher and Phil Piratin.

The other encouraging development took place in the South. The Fianna Fail party had for long relied for much of its support on its mildly radical Republican image; but the jailings, internments and executions during the war had made a considerable dent in the image, and in a presidential election in early 1945 Dr Patrick McCartan won a sizeable vote as an Independent Republican[10]. At the end of the war there were still a lot of political prisoners in jail, so a Release the Republican Prisoners Association was set up in late 1945 bringing together a lot of former Republicans and IRA men. Then on 11 May 1946, Sean McCaughey, a Belfast man and former IRA chief of staff, died after 23 days on hunger and thirst strike in Portlaois prison. It was only after his death that the details of the Fianna Fail government's treatment of political prisoners in Portlaois came out: it emerged that because McCaughey and his colleagues had refused to wear prison clothes, they had been kept naked in their cells since 1941. McCaughey had been allowed no visitors in all that time.

This case so shocked many Fianna Fail supporters that when two months later a new party was launched called Clann na Poblachta, it threatened to transform party politics in the South. It was led by Sean McBride, the lawyer for McCaughey's next of kin and defence counsel in many Republican cases, son of one of the men executed after the 1916 Rising, and a former IRA chief of staff himself. Clann na Poblachta was a newer version of Fianna Fail, flamboyant, verbally militant about partition but unconnected with physical force. Its social policies were vague but radical. A populist organisation, it tried to tap the latent Republicanism and social discontent of the Southern working class and small farmers after years of war-time stagnation. It caught the mood of the times and attracted a highly diverse membership, including an intense young doctor and social reformer called Noel Browne. After fourteen years of Fianna Fail government it generated so much energy and enthusiasm that in October 1947 it won two by-elections, putting McBride and one of his colleagues in the Dail.

Alarmed by the threat to Fianna Fail, De Valera called an election in February 1948 in an attempt to minimise the damage and stop Clann na Poblachta before it became too powerful. He was only partly successful. Clann na Poblachta won ten seats – mostly from Fianna Fail. It was less than they had hoped for but enough to tip the balance in the Dail. Fianna Fail had

68 seats, the combined opposition 78. In a truly extraordinary parliamentary deal, Clann na Poblachta agreed to form a Coalition government with the Southern Labour Party and the conservative anti-Republican Fine Gael Party – the government party during the civil war and the party which had toyed with fascism and General O'Duffy's Blueshirts in the 1930s. John A. Costello of Fine Gael became Taoiseach (Premier), McBride became Minister for External Affairs and Noel Browne, Minister for Health.

The rise of Clann na Poblachta, however contradictory its political position, was a boost to the Northern Nationalists. From the beginning the new party had stressed the partition issue and promised to launch an international campaign over it, and they were pledged to declaring the South a Republic. Their arrival in the Dublin government came just when Nationalist parliamentary strategy seemed exhausted in the North. Their first actions were encouraging: they quickly released the remaining Republican prisoners and attempted to raise the partition issue at the Council of Europe. They tried to give Northern Nationalists some voice in Southern affairs by appointing Denis Ireland of the Ulster Union Club to the Seanad (the Southern Senate), and Dr Eileen Hickey, an Independent Nationalist MP for Queen's University, to the National Health Council in the South.

Meanwhile De Valera, his 'Republicanism' successfully challenged and his government out of office for the first time in sixteen years, went on a speaking tour of the US, Australia, and New Zealand attacking partition, in an attempt to rehabilitate Fianna Fail. Clann na Poblachta was not to be outdone and after some pressure the Taoiseach announced in Canada on 7 September 1948 that his government intended to declare the South a Republic and take it out of the Commonwealth. It was assumed in the North by Unionists and Nationalists alike that this would be followed by a major effort to end partition.

The Unionists reacted sharply. Brooke went on a speaking tour of England to defend the Unionist position, and Stormont put pressure on the Westminster government to back them up. On 28 October Attlee, the British Premier, said at Westminster: 'The view of His Majesty's government in the United Kingdom has always been that no change should be made in the constitutional status of Northern Ireland without Northern Ireland's free agreement'[11]. Brooke saw Attlee in London in November and again in January 1949 to discuss the situation. In the meantime the Dail discussed and passed the Republic of Ireland Bill at the end of December

1948. Inevitably there would be consequential legislation at Westminster and partition would be attacked. To strengthen the Unionist position Brooke called a general election for 10 February 1949.

The election would be tantamount to a referendum on the border. Brooke made sure of that when he announced it: 'We are going to the country on one question and one question only: whether this country is as determined as it was in the past to remain part of the United Kingdom'[12]; and again in his manifesto on 23 January, when he said:

'Our country is in danger ... today we fight to defend our very existence and the heritage of our Ulster children. The British government have agreed to abide by the decision of the Ulster people. It is therefore imperative that our determination to remain under the Union Jack should be immediately and overwhelmingly re-affirmed ... "No Surrender, We are King's men" '[13].

In the South, there was now an intense conflict between Fianna Fail and the Coalition government as to who were the better Republicans, and the Northern election presented the government with a golden opportunity. Under Clann na Poblachta pressure Costello summoned the leaders of the parties in the Dail to a conference in the Mansion House in Dublin on 27 January. It was attended by De Valera for Fianna Fail, General Mulcahy for Fine Gael, William Norton of the Irish Labour Party, Sean McBride and the Lord Mayor of Dublin. They agreed unanimously to establish 'an anti-partition fund to be created by subscriptions and the holding of a national collection in all parishes on Sunday next'[14]. The money would be used to finance anti-partitionist candidates in the elections in the North.

The Southern parties had given no thought to the effect in the North. The collection was taken up at church gates all over the South on Sunday 30 January and brought in about £46,000. Church gate collections are normal procedure for all parties in the South, and this one was taken up outside Protestant as well as Catholic churches – in fact a number of Protestant clergy of Northern origin objected – but inevitably the bulk of the money came from outside Catholic churches. Unionist spokesmen denounced the fund as an attempt by the Catholic Church to win control of the North, and consequently abused their opponents in the election as hired agents of the Vatican or Maynooth (the headquarters of the Irish hierarchy). It made the election bitterly sectarian and won the Unionists thousands of extra votes. The contest became known as the 'Chapel Gates election'.

Northern anti-partitionists had not even been consulted about the Mansion House conference, which seems to have had more to do with the Southern parties' attempts to out-Republican each other than with any real concern about the North. The Northern Nationalists were by no means all in favour of the fund: the *Irish Times* quoted one, unnamed, as saying 'the decision to float the fund is mis-judged, mis-timed and mis-directed'[15]. The *Manchester Guardian* commented:

'What the Zinoviev letter did for the English Tories in 1924, the anti-partition fund can be made to do for the Orangemen in 1949. If Mr Costello's countrymen really want to see the end of the partition of Ireland, they are going the longest way about it'[16].

The effect of the fund was to unite and solidify the Unionist camp. A long-standing dispute between the government and the Protestant churches over education was put aside and a number of dissident Unionists who had been going to contest the election withdrew. It also papered over the divisions on the anti-Unionist side. Anti-partition Labour candidates had intended to challenge the conservative APL in South Down and Derry, but they withdrew as well. The Mansion House Committee sent a four-man team to Belfast who worked hard to secure a single agreed anti-partition candidate in each constituency: they had a powerful argument in that they could offer £300 apiece to candidates they endorsed.

The Anti-Partition League nominated a record seventeen candidates, all outside Belfast. They contested every seat in Counties Tyrone and Fermanagh, and a number of others which had large Catholic minorities. The Unionists in turn contested some traditionally Nationalist seats. There were five anti-partition Labour candidates, all in Belfast, and two of them, Diamond and Hanna, were elected unopposed. There were ten pro-partition official Labour candidates, but even so 20 of the 48 constituencies were unopposed.

The APL manifesto focussed on partition and the treatment of the minority:

'The outstanding issue in Irish politics today is whether 65 per cent of the people in the six north-eastern counties of the nation's 32 can defy the will of the nation . . . no election or plebiscite in these six counties can justify partition not even if it were a valid and free election instead of being, as this is, a spurious and fraudulent one . . . . The large minority in this area have been denied almost all the rights which free men enjoy in every free country. In this area the 35 per cent minority holds less than

seven per cent of the public positions. In the 26-county area in comparison a six per cent minority [the Southern Protestants] **holds over 35 per cent of public appointments'**[17].

And, answering criticism that the League had been ineffective, McSparran the leader was quoted by the *Irish News*:

'Some people said that the anti-partition movement had not made great progress. That was not fair to those who worked to end partition. Until the anti-partition party came into parliament, it was a subject hardly ever mentioned. Through their efforts and the co-operation of the people the position was now that partition was not merely a national but an international question and the matter had been taken up, not merely in their own country, but was of lively interest to the people in the United States and the colonies'[18].

It was a turbulent contest. Already a Westminster by-election in Co.Armagh the previous year had produced ugly incidents with Nationalist agents being attacked and B Specials celebrating the Unionist victory by firing volleys in the air. On 1 February Jack Beattie, who was standing as anti-partition Labour, and had got money from the Mansion House Fund, tried to hold a meeting in Templemore Avenue in East Belfast. Several thousand Loyalists stoned him and broke up the meeting. He had to leave the area in a police car, though the RUC had done little to protect him earlier. Beattie went to London the next day to see Attlee and demand protection for anti-Unionist candidates. The Unionists were unconcerned. Lord Glentoran, later Minister for Commerce, seemed to encourage further violence with his comment that it was only natural 'to expect excitement in Ballymacarrett where Mr Beattie was born and bred and where he has now turned his back on his own people and his own king'[19].

The next night the anti-partition Labour candidate in Cromac had a meeting in Havelock Street broken up by Loyalists. The British Home Secretary told Beattie he had no power to intervene in Northern Ireland, and when Beattie and Willie Gallacher MP tried to raise it at Westminster they were ruled out of order.

The violence continued. Smoke-bombs and fireworks as well as three Orange bands were used to break up an anti-partition meeting in Garvagh in Co.Derry and the candidate and agent had to take refuge in the RUC barracks. Beattie wore a steel helmet at meetings but he was effectively confined to the Catholic Short Strand.

Even the official Labour Party, despite strenuous efforts to prove their loyalty, ran into trouble. Alderman W.J.Leeburn, the Labour candidate for Willowfield, declared that 'he took second place to no man in his allegiance to Ulster's constitutional position. He had fought for that cause in his own time and his family had fought in theirs'[20]. But he was shouted down just the same. The Labour candidate in Antrim had to abandon all public meetings after being stoned off several platforms. It was the most violent election campaign since 1921 and there was widespread intimidation.

The Unionists went all out to create sectarian hysteria. Harry Midgley, who was now a member of the Unionist Party, denounced 'the twin evils of Republicanism and Communism'[21]. Colonel Hall-Thompson, the Minister for Education, rode round his constituency on a white horse to imitate William of Orange, and brandished a blackthorn stick belonging to Edward Carson. Carson's widow and son, the Hon.Edward Carson, a British Tory MP, were brought over from England and the Hon.Edward beat a Lambeg drum[22] at the final Unionist rally in the Ulster Hall. Brooke's last appeal to the electorate was: 'I ask you to cross the Boyne . . . with me as your leader and to fight for the same cause as King William fought for in days gone by'[23].

Even Attlee, who was not sympathetic to the anti-partitionists, was disturbed by the violence. When a Unionist MP asked him at Westminster about Nationalist disturbances in Strabane, he replied, 'I have not had information of that incident but I have had news of quite a number of incidents in Northern Ireland which show that elections there are not conducted on quite the same lines as we have over here'[24]. And some two hundred Labour MPs signed a motion at Westminster calling for the suspension of all elections in Northern Ireland until they could be held in free and democratic conditions. It was never debated however.

The result was a foregone conclusion. The Unionists got 234,202 votes, the Anti-Partition League and Anti-Partition Labour 106,459 and the Labour Party 26,831. The Unionists gained three seats, the APL held their nine, Anti-Partition Labour got two and Beattie and the two official Labour MPs were defeated.

One significant side-effect of this election was that for the first time since 1925 the effective opposition at Stormont was entirely Catholic. Sir Basil Brooke could congratulate himself. Not only had the election demonstrated that the Unionists had a solid majority in the six-county area, but they had routed the Labour challenge more decisively and completely than ever before. All the Labour candidates had been heavily defeated, three of them by more than ten thousand votes.

The anti-partitionists' only consolation was that they had won a majority in Counties Fermanagh and Tyrone. In Fermanagh the APL got 15,482 votes to the Unionists' 13,895, and in Tyrone the APL got 35,773 to 32,408 for the Unionists. They also won a moral victory in Derry City where the Unionists held the City seat by 3,359 and didn't contest the Foyle seat where there was a massive Nationalist majority. The border counties and Derry were still against the Union.

The election ended with another burst of rioting. The RUC baton-charged a Nationalist victory parade in Newry. And when Brian Faulkner, the new MP for East Down, led a Unionist victory parade through the Catholic town of Downpatrick they baton-charged Catholic protestors and there was a fierce riot. There was trouble as well in Castlederg in Tyrone and Keady in South Armagh.

The election had served its purpose however. Fortified with this mandate Brooke could demand that the Westminster government guarantee the position of Northern Ireland, when they were proposing legislation consequential on the South leaving the Commonwealth. On 3 May 1949 the Labour government introduced the Ireland Bill. Most of it concerned Britain's relations with the South and the status of citizens of the Irish Republic in Britain, but clause 1(1)B read:

'Parliament hereby declares that Northern Ireland remains part of His Majesty's Dominions and of the United Kingdom and affirms that in no event will Northern Ireland or any part thereof cease to be part of His Majesty's Dominions and of the United Kingdom without the consent ot the Parliament of Northern Ireland'.

It was, if anything, a strengthening of the original Government of Ireland Act.

Beattie proposed an amendment to deny the Bill a second reading. It was seconded by Anthony Mulvey of the APL and backed by Hugh Delargey and other members of the Friends of Ireland group, Neil McLean and John McGovern of the ILP and Gallacher and Phil Piratin of the Communist Party. It was defeated by 317 to fourteen. A number of other amendments were proposed at the committee stage but even the most moderate one – to substitute 'without the consent of the people of Northern Ireland' for 'without the consent of the parliament' – was defeated by 314 to 56. The Bill was passed and had received the Royal Assent by 2 June.

The most immediate effect of the declaration of the Republic and the anti-partition campaign had been to reinforce and strengthen partition and to confirm the Unionists' hold over the Protestant population in the North. It had been inevitable. Any election fought solely on the partition issue in the North was bound to reproduce the Unionist majority of 1918 or 1921, even without the 'Chapel Gates' collection. As for the international campaign, moral force alone was unlikely to persuade Britain to renounce an area where she had considerable investments, whose strategic importance had been graphically demonstrated during the war, a majority of whose population would oppose any hand-over to the South, and which had close ties with the British military and political establishments. The anti-partitionists' only weapon was moral force and they quickly discovered, like Nationalists before and since in other corners of the Empire, that Labour governments in Britain were little different from Conservative ones as far as colonial policies were concerned.

In the meantime moreover, another aspect of the Labour government's policies was being implemented in the North which would eventually strengthen the link with Britain. The government implemented the war-time Beveridge Report on the Social Services, bringing in a comprehensive National Health Service and social insurance scheme. The war-time Coalition at Westminster had already provided for free secondary education for all, and university scholarships based on merit. The Ulster Unionists at Westminster had voted solidly against the welfare state proposals but, anxious not to provoke a constitutional clash with Britain or create a major social and administrative gap between the North and the rest of the UK, and concerned not to strain the patience of their working-class supporters too far, Stormont adopted a policy of parity with social services in Britain. Since the North was poorer than any British region Westminster agreed in two social services agreements, signed in 1946 and 1948, to subsidise the cost of maintaining parity.

Between 1945 and 1950 a series of bills at Stormont parallel to those at Westminster established the basis of free, comprehensive, health and education services and a greatly improved social insurance scheme, all heavily subsidised by Britain. The Unionists quickly claimed credit for what they had initially opposed, and by the late 1950s a substantial social services gap had opened between the North and the South which helped cement the loyalty of the Protestant population and was to make many Catholics rethink their outright opposition to partition.

The anti-partition campaign had had a traumatic effect on the Labour movement in the North, and in the long run was to lead to its disintegration. Though they had failed to make a breakthrough during the Andrews crisis and had lost Midgley and Beattie (again) the Labour Party and even the Communist Party had grown steadily during the war: Labour participation in the war-time Coalition government in Britain had won them prestige and respect, and the alliance with Russia and the temporary cessation of anti-communist propaganda had buried the red scare for a while.

In the 1945 Stormont election Labour nominated a record fifteen candidates and the Communist Party three. There were three anti-partition Labour candidates including Beattie and two Socialist Republicans – one, David Wylie, a Protestant on leave from the RAF. Harry Midgley's Commonwealth Labour Party, the pro-Unionist group he formed when he left the Labour Party in 1943, put up six candidates, though the chairman and vice-chairman resigned and worked for the official Labour Party. Midgley himself had resigned from the cabinet when the war in Europe ended as there was no longer any argument for a 'coalition' government and his position was untenable.

The Labour candidates polled well, they got 66,053 votes, but they won only two seats, Dock and Oldpark, in Belfast and they lost South Armagh. Oldpark was new ground for Labour, but, like Dock and Pottinger, it had a sizeable Catholic minority in Ardoyne and the Bone. Labour had still failed to win any solidly Protestant seats. The three Communists did remarkably well, getting 12,456 votes, but they had discreetly abandoned their anti-partitionism and taken up a more pro-Unionist position than the Labour Party, calling for a united front with the Midgley supporters while Labour was standing against them. Midgley himself was re-elected, but none of his supporters got in. Beattie was re-elected in Pottinger and Harry Diamond as Socialist Republican in Falls. A year later Labour won the Belfast Central seat in a by-election.

Labour nominated five candidates in the 1945 Westminster election as well. They did well in North and East Belfast and won another 65,000 votes but didn't seriously shake any of the Unionists.

The Labour success in Britain encouraged the local party and kept the Labour revival going for a while. In 1946 they won eight seats on Belfast Corporation and won control of Warrenpoint and Newry Urban Councils.

The party chairman, Jack Magougan, was in a confident and determined mood at the 1946 conference:

'The past year has seen the further decline of the once powerful Nationalist Party. Its degeneration into a narrow sectarian organisation had been in progress for a number of years but as far as Belfast was concerned it was a spent force . . . We oppose the Unionist Party on every aspect of its political philosophy but realise that it is a powerful force. On a sectarian basis it has a permanent majority and it is only through the building of an organisation on a broad basis that we can hope to create the machine essential for its overthrow'[25].

There was considerable industrial militancy in the North at the time and it met with the usual response from the authorities. In March 1946 there was a strike at Dunbar and McMasters' mill in the tiny Armagh village of Gilford over the refusal of a few workers to join the union. Nine non-union members blacklegged and kept the factory open. After three weeks the strike grew violent and pickets attacked the blacklegs leaving the mill. Eventually the RUC had to take them out in police tenders. On the next few nights windows were broken in the blacklegs' homes and on the night of 10 April as the strikers paraded round the town the RUC blocked both ends of the narrow main street and then attacked the parade, baton-charging repeatedly from both ends of the street.

In December 1947 there was a three-week strike by 5,000 men in Shorts' aircraft factory over the dismissal of the chairman and secretary of the Works Committee, Andy Barr, a Communist, and Andy Holmes, a left-wing Labour Party member. They were re-instated. But by now both unions and shop stewards were keeping strikes determinedly non-political. The Communist Party secured a dominant position on the shop-floor and in some of the unions but it was never reflected in its political support, even though the party avoided the constitutional issue and adopted different tactics in the North and South.[26]

Midgley and his Commonwealth Labour Party soon ceased to confuse the Labour scene. Midgley had been becoming steadily more Unionist and in October 1945 he had physically attacked Beattie at Stormont and had been suspended. In May 1946 when the local Labour Party nominated a young left-wing member of the British Labour Party, Desmond Donnelly[27], for a Westminster by-election in Co. Down, the Commonwealth Labour Party backed the Unionist candidate. Finally in

September 1947 Midgley wrote to Brooke applying to join the Unionist Party saying:

> 'For some time past I have been greatly perturbed by the repeated attacks being made on Ulster's constitutional position ... I have now reached the conclusion that there is no room for division among those ... who are anxious to preserve the constitutional life and spiritual heritage of our people'[28].

He hadn't consulted his own party and they condemned him bitterly but they soon faded out of existence.

Midgley was readily accepted by the Unionists and he later played a major role in the 1949 election, attacking his old colleagues in the Labour Party. He was rewarded with the post of Minister for Labour in 1949 and joined the Orange Order and the Apprentice Boys.

The Labour Party had been ambiguous about the constitutional position in the 1945 elections, but a growing left wing, an influx of Catholic members and sheer pressure of events pushed them steadily towards a more anti-Unionist and then anti-partitionist stance. In May 1946 a Joint Committee of the Northern and Southern Labour Parties was established at a meeting in Dublin. In October 1946 the party conference called for the repeal of the Special Powers Act and the disbanding of the B Specials, while its MPs were already co-operating with the rest of the opposition in calling for an end to internment, the release of political prisoners and an enquiry into gerrymandering. The activities of the Friends of Ireland group at Westminster also rubbed off on them.

The election of the Coalition government in the South with its anti-partition policy and a Labour Tanaiste or Deputy Prime Minister inevitably affected the Northern party as well, and a number of Presbyterian members of the party, notably Jack Magougan and Harold Binks, were prominently involved in a committee organising the commemoration of the 150th anniversary of the 1798 Rebellion.

At the party's 1948 conference in September the fraternal delegate from the Irish Labour Party, Roddy Connolly TD, removed any ambiguity about their position:

> 'We in the South are unrepentant anti-partitionists. So long as the north-east corner is governed by a Tory gang we will feel that our liberties are endangered. The Labour movement in Great Britain, the South of Ireland and the North of Ireland are agreed that we should get rid of the border and have a united Ireland. I hope the time will soon come when we

in the South will be marching hand in hand with the Labour men of the North to take over a free Ireland for the Labour Party'[29].

Bob Getgood, MP for Oldpark, replying said 'they had a common objective and that was to see a socialist Ireland established'[30].

But there was a backlash coming. At the same conference two British based unions, the ATGWU and the shop-workers' union, USDAW, proposed a resolution barring all outside speakers from Labour Party meetings without the express permission of the executive. It was aimed at the Friends of Ireland group, but a delegate from Derry pointed to the real implications: 'Partition is what the Northern Ireland Labour Party is afraid of, not Geoffrey Bing'[31]. The resolution was carried by 183 to 96 on the card vote of the big unions. The party's ambiguity on the border issue had enabled them to win many basically Unionist supporters during the war, while the membership of the affiliated trade unions was overwhelmingly Unionist in attitude. Now both were beginning to react against the anti-partitionist swing by the party activists.

After that events moved fast, with the Republic of Ireland Bill in the Dail, Brooke's campaign in England and Attlee's support for the North's constitution.

The West Belfast branch of the party called a rank and file conference in November 1948 to protest about the ban on speakers and to campaign for the selection of candidates pledged to work for a united socialist Ireland in the coming Stormont elections. They also protested against the appointment of a British Labour Party official as a full-time organiser for the Northern party, paid for by Transport House. They saw this as a move to strengthen links with the British Labour movement instead of the Southern one. The pro-constitution party executive, heavily weighted with trade union representatives, promptly expelled West Belfast who then set up an Irish Labour Association opposed to partition.

The party executive, desperate to prove their loyalty to the constitution in the hysterical atmosphere at the end of 1948, requested a meeting with Morgan Phillips, General Secretary of the British Labour Party, to discuss affiliating to the British party as a local section[32]. It was an attempt to manoeuvre the party into a partitionist stance without a formal decision. Once part of the British party they could claim Attlee's declaration on the constitution as their own and point to their links with London as proof that their loyalty lay with Britain and not the South. Bob Getgood MP, the party chairman, and Joe Corrigan, the secretary, resigned in protest and the Irish Labour Party in the South warned that if the merger went through they would organise in the North in competition.

The meeting with Phillips took place but was inconclusive. The British Labour Party wasn't enthusiastic. But by then it was too late. The Attlee declaration, the merger proposal, and the obvious determination of the executive to back the constitution were too much for most of the leftist and anti-partitionist members. In January 1949 Roddy Connolly and Senator Luke Duffy, the secretary of the Southern Labour Party, met dissident members of the Northern party from Belfast, Derry, Armagh, Fermanagh and South Down who agreed to form a Northern section of the Irish Labour Party. A provisional committee was established but progress was interrupted by the 1949 election. Two ex-Labour Party members, Frank Hanna in Central and O.J.Keane in Clifton, stood as Independent Labour however.

On 31 January the official party stated their position on partition:

'The Northern Ireland Labour Party, being a democratic party, accepts the constitutional position of Northern Ireland and the close association with Britain and the Commonwealth. Furthermore we are not seeking any mandate to change it'[33].

During the election they went to extraordinary lengths to prove their loyalty. David Bleakley, the young candidate for Victoria, was presented with red, white and blue rosettes and declared that he was 'as British as any Unionist and was proud to be a citizen of the Commonwealth'[34].

It didn't do much good. They put up eight candidates, lost all three seats they had held and won only 26,831 votes compared with 66,053 in 1945.

After the election the break-up continued. The official party, now called the Northern Ireland Labour Party (NILP) held a special delegate conference on 8 April 1949. It passed the following motion:

'The NILP will maintain unbroken the connection between Great Britain and Northern Ireland as a part of the Commonwealth and to implement this hereby instructs the executive to proceed at once to take all necessary steps to seek the closest possible means of co-operation with the British Labour Party'[35].

The voting was 20,000 for and 700 against. The opposition had almost all gone. The NILP was now an uncontestably partitionist party. They had no MPs at Stormont or Westminster and soon lost all but one seat on Belfast Corporation. But they had trade union affiliations, trade union money and help from the British party. They kept going in the hope that their new position on the constitution would enable them to make a breakthrough among the Protestant working class.

Meanwhile the dissidents were negotiating with the Irish Labour Party and the other anti-partitionist Labour groups. On 4 April 1949 members of the Socialist Republican Party, the Irish Labour Association, supporters of Jack Beattie, and ex-members of the NILP agreed to merge into the Irish Labour Party (IrLP) and elected a temporary committee. The officers were: chairman: Harry Diamond MP (Socialist Republican), vice-chairman: Frank Hanna MP (ex-NILP), secretary: Jack Magougan (ex-NILP) and treasurer: Jack Beattie – still a Westminster MP though he had lost his Stormont seat.

The new group was unique in Northern politics in that it was firmly anti-partitionist yet had a substantial Protestant membership. Most of the left wing of the NILP joined it and in the 1949 local elections they won all seven seats for Falls and Smithfield wards in Belfast and controlled the Warrenpoint and Newry Councils where the entire NILP branches had gone over to the IrLP.

For a while the IrLP was very active and it figured in some spectacular developments in West Belfast. In the 1950 Westminster election they nominated Beattie again. It was a heated contest, a repeat of the 1949 election, and the Unionists nominated the Rev Godfrey McManaway, Stormont MP for Derry City whose stridently sectarian speeches pushed the Unionist vote up by 7,000 and ousted Beattie[36]. But when McManaway took his seat Geoffrey Bing of the Friends of Ireland Group challenged his right to sit and one of Bing's associates took a common informer action against him, based on the Clergy Disqualification Act of 1801, which debarred Anglican clergymen from sitting in the Commons. The issue was referred to the Judicial Committee of the Privy Council.

The Attorney General warned McManaway not to speak or vote in parliament until the committee reported, but he insisted on voting against the Labour government with its tiny majority in the crucial vote on nationalising the steel industry. In October 1950 the Privy Council ruled that McManaway was ineligible to sit and he was allowed to make his first and only speech explaining his position before parliament declared his seat vacant. Herbert Morrison, the Home Secretary, commented, 'It might be held that his action in sitting and voting in a crucial division which might have had serious constitutional consequences was irresponsible, provocative, and undemocratic' but the Tories backed him strongly and he was indemnified against any penalties. The Nationalists promptly queried McManaway's eligibility for the Stormont parliament as well and he resigned in January 1951 to forestall a further enquiry into his position.

There was a by-election in West Belfast in November 1950 and McManaway had a worthy successor in Tom Teevan, a young law lecturer from Co.Derry who was also noted for his violent sectarianism[37]. It was another heated campaign and Teevan won by 31,196 to Beattie's 30,883 – a margin of 913. But the story wasn't over yet. There was another Westminster election in October 1951 and Beattie and Teevan stood again. This time Beattie won by 33,174 to 33,149, a margin of 25.

The whole saga of the break-up of the Labour Party over the partition issue had shown once again, as in 1920 and 1935 though on a smaller scale, how easily a fragile working-class unity built up on social and economic issues, but ignoring, or ambiguous about, the constitutional question, could be fragmented when the basic issue of the existence of the state came to the fore. The bulk of the Protestant members of the Labour Party retreated towards the Unionist camp, the bulk of their former supporters at the polls deserted them completely and fled into the Unionist camp. As before a small but significant group of Protestant radicals went the whole way and joined the anti-partitionist ranks but, just as the events which decided them were not as dramatic as those of 1919 or 1932-33, so they didn't go as far and they became neither Republicans nor Communists, but left-wing members of the Irish Labour Party. Meanwhile the mass of the Protestant workers had had their loyalty cemented to a Unionist government which even at the close of 1949 contained four landowners and four substantial company directors out of fourteen members, with only one token former worker.

After the 1949 election most of the Nationalists went back to Stormont but Paddy Maxwell, the MP for Foyle, didn't attend again and the rest of his colleagues weren't very active. The Unionists were in an intransigent mood. A row had been brewing over education since 1945, when the Protestant churches had protested against an attempt in a new Education Act to restrict their power to insist on the appointment of Protestant teachers to state schools. They suspended their agitation in the interests of Unionist unity during the 1949 election, but when Hall-Thompson, the Minister for Education, proposed to increase state grants to voluntary (mainly Catholic) schools, from 50 per cent to 65 per cent and to pay the insurance contributions of teachers in these schools, it was too much. Hall-Thompson was forced to resign in December 1949 by pressure from the Orange Order and Unionist back-benchers. Faced with attitudes like these, the APL members quickly grew frustrated again and when the Unionists commented on the absence of Malachy Conlon MP, the APL secretary, Cahir Healy replied:

'He has spoken here and he hasn't had much success. If Hon.Members would pay more attention to what is said by the large minority probably their members would have more confidence about coming here. I do not see any use in the Hon.Member for South Armagh wasting time and energy doing something which is of no value whatsoever. This House is not going to determine when partition will end. The Irish people and Westminster will determine that question and when that hour comes they will not give a tinker's curse what you think about it'[38].

Healy indicated the way the APL was thinking. Members concentrated their energies on extra-parliamentary activities and launched a series of meetings in Britain with the Friends of Ireland Group while the Ireland Act was being discussed. In the South the Mansion House Committee stayed in existence and used the surplus from the 'Chapel Gates' collection to finance a series of pamphlets on partition, gerrymandering and discrimination in the six counties.

In November 1949 the Dublin government established an Irish news agency[39] to spread anti-partition and anti-Unionist propaganda abroad. In December Malachy Conlon and Senator Gerry Lennon of the APL and Tom Barry, a veteran of the War of Independence, toured the US where a boycott of Northern goods was being organised. In March 1951 Sean McBride went to the US as well and addressed the House of Representatives while resolutions condemning partition were proposed in both Houses of Congress.

Abstentionist feeling was growing again. Fermanagh and Tyrone had been divided into two constituencies and at the convention for the 1950 Westminster election in Mid-Ulster there was a narrow majority in favour of abstention (83 votes to 78). In Fermanagh-South Tyrone the question was raised but deferred until after the election when another convention voted for abstention.

In May 1950 at the annual conference of the APL there was a motion calling for abstention from Stormont. It was defeated by 89 votes to 32 but there was clearly an undercurrent of abstentionist thinking in the party. In December, following the death of Conlon, there was a by-election for South Armagh and the local convention selected Charles McGleenan to stand as an abstentionist in defiance of the official policy. The APL executive made no effort to intervene and McGleenan defeated an Irish Labour candidate. Meanwhile Anthony Mulvey, the MP for Mid-Ulster, had decided to return to Westminster because of the Labour government's narrow majority and to support Geoffrey Bing's efforts to amend the Ireland Act to provide safeguards against discrimination and gerrymandering. The Anti-Partition League seemed to be falling apart. It had no consistent policy and no way of enforcing one if it had. Its MPs decided their own policies without reference to the organisation. It had one MP attending and one abstaining at Westminster and two MPs abstaining and seven attending intermittently at Stormont. After the 1951 Westminster election the two MPs decided to take their seats again though they got an even less sympathetic hearing from Churchill's Tory government.

In March 1951 four APL MPs, McGleenan, Cahir Healy, Joe Connellan (South Down) and E.V.McCullagh (Mid-Tyrone), and two Senators sought admission to the Dail as elected representatives of part of the national territory, but they found the Dublin government's Republican-ism and anti-partitionism didn't extend as far as giving a vote in their parliament to an unpredictable group of Northerners – who could conceivably make or break Southern governments – or to issuing such a direct challenge to Stormont and to Britain. They were refused.

Shortly afterwards the inter-party government collapsed when the Catholic hierarchy in the South vetoed a plan by Dr Noel Browne, the Minister for Health, to introduce a comprehensive health service for mothers and children, and most of Browne's colleagues in the cabinet and Clann na Poblachta deserted him and fell over themselves to show what good Catholics they were. The incident showed that the Catholic Church held as tight a grip on the Southern government as the Protestant churches had on the Northern one, and provided ammunition for Unionist orators for years afterwards.

Meanwhile politics in the North had moved to the streets. Even before the 1949 election Northern Nationalists had begun to organise parades and demonstrations and had been met with government restrictions and bans. In March 1948 Edmond Warnock, the Minister of Home Affairs, had banned an APL StPatrick's Day parade in Derry. The parade was to carry the tricolour, the emblem of the Republican movement and the flag of the Southern state. It was banned under the Special Powers Act and Warnock said at Stormont: 'So long as this government lasts and so long as I am Minister of Home Affairs, I shall not permit the Republican flag to be carried through Derry City ... No Surrender'[40]. The Rev McManaway commented: 'The Minister was perfectly right in suppressing that demonstration for if he had not done so we [the Derry Unionists] would'[41]. The ban and the Minister's capitulation to the threats of the local Loyalists caused deep resentment in the Catholic-majority city, where the Protestant Apprentice Boys were allowed to march every year.

In September 1948 the government banned rallies planned for High Street in the centre of Belfast to commemorate the anniversary of the 1798 Rebellion – Henry Joy McCracken, one of the Protestant leaders of the Rising, had been hanged in High Street – and restricted a commemorative parade to the Falls Road area. Belfast Corporation tried to follow suit by cancelling the Commemoration Committee's booking of the Ulster Hall for a Ceili, but the committee (which had a substantial Protestant membership) took them to court for breach of contract and won.

In February 1950 the Nationalists held a victory parade through Enniskillen after the Westminster election. The RUC baton-charged the crowd and seized the tricolour after fierce fighting. In March a StPatrick's Day parade was banned from Moneymore in Co.Derry and in Aughnacloy in Co.Tyrone the RUC again baton-charged a parade and seized the tricolour. In August, cars, buses and a band going through Cookstown, Co.Tyrone, to a Gaelic football match in Magherafelt were attacked and stoned by a Loyalist crowd and the RUC refused to intervene. On StPatrick's Day 1951 Eddie McAteer MP and a number of APL councillors tried to carry the tricolour in a token march in Derry but the RUC attacked them, seized the flag and arrested three of the councillors. The following day they stopped a parade by a local band even without the tricolour. In May they stopped an Irish Labour Party parade to commemorate James Connolly from carrying the tricolour.

In the meantime the Nationalists had gone to the courts however. In the Cookstown case Tyrone County Court awarded compensation to the band, fined a number of Loyalists including the local commandant of the B Specials for attacking it, and ruled that all citizens were entitled to the protection of the police on the public road. And in April 1951 James McSparran MP successfully challenged the ban on the tricolour in the High Court on a technicality.

The government hurriedly drafted a Public Order Bill requiring 48 hours' notice of all parades other than traditional – i.e. Orange – ones, and giving the government or the RUC power to ban or re-route parades at will if they thought they might lead to a breach of the peace. There was no appeal from a ban or a re-routing order. The opposition denounced the bill but it was rushed through parliament by 3 July 1951.

Eddie McAteer MP declared that 'the immediate duty of the people of Derry is to meet the bill with determined disciplined disobedience'. But the first clashes were in Enniskillen. Even before the bill became law the RUC attacked an AOH parade on 15 August batoning men and women and seizing the tricolour. Later they cut down tricolours from several private houses in the town, including Cahir Healy's. Again the government was responding to pressure from local Loyalists. T.C.Nelson, the Unionist MP for Enniskillen, said 'Had the Minister for Home Affairs refused to forbid the tricolour being carried through Enniskillen then we would have taken steps to see it wasn't carried'[42]. It was no idle boast. A few days later three hundred Loyalists armed with clubs and cudgels prevented a local Catholic band from parading through the village of Tempo near Enniskillen.

The government were intent on taking a tough line. In May 1951 they used the Special Powers Act to intern a number of Republicans during a royal visit to the North. And at the end of 1950 they had established a Reserve or Commando force of 100-150 men inside the RUC. The Commandos were to be a highly-trained, self-contained mobile force which could be used either against the IRA or as a riot squad. In fact it was this squad who were used in most of the tricolour riots. Despite all the criticism of the Stormont government by Labour backbenchers, the Labour government agreed to the RUC Commandos being trained by the British Army at Ballykinlar barracks in Co.Down and supplied with automatic weapons and equipment by the War Office.

The Anti-Partition League had tried working in the Stormont and Westminster parliaments without success; they had launched an international publicity campaign with the same result; they had turned to street demonstrations in the North only to be batoned off the streets. It was inevitable that the thoughts of some sections of the Nationalist population should turn again to physical force. As early as June 1949 Malachy Conlon had hinted at force at a rally in Armagh when he talked of a 'final move to end partition . . . in which every nationalist man or woman, boy or girl, would be called upon, not just to attend meetings and wave flags but to make sacrifices [and] stand the strain which so many generations have stood before'[43], and touring America with Conlon, Tom Barry had advocated that the South should declare war on the North. Early in 1950 Capt. Peadar Cowan, an ex-Clann na Poblachta TD in the South, had talked of raising an army to invade the North. Most of this was just talk, certainly the parliamentarians of the APL had no intention of fighting anybody, but it was symptomatic of the frustration of Northern and Southern Nationalists.

Meanwhile the IRA had been slowly re-organising itself and had decided on another campaign in the North. In May 1951 they established a military council to draw up plans for it, and in June they launched a successful attack on Ebrington military barracks in Derry, getting away with six machine guns, two Bren guns, 20 Sten guns, 20 Lee Enfield rifles and a quantity of ammunition. Once again Unionist intransigence was driving a section of the Nationalist population towards war.

9

The Fifties Campaign

The decade of the 1950s was dominated by the most serious physical force campaign launched against the Northern state since 1922. The collapse of the anti-partition campaign had closed another door on the Northern minority. They had failed to reform the Northern state from within, they had been unable to end its existence by constitutional means. And throughout the 1950s the Unionists seemed determined to drive home the lesson. They repeatedly banned and broke up anti-Unionist rallies and demonstrations, even in solidly Nationalist areas, and then forced Orange parades through Catholic areas.

The result was inevitable. In elections in 1953 and 1955 the minority population, first in Co.Tyrone and then across the North, rejected the parliamentary Nationalists for candidates who supported or were actually involved in the use of physical force. And when the military campaign finally began in 1955 it was not the Southern-based IRA who launched it, but a new Northern organisation born directly out of the frustration of the minority.

The campaign proved better organised and better planned than the war-time one and won a remarkable degree of public support both North and South of the border; but it avoided striking at the North's most vulnerable point, the industrial, commercial and administrative complex of Belfast, and it was conceived in purely military terms with no corresponding political campaign to sustain its public support in face of harassment and repression. Internment and jailings North and South broke the back of the campaign by 1960 but even so 100,000 people still voted Republican in elections in 1959 and 1961 in the two states. The grievances which had provoked the military campaign were still there and when it was formally ended in 1962 the conflict had only been adjourned, not resolved.

The fifties campaign was a rural one. In Belfast the Unionists reigned securely for most of the decade. The Labour Party had been shattered by the partition issue, and the more vigorous and radical Irish Labour Party was forced to retreat into the Catholic ghettos where it was destroyed by Catholic bigotry and ghetto sectarianism. The partitionist rump of the Northern Ireland Labour Party seemed of little consequence. But unemployment was steadily rising, the economy was stagnating and the Brookeborough government seemed quite uncaring. The NILP had now established themselves as solidly loyal on the constitution. In 1958 they suddenly won four seats in a Stormont general election. It was a signal that economics were going to play a more direct part in Northern politics during the coming decade.

The 1951 Public Order Act did not end street politics by the Nationalists. On 17 March 1952 the APL held a rally in the Diamond in the centre of Derry. The RUC didn't intervene and the rally went off quietly, but the crowd then staged an impromptu march, headed by the tricolour. The RUC baton-charged them, seized the flag and arrested two men. A large crowd then beseiged and stoned Victoria RUC Barracks and the RUC made repeated baton-charges in the centre of the city. Two dockers on their way home for lunch were arrested and the entire dock labour force held a lightning strike and marched into the city centre to demand their release. That night there was fierce fighting between the RUC Commandos and youths from the Catholic ghetto of the Bogside. Twenty-two people were treated in hospital for injuries. It was the most violent clash in Derry since the 1920s.

The tough police action in Derry angered an already alienated population and pushed the Nationalists further towards extra-parliamentary agitation. Already Eddie McAteer, now vice chairman of the APL had published a half humorous pamphlet called *Irish Action*, advocating civil disobedience, though he had no intention of going too far:

'Most Irish people who are active in seeking freedom used to believe that it would come to us by force of either constitutional action or by violence. Then the mighty spirit of the late Mahatma Gandhi pointed a third road – non-co-operation, non-violence...

'Nowadays governmental machinery works largely through the agency of myriads of forms which are showered on the helpless citizens ... All such forms should be lost and if needs be – under threat of active compulsion for example – you can cause the department concerned to issue a duplicate ... if it pays you to fill in a form, fill it. If it doesn't, throw the form in the fire. Increased cost and difficulty in administration here will quickly make itself felt in Whitehall. Should it happen that you

have the leisure to go to the department, act stupid, demand explanations, object, anything at all that will clog the departmental machinery'[1].

McAteer and his colleagues went in for symbolic gestures. In February 1952 when the gerrymandered Derry Corporation gave a civic reception to the Governor of Northern Ireland, Lord Wakehurst, McAteer, who was an Alderman on the Corporation, got up and made a speech in Irish during the Governor's address. In May he took the Mayor's seat at a Corporation meeting and refused to leave, claiming that he represented the majority of the people of the city.

During the coronation celebrations of Elizabeth II, the nine Nationalist MPs at Stormont, Harry Diamond MP, the five Nationalist Senators and the two Westminster MPs, issued a proclamation of their own repudiating her authority and had it posted on walls in Nationalist areas:

'Whereas we, the undersigned, are the elected representatives of the greater portion of Ireland over which the British Crown and Government claim sovereignty and jurisdiction . . . and whereas Queen Elizabeth of England has been crowned with the title of Queen of Northern Ireland . . . now we, in the name of the people we represent . . . hereby repudiate all claims now made or to be made in the future by or on behalf of the British Crown and Government to jurisdiction over any portion of the land of Ireland or of her territorial seas'[2].

The coronation provided other irritants as well when Belfast Corporation and several local councils insisted on putting up festive decorations in Catholic areas. In Cookstown, when the bunting was pulled down it was re-erected and guarded by the RUC until the celebrations were over. When an Orange band planned to march through the overwhelmingly Catholic town of Dungiven, local Nationalists, enraged by the constant bans in Derry, threatened to block the route and prevent the march. The RUC, caught with inadequate forces in the area, were forced to stop the band and a children's parade went ahead without Union Jacks.

In Stormont the Unionists seemed determined to treat the opposition with contempt. When Cahir Healy raised the question of a council by-election in Lisnaskea where more votes were cast than there were electors on the register – the Unionist candidate won of course – or the case of Catholic workmen sacked by Enniskillen Council for going to mass during working hours on a Catholic holiday, the government ignored him.

Empty proclamations didn't satisfy some of the frustrated Nationalist population. The IRA were already re-organising but even they weren't moving fast enough for some people. In October 1951 the IRA expelled Liam Kelly of Pomeroy for taking unauthorised action. He took most of the IRA membership in Co.Tyrone with him and set up a new armed organisation called Saor Uladh (Free Ulster). Kelly had a flair for the dramatic and on Easter Monday 1952 armed members of Saor Uladh took over Pomeroy in the early hours of the morning, cut the telephone wires, set up road blocks and read the Proclamation of the Republic in the centre of the village.

When a Stormont election was held in October 1953 Kelly sought a mandate for his militant policy by standing as an abstentionist in Mid-Tyrone. The growing dissatisfaction with the parliamentary policy was shown by the fact that another abstentionist stood against an APL candidate in Mid-Derry while the sitting MP, Joe Stewart, only won the nomination from an abstentionist in East Tyrone by the toss of a coin. Almost every APL convention idscussed the question of abstention and of course one APL member, McGleenan in South Armagh, was already an abstentionist.

Liam Kelly defeated the outgoing Nationalist in Mid-Tyrone by 4,178 votes to 3,376, while in the neighbouring Mid-Derry the abstentionist was defeated by only 584 votes. Kelly had made his views quite clear before the election.

'I will not take the Oath of Allegiance to a foreign Queen of a bastard nation. I took an Oath of Allegiance to the Irish Republic when I was sixteen. I have kept that oath and I intend to keep it.

'I do not believe in constitutional methods. I believe in the use of force; the more the better, the sooner the better. That may be treason or sedition, call it whatever the hell you like'[3].

If the people of Mid-Tyrone had shown their lack of confidence in the parliamentary road by electing Kelly the government quickly confirmed their views. A month after the election Kelly was arrested and charged with making a seditious speech. He was tried on 4 December and made a long political statement outlining his own and Saor Uladh's policies. They were very close to Clann na Poblachta in the South and Kelly had been in contact with Sean McBride. They accepted the 1937 Southern constitution which claimed the North as part of the National territory, and their aim was to put that claim into effect. They also accepted the legitimacy of the Dail and the Dublin government in the South, but rejected the authority of Stormont or Westminster in the North.

It was a position calculated to make it difficult for the Southern government to act against Saor Uladh. Kelly concluded: 'Those, who in this part of Ireland seek to uphold the authority of a foreign power, realise that my election by the people of Tyrone is but the first indication of a new awakening'[4].

Kelly was convicted and bound over to keep the peace for five years. He refused to give any undertaking and was jailed for twelve months. The case caused widespread indignation and Sean McBride put down a motion in the Dail condemning his imprisonment. A few days later 600 people attended a convention in Pomeroy and set up a new political party called Fianna Uladh whose aim was, 'To develop an organisation of Republicans in occupied Ireland into a disciplined political movement and to use every legitimate means to bring about the re-unification of the territory of the Republic of Ireland'[5]. An executive committee was elected and Kelly appointed chairman.

In May 1954 a new Coalition government was formed in the South. Clann na Poblachta had been reduced to three seats in the Dail and McBride refused a place in the cabinet, but the Coalition was dependent on Clann na Poblachta's votes. In July, Kelly, who was still in jail, was elected to the Southern Seanad on McBride's nomination. On 19 August 1954 he was suddenly released from jail a fortnight before his sentence was up. The government was trying to avoid demonstrations to welcome him home, but their efforts were in vain. A large crowd met him in Dungannon and 10,000 people, including Sean McBride, turned out for a rally that night in the Nationalist village of Pomeroy – normal population 340. A big force of RUC was drafted in and when the demonstrators tried to march down the street with the tricolour a pitched battle broke out and lasted several hours, leaving twelve RUC and 40 civilians injured. The vice-chairman of Fianna Uladh, Laurence Loughran, and a couple of committee members were among those jailed afterwards.

The RUC action in Pomeroy was bitterly resented. A fortnight later the local Nationalists in Newry called a protest march to the town hall where the chairman of the Nationalist-controlled urban council and the local MP were to speak. There were 10,000 people on the march but the RUC barred them from the town hall and the centre of the overwhelmingly Nationalist town, and when an impromptu meeting was held they protected a small group of Unionist hecklers who disrupted it. They seemed to be out to provoke a confrontation.

In fact the government had acted with a heavy hand throughout

1954. In February they had brought in the Flags and Emblems Act to block up any loop-holes in the Public Order Act. The new act made it illegal to interfere with the display of the Union Jack anywhere except on one's own private property, but gave the RUC power to take down any other flag or emblem on public or private property at will if they thought it might lead to a breach of the peace.

It was obviously aimed at the tricolour, and both the Public Order Act and the Flags and Emblems Act were used in July 1954 to prevent the flying of the tricolour or a parade during a Nationalist feis or festival in the Fermanagh village of Newtownbutler.

This tough line was a response to back-bench pressure. The government had been under fire for alleged 'appeasement' of the minority ever since the education controversy in 1949, and were anxious not to appear soft on law and order issues. But they weren't tough enough for some of their supporters. With attention in England and abroad focused on Northern Ireland by the anti-partition campaign, they were hesitant about imposing a policy of open and naked Orange supremacy. But that was what the local Orange Lodges and Unionist Associations were demanding, and so there had been a major clash over the Longstone Road affair.

In June 1952 Orangemen from Annalong in Co.Down announced their intention of marching over the Longstone Hill, a small Catholic area near Annalong. It was not their usual route – in fact they would be making a deliberate detour to go there – and no Orangemen had marched there for 25 years. It was very much a case of parading the flag in hostile territory. Having banned Nationalist marches from the centre of Nationalist-majority towns like Derry and Enniskillen, the Minister of Home Affairs, Brian Maginess, could hardly permit this. He banned the march. The decision caused uproar and Maginess yielded, allowing another Lodge to march by the Longstone Road on 3 July. When they got to the Longstone Hill a group of local Nationalists blocked the route and the RUC hadn't enough men to force a way through so they stopped the Orangemen.

The government came under fierce attack over the Longstone Road and Dungiven incidents, and in a general election in 1953, both Maginess and Hall-Thompson, the ex-Minister for Education, were opposed by hard-line Independent Unionists. Maginess was constantly heckled and had to call in the RUC to protect him at his final rally, while Brooke himself, now Lord Brookeborough, had to defend his minister's action. In the event the cautious rural voters stayed loyal to the Unionist leadership, and Maginess was re-elected by 6,400 votes to 4,850 in Iveagh in Co.Down; but in Belfast Hall-Thompson was defeated by 345 votes by Norman Porter, secretary of the National Union of Protestants, a Protestant lay preacher and an extreme Loyalist.

The pressure was kept up and Brookeborough had publicly to defend Maginess again in November, while in January 1954 a big rally in the Ulster Hall, called by the Orange and Protestant Committee and addressed by Porter, passed a vote of no confidence in the government. In May the same group organised a mass rally in Antrim to protest against the Gaelic Athletic Association being allowed to hold a carnival on a Sunday. One of the speakers was the official Unionist MP for Antrim, Nat Minford, who had earlier declared at Stormont, 'I said before in this House and I repeat it; that Ulster is a Protestant country, and that this is a Protestant parliament for a Protestant people'[6].

Maginess was moved from Home Affairs early in 1954 and replaced by G.B.Hanna, but the new minister repeated the ban on the Longstone Road march, spelling out the reasons clearly:

'I am quite satisfied that, were I to ban a Republican or any other opposition procession or meeting in one part of the country and, not only to permit an Orange procession in a Nationalist district, but to provide police protection for that procession, I would be holding our entire administration up to ridicule and contempt'[7].

A year later however, Hanna lifted the ban and on 12 July 1955 15,000 Orangemen, led by Brian Faulkner, Stormont MP for East Down, Captain L.P.S.Orr, Westminster MP for South Down and Norman Porter MP, paraded twice along the Longstone Road. Local feeling had been expressed by three bombs which blew holes in the road the day before, but they had been hurriedly repaired and 300 RUC lined the road equipped with police tenders, jeeps and walkie-talkies while the parade was preceded by more RUC in riot gear.

Two weeks later a parade in connection with the Newtownbutler Feis was banned again and a large force of RUC and Commandos drafted into the village. A group of men from Clones in Co.Monaghan tried to march, the RUC attacked them, and there was a serious riot with the RUC using water cannon for the first time in the North. Twelve civilians were injured and two members of Clones Urban Council were among those arrested.

Meanwhile, despite the Kelly defection, the regular IRA had

continued their preparations. In July 1953 they staged an unsuccessful arms raid on Felstead OTC camp in England and three men, Manus Canning from Derry, Cathal Goulding of Dublin and John Stephenson, or Seán McStiofain, of London, were jailed for eight years each. A year later they had a striking success. On 10 June 1954 a raiding party got into Gough military barracks in Armagh and escaped with a massive haul of 250 rifles, 37 Sten guns and nine Bren guns. The Gough barracks raid was a great boost to IRA morale as well as striking power, and recruiting increased sharply. In October 1954 they tried to repeat their coup at Omagh barracks but it misfired, and eight IRA men were caught and sentenced to long jail terms for 'treason felony'. However the Omagh raid proved almost as valuable as the Armagh one because the eight prisoners became heroes and martyrs to much of the Nationalist population.

When a Westminster election was called in May 1955 the IRA decided, following Kelly's example, to contest it and get a popular mandate for their campaign. They named candidates for all twelve seats, half of whom were in jail for the Omagh raid, and made it clear that they would not stand down for anyone. When the Nationalist conventions for Mid-Ulster and Fermanagh-South Tyrone were held the Republican candidates' names were put forward for selection. The Anti-Partition League had not been able to change the traditional loose structure of these conventions, which consisted of local councillors and delegates elected at meetings in each parish, and at which anyone could be nominated. In Fermanagh-South Tyrone the Republican, Phil Clarke, was selected by 114 votes to 71 against strong opposition from Cahir Healy, who denounced the policies of physical force and abstentionism despite his own abstention from both Westminster and Stormont in the past. In Mid-Ulster the nomination of the Republican, Tom Mitchell, was vehemently opposed by E.V.McCullagh the ex-MP for Mid-Tyrone, who had been ousted by Liam Kelly, and the convention took no decision.

In the event no Nationalist stood and the election was a massive success for the Republicans. They got a total of 152,310 votes and won the two Nationalist seats of Mid-Ulster and Fermanagh-South Tyrone by 260 and 261 votes respectively[8]. It was the biggest anti-partition vote since 1921 and nearly 50,000 more than the total anti-partition vote in 1949. Despite the antagonism of the Nationalists in Mid-Ulster and Fermanagh-South Tyrone, Mitchell and Clarke had come within a few thousand of the 1951 Nationalist vote there. The message was clear. The Republicans had won the allegiance of the minority population, for the moment at least. The Unionists' utter lack of response to the Stormont opposition and their rigorous suppression of all extra-parliamentary protest had reaped their reward.

The election had an interesting sequel. The new MPs Tom Mitchell and Phil Clarke were both in jail serving ten-year sentences for the Omagh raid. It was doubtful if they were legally eligible to be elected. The defeated Unionist candidate in Fermanagh-South Tyrone, Colonel Robert Grosvenor, filed an election petition in June seeking to have Clarke unseated and himself declared elected. There was no petition in Mid-Ulster and on 18 July the British Attorney-General proposed at Westminster that the seat be declared vacant and a by-election held. The motion was opposed by the Labour MP Sidney Silverman who expressed some sympathy with Mitchell's views and argued that if the electors of Mid-Ulster didn't want to be represented at Westminster it would be undemocratic to force them to be. Most of the left-wing Labour members voted against the motion but it was carried by 197 votes to 63.

The by-election was held on 11 August 1955 with the same two candidates: Tom Mitchell and Charles Beattie, Unionist. Mitchell won again, increasing his majority to 806 in a 90 per cent poll. This time Beattie did lodge an election petition and in September and October election courts ruled that both Republican candidates had been ineligible to be elected. The seats were awarded to the defeated Unionists. There was a formal motion at Westminster to seat both men and it was again opposed by Silverman and the Labour left but passed by 280 to 99.

The Fermanagh-South Tyrone saga ended there, with Westminster rather shamefacedly seating Colonel Grosvenor; but the Mid-Ulster story took another turn. On 1 December Westminster was informed that Beattie was a member of various national insurance tribunals which might disqualify him too. Early in 1956 a Select Committee ruled that he was indeed ineligible and he left Westminster without ever speaking there.

A second by-election was held on 8 May 1956. The Republicans nominated Mitchell again. The Unionists announced they would not contest it, and the Nationalists then put up Michael O'Neill the former MP. Near nomination day a prominent local Unionist, George Forrest, went forward as an Independent. In fact he was fully supported by the Unionist machine and the Independent tag appears to have been only a subterfuge to ensure a divided anti-Unionist vote. The election was very bitter on the

Nationalist side, with O'Neill denounced as a vote-splitter and his few election meetings shunned. He said his main concern in the contest was:

'to see that all the Nationally-minded people were not misrepresented as being unanimously in favour of a policy of physical force which was contrary to the advice of the leaders of the Dail'[9].

O'Neill's intervention was effective: Forrest was elected. The figures were: Forrest 28,605 votes, Mitchell 24,124 O'Neill 6,421. But the real battle had been inside the minority community. The *Belfast Telegraph* described it as a 'crushing defeat' for the Nationalist Party. It certainly was. There had been no opportunity to choose between Nationalist and Republican in the general election. The last opportunity had been in 1953 and the Mid-Ulster verdict was much more decisive than the Mid-Tyrone one. Mitchell had won almost four times as many votes as the candidate of what had been the main opposition party. O'Neill had lost his deposit.

The alienation of the Catholic minority from the Northern state seemed almost complete. The government had helped to put the finishing touches to it. After the Armagh and Omagh raids the B Specials had been sent out on patrol and the aggressive behaviour of this entirely Protestant and Unionist force had enraged many Catholics, especially in rural areas. Proof of identity was demanded from next-door neighbours and abuse and rough searching were commonplace. Catholics were searched while Protestants were waved on, and Catholics with known Republican sympathies were constantly harassed. The nervous, untrained Specials were quick to open fire and on 5 March 1955 a Special patrol shot an eighteen-year-old youth dead and wounded his girl-friend as they came home from a dance near Keady in South Armagh. The following night another patrol shot and wounded a man near Aughnacloy. Not only was he not an IRA man but he was an off-duty B man himself. These were only the first of many shooting incidents by B men which did much to inflame Nationalist feeling.

The frustration of the minority was dramatically illustrated on 2 July 1955, when a car blew up in the grounds of the Stormont parliament buildings killing the driver. The dead man was Brendan O'Boyle and he was on his way to blow up the Stormont telephone exchange when the bomb exploded prematurely. Like Liam Kelly, he was a former member of the IRA and had left to set up his own small group Laochra Uladh. O'Boyle's death was the end of his organisation, but the drift towards violence had begun.

On 26 November 1955 a bomb blew in the side of Roslea RUC barracks in Co.Fermanagh and a group of armed men tried to shoot their way inside. They were eventually driven off but one RUC man was seriously injured. No organisation claimed responsibility for the attack and the IRA condemned it.

In fact the raid had been carried out by Saor Uladh and it had an extraordinary sequel. One of the raiders, Connie Green, an ex-British soldier from Derry, had been wounded in the attack, and died across the border in Co.Monaghan. Saor Uladh didn't want to attract police attention by revealing their part in the incident, and since news of Green's death would have pointed the finger at them, they contacted Clann na Poblachta in Dublin to get the death hushed up. On instructions from Dublin the local Gardai took the coroner to a farmhouse where the body was already lying in a coffin and he made out a death certificate for an unknown man who had died from gunshot wounds. Green was then buried quietly in the nearby Carrickroe churchyard.

A Dublin newspaper revealed the story a few days later however, and there was a storm of protest from the Northern Unionists who demanded extradition of political offenders from the South. J.A.Costello, the Taoiseach, made a statement in the Dail on 30 November.

'We are bound to ensure that unlawful activities of a military character shall cease and we are resolved to use, if necessary, all the powers and forces at our disposal to bring such activities effectively to an end'[10].

He ruled out any question of extradition however.

Saor Uladh finally accepted responsibility for the Roslea raid on 16 December and re-stated their position:

'Saor Uladh accepts the constitution of the Republic enacted on 1 July 1937 and recognises that Oireachtas Eireann [the Southern Dail and Seanad] **is the sole legitimate authority in Ireland.**

'Saor Uladh is organised solely in the six counties. Application of the laws enacted in the constitution is, by the constitution itself, restricted to the 26-county area. It is apparent therefore that these laws are not applicable in the case of Saor Uladh'[11].

If they thought that such legal niceties would prevent the Southern government acting against them they were soon to be disillusioned.

The statement underlined one of the differences between Saor Uladh and the IRA, in that the IRA refused to recognise the Southern government as well as the Northern one, though they had introduced a regulation forbidding the use of arms against 26-county forces in the hope of avoiding another round of shootings and executions like those during the second world war.

An ironic footnote to the raid was that though Liam Kelly was believed to have led it himself, he spoke in the Southern Seanad shortly beforehand and was back in his place early in 1956.

The Northern government quickly banned Saor Uladh under the Special Powers Act and after a few months they banned Fianna Uladh and Sinn Fein as well. They strengthened the RUC Commandos or Reserve force, who were transformed from a riot squad into a crack para-military unit armed with Bren guns, anti-tank guns, mortars and grenades. During 1956 they also mobilised over two hundred B Specials for full-time service to reinforce the RUC.

The Nationalists, alarmed by the Westminster election results and under pressure from their constituents, walked out of the two-day Stormont debate on the Roslea raid. The Catholic Church was sufficiently worried about the growing support for violence for Cardinal D'Alton, the head of the Catholic Church in Ireland, to denounce it on Christmas Eve 1955, and for the Catholic hierarchy to issue a statement condemning violence and have it read in all churches in January 1956. On 12 February they declared it a mortal sin to be a member of an illegal organisation.

The Unionists meanwhile added fuel to the flames. On Easter Monday 1956 the Orangemen marched on the Longstone Road again, protected by the RUC. The local people blocked the road with boulders and farm machinery and there was a pitched battle between farmers armed with spades and pitchforks and the RUC in riot gear. Ten civilians and four RUC were injured before the road was cleared, and over thirty people were prosecuted.

Early in May the British government announced increases of two shillings a week in family allowances for third and subsequent children in a scheme to help impoverished large families. Up to this, Unionist policy had been to maintain parity with Britain in the field of social services. But on 18 May Ivan Neill, the Stormont Minister for Labour, announced that he was departing from the British scheme and would increase the allowances for second and third but not for subsequent children. The alteration would obviously penalise large families in Northern Ireland and ran completely counter to the idea of the original scheme. The reason for the change was that Catholics in the North tended to have larger families than Protestants and the Unionists had become alarmed at the increasing Catholic birth-rate. Despite the fact that nearly 60 per cent of emigration from the North was by Catholics, the percentage of Catholics in the population was slowly rising. It went from 33.5 per cent in 1926 to 35 per cent in 1961[12]. Eventually the increasing birth-rate might endanger Unionist control in the North as a whole. In the short term it threatened their grip on some of the elaborately gerrymandered local authorities. The *Irish Times*, commenting on rumours of the move, said: 'Belfast fears the growth of the Catholic Nationalist population and it will do anything to stop it'[13].

There was a storm of protest from the opposition at this crude party manoeuvre. The Irish Congress of Trade Unions and the Presbyterian Church condemned it as penalising the poorest section of the community of whatever religion. Six days after the second reading of the bill began Brookeborough announced that the government was going back to a policy of strict parity with Britain.

The simmering frustration of the Northern Nationalists was spreading to the South, where eager young Republicans were joining the IRA looking for action. But the IRA had still not begun its long-planned Northern campaign. In June 1956 the IRA expelled one of its most militant and energetic activists, Joe Christle. Christle, a night-student at University College Dublin, was constantly impatient with the cautious IRA leadership. When he went he took most of the young Dublin members with him. By September he had linked up with Saor Uladh and they were getting ready for action.

On 11 November 1956 Saor Uladh and the Christle group combined to attack six customs posts along the border in one night. It was quite an effective operation and between them they could muster a small but efficient striking force; but they had no overall plan of campaign and no political arm to generate mass support – Fianna Uladh had been allowed to fade away. They were also very localised. Saor Uladh was virtually confined to Tyrone, Fermanagh and Monaghan and the Christle group were mostly from Dublin and operating far from home. Their main effect was to force the IRA into action.

The IRA had been arming and training for a Northern campaign for nearly five years; but the leadership, who had slowly re-built the organisation after the war years, were reluctant to take the final step. At the beginning of 1956 a recent recruit, Sean Cronin, who had been an officer in the Irish Army, presented them with a plan of campaign called 'Operation Harvest'. The Army Council agreed to launch the attack that winter – the Kelly-Christle link-up left them with no option if they wanted to keep their members.

At the beginning of December 1956 four columns of 25 men each were sent to the border. They were to operate from base areas in the South and link up with IRA units inside the six counties. The ambitious Operation Harvest called not only for attacks on Crown forces and military and police installations, but also for sabotage of communications and attacks on public buildings and property. The aim was to drive the Crown forces out of whole areas in the North and prevent the civil administration from functioning, thereby creating 'liberated zones'.

On the night of 11-12 December about 150 IRA men attacked ten targets in all six counties. The targets were in line with the Operation Harvest strategy. A BBC transmitter was destroyed in Derry, and a Territorial Army building in Enniskillen. A courthouse in Magherafelt, Co.Derry, a B Special hut in Newry and a number of bridges in Co.Fermanagh were damaged. The following night the RUC barracks in Lisnaskea and Derrylin in Fermanagh were attacked. Sinn Fein issued a statement saying:

'Irishmen have again risen in revolt against British aggression in Ireland. The Sinn Fein organisation say to the Irish people that they are proud of the risen nation and appeal to the people of Ireland to assist in every way they can the soldiers of the Irish Republican Army'[14].

On 14 December Costello threatened stern action in the South if the campaign continued. At Westminster the twelve Ulster Unionist MPs met the Home Secretary to demand support in face of this attack, and the British ambassador was instructed to protest to the Dublin government. Brookeborough made a television broadcast in the North and asserted his government's determination to crush the IRA campaign. Stormont debated the raids, with the opposition walking out again. On 19 December the British Premier, Sir Anthony Eden, said:

'In the Ireland Act 1949 the Parliament of Westminster declared Northern Ireland to be an integral part of the United Kingdom. This is a declaration which all parties in this House are pledged to support. The safety of Northern Ireland and its inhabitants is therefore a direct responsibility of Her Majesty's Government which they will, of course, discharge'[15].

On 21 December the RUC arrested a large number of Republicans, both IRA men and Saor Uladh supporters, and detained them under the Special Powers Act. Internment had been reintroduced. Eventually some 256 men and one woman were to be interned. The next day a large number of border roads were cratered or spiked, and bridges on them blown up, leaving only seventeen roads across the border passable. As a result of Eden's statement RUC and B Special patrols were now joined by British Army scout cars, and in January 1957 a joint planning committee was established, consisting of the British Army's GOC Northern Ireland and the commander of the British 39th Infantry Brigade, together with senior officers of the RUC and B Specials. Its purpose was to co-ordinate resistance to the IRA campaign, and from then on the RAF assisted the RUC with aerial reconnaissance while the British Army backed up the RUC and Specials; though the situation never became serious enough to involve them on a major scale.

There was a lull in the campaign over Christmas; but on New Year's Eve two RUC barracks were attacked in Fermanagh. At Derrylin an RUC man was killed and at Brookeborough two IRA men, Sean South from Limerick and Fergal O'Hanlon from Monaghan, were killed and several others wounded. The Brookeborough attack was a military debacle but a propaganda victory. South and O'Hanlon became national heroes in the 26 counties and thousands flocked to their funerals from all over the South. An estimated 50,000 people followed South's funeral in Limerick. There was a great emotional upsurge of support for the IRA, and when Costello again threatened action against them on 6 January and most of the Army Council were rounded up and jailed for short terms under the Offences Against the State Act, his action was widely resented. On 28 January in the Dail Sean McBride tabled a motion of censure on the government because of their economic policy and their harassment of the IRA. It brought down the government. Costello dissolved the Dail on 12 February and there was a general election on 5 March 1957.

The campaign in the North had slowed down in the meantime, with only three major incidents in three months – the destruction of Dungannon Territorial Army centre on 18 January, the hijacking and destruction of a Strabane-Derry freight train on 2 March and another attack on Derrylin RUC barracks. The IRA decided to put their energies into the Southern election for the moment. Sinn Fein nominated nineteen candidates and in a great wave of enthusiasm four of them were elected; one, John Joe McGirl, topping the poll in the Sligo-Leitrim constituency. The other successful candidates were Fergal O'Hanlon's brother Einachan in Co.Monaghan, Ruadhri O'Bradaigh in Longford-Westmeath, and John Joe Rice in Kerry. Altogether Sinn Fein got 65,640 votes, their highest total in the South since 1927. They seemed on the crest of a wave. They had just won remarkable successes in elections North and South and they had launched their long-awaited campaign.

But their success in the Southern election was a pyrrhic victory. The Sinn Fein TDs didn't take their seats, McBride lost his and Fianna Fail had a clear majority and formed the government. They were not dependent on IRA-supporting Clann na Poblachta members for their majority and after the war years they had no inhibitions about suppressing the IRA. The Southern economy was in difficulties, there was a balance of payments deficit, unemployment had reached 70,000 and emigration was at its highest point since the 1880s. The Fianna Fail government badly needed to increase exports and were anxious to improve trading relations with Britain. They were not going to let the IRA jeopardise their chances. On 4 July an IRA unit ambushed an RUC patrol at Forkhill in South Armagh and one RUC man was killed. De Valera acted swiftly. On 7 July 1957 internment was re-introduced in the South, dealing the IRA a body blow.

IRA activity had been fairly constant in the North in the spring and early summer, though the only major incident had been when the Kelly-Christle group had blown up the lock gates of the Newry ship canal in May, causing considerable damage. In early August there was a series of blasts in Newry and a government-owned barge was blown up on Lough Neagh. The government responded on 12 August with a curfew from 11pm to 5.30am in the Newry area, which lasted for a month. A few days later an RUC man, Sergeant Ovens, was killed and a couple of British soldiers injured in a booby-trap explosion near Coalisland in Co.Tyrone.

The campaign continued throughout the winter, but the IRA were forced to concentrate on trying to ambush RUC or B Special mobile patrols rather than attack fixed targets like barracks which were now well defended. They had no notable successes and sustained one very heavy blow: on 11 November four IRA men and a local sympathiser were blown up while preparing a bomb just across the border at Edentubber in Co.Louth. By the end of 1957 there had been a total of 366 incidents since the campaign began and the death-toll was three RUC men and seven Republicans.

In terms of Operation Harvest the IRA had made little progress.

They hadn't inflicted many casualties on the Crown forces or seriously disrupted the civil administration, and they certainly hadn't created any 'liberated zones'. The IRA had deliberately avoided action in Belfast, partly because they were doubtful about security in the Belfast units but mainly because they were afraid it would provoke a sectarian backlash against the Catholic ghettos. But the basis of their plan of campaign was to cripple the administration and infrastructure of the Northern state, and in the light of this objective, a campaign which avoided Belfast, the political, administrative and economic centre of the six counties, could be of only marginal effect – especially one concentrated in the remote and backward border areas. In an inherently sectarian state the danger of a backlash was always there; indeed the size of the backlash might well have been a measure of the effectiveness of the campaign. That there was virtually no backlash, no attacks on Catholic ghettos and no unofficial Protestant violence probably indicates that the state was never seriously challenged.

There was a flurry of activity at the start of 1958, but by now the weight of repression on both sides of the border was having its effect. There were now 187 men interned in the South as well, and the IRA command structure was badly hit. What was left could not cope with the forces ranged against them. The crack RUC Reserve force was expanded to over 500 men, half of them B Specials mobilised full-time. They were equipped with British Army Ferret cars and operated out of strategically-placed bases spending all their time combatting the IRA campaign. Altogether some fifteen hundred B men were mobilised for full-time duty, while the Specials as a whole were expanded to 13,000 strong. There were Special patrols every night in almost every area, and Special guards on every important installation. By mid-1958 they had sapped the IRA's capacity to launch more than pin-prick attacks.

At the same time however two actions by the RUC themselves helped revive support for the flagging campaign. On 19 November 1957 the RUC arrested two Republicans, Kevin Mallon[16] and Francis Talbot, in connection with the Sergeant Ovens killing in August. At his trial in July 1958 Mallon told how he was beaten continuously for several days, threatened several times with a loaded gun, and his lips were burned with lighted cigarettes until eventually he signed a confession admitting possession of explosives and making the phone call that lured Ovens to his death. Talbot got the same treatment and signed a similar statement. They were charged with the murder of Ovens.

Normally Republicans refused to recognise courts North or South of the border – a practice which made it only too easy for the state to get convictions – but because Mallon and Talbot were charged with a capital offence this practice was waived and they were defended by Elwyn Jones QC, later Attorney-general in the British Labour government. Both men repudiated their statements and complained of the brutality they had undergone. The jury cleared them, but they were promptly re-arrested and charged with possession of explosives. The same confessions were used as evidence but this time Mallon and Talbot refused to recognise the court and were undefended. They were convicted and sentenced to a total of 22 years in jail.

On 12 March 1958 warders in Crumlin Road prison discovered a tunnel being dug by the internees. When the internees resisted a follow-up search, the RUC Reserve force were called in and there was a violent clash, with some internees severely beaten up – one man had a broken leg and several broken ribs. A couple of the prisoners took an action for damages which was unsuccessful but publicised the details of the case. The two incidents and the RUC brutality involved served to anger many Catholics not normally sympathetic to the IRA.

In the meantime there was a Stormont election in the North. The law had been changed since 1953 so that candidates had to take an oath of allegiance before nomination. That ruled out both Sinn Fein and Fianna Uladh, since neither would take the oath even to break it. Anyway, with internment in operation and both organisations illegal, it would have been difficult for them to campaign since their election workers would have been liable to arrest. Liam Kelly and Charles McGleenan, the other abstentionist MP, stood down. Sinn Fein toyed with the idea of write-in candidates or a spoiled vote campaign but did nothing about it. The initiative was left with the Nationalists whose leader, McSparran, had recently repeated their opposition to the IRA campaign: 'The Anti-Partition League was formed for the purpose of endeavouring to secure the unity of this country by peaceful means and without resort to force ... and had vehemently condemned the use of force'[17]. They won eight seats, losing Mid-Tyrone where two Nationalists split the Catholic vote and let a Unionist in.

Both the IRA and Saor Uladh tried to keep the military campaign going and lost some more men. Alo Hand of Saor Uladh was shot dead by the RUC near Newtownbutler on 2 July 1958; Pat McManus, the IRA commander in Fermanagh, was killed by a premature explosion on 15 July;

and James Crossan, another IRA man, was shot unarmed by the RUC as he walked across the border in South Armagh. An RUC man was blown up by a land-mine in South Armagh as well. But by September 1958 almost all the IRA's army council were jailed or interned in the South, and their plans for a winter offensive had to be called off. The campaign was petering out. Soon the Southern government began releasing their internees again and in March 1959 they closed down the Curragh internment camp. Liam Kelly recognised that this round of the struggle was over and left for America.

In October 1959 there was a Westminster election. Sinn Fein decided to stand again – there were no restrictions on Westminster candidates and Stormont was chary of interfering with the election campaign. The Nationalists gave them a clear field and they contested all twelve seats. They got 73,415 votes, less than half of the 1955 total. In Fermanagh-South Tyrone they dropped from 30,529 votes in 1955 to 7,348 and lost the seat, in Armagh from 21,363 to 6,823. Only Tom Mitchell in Mid-Ulster held his vote, getting 24,170, slightly more than in the 1956 by-election, but he was easily defeated. It was a heavy blow, after 1955. The emotional support they had won then was evaporating, faced with the attrition of arrests, internment, and constant security operations. The people had no stomach for continuing a campaign which had failed.

The IRA were beaten but they wouldn't accept it. There were occasional incidents, 27 in 1959, 26 in 1960 but no one was killed. In January 1961 an off-duty RUC man suspected of spying in Co.Cavan was shot dead near Roslea but soon afterwards even the Stormont government felt they could relax their vigilance and the last of the Northern internees was released in April 1961. In October there was an election in the South and Sinn Fein stood again. It was a repeat of the Northern debacle: their vote went down from 65,640 to 36,393 or three per cent of the total poll. They lost all four seats they had won in 1957. The political backing for the campaign had disappeared on both sides of the border.

But the IRA still wouldn't accept it. In November 1961 there were a few more ambushes on RUC patrols. One on 12 November at Jonesborough in South Armagh was only too successful. Another RUC man was killed. Brian Faulkner, the Northern Minister for Home Affairs, threatened the death penalty against the IRA. The Dublin government quickly introduced military courts in the South. By the end of the year they had sentenced 25 men. The IRA army council finally accepted the inevitable. They ordered their volunteers to dump arms and on 26 February 1962 they announced the end of the campaign. Eight IRA men and one sympathiser, two Saor Uladh members and six RUC men had been killed. The damage caused was estimated at a million pounds, the cost of increased security in the North at ten million[18].

The IRA statement said:

'The decision to end the resistance campaign has been taken in view of the general situation. Foremost among the factors motivating this course of action has been the attitude of the general public whose minds have been deliberately distracted from the supreme issue facing the Irish people – the unity and freedom of Ireland'[19].

For the IRA to blame the people for not supporting them was an inadequate explanation for the failure of a long-planned and prepared-for campaign. In fact the rural Catholic population, frustrated with Unionist intransigence and the failure of parliamentary politics, did support them in 1955. But the IRA was in possibly the most unpolitical phase of its history – this was the period of the cold war and militant Catholic anti-communism, and the IRA, while despising parliamentary politicians, was deeply suspicious of left-wing politics. They had no policy other than physical force and no serious political organisation to mobilise their supporters and channel their energies into the mass resistance which is complementary to all guerrilla campaigns, and which might have steeled the Nationalist population to continue active support despite RUC and B Special harassment. Sinn Fein was only a convenient title for the IRA to use in elections, and the campaign was a purely military one. As a result, when the military effort flagged, the supporters quickly lost heart and after the first few months the campaign was an irritant rather than a threat to the Northern government.

After 1962 the IRA and Saor Uladh seemed to be spent forces; but in fact, though they had taken a beating in the 1959 and 1961 elections, 73,000 people in the North and 36,000 in the South had still voted for a policy of violence. It was a sizeable hard core of intransigents for any state to have. And the policies which had produced the IRA campaign hadn't changed.

The Unionists had certainly not grown any more conciliatory. In February 1957 Harry Midgley, former socialist, former anti-partitionist, now Unionist Minister for Education, speaking in the Orange Hall in Portadown, had said, 'All the minority are traitors and have always been traitors to the government of Northern Ireland'[20]. The government were still under pressure from more extreme Unionist elements. In the 1958 election Norman Porter led a team of four Independent Unionists who condemned 'appeasement' of the minority and stressed 'the vital need of maintaining a Protestant Ulster and Protestant principles'[21]. A 'Protestant Unionist' stood against Maginess, the ex-Minister of Home Affairs in Iveagh. They were all defeated but Porter actually increased his vote by a thousand and was only beaten by a margin of 45 when a number of mainly middle-class Catholics voted for the official Unionist in order to keep Porter out[22].

At Easter 1958 an Orange parade was again forced through the Longstone Road by 300 RUC, and on 3 July the Bovevagh Orange Lodge, which had caused the trouble in 1953, marched through Dungiven with a heavy RUC escort taking the local people by surprise. The Minister of Home Affairs, W.W.B.Topping, had privately agreed to the march without informing anyone. It was bitterly resented and tension was high in the town for a few days, with Catholics boycotting Protestant shops. The local rural council, which was Nationalist-controlled, strongly condemned the minister's action.

The Bovevagh Lodge proposed to march again in 1959, but it would have been impossible to keep it quiet this time and there was bound to be a riot. Even the Protestants in Dungiven protested against the march and Topping was forced to ban it. The hard-liners were outraged and Topping was booed and jeered at the main Orange Parade in Belfast on 12 July. In December he was removed from the Ministry of Home Affairs and made a judge. He was succeeded by Brian Faulkner, the man who had led the first Longstone Road march.

Faulkner immediately banned a cross-country race by a mainly-Catholic sporting body in the same area and in July 1960 he allowed the Orange parade in Dungiven. The townspeople were enraged and held a protest march and meeting the day before. On 10 July 200 RUC baton-charged local youths off the streets in Dungiven, and 10,000 Orangemen led by Robert Chichester-Clark, Westminster MP for Co.Derry, and Norman Porter paraded twice through the town. That night and the next there was fierce rioting between the RUC and locals in the town.

The Unionist leadership even made it clear that they didn't want Catholic support. In November 1959 Sir Clarence Graham, an industrialist and chairman of the standing committee of the Unionist Council, suggested that suitable Catholics might be permitted to join the Unionist Party and even be selected as candidates. There was by now a small group of Catholic business and professional men who had developed a vested interest in the Northern state, while others were influenced to support the link with Britain by the vastly superior social services in the North. They represented only a small section of the minority population, but Sir George Clark, the Orange Grand Master and a Unionist Senator, replied to Graham: 'It is difficult to see how a Catholic with the vast differences in our religious outlook, could be either acceptable within the Unionist Party as a member or for that matter, bring himself unconditionally to support its ideals'[23]. Brookeborough supported Clark and a week after his first statement Graham had toed the line and signed a statement by the executive committee of the Unionist Council reiterating the basic aims of the party and its determination: 'To welcome to our ranks only those who unconditionally support these ideals'[24]. In fact as late as 1969 two Catholics were refused membership of the Unionist Party in North Belfast, and in South Belfast in 1970 a man who was married to a Catholic was admitted only by thirteen votes to eleven[25].

The activities of Saor Uladh and the IRA dominated events in the countryside in the 1950s, but in industrial Belfast the political opposition was provided by some form of Labour. The new Northern section of the Irish Labour Party had a promising beginning. It had two MPs at Stormont, one at Westminster, and a firm foothold in local government. It was part of an all-Ireland party with members in the Dublin government. But it quickly began to fall apart. Frank Hanna MP left almost immediately having secured his seat in Belfast Central. Early in 1951 there was a violent split between Harry Diamond and the majority, led by Jack Beattie and Jack Magougan. It was at least partly over the majority's call for changes in the ultra-Catholic laws and constitution of the South.

In the summer of 1951, when the party nominated Beattie for a vacancy for the Belfast Corporation in Smithfield ward, Diamond resigned his own seat to oppose him. It was a bitter, sectarian contest but the verdict was clear. In a Catholic ward the Protestant Beattie won by 1,402 votes to 312. In September Diamond and his supporters were expelled by the Dublin executive of the party, and he replied with a 'red scare': 'We are relieved that we have got rid of the pro-Communist group in Belfast which had been retarding our progress up to now'.

In the 1953 election the official party put up five candidates, four in

Belfast, including Magougan and Beattie in Falls and Central, and one in South Down against a Nationalist. By now Diamond had split with most of his supporters and there were four different splinter groups of Irish Labour in the election. It was a dirty election. Frank Hanna, a wealthy solicitor and a prominent member of the Clonard Catholic Confraternity, – something he didn't let his constituents forget easily – declared 'The Irish Labour Party, by adopting two non-Catholic candidates for those two constituencies, [Falls and Central] is in effect trying to deprive Belfast of any Catholic representation in parliament'[26]. The official party fared disastrously, coming bottom of the poll in each constituency.

In the 1955 Westminster election Beattie got twice as many votes as the Republican candidate in West Belfast – with no political programme the Republicans made little impact on the more class-conscious workers of West Belfast – but was easily defeated[27]. In the 1958 Stormont election the official party again failed to win a single seat and a few months later they were all – including Beattie – eliminated in the Corporation elections by a new Catholic grouping led by Hanna. Beattie died a few months later and the Irish Labour Party faded from the scene in the North.

Under the pressure of Orange sectarianism they had been forced to confine themselves to the Catholic ghettos, only to be shattered and destroyed by the virulent anti-communism and anti-socialism of the Catholic Church of the 1950s and ghetto sectarianism against a mainly Protestant-led party.

The pro-partition NILP had its troubles too at the start. Despite the 1949 conference decision on partition, it still wasn't Unionist enough for some and Harry Holmes, a former chairman of the party, went the way of Harry Midgley, joining the Unionist Party and becoming MP for Shankill in 1953. The NILP put up eight candidates in the 1953 election and improved their position somewhat as their pro-partition stance gradually won acceptance. In a by-election in Woodvale in 1955 their candidate was beaten by only 436 votes. Then in the 1958 election, with their candidates denouncing the IRA as vehemently as any Unionist, they won four seats, all in Belfast: Pottinger, Oldpark, Woodvale and Victoria.

The Unionists were shocked. The loss of Pottinger and Oldpark was not surprising – they were former Labour seats with substantial Catholic populations – but Woodvale and Victoria were a different matter. They were solidly Protestant and mainly working-class. If they could fall to the

NILP even with tiny majorities – 80 votes in Woodvale, 147 in Victoria[28] – nearly every seat was vulnerable.

There was little doubt why the NILP had done so well. An expanding world economy after the war, with a big demand for peace-time products to make up for lost production, had kept factories fully occupied and unemployment low until the early 1950s. Then a recession had hit the linen trade and gradually spread to industry in general, until in 1957, 13,500 people emigrated from the North, the largest figure since the war, and in 1958 the unemployment figure reached 48,000 or 10.7 per cent, again the highest total since the war. Unemployment was making its presence keenly felt on the Protestant Shankill and Newtownards Roads as well as the Catholic Falls. The shipyard was hard-hit and the new MPs for Victoria and Woodvale, David Bleakley and Billy Boyd, were ex-shipyard workers. They were also Protestant lay-preachers and at least as 'loyal' on the border issue as the Unionist Party.

Once in Stormont the NILP group spared no effort to prove its loyalty. In his maiden speech David Bleakley, the most articulate of the four, attacked the Nationalists as sectarian for complaining about discrimination. He didn't condemn discrimination itself. At the end of his speech Robert Nixon, a right-wing government backbencher, welcomed him as a fellow Unionist. After the border raid at Newtownbutler in July 1958 in which a Saor Uladh man was killed Bleakley declared: 'We most emphatically deplore these murderous incursions into our territory. Like all decent people we re-affirm our determination to give every possible support to those who are preserving law and order and civilised standards in our community'[29]. He said nothing about the grievances and frustrations which had caused the campaign of violence. The four MPs consistently supported internment and the actions of the RUC and Specials, and voted against motions for the release of internees and political prisoners. And in November 1961 when the last RUC man was killed, Bleakley suggested using capital punishment against IRA men. The NILP men were fairly accurately described as 'pale pink' Unionists.

The NILP group had been elected because of the worsening economic situation and the Brookeborough government's complacency and inactivity. They took up the position of official opposition, vacant since 1929, and concentrated on the economic situation. Their programme was hardly revolutionary: economic planning, government aid to ailing industries and measures to attract new ones, co-operation with the trade unions. But it was resisted by Brookeborough and the landlord and factory-owning Unionist establishment. Discontent grew. Soon even the liberal Unionist *Belfast Telegraph* was tentatively supporting NILP policies. It looked as if the government would have to change its attitude if it was not to lose another few seats at the next election.

The Rise and Fall of Terence O'Neill

The Northern economy was in difficulties in the late 1950s. The three traditional industries on which it was based, agriculture, textiles and engineering including shipbuilding, were simultaneously in decline with no prospect of substantial long-term improvement. Employment was dropping steadily in all three. The number of insured employees in agriculture went down from 21,400 in 1950 to 13,100 in 1961, in textiles from 72,800 in 1950 to 56,300 in 1961, and in shipbuilding from 24,200 in 1950 to 20,200 in 1961[1]. Unemployment had reached an unacceptable level among Protestant skilled workers as well as Catholics. In the first nine months of 1961, ten thousand men were laid off in the Belfast shipyard alone.

There were other social problems too. Average weekly earnings in Northern Ireland were only 78 per cent of those in Britain. Housing was grossly inadequate with 19·3 per cent of houses having no piped water supply and 22·6 per cent of houses with no flush toilets[2]. A government report in 1962 severely criticised the house-building rate in Northern Ireland – 6,000 a year – and said it would have to be nearly doubled, to 10,000, for Northern Ireland even to stand still in housing development[3].

The government's response was complacent and lethargic. Brookeborough, who divided his time between running the government and his estates in Fermanagh, was vehemently opposed to planning and co-operation with the trade unions. Under him the Unionists relied on traditional methods to keep their supporters loyal. As late as March 1961 an aspiring Unionist barrister (later an MP), Robert Babington, could say,

'Registers of unemployed Loyalists should be kept by the Unionist Party and employers invited to pick employees from them. The Unionist Party should make it quite clear that the Loyalists have the first choice of jobs'[4].

Nonetheless the government was forced to take some initiatives. A Northern Ireland Development Council under Lord Chandos was set up in 1955 but it did little more than wine and dine visiting industrialists and had little success. A scheme of industries development grants and capital grants was established to encourage new industries. Firms could get rent-free advance factories, grants of one third or more of their capital costs, re-training grants, generous loans, a coal subsidy, and 75 per cent de-rating. Some £55 million was paid out in grants and subsidies between 1955 and 1961, but it barely absorbed the natural increase in the labour force, never mind reducing the unemployment rate. A working party of senior civil servants from Stormont and Westminster, the Hall Committee, was established in May 1961 to study the Northern Ireland economy.

It was not enough to defeat the NILP challenge. There was a Stormont election in May 1962. The NILP encouraged by its success in 1958, launched its biggest challenge since 1945, putting up fourteen candidates. The IRA campaign was over, there was no serious threat to the constitution and anyway the NILP had amply shown its 'loyalty over the past four years. Protestant workers were able to register a protest vote against government economic policy without rocking the boat too much.

The NILP got 76,842 votes, their highest total ever, and held all four seats won in 1958 with substantially increased majorities[5]. They didn't win any new seats but sharply reduced the Unionist majority in some. To the Unionists they were still a serious threat, though in fact their failure to improve on their 1958 position probably meant they had reached the limit of the Protestant protest vote.

The Hall Committee reported in October 1962, but it recommended little except the establishment of an economic advisory council. It even suggested that the unemployed be encouraged to emigrate to Britain. In February 1963 unemployment had again reached 45,000 or 9·5 per cent and, with his Loyalist constituents being paid off, a government backbencher, Desmond Boal, MP for Shankill, voted with the NILP on a censure motion on unemployment and called on Brookeborough to retire. Shortly afterwards ten backbenchers also signed a memorandum calling for his resignation. Brookeborough had a diplomatic duodenal ulcer operation and resigned on 23 March 1963.

His successor, selected by discreet consultations among the Unionist bosses and the landed gentry, was Finance Minister Captain Terence O'Neill, an old Etonian and ex-Guards officer. O'Neill was a colourless figure who was largely a mouthpiece for technocrats in the civil service. Though an Orangeman he had no record of drum-beating militancy or fundamentalist Protestantism, and regarded the Orange Order with snobbish disdain. As a former Finance Minister he was acutely aware of the North's economic problems and was more interested in solving them and warding off the NILP challenge than in traditional Unionism. From the beginning the Unionist hard-liners distrusted him and would have preferred Brian Faulkner, the ambitious and hard-line Home Affairs Minister.

The beginning of O'Neill's premiership saw a flood of economic reports collected and codified in the Wilson Plan of December 1964, which became the basis of the government's economic policy. It involved one fundamental decision: to accept as irreversible the decline of the North's traditional industries and to concentrate on attracting new industry from outside to replace the lost jobs. The strategy of the £450 million plan was to create a modern economic infrastructure and a series of growth-centres which, together with even more lavish grants, would make the North a Mecca for foreign capitalists.

The government decided to create a new city of a hundred thousand people out of the adjoining towns of Lurgan and Portadown in North Armagh, and to develop seven other towns as industrial growth centres, to undertake a massive road-building programme including four motorways and a £35 million ring road for Belfast, and to build a second University at Coleraine.

A logical corollary was recognition of the trade unions. Union co-operation and good labour relations were essential if foreign capitalists were to be attracted. Brookeborough had always refused to recognise the Irish Congress of Trade Unions, partly because it was an all-Ireland body and partly because he was violently anti-trade union anyway[6]. In August 1964 the government recognised an autonomous Northern Committee of the ICTU and the way was open for the establishment of an employer-labour-government economic council.

Eventually the government's strategy was successful in attracting a number of big international combines such as Michelin, Goodyear, Du Pont, Enkalon, ICI and Courtaulds, and Northern Ireland became a major centre of the artificial fibre industry. It also changed the traditional power balance in the North, as economic power shifted from the old-established family firms which had been the backbone of the Unionist Party to new British, American or continental firms. Political influence followed: more slowly, but in the direction of a modernised, less sectarian Unionism. And the changing economic structure had another side-effect. The decline of traditional industries, where discrimination and Protestant privilege were well-entrenched, and the rise of new firms which didn't discriminate or which employed a lot of mainly Catholic semi-skilled or female labour, left the Protestant working class feeling threatened and insecure. The days of easy sectarian ascendancy, of recruitment and advancement through the Orange Lodges, seemed to be coming to an end. Soon there were rumblings of discontent in the Unionist Party both from the traditional power elite and from the working-class grass roots.

The new technocratic Unionism quickly trod on some traditional toes, and in October 1963, after only six months, Edmund Warnock, an ex-Attorney-General, launched an oblique attack on O'Neill by condemning the way he had been selected and naming Faulkner as a rival contender. Warnock claimed the support of eight other MPs out of a backbench party of nineteen, but he didn't push the issue to a confrontation.

Meanwhile, in the South, a process similar to the Brookeborough/O'Neill transition and the new economic strategy had been going on as well. Unemployment and emigration had been consistently high in the South since the Second World War, reaching a peak under the second Inter-Party government (1954-57). The new Fianna Fail government elected in 1957 reversed their traditional policy of trying to develop native industry by high tariff barriers, and partially repealed the Control of Manufactures Act in 1958[7]. At the end of 1958 they adopted their first Programme for Economic Expansion and based their economic policy on the attraction of foreign investment with even more lavish subsidies than the North, the development of free trade with Britain and eventual entry, together with Britain, into the Common Market.

In June 1959 De Valera became President in the South and was succeeded as Taoiseach by Sean Lemass, Minister for Industry and Commerce and architect of the new economic policies. The new line was confirmed. With De Valera, who had some marginal commitment to the old Republican ideal of economic independence, out of the way Lemass quickly jettisoned the last vestiges of Republicanism. In July 1959 he initiated Anglo-Irish trade talks in London and a trade agreement was signed in 1960. In September 1959 Lemass had suggested a logical corollary, economic co-operation between North and South in Ireland, but Brookeborough wasn't interested.

The new economic policy was very successful for a time. By March 1965, 234 new foreign enterprises had been established, 40 per cent of them British. Trade ties with Britain became closer, especially after the election of a Labour government at Westminster, and an Anglo-Irish free trade area was agreed on in December 1965. By 1968 the South had become the fifth largest importer of British goods. The balance of economic power and political influence was shifting there as well. Everything tended towards better North-South relations – British influence and the US and continental interests on both sides of the border.

On 14 January 1965 Lemass went to Belfast and met O'Neill at Stormont. It was the first such meeting since 1925. They issued a brief communique:

'We have today discussed matters in which there may prove to be a degree of common interest and have agreed to explore further what specific measures may be possible or desirable by way of practical consultation and co-operation.

'Our talks – which did not touch upon constitutional or political questions – have been conducted in a most amicable way and we look forward to a further discussion in Dublin'⁸.

Public reaction was largely favourable. Northern business circles welcomed the meeting for very tangible reasons. The North had a £10 million annual trade deficit with the South and increased trade might help to reduce it. In general, cross-border co-operation on tourist promotion, electricity generation etc. could lead to considerable savings. It was very much in line with the new technocratic policies at Stormont and O'Neill's autobiography records how large a part senior civil servants North and South played in arranging the meeting.

O'Neill returned the visit in February 1965 and a whole series of meetings began between Stormont and Dublin ministers to discuss co-operation between their departments. Ironically, two of the ministers who got on best together were Harry West, Northern Minister of Agriculture and later leader of the extreme Loyalist United Ulster Unionist Council (UUUC) and his opposite number Neal Blaney, later to figure in the Dublin arms trial. In May 1965 O'Neill met Harold Wilson in London and he strongly endorsed the cross-border talks.

The idea was not so popular in the Unionist Party however. The meeting was denounced by Warnock and Desmond Boal in a debate at Stormont in February. Warnock argued that it had always been Unionist policy not to co-operate with the Dublin government until they formally recognised the North. He said, 'It is an unwarrantable assumption of personal dictatorship by the Prime Minister to reverse that policy without the consent of the people who support his government'⁹. In April Robert

Nixon MP called on O'Neill to resign and suggested Faulkner as an alternative leader.

However, Warnock, Boal and Nixon represented the extreme right wing of the party. Their opposition was expected. More serious was the fact that O'Neill hadn't consulted his own cabinet beforehand. Evidently he couldn't trust all his colleagues.

In November 1965 O'Neill called a snap election to consolidate his position. It seemed to work. He had a remarkable success. In the Westminster election of October 1964 the NILP had still posed a threat, contesting ten seats and winning 103,000 votes, though no seats. Now they were routed. They lost their two solidly Protestant seats in Woodvale and Victoria and their majority in Pottinger was halved. Their vote was down in every single constituency. Their total vote, despite three extra candidates, was 66,323, 10,000 less than in 1962.

The NILP with its constant assertions of loyalty on the constitutional issue had previously picked up a sizeable Unionist protest vote; but now O'Neill with his economic planning, public investment, co-operation with the trade unions, and finally cross-border talks, had stolen their policies. If anything O'Neill was beginning to appear more liberal than the NILP. In November 1964 a motion to open public play centres on a Sunday had been defeated by one vote at Belfast Corporation. Two Labour members, one of them Billy Boyd MP, had voted to keep the play centres closed. The incident confirmed the NILP's image as a sabbatarian Protestant party and alienated many of their supporters.

O'Neill had campaigned personally against the NILP and was well pleased with his victory; but it had one unforeseen consequence. The new MP for Woodvale was an extreme Unionist docker, John McQuade, who was closely connected with a fundamentalist Protestant preacher, Ian Paisley. Paisley now had two allies on the Unionist backbenches – Desmond Boal was also associated with him – and O'Neill had four open enemies in his parliamentary party. Paisley had already caused O'Neill quite a lot of trouble the previous year. He was shortly to cause him a great deal more.

Ian Paisley had started his own violently anti-Catholic Free Presbyterian Church in 1951, and he has been its permanent Moderator or Head ever since. He was an extreme Unionist and was actively involved with Norman Porter, the Protestant Unionist MP, in the early 1950s. They were in a long tradition of political pastors and right-wing politico-religious groups in the North, stretching back to the Rev Henry Cooke and Hugh

(Roaring) Hanna in the nineteenth century, and including the Belfast Protestant Association at the beginning of this century and the Ulster Protestant League in the 1930s. Extreme Protestantism had always provided the ideology for the violent fringes of the Unionist Party.

Paisley won some notoriety by his association with the kidnapping and proselytising of a fifteen-year-old Catholic girl called Maura Lyons in 1956, by abusing and heckling liberal Protestant leaders such as Rev Donald Soper, and by getting arrested in Rome for protesting at the opening of the Vatican Council in 1962. As unemployment grew in the late 1950s he built up an organisation called Ulster Protestant Action (UPA) whose aim was 'To keep Protestant and loyal workers in employment in times of depression, in preference to their Catholic fellow workers'[10]. In June 1959 a mob attacked a Catholic-owned fish and chip shop on the Shankill Road after Paisley and Unionist Councillor Charles McCullough had addressed a 1,500-strong UPA rally there. In 1961 the UPA was giving out leaflets at factories and in the shipyard condemning the allocation of Corporation houses to Catholics, and in February 1961 they had their first major success when they won control of Shankill Unionist Association and got Desmond Boal adopted as the Unionist candidate in a by-election.

With the accession of O'Neill, Paisley stepped up his activities and serious trouble came with the Westminster election of October 1964. Sinn Fein was contesting the West Belfast seat and had a tricolour in the window of their election headquarters in Divis Street on the Falls Road. Even the RUC had given up interfering with tricolours in Catholic areas, but on Sunday 27 September Paisley threatened at a meeting in the Ulster Hall that if it wasn't removed within two days he would lead a march to Divis Street to remove it himself.

The government was in a dilemma. West Belfast was a marginal seat and there were four candidates: James Kilfedder, Unionist; Billy Boyd, NILP; Harry Diamond, Republican Labour and Liam McMillan, Sinn Fein. If Boyd took enough Protestant votes off Kilfedder and Diamond got most of the Catholic votes, they'd lose the seat. It was no time to alienate their Loyalist supporters.

The day after Paisley's threat 50 RUC men led by District Inspector Frank Lagan broke down the door of the Sinn Fein office and seized the flag, while the Minister of Home Affairs saw Paisley and appealed to him to call off his march. His object achieved, Paisley contented himself with a rally at the City Hall. But on the Falls Road, a crowd of several thousand had gathered waiting for Paisley and when he didn't come a few buses were burnt. The next night there was fierce rioting after a Sinn Fein meeting, and the RUC made several baton charges. On Thursday the flag was put up again and the RUC broke in with pick-axes to take it down. That night Belfast had its worst riots since 1935. The RUC used armoured cars and water-cannon and the rioters replied with petrol-bombs. A bus and an RUC armoured car were burnt. The *Newsletter* quoted an RUC officer as saying, 'Things were clearly beyond RUC control and the Army might be called in'[11].

Three hundred and fifty RUC wearing military helmets and backed by armoured cars were sent into the Falls on the Friday night and smashed the resistance there. Fifty civilians were taken to hospital. In Dublin a thousand demonstrators marched on the British Embassy and stoned the Gardai surrounding it. By now Diamond, Eddie McAteer the Nationalist leader, his brother Hugh the Republican, and Sinn Fein all appealed for peace. The RUC backed off a little and when the tricolour was carried at a Republican parade on the Sunday they didn't interfere. The Divis Street riots were over. The Unionists held West Belfast quite safely[12].

O'Neill's liberal image was slightly tarnished when he commented, 'Today certain Republican candidates, many with backgrounds in the IRA . . . now appear to be using a British election to try to provoke disorder in Northern Ireland'[13].

The episode was significant. It showed that for all the liberal image, Stormont governments would still capitulate to pressure from the extreme right. And the violence of the rioting showed the depth of alienation among the Catholic working class in the ghettos. The Divis Street riots also served to focus British attention on the Northern Ireland situation at the very time when a new Labour government was coming into office.

The Lemass-O'Neill meeting gave Paisley new ammunition, and in February 1965 a massive Paisley rally outside the building forced O'Neill to abandon a function in the Unionist Party headquarters. For the rest of the year Paisley stomped the country denouncing 'O'Neillism'. He was an effective demagogue and his extreme sectarian Loyalism promised a continuation of Protestant supremacy and provided reassurance to grass-roots Unionist supporters who felt betrayed by O'Neill. His jibes at the 'Big House' Unionists and the 'fur-coat brigade' articulated the vaguely felt resentment of the Protestant working class and petty bourgeoisie. He built up a substantial following and in February 1966 launched a weekly paper, the *Protestant Telegraph*, which poured out a steady stream of hysterical anti-Catholic and anti-communist propaganda. In April he set up a twelve-man Ulster Constitution Defence Committee to co-ordinate his movement, with the Ulster Protestant Volunteers as its vanguard.

Paisley's activities were reaching a climax. In March 1966 he brought Edward Carson's son, an unstable Tory ex-MP, to Belfast, where he dutifully denounced O'Neill and said his policies 'can only lead to a destruction of Ulster's hard-won constitution and liberties'. In April Paisley forced the government to mobilise the B Specials for a month and ban trains from the South[14] from coming to commemorations of the 50th anniversary of the 1916 Rising, and then denounced them for not banning the parades altogether.

On 6 June he led a turbulent parade through the Catholic Cromac Square, where local residents tried to block the road and were cleared by the RUC after a short sharp riot, and on to the Presbyterian General Assembly where the marchers tried to attack the Governor of Northern Ireland. This time he had gone too far. O'Neill and his Minister of Home Affairs were in London being ticked off by Wilson that very day. Paisley was prosecuted on 18 July and went to jail for three months when he wouldn't agree to be bound over for two years.

His followers reacted violently. There was a serious riot with Loyalists fighting the RUC outside the prison on 22 July. The next day the RUC tried to block a 4,000-strong Paisleyite protest march from the centre of Belfast, but the marchers broke through and rampaged through the centre of the city breaking shop windows, stoning the Catholic-owned International Hotel, and going on to Sandy Row where they tried to burn down a bookie's shop which employed Catholics. That night there was savage rioting outside the jail with repeated baton-charges by the RUC. Only heavy rain finally stopped it. The government banned all meetings and parades in Belfast for three months, and gave the RUC power to break up any gathering of three or more people.

Meanwhile there had been more alarming developments. In February, March and April 1966 there had been a number of petrol-bomb attacks on Catholic shops, homes and schools in Belfast. On 7 May an elderly Protestant woman, Mrs Gould, was killed in a petrol-bomb attack on a Catholic pub next door to her home. On 27 May a Catholic man, John Scullion, was shot and wounded in Clonard Street off the Falls Road and died on 11 June. Then on 26 June three Catholic barmen from the

International Hotel were shot as they left a pub in Malvern Street, on the Shankill Road. One of them, Peter Ward, was killed. Three men, 'Gusty' Spence, Robert Williamson and Hugh McLean, were quickly arrested and charged with the murder of Ward. Spence was also charged with murdering Scullion. Other arrests were made and the story began to unfold.

On 22 May Belfast papers had received communiques from a group called the Ulster Volunteer Force – after the UVF of the 1912-22 period – saying 'From this day on we declare war against the IRA, and its splinter groups. Known IRA men will be executed mercilessly and without hesitation'[15]. The UVF also claimed responsibility for the shooting of Scullion but at the time no one paid much attention.

In fact the UVF was a small group of Paisley supporters who, alarmed by his denunciations of the Unionist sell-out, had set up an armed organisation. They were in a tradition of violent Protestant and Unionist groups which included the original UVF and the re-formed UVF of the 1920s, the Ulster Protestant Association of 1920-23 and the gunmen on the fringes of the Ulster Protestant League in 1935. Like their predecessors they were virulently anti-Catholic and attacked Catholic homes and Catholic civilians. The moving spirit of the UVF was 'Gusty' Spence, a brother of the Unionist election agent for West Belfast, ex-British soldier and military policeman in Cyprus, shipyard worker and former Ulster Protestant Action activist.

The UVF had been responsible for the petrol-bombings earlier in the year and had killed Scullion and Mrs Gould. Scullion was killed by a group who had been looking unsuccessfully for a prominent IRA man, Leo Martin. Ward was killed when they had again failed to locate Martin and returned to their local pub to find four young Catholics drinking there. They decided to kill them instead. Their attitude to Catholics was the logical outcome of years of discrimination and Unionist propaganda that all, or almost all, Catholics were 'disloyal'.

In court, the RUC gave evidence that McLean, when charged, said 'I am terribly sorry I ever heard of that man Paisley or decided to follow him'[16]. Paisley immediately denied all knowledge of McLean or the UVF. It was not a very plausible story. Spence had been actively associated with Paisley and Paisley had publicly thanked the UVF for taking part in a march on 17 April, and referred to them again on 16 June. Soon a closer connection was established. The government banned the UVF under the Special Powers Act and O'Neill announced that a leading member of the

UVF was also a prominent official of Paisley's Ulster Constitution Defence Committee.

The man was Noel Doherty, the secretary of the UCDC. He was a printer by trade, a B Special, and had been a Protestant Unionist candidate in the Belfast Corporation elections in 1964. He was very closely involved with Paisley, had set up the presses for the *Protestant Telegraph*, suggested the idea of the UCDC and the Ulster Protestant Volunteers, and played a leading part in organising them. On 21 April on his way to Armagh Paisley had dropped Doherty off in the village of Loughgall and picked him up later. In Loughgall Doherty was discussing with the local UPV members the possibility of getting arms and explosives for use against the IRA. In May Doherty put members of the Shankill Road-based UVF in touch with Loughall UPV, who supplied them with gelignite. By mid-June rumours of the activities of the two groups were common in the shipyard and Tom Boyd, the Labour MP for Pottinger, had called on the government to act against them on 23 June – three days before the Malvern Street murder.

Doherty and his Loughgall associates were caught in the general roundup after Malvern Street. Paisley had just dismissed him from the UPV and UCDC and managed to stay aloof from the proceedings. This wasn't the 1920s: the Unionist leadership had no use for Loyalist gun-men. In fact the killings had brought the North some very ugly publicity which could harm the industrial drive. The UVF and UPV men were tried in October 1966. Spence, Williamson and McLean were convicted of the murder of Ward and sentenced to life imprisonment with a minimum term of twenty years. Doherty was jailed for two years for trafficking in explosives. Two other men were jailed on fire-arms charges.

In the meantime there had been a growing fundamentalist backlash against 'O'Neillism'. The official resolutions passed at the Orange rallies on 12 July 1966 condemned the so-called 'Romeward trend' of the Protestant churches, and several government ministers were shouted down by Paisley supporters. On 23 September O'Neill returned from a holiday in England announcing that a conspiracy had been mounted against him. Desmond Boal had been given a junior post in the government earlier in the year to placate him, but he had strongly supported Paisley during June and resigned again. Now he had organised a petition for the removal of O'Neill and got the signatures of twelve of the 25 backbenchers. A parliamentary party meeting was called for 27 September and in the interim Boal got another signature. Warnock called for Faulkner to replace O'Neill and caucus meetings were held in Faulkner's house. Publicly Faulkner dissociated himself from the conspiracy but refused to back O'Neill. Three other ministers, Harry West, Ivan Neill and William Morgan, out of the nine-man cabinet, also refused to support O'Neill.

The party meeting was an anti-climax. The conspiracy collapsed. Faulkner had gone to America and four of the rebels, Boal, Nixon, Walter Scott and Tom Lyons, left before the vote. O'Neill got a vote of confidence with one against and one abstention. The Chief Whip – and O'Neill's cousin – Major Chichester-Clark, announced blandly, 'The rebels are now satisfied. There will be closer liaison between the government and the party'[17]. But the confrontation was only postponed. O'Neill could not go on indefinitely with half his cabinet and half his parliamentary party against him.

The next round came seven months later. On 26 April 1967 O'Neill sacked Harry West, the Minister for Agriculture, for his part in a land deal in Co. Fermanagh. The Unionist Party wasn't used to rigorous standards about ministers' profiteering. It was reckoned that O'Neill was settling accounts for the September conspiracy, especially when he replaced West with his faithful supporter Chichester-Clark. There was another storm. Faulkner said he was sure West was blameless. There was a backbench meeting on 2 May and O'Neill's action was backed by a majority of one. The backlash was gathering strength. It would be only a matter of time before O'Neill was ousted. The grass roots hankered after the old Orange ascendancy; the Unionist Party would not let itself be transformed into a non-sectarian conservative party.

The beginning of the O'Neill era had coincided with a change in the mood of the Catholic minority. The failure of the fifties' IRA campaign had turned their attention back to parliamentary politics. At the same time the post-war free education system and the increase in university scholarships was creating a much larger, better-educated Catholic middle class, ambitious, anxious to participate in politics and to end their second-class status. Free education and the welfare state also made them less anxious for immediate unity with the South with its inadequate social services, and more willing to work within the Northern system.

In November 1959 a group of Catholic graduates set up National Unity, a body which, though supporting a united Ireland, accepted the Northern constitution and was opposed to violence. They aimed to work for reforms within the North and act as a sort of Bow Group to the talentless Nationalists, since the Anti-Partition League had now collapsed irrevocably.

At first the Nationalists were not interested, but the accession of O'Neill gave a major boost to the new attitudes. A Prime Minister who wasn't an evident bigot and who talked of reconciliation seemed to offer the prospect of reform at last. In April 1964 National Unity held a convention of all anti-partition groups in Maghery in Co.Armagh and attacked the Nationalists for their lack of policies or a democratic party structure. The convention established a national political front of the Nationalist MPs, Harry Diamond, Frank Hanna, the new MP for Dock, Gerry Fitt, and the National Unity activists.

The front split up in a couple of months; but in November 1964 the Nationalists published a 39-point policy statement committing them to work within the constitution, and calling for industrial training schemes, action to end unemployment, public ownership of essential industries and support for agricultural co-operation as well as an end to discrimination, gerrymandering etc. They also promised the establishment of a new democratic party structure with annual conferences. It was hardly a revolutionary document, but it was the first comprehensive policy statement to deal with anything more than Irish unity and minority grievances since Joe Devlin's time. In February 1965 after the Lemass-O'Neill meeting, and advised by Lemass, they took up the position of official opposition for the first time in the state's history, with Eddie McAteer as leader.

At the same time the ambitious young graduates of National Unity, who hadn't been able to break into the charmed circle of the rural Nationalists, had given up waiting for the promised democratic structure and gone ahead and formed their own National Democratic Party. Slightly more radical than the Nationalists it was even more committed to the concept of working for social and economic reforms within the Northern state.

The wheel had come full circle since 1925. Then the Nationalists had shelved their opposition to partition and entered the Northern parliament to work within it for immediate reforms. The total lack of response had forced them into fruitless abstentionism and then, when they returned to parliament after the war, they had put immediate reforms in second place to the campaign to end partition and the whole system which had produced their grievances. Throughout the 1950s they drifted directionless, but now they had committed themselves more completely than ever before to working within the system to reform it.

O'Neill enjoyed a honeymoon period with the Catholic minority. He talked of building bridges between the two communities, he visited Catholic schools and was photographed chatting with priests and Reverend Mothers. He even met the Catholic Cardinal. It was an indication of how deeply divided the Northern population had become that such trivial gestures made headlines in the press, were received with pathetic gratitude by the Catholics and enraged the Loyalists. But then, as O'Neill himself said of Brookeborough, 'In twenty years as Prime Minister he never crossed the border, never visited a Catholic school and never received or sought a civic reception from a Catholic town'[18]. The Lemass-O'Neill meetings and the attacks by Paisley confirmed and strengthened his popularity among the Catholics.

In reality little had changed however. O'Neill was still a Unionist and an Orangeman and marched with his Lodge every 12 July. He even joined two other offshoots of the Orange Order, the Apprentice Boys and the Royal Black Preceptory, after he became Prime Minister. He made no move to end the minority's three main grievances: gerrymandering of local government, discrimination, and the existence of the Special Powers Act and the B Specials. He admitted after he resigned that 'As the party would never stand for change I was really reduced to trying to improve relations between North and South; and in the North itself between the two sections of the community'[19]. The new regime was based on an illusion.

In fact some of the new economic policies worsened the minority's position. There was already an economic imbalance between East and West in Northern Ireland, or more precisely between the areas of Antrim, Down and North Armagh within 30 miles of Belfast, and Fermanagh, Tyrone and Derry in the West and Newry in the South. The West and South suffered from consistently higher unemployment and emigration than the East, especially Derry, the second city of the North, with a population of over 50,000 and permanent male unemployment of nearly 20 per cent. The East was overwhelmingly Protestant, the West and South mainly Catholic.

The new economic strategy did nothing to remedy the situation. Its purpose was, by providing fast, efficient transport and communications, advance factories, industrial sites and services, greatly improved education facilities and social amenities, to attract new industry and to divert it away from the congested and unhealthily overdeveloped Belfast area. (40 per cent of the total population of Northern Ireland lived within the Belfast urban area – including Newtownabbey, Holywood, and Lisburn – in 1971)[20]. But under the Benson Report the railway line to Newry and the line to Derry through Omagh and Strabane were axed, leaving the three towns with no fast efficient transport system. The new motorways went to Ballymena in Co.Antrim and Lurgan and Portadown in North Armagh, not to Derry or Newry. But the Matthew Report was the crucial one. It recommended the development of a new city with a massive injection of capital as an alternative focus to Belfast – but not the existing city of Derry with some established industry, its own port and a nearby airport. In fact Derry wasn't even among the other seven growth centres listed, nor was Newry. The new city – based on Lurgan and Portadown – and six of the seven growth centres were within a 30-mile radius of Belfast. The only exception was Coleraine – a solidly Protestant town in North Derry. Only one of the eight centres had a Catholic majority – Downpatrick in Co.Down.

The final insult came with the Lockwood Report at the end of 1964. It recommended a second university for Northern Ireland, but again not in Derry, the second largest centre of population, where there was already an old-established University College. The university was to go to Coleraine. There was a big protest campaign in Derry backed even by liberal Unionists, and it came out that hard-liners in the Derry Unionist Party had lobbied against their own city because investment and development would swell the already growing Catholic majority to such a size that no gerrymandering could keep the city in Unionist hands. The government endorsed the Lockwood decision.

The O'Neill administration could argue that the original economic imbalance between East and West was none of their doing; but their development policies not only did nothing to remedy the situation, they actually increased the imbalance. The Catholics in the West had to watch while investment and industry poured into areas of virtually full employment, while their depressed areas declined even further. After Lockwood, Derry became a powder-keg. And it was not as if Catholics in the more prosperous East were benefitting greatly either. Unemployment in the Catholic ghettos of Belfast remained consistently higher than in neighbouring Protestant areas[21], and none of the new industry was pumped into depressed West Belfast.

Indeed it seemed clear that the Unionists, with their obsessional fears about the higher Catholic birth-rate – and the percentage of Catholics among school-children (46·6 per cent in 1962)[22] was considerably higher than in the population as a whole – were anxious to maintain the high rate of emigration from the mainly Catholic West, by denuding it of industry and siting new development only in areas where the Protestant majority was virtually impregnable. Derry City was a special case. Not only were the Loyalists determined to keep control of the city which held a central place in their mythology, but they foresaw that a growing and expanding Derry with its own university could provide leadership and a rallying point for the minority throughout the province.

And there was no evidence of change even in areas where no new legislation, no drastic shifts in policy, were required. In September 1967, four years after O'Neill came to power, the government reappointed members of three public boards. The figures were: Youth Employment Board, 33 members, three Catholics; Hospitals Authority, 22 members, two Catholics; General Health Services Board, 24 members, two Catholics. The functions of these boards affected Catholics as much as Protestants, appointment was simply a matter of government nomination, and there was no shortage of middle-class Catholics eager to serve on them. Even the liberal Unionist *Belfast Telegraph* said the appointments made a mockery of O'Neill's professions of goodwill[23].

Disillusion was beginning to set in by the end of 1965. It affected the political activists first and it was all the sharper because the minority's hopes had been raised so high. It was first articulated, ironically enough, by the NILP in their manifesto for the 1965 election:

'When Captain O'Neill became Prime Minister two years ago, he encouraged hopes that he would turn his back on the past and that we would see a new era of bridge-building within our divided community, of progress in the economic field. Both these hopes have been disappointed . . .

'No attempt has been made by the Northern Ireland government to knit the community together; there have been no electoral reforms, no review of electoral boundaries, no financial arrangements with the Mater Hospital[24]; there is to be no ombudsman. The siting of the new university, the siting and naming of the new city, the appointment of its commission, all have been handled, whatever their merits, in such a way as to give the maximum offence. Not merely has Captain O'Neill dashed the hopes he himself raised, he has added a new bitterness and disappointment to the grievances of the minority'.

When the Nationalists finally held their first annual conference in

May 1966, McAteer took the opportunity to express his frustration at the lack of results after a year as the official opposition. It was a theme he returned to. Early in December 1966 he warned that if there weren't major civil rights reforms in the forthcoming Queen's Speech, the Nationalists might give up the role of official opposition. There weren't, and at the second Nationalist conference in July 1967 he commented that 'It was a matter of disappointment that each concession and each gesture they had made so far had met with little or no response'[25].

By now politics in the North had become centred on the question of civil rights for the Catholic minority. In January 1964 a group of middle-class and professional Catholics established the Campaign for Social Justice and began to collect and distribute facts and figures about gerrymandering and discrimination. They were backed by the Nationalists and the new National Democrats of course, but support also came from an unexpected quarter.

The NILP was changing. After the collapse of the Irish Labour Party there was a vacuum in Northern politics. Gradually, despite its ultra-constitutionalism, Catholics, liberals and leftists began to join the NILP and its complexion changed. In 1965, despite opposition by Bleakley, the party conference voted for repeal of the Special Powers Act. Ironically, the loss of two seats in the 1965 election strengthened the leftward trend by weakening the influence of the pro-Unionist ex-MPs Bleakley and Billy Boyd. In September 1966 the NILP and the Northern Committee of the ICTU presented a joint memorandum to the government demanding 'One man, One vote' and fair boundaries in local elections, measures to end discrimination in housing and employment, fair representation for the minority on public boards and the appointment of an ombudsman. It was a significant development coming from two mainly Protestant bodies. However when a joint NILP/ICTU delegation met the cabinet in December 1966 to press their demands they got no satisfaction. When William Craig, then Minister for Home Affairs, was questioned about the difference between the restricted local government franchise in Northern Ireland and the universal franchise in Britain, he said Britain was out of step with the North.

Faced with attitudes like this in the North, and encouraged by the election of a Labour government at Westminster in October 1964, opposition politicians began to look to Westminster for intervention. In June 1965 a group of backbench Labour MPs, some of them veterans of the

Friends of Ireland Group, set up the Campaign for Democracy in Ulster to call for a Westminster enquiry into affairs in Northern Ireland. They based their demand on Section 75 of the Government of Ireland Act 1920:

'Notwithstanding the establishment of the Parliament of Northern Ireland or anything contained in this Act, the supreme authority of the Parliament of the United Kingdom shall remain unaffected and undiminished over all persons, matters and things in Northern Ireland and every part thereof'.

The CDU campaign got a major boost in March 1966 when Gerry Fitt was elected MP for West Belfast. Fitt was a hustling local politician connected with one of the many splinters of the old Irish Labour Party. He was elected to Stormont for the Dock constituency in 1962, and held the seat again in 1965, the first man to do so. By 1966 he had acquired enough prestige to keep other opposition groups out of West Belfast, and won it in a straight fight with the Unionist[26]. Now for the first time since 1950 there was both a spokesman for the Northern minority at Westminster and a Labour government to hear him.

The Malvern Street murder gave the campaign for an enquiry another boost, with Harold Wilson himself denouncing the ultra-Unionists as 'quasi-fascist'. In November 1966 the Home Secretary Roy Jenkins told a CDU delegation that the government was pressing Stormont hard to bring in reforms. In March 1967 the NILP conference backed the demand for an enquiry and in April three backbench members of the CDU, Paul Rose, Maurice Macmillan and Stanley Orme[27], visited the North for discussions with opposition politicians.

The pressure for reform seemed irresistible but no reforms were coming. Instead in March 1967 William Craig used the Special Powers Act to ban Republican clubs.

After the collapse of the IRA campaign in 1962 the Republican movement had changed. Many dropped out, disillusioned; others rethought their position, realising the need for mass involvement and participation in their struggle, and turned towards left-wing politics and social agitation. They revived the radicalism of the IRA in the thirties, getting involved in strikes, struggles over foreign ownership of land and fishing rights. They also abandoned the formal legalism of the past, with its belief in the army council of the IRA as the legitimate government of Ireland, in favour of a more flexible policy of working within the system to bring it down. They set up Republican clubs as part of this strategy. Since

Sinn Fein was illegal in the North, the Republican clubs were an attempt to organise openly and legally for legal political action.

Craig's ban seemed an attempt to suppress even quite legitimate non-violent opposition. It led to widespread protest and within days of the announcement left-wing students and Young Socialists held two protest marches in Belfast. Later, in November, 1,500 students and Young Socialists tried to march to the City Hall in Belfast, but were re-routed by the RUC when Paisley held a counter-demonstration in Shaftesbury Square.

The Young Socialists who were behind the marches had also been responsible for much of the leftward movement of the NILP, but were now moving away from conventional politics towards extra-parliamentary action and marxism[28]. Their impatience with the reforms which never came was soon to communicate itself to the rest of the opposition and to the minority as a whole. Speaking at a Connolly Association rally in London in June 1967, Gerry Fitt warned dramatically that continued frustration in the North would lead to violence again. He spoke much truer than he realised.

Another of the Republicans' legal activities had been the setting up of Wolfe Tone Societies as discussion forums for Republicans, communists, socialists and other radicals – the Republicans were strongly influenced by the Communist Party at the time. In the North the Wolfe Tone Society and the Campaign for Social Justice combined to establish a Northern Ireland Civil Rights Association (NICRA), along the lines of the National Council for Civil Liberties in Britain. The NICRA was a sober, moderate body, and when Craig banned a Republican parade through Armagh at Easter 1968, after pressure from Paisley, it held protest rallies in Armagh and Newry. But pressure was growing for more direct action.

In Derry since the beginning of the year the local Republican club and the left-wing local Labour party, led by Eamonn McCann, had formed a Housing Action Committee and were encouraging squatting and disrupting traffic and corporation meetings. They were loudly denounced as 'communist agitators' by the local Nationalists who had evidently forgotten the early 1950s. In Caledon, Co.Tyrone, the local Republican club was also encouraging homeless Catholic families to squat in newly-built council houses, since the Unionist-controlled Dungannon Rural Council wouldn't allocate the houses to them. In June the families were evicted and the council allocated one of the houses to the local Unionist candidate's secretary, an unmarried girl. Austin Currie, a Nationalist MP, occupied the house in protest and was evicted and fined.

In August 1968, fed up with both the rural council and the gerrymandered urban council, the Dungannon-based Campaign for Social Justice decided to hold a protest march from Coalisland to Dungannon. NICRA rather hesitantly agreed. The march surprised the organisers. 2,500 people, twice the population of Coalisland, turned up. Many of the marchers, hitherto uninvolved in politics, saw the occasion as a way of demonstrating their frustration.

Paisley's UPV announced a counter-demonstration for the centre of Dungannon, and the RUC promptly barred the Civil Rights march from the centre of the town – the Catholics were to be kept in their ghettos. The organisers stopped the march and held a rally. Some Young Socialists tried to get through the RUC cordon and were beaten back and there was a few minutes' turmoil. It was a small enough affair but it had started an idea.

Derry was the obvious centre for another march. The local Derry activists suggested it and NICRA again agreed, but even more hesitantly because the local Nationalists wouldn't support it – though McAteer eventually marched. The march was planned for 5 October and the route was to be along business streets from the Waterside Station on the East side of the Foyle, across Craigavon Bridge and to the Diamond in the centre of the city. The Derry Unionists were up in arms. The Diamond was the centre of the plantation walled city, the symbol of Protestant supremacy perched above the Catholic masses in the Bogside. No anti-Unionist parade had ever gone through the walled city – or attempted to – since the RUC had batoned the Anti-Partition League off the streets at the start of the 1950s.

On 1 October the Apprentice Boys[29] gave notice of an 'annual' parade on 5 October over the same route as the Civil Rights march. No one in Derry had ever heard of the 'annual' parade before but it served the purpose. Craig banned all parades, except in the ghetto, on 5 October.

NICRA dithered and were about to call it off when the Derry groups and the Belfast Young Socialists said they would go ahead regardless. NICRA hurriedly agreed and the march assembled on 5 October. Craig had drafted in a massive force of police, including the RUC Reserve force and two water cannons. He boasted that this would not be another Armagh – where the Republicans had successfully defied his ban at Easter.

Two thousand marchers set off from the Waterside station and got about 200 yards. They were met by a solid wall of RUC, who batoned Gerry Fitt, at the head of the march. Crushed in the narrow street most of the marchers didn't even see this, and the organisers tried to hold a meeting.

The Young Socialists made a determined effort to get through however and the RUC baton-charged. The marchers were caught between two lines of police, batoned savagely and then hosed with the water cannon. Even the government-commissioned Cameron Report later criticised the indiscriminate violence of the police.

Scattered fighting broke out throughout the city as the RUC charged groups of marchers and ended up in the Bogside, where barricades were put up that night and petrol bombs used for the first time in Derry. 77 civilians were injured[30] and a number arrested, though the charges were later dropped.

The march had been well covered by television. Viewers all over Ireland and Britain saw the RUC smashing up a peaceful demonstration. A wave of anger swept through the frustrated minority, and stirred liberal opinion in the North. The Young Socialists and student left were organising. On 9 October a thousand students set out to march to the City Hall in Belfast. Paisley held a counter-demonstration at Shaftesbury Square and the RUC rerouted the students. They accepted, only to be stopped again nearer the city centre because half a dozen Paisleyite women had blocked the road. The students (including the author, then a postgraduate student and teacher) held a three-hour sit-down in the street and then went back to the university. That night they set up the Peoples Democracy (PD), a loose activist body committed to civil rights reforms, but with a tough Young Socialist hard core. It was to become the dynamic driving force of the Civil Rights movement.

Things were moving fast. On 15 October the Nationalists withdrew from their position as official opposition. The next day the PD held another march, 1,500-strong, to the City Hall. This time a worried RUC let them through. It was to be the last anti-Unionist march allowed into the city centre to date. On 21 October Harold Wilson expressed his concern about the situation in the North and said there must be reforms. On 24 October the PD took over the parliament buildings at Stormont and held a nine-hour sit-in there. The next day Jack Lynch, the new Southern Taoiseach, saw Wilson in London to protest about the events in Derry. On 3 November Wilson saw O'Neill, Craig and Faulkner and demanded that they introduce reforms urgently.

There was to be another march in Derry over the original route on 16 November. Craig banned all marches inside the walled city for a month. 15,000 people marched on the 16th but were stopped again by a massive force of RUC. The organisers, a 'moderate' Citizens' Action Committee led by John Hume and Ivan Cooper[31], who had ousted the original activists, prevented a confrontation. It didn't matter, the march had shown the strength of the new Civil Rights movement and for the next few days, despite the efforts of the CAC, Derry factory workers marched in, out and around the walled area, breaking Craig's ban several times a day. The city was in revolt. The government had to do something. On 22 November O'Neill announced a package of reforms. Derry Corporation would be abolished and replaced by a nominated commission, there would be an ombudsman, local authorities would be encouraged to adopt a points system for allocating houses, the company vote would be abolished for local elections and the government would consider suspending parts of the Special Powers Act.

It was too little, too late. It was enough to outrage the Loyalists without satisfying the Civil Rights movement at all. The whole campaign began to centre around 'One man, One Vote' – effectively around who controlled the gerrymandered councils. O'Neill wouldn't concede it – it would have split the Unionist Party. The Civil Rights movement wouldn't be satisfied without it. NICRA decided to go ahead with a march in Armagh on 30 November.

Paisley and his right-hand man, a retired Army Major, Ronald Bunting, threatened a counter-demonstration and Paisley saw Craig the day before but there was no ban. The government didn't want a repetition of the massive Derry march. At 1am on the morning of the demonstration Paisley and his supporters occupied the centre of the town. Throughout the morning their numbers swelled and they armed themselves with cudgels and clubs. There were 350 RUC in Armagh but they made no effort to remove the Paisleyites. The Civil Rights march, 5,000-strong, was stopped as it reached the edge of the Catholic ghetto. The march was legal, the Paisleyite counter-demonstration illegal, yet the RUC capitulated to the armed Loyalist mob.

What support O'Neill's package of reforms had won among the minority, the capitulation in Armagh lost again. On 9 December he made another attempt to regain credibility with the minority and get support against the hardliners in the Unionist Party. He made a mawkish appeal on television, addressing himself to the Civil Rights demonstrators: 'Your voice has been heard and clearly heard. Your duty now is to play your part in taking the heat out of the situation'[32]. Craig attacked the speech the following day and O'Neill sacked him on 11 December. The appeal was highly successful. Many Catholics were flattered at the idea of a Unionist Prime Minister appealing directly to them. The Protestant middle class were appalled at the spectacle of violence which loomed in front of them. The *Belfast Telegraph*, the organ of the modernising businessmen – it had recently been taken over by Lord Thomson – printed 'I back O'Neill' coupons to be cut out and posted to him. In a wave of emotion tens of thousands of coupons were returned and the Derry Citizens' Action Committee called off all protests for a month.

But when the emotion subsided 'One Man, One Vote' was no nearer. O'Neill's speech had solved nothing. Even Wilson acknowledged as much at Westminster on 12 December when he said that universal franchise must come in Northern Ireland. The Peoples Democracy decided to go ahead with a four-day march from Belfast to Derry, starting on 1 January. The march would be the acid test of the government's intentions. Either the government would face up to the extreme right of its own Unionist Party and protect the march from the 'harassing and hindering' immediately threatened by Major Bunting, or it would be exposed as impotent in the face of sectarian thuggery, and Westminster would be forced to intervene, re-opening the whole Irish question for the first time in 50 years. The march was modelled on the Selma-Montgomery march in Alabama in 1966, which had exposed the racist thuggery of America's deep South and forced the US government into major reforms.

The march was denounced by every establishment organ, by almost the entire middle class, Catholic as well as Protestant, and by Eddie McAteer, whose comment was 'Half a loaf is better than nothing.' Even NICRA was divided. There was no ban. The government hoped the march would peter out of its own accord.

About eighty marchers set off from the City Hall in Belfast at 9am on 1 January 1969. The author was the march organiser. The plan was to stop in Antrim for tea and then to march to a country hall for the night. The first leg was fairly uneventful. A few Paisleyites marched in front with a Union Jack but gave up after a mile or two. The march reached Antrim about 4pm and a handful of Paisleyites gathered on the bridge outside the town. The RUC immediately stopped the march and mingled with the Paisleyites while a lambeg drummer summoned more Loyalists to block the bridge. There was stalemate till nightfall, when the RUC had to transport the marchers to the hall.

The next morning was the same. The police stopped the march outside Randalstown while a group of Paisleyites armed with sticks and cudgels blocked a bridge. The march was allowed through the Catholic village of Toome and then blocked again. This time the Minister for Agriculture and local MP, Major Chichester-Clark, was lurking in the background. Now came the first evidence of active RUC-Paisleyite collusion. The march was diverted up a side-road on the pretext that a hostile crowd was blocking the main road, but in fact the hostile crowd was waiting at an isolated cross-roads on the diversion route.

Eventually the march reached another Catholic village – Gulladuff. By then it was dark, and hearing that a crowd of Loyalists were waiting on the road to Maghera – that day's destination –, the marchers decided to halt till morning. Deprived of their prey the Loyalists rampaged through Maghera attacking Catholic shops and homes. Chichester-Clark met a deputation of Loyalists that night at his home and promised to try to get the march banned next day.

In the morning the RUC blocked the march going into Maghera. It proceeded over the Sperrin mountains to Dungiven where it got a warm reception, only to be blocked again outside the town. The RUC claimed there were hostile crowds in the villages of Feeny and Claudy on the main road, but the marchers had had enough. They broke through the police cordon and went straight through the villages. There was no hostile crowd. There was one on the diversion suggested by the RUC however.

That afternoon the new Home Affairs Minister, William Long, had what he described as a 'congenial' meeting with Paisley and Major Bunting, the self-confessed organiser of the 'harassing and hindering'. But there was still no ban, and Paisley and Bunting went on to address a Loyalist rally in the Guildhall in Derry where the next day's 'harassment' was organised.

On 4 January the march set out from Claudy swelled by several hundred supporters who had come out from Derry. A few miles out from the village they were halted again and then allowed to proceed with a warning that there might be some stone-throwing ahead. A bit suspicious of the RUC's sudden willingness to let them march they went ahead. At Burntollet Bridge several hundred Loyalists hurled rocks and bottles and then charged, armed with clubs and iron bars. It was an ambush. The spot was well chosen, the Loyalists were on a height and dozens of marchers were driven off the road and into the river Faughan, some quite badly injured.

There was no doubt that it was a trap. The RUC knew an ambush had been prepared. Heaps of stones had been collected the night before and crowds of cudgel-wielding men had been gathering since early morning while RUC men stood among them laughing and chatting. During the ambush some of the RUC joined in and attacked the marchers too. After the attack they made no attempt to arrest any of the Loyalists. I remember going back to the bridge and finding RUC and ambushers sitting about relaxing. It later turned out that nearly a hundred of the ambush party were off-duty B Specials[33].

The battered remnant of the march trudged on to Derry. At Irish Street estate on the outskirts of the city there was another ambush with stones and petrol-bombs, and in Spencer Road the RUC stopped the march while Loyalists pelted it with rocks from a hilltop quarry. But eventually it arrived to a rapturous welcome from a huge crowd in Guildhall Square. That night the RUC Reserve force, drunk, and apparently furious that the marchers had got through, ran amok in the Catholic Bogside breaking windows and doors and beating up anyone in sight. The people were outraged, barricades were built and Free Derry was born. The RUC were kept out of the area for a week.

O'Neill, who had been silent throughout the march, issued a statement on 5 January.

'The march to Londonderry planned by the so-called Peoples Democracy, was, from the start, a foolhardy and irresponsible undertaking. At best those who planned it were careless of the effects which it would have; at worst they embraced with enthusiasm the prospect of adverse publicity causing further damage to the interests of Northern Ireland as a whole . . .

'Some of the marchers and those who supported them in Londonderry itself have shown themselves to be mere hooligans ready to attack the police and others. And at various places people have attempted to take the law into their own hands in efforts to impede the march. These efforts include disgraceful violence offered indiscriminately both to the marchers and the police who were attempting to protect them.

'Of course those who were responsible for this violence were playing into the hands of those who are encouraging the current agitation. Had this march been treated with silent contempt and allowed to proceed peaceably the entire affair would have made little mark . . .

'Enough is enough. We have heard sufficient for now about civil rights; let us hear a little about civic responsibility'[34].

He also threatened to mobilise the B Specials, who had provided many of the attackers. The venom of O'Neill's attack on the marchers, the mildness of his rebuke to the Loyalists and his silence about the conduct of his police enraged the minority, and lost him all the sympathy his television broadcast had gained. Most Catholics and the small group of liberal Protestants who supported the Civil Rights movement had originally opposed the march and had been prepared to give O'Neill a chance. But they had watched the marchers being blocked, re-routed and harassed for three days and ambushed on the fourth, while the RUC stood by and watched or even joined in, and government ministers held meetings with the attackers. Burntollet was the turning point for the Civil Rights movement. They would accept no further promises or excuses, they wanted civil rights – especially 'One Man, One Vote – immediately.

There was a march in Newry on 11 January, which erupted in violence when the government banned a section of the route through the centre of the 80 per cent Catholic town. Even the local Protestant businessmen protested at the ban. From the nonchalance with which the RUC watched the crowd burn a few worn-out police tenders and throw them in the canal, it looked as if the incident was set up to discredit the Civil Rights movement.

It made no difference. Things were moving fast again. On 15 January O'Neill announced a government commission to investigate the recent disturbances and their underlying causes. It consisted of a Scottish judge, Lord Cameron, and two local academics, one Catholic and one Protestant. The official enquiry had come at last. On 23 January Faulkner resigned from the government. He said the commission was a political manoeuvre. It would recommend 'One Man, One Vote' and get the government off the hook. In an extraordinary personal *volte face* he argued that the government should make the decision itself and then sell it to the party. In an extremely bitter reply O'Neill pointed out that Faulkner had always opposed 'One Man, One Vote' and accused him of disloyalty during successive party crises. In a revealing aside he said,

'You knew perfectly well, following the party meeting at which these proposals were discussed, that any change in the declared policy [on the franchise] **was not acceptable at the present time to the vast majority of our parliamentary colleagues'**[35].

The Unionist Party simply wouldn't concede the only reform which might have satisfied the Civil Rights movement.

The next day William Morgan, another cabinet hard-liner, resigned as well. On 29 January Paisley and Bunting went to jail to serve three-month sentences for the Armagh affair. On 3 February twelve Unionist backbenchers met in a hotel in Portadown and called for O'Neill's resignation[36]. There was now a majority of the backbench party against him. That evening he announced an election for 24 February. He hoped to get a mandate against the hard-liners by rallying the Protestant moderates and winning a substantial Catholic vote.

It was an extraordinary contest. Both O'Neill and his hard-line opponents were still in the Unionist Party, but where the official Unionist candidates were anti-O'Neill they were opposed by unofficial pro-O'Neill candidates or vice-versa, while some candidates managed to keep a foot in both camps. Protestant Unionists also stood against a number of O'Neillites. Paisley himself appealed his sentence and got out of jail to challenge O'Neill in Bannside, where he had been unopposed since 1946. If O'Neill was wooing the Catholic vote he wasn't offering much. His manifesto promised no new reforms and certainly not 'One Man, One Vote'. In general O'Neill was backed by the landed gentry, the modernising businessmen, the media and the professional middle class. The hard-liners, led by Faulkner, were backed by the Protestant working class, farmers and petty bourgeoisie. Most of the Catholics remained unimpressed.

But there were other battles being fought. On the opposition side some of the new leaders of the Civil Rights movement stood against the traditional Nationalists. The PD put up eight candidates on a militant leftist and Civil Rights platform, challenging both Unionists and Nationalists and intervening in the pro-and anti-O'Neill contest. The aim was threefold: to win mass support for an intensified and broadened Civil Rights campaign criticising the South as well, to oust the 'Old Guard' Nationalists and, perhaps most important, to combat the notion that the minority should back O'Neill in the power struggle in the Unionist Party – and by implication reduce their demands to what he could persuade the Unionists to accept. The PD, was firmly, if instinctively, convinced that the Unionist Party, being based on sectarianism and Protestant supremacy, could never dismantle the Orange state. Accordingly PD decided to oppose O'Neill himself in Bannside – the author was the PD candidate against both O'Neill and Paisley and managed to save his deposit in a fiercely Loyalist constituency.

The election ended in confusion and stalemate. In the 23 constituencies where pro-O'Neill candidates faced anti-O'Neillites or

Protestant Unionists, the pro-O'Neillites got 141,914 votes and eleven seats, their opponents 130,619 votes and twelve seats. O'Neill himself had suffered a severe rebuff when he scraped home without an overall majority in Bannside[37]. He was left with a party more bitterly divided than ever in which neither side had the upper hand.

On the opposition side the most startling result was the ousting of Eddie McAteer by John Hume, one of the new Civil Rights leaders, by a majority of 3,653. A second Nationalist was ousted in Mid-Derry by another Civil Rights leader, Ivan Cooper, a Protestant, and a third went out in South Armagh. The Nationalists had lapsed into easy acceptance of the Northern status quo and had come to terms with their Unionist masters. They had been slow to sense and respond to the growing militancy of their constituents. Now they were paying the price. Within four years they would virtually have disappeared from the Northern scene. The PD candidates got 23,645 votes and narrowly failed to oust another Nationalist in South Down. The NILP, who had already lost most of their left-wing militants to the PD, made little impact. They lost their seat in Pottinger, held Oldpark, and narrowly won in Falls, where their candidate, Paddy Devlin, had been active in the Civil Rights movement. But the shape of opposition politics was changing fast. Within a year Devlin and two of the six remaining Nationalists had broken with their parties.

When Stormont re-assembled O'Neill was faced with a parliamentary party of 35 which contained most of his bitterest opponents and a number of fence-sitters. He had three supporters who weren't members of the parliamentary party. On 28 February the party met and O'Neill was re-elected leader by 23 votes to one with one abstention, after ten of his opponents had walked out. But from the beginning at least eight of his majority were unreliable. How long could he last?

He tried to carry on. The Queen's Speech promised legislation to implement the November package of reforms. To balance it, on 12 March the government introduced a stiff Public Order Bill requiring longer notice of parades, outlawing counter-demonstrations and banning sit-downs, occupation of public buildings and other civil disobedience tactics.

But things were moving fast again. A new, more radical NICRA executive had been elected including two PD members – the author was one of them. On 14 March, four of the 'Old Guard' members – including Betty Sinclair of the Communist Party – resigned in protest at its increased militancy but the membership backed the new tough line – the Public Order

Bill was evidently aimed at the Civil Rights movement, while police brutality at a PD march in Lurgan showed that the RUC hadn't changed their attitude. The new NICRA executive showed its teeth on 22 March with simultaneous demonstrations against the Public Order Bill in six different towns, while the opposition MPs staged a sit-down in the parliament at Stormont.

Meanwhile Paisley and Bunting went back to jail on 25 March, and the Unionist right wing were full of discontent. On 30 March a massive explosion rocked an electricity station at Castlereagh outside Belfast, causing damage estimated at £2 million. The *Protestant Telegraph* immediately blamed the IRA and the hard-line Unionists demanded an end to all concessions and tough repressive measures rightaway.

On 17 April there was a by-election for the Mid-Ulster seat at Westminster. Bernadette Devlin, a 21-year-old student member of PD, had won the nomination as a united anti-Unionist candidate. She won the election with the biggest anti-Unionist majority since the seat was created in 1950[38]. It was a convincing demonstration that almost the entire minority had swung behind the militant Civil Rights campaign.

Two days later there was a minor riot in the centre of Derry. The RUC beat the rioters back to the edge of the Bogside. A group of RUC men broke into a house in William Street and beat the owner, Sam Devenny, unconscious in front of his family. He died three months later. The rioting intensified and that night the RUC Reserve force in full riot gear occupied the Bogside. In the morning, as Bogsiders awoke to find their narrow streets occupied by armed police and as word of the Devenny beating spread, the atmosphere was electric. Most of the people evacuated the area and the menfolk gathered on Creggan Heights arming for a fight. For a couple of hours Derry was on the brink of open war until a frightened Minister of Home Affairs ordered the RUC to withdraw.

But already NICRA and PD had organised a series of protests in Belfast and across the North, most of which ended in riots, and in Belfast the IRA, in its first action since the Civil Rights campaign began, petrol-bombed a number of post offices. The same night there were much more effective blasts at the Silent Valley reservoir in Co.Down and an electricity link-up in Portadown.

Rioting continued on the Falls Road for several days, and on 22 April, O'Neill took the only step which might placate minority feeling and defuse the situation: he accepted the principle of 'One Man, One Vote'. The next morning his cousin Chichester-Clark resigned. The following day the full parliamentary party of MPs and Senators accepted the change by 28 votes to 22. Faulkner voted against. That night and the next there were two more blasts at water pipe-lines, leaving the whole of Belfast short of water.

The bombs were turning the waverers against O'Neill. There would soon be a meeting of the Unionist Party Standing Committee. He was unlikely to survive it. On 28 April he resigned, and appeared on television saying,

'I have tried to break the chains of ancient hatreds. I have been unable to realise during my period of office all that I had sought to achieve. Whether now it can be achieved in my life-time I do not know. But one day these things will be and must be achieved'.

Months later it was revealed that the series of bomb blasts in March and April were organised by the UVF to simulate IRA attacks and panic the Unionist Party into bringing O'Neill down. He went, detested by the Loyalists, who refused to sacrifice their ascendancy and come to terms with a new self-confident minority unwilling to tolerate second class citizenship any longer. He was unlamented by the minority whose hopes he had raised but couldn't fulfill. The Unionists had built their state on sectarianism and Protestant supremacy. They could not jettison them now without shaking the state to its foundations, perhaps even destroying it.

If any of the minority had shed tears over O'Neill's downfall they dried them shortly after it when, with sublime paternalist arrogance, he said:

'It is frightfully hard to explain to Protestants that if you give Roman Catholics a good job and a good house they will live like Protestants, because they will see neighbours with cars and television sets.

'They will refuse to have eighteen children, but if a Roman Catholic is jobless and lives in the most ghastly hovel, he will rear eighteen children on National Assistance...

'If you treat Roman Catholics with due consideration and kindness, they will live like Protestants, in spite of the authoritative nature of their Church'[39].

The Drift to Disaster

The fall of Terence O'Neill solved nothing. The forces which brought him down were still at work and would bring down his successors just as surely. O'Neill had been caught between the hammer and the anvil: between the minority's revolt against Protestant supremacy and the Loyalists' determination to cling to that supremacy. The middle ground was being swept away, those who tried to occupy it were destined to be swept away as well. On 1 May 1969 the parliamentary Unionist Party elected Chichester-Clark as leader with a majority of one over Faulkner. O'Neill's own vote carried the day; he backed Chichester-Clark. In fact he seems to have timed his resignation to ensure Clark's election. He commented,

'Had I stayed on even for another week I think there's no doubt about it that two members of the [parliamentary] **party would have changed sides. Then the moderates would have been in a minority of one . . . by getting out when I did I saved both my cabinet and my policies'**[1].

Chichester-Clark, despite his resignation from O'Neill's cabinet, was basically an O'Neillite, but the resignation had won him some credibility with the hard-liners. As a member of the landed gentry and of a leading Unionist family – his father and his grandmother, Dame Dehra Parker, had held the South Derry seat before him, his grandmother had been a cabinet minister and his brother was an MP at Westminster – he had the support of the traditional Unionist establishment. He was a keen Orangeman and a popular, uncontroversial figure. O'Neill hoped that he could hold the Unionist Party together while putting through the now inevitable 'One Man, One Vote'.

But the basic contradiction of the Northern state was now out in the open. The Catholics, with new self-confidence, would no longer tolerate second-class citizenship and discrimination; the Unionist grass roots, kept loyal for nearly fifty years by anti-Catholic propaganda and Protestant privilege, would tolerate no concessions and every escalation of minority agitation only made them more intransigent. No change of personalities could resolve the contradiction, especially when the minority knew O'Neill had been ousted because of his willingness to make some concessions, and when his successor was as dull and stumbling as Chichester-Clark.

Nonetheless Clark had a brief honeymoon. He brought Faulkner back into the cabinet, temporarily re-uniting the party. He announced an amnesty for all offences connected with political protests since 5 October 1968: this got Paisley and Bunting out of jail and got the RUC out of having to prosecute some of the Burntollet ambushers, including the B Specials who were involved, but it also affected some Civil Rights demonstrators. On 9 May the Unionist Party Standing Committee accepted the principle of 'One Man, One Vote'. On 21 May Chichester-Clark, Faulkner and two other ministers saw Harold Wilson and James Callaghan, the Home Secretary, in London and Wilson announced that the next local elections in the North would be held under 'One Man, One Vote'.

NICRA called a temporary halt to demonstrations, but the logic of events was taking over. RUC intervention in a row in a pub on Belfast's Crumlin Road sparked off the smouldering hatred of the Catholic working class for the RUC and led to several weekends of fierce rioting in Ardoyne, a tough depressed ghetto in North Belfast. It also led to the formation of the extreme Unionist Shankill Defence Association (SDA), led by John McKeague, in the adjoining Protestant area. There was trouble in June, as two Orange parades were forced through Dungiven, while a proposed Connolly commemoration parade was banned from the centre of Belfast and John McKeague and his supporters were allowed to occupy the centre of the city to prevent it.

On 12 July an Orange parade was stoned in Derry and rioting between Bogsiders and the RUC lasted for three days, with an RUC man shooting and wounding two civilians. In Dungiven a third Orange parade led to two days of rioting and attacks on the Orange Hall. A 66-year-old Catholic man, Francis McCloskey, was killed in an RUC baton-charge, and a platoon of B Specials fired over the heads of a Catholic crowd coming out of a dance. The Orange Hall was burnt down and several police tenders wrecked.

On 26 July a PD march was banned in Fermanagh and 37 PD supporters arrested. On 2 August an Orange march past the Catholic Unity Flats in Belfast led to major rioting and Patrick Corry, a Catholic, died in an RUC barracks after a beating-up by police. The rioting went on for three days, with Loyalist crowds, led by the SDA, trying to attack Unity Flats and Ardoyne and clashing with the RUC. Eventually the Loyalist rioting was stopped by mobilising the B Specials and using them to replace the RUC on the Shankill Road. Meanwhile the Ardoyne rioting had seen a sinister new development. A number of Catholic families were forced out of their homes in the mainly Protestant area opposite Ardoyne, while the SDA also put pressure on Protestants living in Ardoyne to move out. It was the start of what was to be a massive intimidation campaign.

There was another significant development during the riots at the beginning of August. A detachment of British troops was moved into the RUC headquarters on stand-by for use in Belfast. As it happened they were not called on, but it was a sign of the growing British involvement in the Northern situation. In fact five hundred extra British troops had been flown into the North in April after the first UVF explosions, and used as guards for vital installations. On 12 July troops had been moved into a naval base in Derry as a precaution, and shortly afterwards Wilson had appointed Roy Hattersley as a Minister of State for Defence with the job of preparing for intervention in Northern Ireland if necessary.

Everyone knew the crunch would come on 12 August. That was the day of the Apprentice Boys' parade in Derry, when thousands of Orangemen from all over the North would come to Derry, and parade through the city and around the walls overlooking the Bogside to commemorate the Siege. It was virtually a direct celebration of the plantation and the Protestant ascendancy and served as a yearly reminder to the Catholic population of who was master even in this Catholic city.

After a year of Civil Rights marches banned from the centre of every town and batoned off the streets of Derry, the Catholics were in no mood to be reminded of their inferiority. If the march went ahead there was bound to be a riot. But if there was a riot it was bound to be followed by an RUC invasion of the Bogside; and so, three weeks before the march, a Bogside Defence Association was set up chaired by Sean Keenan, a veteran Republican. The Bogsiders were determined to have no repetition of 4 January and 19 April.

The Stormont government turned down all appeals to ban the march. A ban would have been Clark's political death warrant. They knew the consequences: on 8 August Clark and Porter, the Home Affairs Minister, saw Callaghan in London to request the support of British troops.

The march went ahead. It was stoned at the fringe of the Bogside, the RUC baton-charged and the siege was on. The Defence Association had built barricades around the Bogside and they were defended with petrol-bombs. The RUC used armoured cars to try to break through and fired CS gas – the first time it had been used in Ireland. The moderate Citizens' Action Committee leaders like Hume and Cooper were swept aside. Leadership was in the hands of the Republican and left-wing activists. The tricolour and the Starry-Plough – the flag of Connolly's Citizen Army in 1916 – were flown from a towerblock of flats. Bernadette Devlin MP was behind the barricades urging on the defenders.

The siege went on all day and all night. The RUC were pressing hard – 700 of their 3,000 men were in Derry at the time. The Bogside defenders appealed for help. NICRA and the PD arranged mass rallies for a dozen centres to stretch the RUC as far as possible. It was understood that they would end in riots. A NICRA delegation saw John Taylor, the hard-line Junior Minister for Home Affairs, to give the government a last chance to call off the Bogside siege. They refused and the rallies went ahead. There were riots everywhere, with the most serious violence in Dungannon and Belfast. In Dungannon armed B Specials were brought in and fired into a Catholic crowd, wounding two men and a girl. In Belfast several buildings were burnt on the Falls Road, two RUC barracks attacked by crowds and a grenade thrown at an RUC vehicle. The RUC fired into a crowd, wounding two men.

The government still would not take the only step that could bring peace – pulling the RUC back from the Bogside. Instead Chichester-Clark announced the recall of parliament for the following day and the mobilisation of the B Specials – a move calculated both to enrage and to terrify the Catholic population.

The Dublin government had been in continuous session all day. They were under considerable pressure. Popular feeling had been growing in the South ever since the beginning of the Civil Rights movement. It had been inflamed by the decision to let the Apprentice Boys' march go ahead and by the attack on the Bogside. Now three cabinet ministers, Neil Blaney, Charles Haughey and Kevin Boland, were demanding that the Irish Army invade the North and seize Derry, Newry and the mainly Catholic area west of the Bann.

There was no real question of invasion. This would bring the South into direct conflict with Britain, and the economic forces which had led to the Anglo-Irish free trade area and the Lemass-O'Neill talks were still in operation. The South could not afford to clash with its economic overlord. It was even doubtful if the three ministers were serious about intervention, for when it was refused none of them resigned or took the issue to the country by publicly calling for the use of the Army. It seems more likely that the demand was part of a move to topple the Taoiseach, Jack Lynch, by outflanking him on the Republican issue.

The result was a compromise. The Southern government would bluster; it would sound militant but do nothing serious about the situation. Lynch went on television that night (13 August) and made a strong speech saying:

'It is evident also that the Stormont government is no longer in control of the situation. Indeed the present situation is the inevitable outcome of the policies pursued for decades by successive Stormont governments. It is clear also that the Irish government can no longer stand by and see innocent people injured and perhaps worse'.

He announced that the Irish Army would establish field hospitals along the border for people injured in the North – a convenient excuse for moving the Army to the border – and called for a UN peacekeeping force in the six counties. He also called for negotiations with Britain about the future of the North, 'recognising that the re-unification of the national territory can provide the only permanent solution for the problem'[2].

The speech had a significant effect in the North. To the minority it was an encouragement to resist. It seemed as if, for the first time since 1922, a Southern government was prepared to intervene in the six counties, and the longer they could hold out the nearer they would be to Irish unity. The Loyalists on the other hand were enraged and alarmed. The result was to be seen the following night.

On 14 August the North was on the brink of war. The opposition boycotted the special session of the Stormont parliament which heard Clark denounce the rioting in a bitter speech,

'This is not the agitation of a minority seeking by lawful means the assertion of political rights. It is the conspiracy of forces seeking to overthrow a government democratically elected by a large majority'[3].

Meanwhile B Specials were replacing the RUC on the edge of the Bogside and preparing for another attack. But if the Bogsiders had resisted the RUC they would fight the B Specials with far greater vigour.

At 5pm British troops moved into the centre of Derry, fully armed. There was an anxious moment as the rioters watched them take up their positions. There were hurried negotiations between the Defence Association and the British commander and then he agreed to pull the RUC and

Specials back behind his troops and not to enter the Bogside. The siege was over. The Bogsiders felt that they had won – not only because they had kept the RUC out of their area but because they had forced the British Army to intervene. They sensed vaguely that direct British intervention re-opened the whole constitutional question.

In Belfast the trouble was only beginning. Tension was at fever pitch. On the Falls Road people were barricading the streets. On the Shankill Road crowds of angry Loyalists filled the streets connecting it with the Falls, and mingling with them were hundreds of the mobilised Specials armed with rifles, revolvers and sub-machine guns. Rioting started at Hasting Street barracks on the Falls. As it continued mobs of Loyalists surged down the side streets towards the Falls, attacking and burning Catholic houses, firing into the Catholic area and eventually planting the Union Jack in Divis Street. The B Specials were prominent among the attackers. Some IRA men with a few weapons, including one Thompson sub-machine gun – most of their weapons had been moved out of Belfast as part of the new political emphasis – fired at the attackers and one Protestant, Herbert Roy, was killed. Eventually the mob of Loyalists and Specials was driven back, but not before they'd burnt out most of the Falls Road, or Catholic ends of Dover Street and Percy Street.

Meanwhile the RUC had brought out their Shorland armoured cars fitted with Browning heavy machine guns, and fired into the Catholic Divis Flats killing a nine-year-old boy, Patrick Rooney, and a young British soldier, Herbert McCabe, who was home on leave. The Shorlands continued to roar up and down the road for most of the night.

Across the city there were similar scenes in Ardoyne. The RUC charged into the Catholic area, followed by a Loyalist mob who burned out half of Hooker Street. In the confused fighting the RUC opened fire with sub-machine guns into the Catholic streets and shot two men dead.

There was rioting in Armagh as well and B Specials were brought in to reinforce the RUC. They opened fire with rifles into a Catholic crowd, killing one man.

The death toll for the night of 14-15 August was six – five Catholics and a Protestant. 150 Catholic homes had been burnt out in Belfast, and overnight the government had reintroduced internment, arresting 24 men throughout the North.

Throughout the day Belfast was in a state of suspended war. Bigger and stronger barricades were built in the Falls, guns rushed up from the

South, preparations made to resist another onslaught. Late in the afternoon British troops began to take up positions on the Falls Road. They made no attempt to breach the barricades and as in Derry their intervention defused the situation.

But they didn't intervene everywhere. While they were taking up positions a Loyalist mob burned down the whole of Bombay Street in the Catholic Clonard area, and a young member of the Junior IRA was killed trying to hold them off. Later in the evening troops went into Clonard as well, but they didn't go into Ardoyne. That night there was another pitched battle there between the Catholics on the one hand and the RUC and Loyalists on the other. One Protestant was shot dead and a whole Catholic street, Brookfield Street, burnt out. The military moved in the next day, 16 August.

The rioting was the most serious and the death-toll the heaviest in a couple of days since the 1920s. There was also massive intimidation, overwhelmingly directed against Catholics. A report furnished to the Scarman tribunal showed that 1,820 families fled their homes in Belfast in July, August and September 1969. 1,505 or 82·7 per cent were Catholics. The report calculated that some 5·3 per cent of all Catholic households in the city had been displaced, compared with 0·4 per cent of Protestant families[4]. For some families it was the second or even the third time in living memory that they had been put out.

Nonetheless morale in the Catholic ghettos was high. Most of the Falls Road and Ardoyne was behind barricades, and the British Army and especially the RUC kept well outside. The IRA had brought in arms and organised the defence of the areas, and the Peoples Democracy was running a powerful pirate radio station and producing a daily newssheet, both pouring out militant propaganda. It was a dual power situation. The IRA and PD drew up a tough set of demands to be met before the barricades would be taken down: Stormont must be suspended, the RUC disarmed, the B Specials disbanded and the Special Powers Act revoked.

The anti-Unionists could afford to wait. Stormont's authority was crumbling. It had been rescued from the effects of its blunders only by the intervention of the British Army. The opposition was boycotting the parliament. The police force had been discredited and was publicly excluded from large areas of the two main cities. In the South the government was still under heavy pressure. The deaths in Belfast and the stream of Catholic refugees across the border to safety in the South had inflamed feeling. There were violent riots in Dublin on 16 August calling for arms for the North. The Southern government mobilised their army reserves and urged Westminster to take strong measures with their Stormont underlings.

With their troops on the streets Westminster had to do something. On 19 August Clark, Faulkner and Porter, the Home Affairs Minister, were summoned to Downing Street to see Wilson, Callaghan and Healey, the Minister for Defence. Clark had been warned that the intervention of the British Army would involve conditions. In the event they were less than the Unionists had feared. The Specials would be put under Army, i.e. Westminster, control, and the pace of reform would have to be speeded up. A bromide communique was drawn up re-affirming Stormont's constitutional position and declaring that:

'The two governments today have re-affirmed that in all legislation and executive decisions of government every citizen of Northern Ireland is entitled to the same equality of treatment and freedom from discrimination as obtains in the rest of the United Kingdom irrespective of political views or religion. In their further meetings the two governments will be guided by these mutually accepted principles'.

But that night on television Wilson said that the B Specials would be 'phased out' and the next day Westminster announced that a tribunal would be set up to investigate the riots and a committee would study the re-organisation of the RUC. It was generally expected that the committee would recommend disbanding the Specials.

A week later Callaghan came to Belfast, met the Stormont cabinet, and outlined his plans. There would be a permanent British government representative in Belfast from now on to keep an eye on them. Three joint working parties of Whitehall and Stormont civil servants would study ways of dealing with discrimination in housing and jobs and how to improve community relations. Callaghan would be back in six weeks to review their progress.

Callaghan also went on walking tours of the riot areas in Belfast and Derry, and got a warm welcome from the Catholics in the Falls and Bogside who felt he was by-passing Stormont to talk to them directly. The Protestants were less enthusiastic. Before he left it was announced that all the men interned had been released and that the Stormont government was appointing a new Minister for Community Relations.

There was a basic ambiguity about the role of the British Army and government at the time which Callaghan exploited to the full. Legally, constitutionally, and in reality the British troops had intervened 'in aid of the civil power', to rescue the Stormont government from the morass it had created for itself. If Westminster was forcing some measure of reform on Clark and his colleagues, its purpose was to strengthen the state by removing some of the more obvious grievances. But to many, probably most, Catholics the troops had saved them from the hated RUC and Specials and Westminster was now forcing the unwilling Unionists to grant civil rights to Catholics. Westminster seemed to be on the Catholics' side. Only the Republicans and the PD were warning that the British guns would eventually be turned on anti-Unionists, and for the moment not many were listening. It was an ambiguity that could not last beyond the first major Catholic riot, but for the moment events helped to sustain it.

The Loyalists were frustrated and angry. They were outraged by the existence of the 'No-Go' areas behind the barricades where Crown forces couldn't penetrate and the Union Jack didn't fly. Parts of their state had virtually seceded. And they sensed that the intervention of the British troops had drastically curtailed the powers of Stormont.

Early in September there were several Loyalist protests demanding an end to the No-Go areas, and on 5 September Unionists clashed with the Army who used CS gas against them. Even when the Catholic barricades came down, Loyalist gangs continued to attack isolated Catholic families; and on 28 September a large Loyalist crowd attacked Unity Flats at the bottom of the Shankill Road, were beaten off and then burned down Coates Street, a tiny Catholic street between the Falls and Shankill. There was more Loyalist rioting in the first week of October. John McKeague of the Shankill Defence Association was arrested on 5 October and later sentenced to three months in jail.

Meanwhile important developments were taking place. On 12 September the Cameron Commission – appointed by O'Neill – reported. It confirmed and documented the existence of discrimination and gerry-mandering against Catholics and vindicated the Civil Rights movement. It reported that there had been 'serious breaches of discipline and acts of illegal violence' by the RUC during the Civil Rights campaign and it described the B Specials as 'a partisan and para-military force recruited exclusively from Protestants'. On 8 October Callaghan returned to Belfast to review the progress of his three working parties. On 10 October the Hunt Report was published and it was announced that the RUC inspector general was being replaced by Sir Arthur Young, a London police chief. The Hunt Report recommended the disarming of the RUC and the disbandment of the B Specials. It also recommended the establishment of a new, part-time military force, later called the UDR, but this was hardly noticed at the time.

The following night crowds of Loyalists gathered on the Shankill Road, tried to attack Unity Flats, and clashed violently with the RUC and British Army. Loyalist gunmen opened fire and killed an RUC man, Constable Arbuckle – the first one killed since 1962. The Army fired back and in a serious gun-battle shot two Protestants dead. Fourteen soldiers, three RUC men and 20 civilians were wounded by gun-fire before the night was out. The next day, 12 October, the Army launched large-scale searches on the Shankill, capturing guns and ammunition and a pirate radio.

The killing of an RUC man by Loyalists protesting at the disarmament of the RUC and the scrapping of the Specials, shocked most Unionist supporters however much they disliked the Hunt Report. They got another shock on 19 October when a man was blown up and killed planting a bomb at an electricity plant at Ballyshannon in Co.Donegal. He was Thomas McDowell from Kilkeel in Co.Down, a member of Paisley's Free Presbyterian Church and of the UVF.

The Unionist Council gave Chichester-Clark a vote of confidence by 426 votes to 89 on 24 October, but it was a confidence that was likely to evaporate as the effect of the Hunt Report and the other reforms began to sink in.

There was more evidence of Loyalist violence before the end of the year. On 31 October a bomb destroyed the Wolfe Tone monument at Bodenstown in Co.Kildare, and on 26 December another one damaged the O'Connell monument in the centre of Dublin. In between, in a round-up following McDowell's death, ten men were charged with causing the explosions which brought down O'Neill. They included John McKeague, and three others who had been closely connected with Paisley's organisations: Trevor Gracey, circulation manager of the *Protestant Telegraph*, Frank Mallon, treasurer of the UCDC, and Samuel Stevenson, Major Bunting's campaign manager in the February elections. Another man, Robert Murdoch, had been charged but cleared in the 1966 UVF trials. Three of the ten were also B Specials. Paisley himself remained just outside the circle.

Stevenson pleaded guilty and implicated the others. He said the purpose of the bombs was to create anti-IRA hysteria, force the government to release Paisley from jail, and bring down O'Neill. He was convicted and sentenced to twelve years. The others weren't tried until early 1970. A bomb rocked the courthouse during the trial – enough to intimidate most juries – and they were all cleared.

It was a period of intense political activity in the minority community. The politicians, the clergy and the Catholic middle class in general had been swept aside in the hectic days after 12 August. They quickly re-asserted themselves, demanding and getting representation on the non-elected Central Citizen's Defence Committee (CCDC) in Belfast. Soon more and more influence was in the hands of Fr Padraic Murphy, the right-wing parish priest of the Lower Falls, and Tom Conaty, a wealthy Catholic businessman. They seemed almost as keen as the British Army and Chichester-Clark to get the barricades down and end the situation of dual power.

On 11 September a CCDC delegation of Murphy, Conaty and the local MPs Gerry Fitt, Paddy Devlin and Paddy Kennedy, saw Callaghan in London and agreed to take the barricades down. The move was unpopular with the people in the ghettos and there was serious opposition when they got home, led by some Republicans, Frank Card, Billy McKee and Leo Martin. Eventually Murphy had to call in the bishop, Dr Philbin, and the barriers came down on 15 September, though not before Philbin had been publicly abused by members of his flock on the Falls Road – a blow to his dignity which gave him a lasting hatred of radical Republicanism.

For months the bulk of the Catholic population was bemused by the series of reports and reforms and by good public relations work. The new head of the RUC Sir Arthur Young was photographed touring the Falls with Jim Sullivan, a prominent Republican, and met the CCDC in their rooms. And of course the Army was busy quelling the Loyalists. The Catholics remained quiescent.

But behind the scenes the Republicans were re-organising and re-arming. The events of August had caught them unprepared. Apart from the shooting in Divis Street, the IRA's only contribution to the crisis was a badly bungled attack on Crossmaglen RUC barracks on 17 August when it was all over. Known IRA men had been jeered at in the ghettos because they were unable to defend their own areas. They were determined it wouldn't happen again. Old IRA men who had little interest in politics and had dropped out because of the new political line rejoined. And there was a steady stream of recruits from young men who had seen houses and streets burnt down by Loyalist mobs and who'd been unable to prevent them.

The Belfast IRA men felt betrayed by the Dublin leadership, and even by the Belfast officers who hadn't foreseen the crisis and had left them undefended. In September the militants staged a minor coup and forced the co-option of three hard-liners, Billy McKee, Seamus Twomey and Sean McNally, on to the Belfast command. But other forces were intervening as well.

As early as February 1969 a group of Fianna Fail TDs approached the IRA in Co.Derry with a proposition. They could see violence coming in the North and they would supply money and arms on condition that a separate Northern command of the IRA was set up. The offer was repeated in June in Dublin to members of the IRA's army council including Cathal Goulding, the chief of staff and Sean McStiofain, the intelligence officer. By now it was clear that TACA – a group of businessmen who financed Fianna Fail in return for favours received – was involved. TACA was closely identified with the three ministers who were to figure in the cabinet crisis in August: Blaney, Boland and Haughey. They were strange allies for the IRA. Boland's father, as Minister for Justice, had been responsible for the internment and executions of IRA men during the war; Blaney had been in the cabinet which introduced internment in 1957; and Haughey as Minister for Justice had re-introduced military courts for Republicans in 1961. They were also, especially Haughey, identified with the aggressively right-wing and capitalist element in Fianna Fail which was constantly attacked by the new leftist Republican movement.

Logically enough there was now a further condition attached to the offer: the IRA must drop its leftist policies and stop agitating against Fianna Fail in the South. The deal had three obvious benefits for the TACA men. It would get the Republicans off their backs; if there was trouble in the North it would confine it there and give them some control over it; and it would give them a 'Republican' image useful in the power struggle with Lynch.

The IRA were divided and the crisis erupted before the negotiations were completed; but during the stormy cabinet meetings in Dublin the dissidents forced Lynch to set up a cabinet sub-committee on the North dominated by Blaney and Haughey, and to give it £175,000 – £75,000 for publicity and £100,000 for 'relief'.

The publicity was two-edged. Fianna Fail – and the minority politicians in the North – were alarmed at the sharply radical turn of the Northern Civil Rights movement, which, under PD influence, was attacking the Southern state as vehemently as the Northern one. In fact since 12

August, the PD in Belfast and the loose leftist group in Derry had been churning out radical leaflets, papers, posters and propaganda non-stop. The Dublin government seconded a dozen PR men from state-sponsored companies to produce anti-Unionist and pro-Fianna Fail propaganda. A 'Civil Rights office' was set up in Monaghan in opposition to NICRA, and a Dublin journalist friend of Blaney's was sent North to produce a Nationalist and anti-marxist paper, *The Voice of the North*.

The publicity campaign petered out eventually. The 'relief' had a more lasting effect. An Irish Army intelligence officer, Captain Kelly, had been visiting the North regularly and reporting back to his chief, Colonel Heffron, who relayed the information to the Minister of Defence, Jim Gibbons. Kelly reported that the Catholic Defence Committees – effectively the IRA – wanted and needed guns. The Dublin government couldn't openly arm the IRA; it would provoke a furious row with Britain. The Northern sub-committee decided to hand over the £100,000 for 'relief' to the Defence Committees through bogus bank accounts, and ask no questions about what it was being used for. The Irish Army also gave some informal help in buying arms.

It all came out at the beginning of May 1970 when £80,000 worth of arms addressed to Haughey's brother were seized at Dublin airport. Lynch sacked Blaney and Haughey from his cabinet and Boland resigned in protest. Three weeks later, Blaney, Haughey and his brother, Captain Kelly, Albert Luykx, a Belgian businessman living in Dublin, and John Kelly, a Northern IRA man, were charged with importing arms. They were tried in September and the defence was simply that the whole enterprise was sanctioned by the government. Gibbons, the Minister for Defence, denied it all but cut a poor figure in the witness box. The charges were dismissed and it was widely believed that the whole cabinet, from the Taoiseach down, had given tacit consent to the operation but had had to stop it when British intelligence tipped off the pro-British opposition party, Fine Gael.

Lynch had taken advantage of the opportunity to get rid of his main rivals in the cabinet. Times had changed since the heady days of August 1969 and the rest of the Fianna Fail Party had accepted economic realities and the South's subservience to Britain. There was no major split over the arms trial and the cabinet sackings. Three backbench TDs were forced out or resigned. Boland alone went to the length of setting up a new party called Aontacht Eireann and challenging Lynch at the polls. Blaney contented himself with securing his own position as Independent Fianna Fail in

Donegal and Haughey stayed in Fianna Fail hoping to rehabilitate himself and replace Lynch eventually[5].

All this was used to put further pressure on the IRA. By now a backlash had begun against the leftist development anyway. Angry militants blamed the August debacle on the new emphasis on politics, forgetting that the Civil Rights movement had shaken the Northern state to its core, forced direct British intervention for the first time since 1922 and secured the disbandment of the B Specials. The frustration exploded at the IRA army convention in December. A proposal to end the traditional policy of abstention from Stormont, the Dail and Westminster crystallised all the resentment and the dissidents walked out. A month later the Ard Fheis of Sinn Fein voted to end abstentionism as well and there was another walk-out.

The dissidents established a provisional army council of the IRA and a caretaker executive of Sinn Fein. The Provos were born. The Provisional chief of staff was, ironically, Sean McStiofain, born in England and jailed for eight years with Cathal Goulding for the Felstead raid in England in 1953. The head of the Provisional Sinn Fein was Ruadhri O'Bradaigh, who had been elected Sinn Fein TD for Roscommon in 1957.

The Provisionals' first public statements strongly attacked the leftward trend in the organisation and were vehemently anti-communist. The caretaker executive of Sinn Fein said in its manifesto on the split:

'There is no doubt that an extreme form of socialism was being pushed on the movement . . . it seems certain that the ultimate objective of the leadership . . . is nothing but a totalitarian dictatorship of the left'.

Of themselves they said 'Ours is a socialism based on the native Irish tradition of Comhar na gComharsan [Neighbourly Co-operation] which is founded on the right of worker-ownership and on our Irish and Christian values'[6]. The Provisional army council of the IRA said in its Easter statement: 'Irish freedom will not be won by involvement with an international movement of extreme socialism'[7]. They quickly attracted many of the right-wing traditional Nationalists who had opposed the swing to the left and dropped out of the Republican movement.

But the split between the Provisionals and the 'Officials' as the other section were called was never a simple left-right division. In their reaction against the unpolitical militarism and nationalism of the 1950s some of the Officials had become so deeply involved in social agitation that they regarded the Northern question as an unwelcome distraction, while others had become reformists quite committed to a strategy of working through parliament. One effect of this was that, while the Provisionals, like the left-wing PD, were from the beginning in favour of forcing the suspension of the Stormont parliament as a major step towards ending the Northern state, the Officials were in favour of retaining and reforming it. They then intended to try to win power in both Stormont and the Dail. This gradualist attitude, even in the face of the events in the North, drove many of the younger militants in the Republican movement especially in the North to join the Provisionals despite their unrevolutionary social attitudes[8]. And it was in the Northern ghettos that the Provos found their strength, based on the promise of arms and militant action.

For the time being the Provos concentrated on recruiting and collecting arms and they weren't too fussy about where they came from; but if the TACA men established any influence over them it was short-lived. The Provos were a product of the Northern situation and their actions were dictated by events in the North not by Southern politicians or businessmen.

After the flurry of reform announcements in September and October 1969, and with the Catholics fairly quiet, Westminster let things take their course. But there was growing resentment among the Unionists and a steady resistance to change in the institutions of the state. A Scotland Yard detective was appointed to investigate the death of Samuel Devenny in Derry in April. He met 'a conspiracy of silence' by the RUC and no one was charged. An internal investigation of police action in the Bogside on 4 January recommended charges against certain RUC men. No action was taken. No one was charged or even disciplined in connection with the B Special shooting of John Gallagher, the man killed in Armagh on 14 August. It seemed the RUC could be disarmed but not reformed. On the other hand Bernadette Devlin MP was charged with riotous behaviour during the siege of the Bogside and sentenced to six months in jail, a decision calculated to enrage Catholics to whom the siege was a heroic episode.

Chichester-Clark began to make concessions to the creeping tide of reaction. He brought John Brooke, Brookeborough's son, a member of the anti-O'Neill Portadown parliament[9] and a hard-liner, into the government on 30 January 1970. He reintroduced the tough Public Order Bill on 5 February. But this didn't satisfy the critics. On 19 March five MPs, William Craig, Harry West, Desmond Boal, John McQuade and Norman Laird, were expelled from the parliamentary party for not supporting a vote of confidence in the government's security policy. The O'Neill process was starting again. On 17 April 1970 there were by-elections for the solidly Unionist South Antrim and Bannside seats – O'Neill had been made a Lord. Paisley and one of his ministers stood and won[10]. Neither had an overall majority, but they got a majority of the traditional Unionist vote which was what mattered. Later, in June, Paisley won the North Antrim seat at Westminster, defeating the sitting Unionist by 2,679 votes. On 24 April the Unionist Party Conference voted against the government's housing policy – one of the reforms – by 281 to 216.

The Southern gun-running story didn't improve matters. By the end of May, Clark's position was very shaky, and he couldn't afford to alienate Unionist supporters any further.

The Loyalist marching season was beginning again. Already there had been serious trouble on Easter Tuesday (31 March) when an Orange parade went past the Catholic Clonard and Ballymurphy areas on the Springfield Road. The result was four days of rioting in Ballymurphy between Catholics and the British Army, who were very brutal, saturating the estate with CS gas and then physically occupying it. The Catholics replied with petrol bombs. It was the first major clash between Catholics and the Army, who now appeared in the RUC role of protectors of triumphalist Orange parades. This episode went a long way towards ending the ambiguity about the Army's role. General Freeland, the British GOC in Northern Ireland, took the process a little further when he went on television and threatened to shoot petrol bombers dead. There was more rioting in Ardoyne and the New Lodge Road, a hitherto peaceful Catholic area, during May.

On 2 June a local Army commander diverted an Orange march away from Ardoyne, where it would have passed the burnt-out mouths of Hooker Street and Brookfield Street. There were two nights of vicious rioting on the Shankill Road. That decided the cabinet. Despite pleas by Sir Arthur Young and the British permanent representative, there would be no more bans or restrictions on the Orange parades. Violence was now inevitable, especially when Bernadette Devlin was jailed on 26 June.

Saturday 27 June was the 'Little Twelfth'[11] with Orange parades due to pass Ardoyne, Clonard, Unity Flats and the isolated Catholic enclave of Short Strand in East Belfast. It would be the first test of the Provos' Defence Committees. Rioting broke out immediately after the march passed Ardoyne. There was a gun-battle and three Protestants were killed.

Across the city in East Belfast there was an attack on the Short Strand with crowds trying to petrol bomb St Matthew's Church which commanded the entrance to the area, and Loyalist gunmen firing into the ghetto from the Newtownards Road. An opposition MP demanded that the Army intervene and protect the area. They refused, saying they hadn't enough men. Instead they sealed the bridges leading to the West of the city.

The 6,000 Catholics in the Short Strand were terrified, marooned amongst 60,000 Protestants and all escape cut off. The Provos went into action and in a major gun-battle two Protestants were shot dead and two fatally wounded. One IRA man was killed and Billy McKee, their Belfast commander, wounded. The Loyalists were held off. The Short Strand battle ensured the growth of the Provos; for if the British Army couldn't defend the Catholics against Loyalist attacks then they would obviously have to defend themselves. Events a few days later finally removed all remaining doubts about the Army's role in the conflict.

Loyalist tempers were at boiling point after 27 June. Chichester-Clark was desperate to appease them. A new Tory government had just been elected in Britain and Maudling, the new Home Secretary, visited Belfast and gave the go-ahead for tough 'law and order' policies.

On 1 July a draconian Criminal Justice (Temporary Provisions) Bill was rushed through Stormont, bringing in mandatory six-month minimum prison terms for rioting. The opposition MPs, panicked by the gun-battles, didn't resist. But even this was not enough. The government seemed anxious to strike an exemplary blow at the IRA before 12 July. On 3 July, with a great display of force, the Army raided a house in Balkan Street in the Lower Falls. They found a small collection of arms – twelve pistols and a sub-machine gun – and provoked a major riot. The people feared they were going to be left defenceless against another Loyalist assault: after the previous weekend they had no confidence in Army protection.

The Army flooded the area with CS gas and suddenly withdrew. It looked like a manoeuvre to draw out the IRA. If so, it worked. Barricades were built and the Official IRA, anxious to prove they were as good as the Provos, took up positions. General Freeland cordoned off the whole Lower Falls, ordered a total curfew and then attacked. There was another heavy gun-battle with the Army firing over 1,500 rounds and killing three civilians, one of them a London-Polish photographer. Another civilian was crushed to death by an armoured car. No British soldiers or IRA men were killed.

The Army occupied the entire area, maintained the curfew for 36 hours and conducted a house to house search, smashing doors and furniture in the process and leaving a trail of destruction behind them. To cap it all, they took two Unionist ministers, John Brooke and William Long, on a triumphal tour of the subjugated area. They found a total of 30 rifles, 24 shotguns and 52 pistols – a paltry enough figure beside the 100,000 licensed guns in Northern Ireland, 80 per cent of them in Protestant hands. They outraged almost the whole ghetto population, to whom the British Army was now just another instrument of the Stormont government for terrorising Catholics in order to appease the Orangemen. Lord Carrington, British Minister for Defence, later admitted that the move had been grossly counter-productive, and the curfew turned out to have been quite illegal.

The battle of the Lower Falls caused an upsurge of feeling in the South, but by now Lynch was firmly in control. As a gesture to the Northern Catholics he sent his Minister of External Affairs, Dr Hillery, to visit the Falls and on 11 July he made a carefully balanced speech. He appealed for no interference with the Orange marches and then said 'it is for political leaders to govern wisely and justly. I accept the guarantees of the British government that they will do so. My government is the second guarantor'[12]. A week after the Falls curfew he had managed to endorse British policy, tempering it of course with a vague hint of action by the Dublin government. On 22 October after a quieter period in the North, he was able to tell the United Nations General Assembly that he supported British policy in the North, this time without qualifications. A few days later he got a vote of confidence from his parliamentary party by 70 votes to three. The Southern establishment was evidently more interested in stability and good relations with Britain than in the plight of the Northern minority.

In the North itself relations between the Army and the minority grew steadily worse. On 31 July in the New Lodge Road, the Army shot dead a local youth, Danny O'Hagan, in a minor riot. A few days later the ex-chairman of NICRA, Frank Gogarty, who was very popular in the area, was arrested, beaten up and jailed for six months. Throughout the winter there was constant small-scale rioting in the ghettos and a steady stream of youths were jailed for the mandatory six months under the Criminal Justice Act, many on perjured evidence. By 7 December 1970, 109 people had been tried on charges carrying mandatory sentences. All had been convicted and only four got off on appeal. The vast majority were Catholics.

The opposition politicians could sense minority support slipping away from them. Self-preservation proved stronger than party loyalty. In an attempt to meet the threat, six opposition MPs came together to form the Social Democratic and Labour Party, on 21 August. It was an extraordinary alliance. Paddy Devlin had been elected as NILP, Gerry Fitt as Republican Labour, Austin Currie as a Nationalist. The other three, John Hume, Ivan Cooper and Paddy O'Hanlon, got in as Independents at the height of the Civil Rights campaign. Gerry Fitt became leader of this alliance of convenience, and the head-without-a-tail appearance of the SDLP was remedied in October when the National Democratic Party joined them *en bloc*. The new party was supported by the Southern government and largely financed by Southern businessmen. From the beginning it was effectively the voice of the Catholic middle class in the North.

The SDLP did not speak for the working class in the Catholic ghettos however. Increasingly the Provos did, and they were flexing their muscles. In July and August there was a series of bombs at banks, electricity stations and judges' homes. On 11 August two RUC men were killed by a booby-trap bomb in South Armagh. No one claimed responsibility but on 4 September a man was killed planting a bomb at an electricity transformer in Belfast. He was Michael Kane, a member of the Provos. In November a Provo supporter was burnt to death trying to fire an Orange Hall near Carrickfergus. The Provos had begun a bombing campaign but weren't prepared to acknowledge it because they weren't ready for an all-out confrontation with the Army.

In fact Catholic frustration forced the pace. On 11 January 1971 violent rioting broke out in Ballymurphy and lasted for five days. Bishop Philbin paid a rare visit to the district and denounced the 'hooliganism'. He was ignored. Even the Provos tried to stop the riot but couldn't. It was a spontaneous outburst of ghetto feeling.

The Ballymurphy riot brought things to a head in the Unionist ranks. The Falls curfew and the Criminal Justice Act hadn't stopped the steady drift to the right. Early in August 1970 Paisley and Craig had called for the re-arming of the RUC, the re-introduction of the B Specials and internment. On 26 August, Porter, the Minister of Home Affairs, and a 'moderate' in Unionist terms, resigned. Chichester-Clark replaced him with John Taylor, a leading right-winger and member of the Portadown parliament. He was trying to satisfy the insatiable.

In September 1970 an alliance of the hard-line constituency associations west of the Bann was formed, called the West Ulster Unionist

Council. The chairman was Harry West, who'd been expelled from the parliamentary party, and it soon became a focal point for discontent. In October Clark's own South Derry branch joined it. At the end of November the powerful Belfast County Grand Orange Lodge passed a vote of no confidence in the government.

One of the hard-liners' central demands was the re-introduction of internment. In December 1970 they got an unexpected boost when Jack Lynch suddenly announced that his government had uncovered a Saor Eire[13] plot to kidnap foreign diplomats and was thinking of bringing in internment to deal with it. After that what could Clark say? A few days later he stated that he would not oppose internment if the Army recommended it.

After the Ballymurphy riots Clark saw Maudling in London to demand more repression. Maudling stalled. On 25 January 1971, 170 delegates to the Ulster Unionist Council called for Clark's resignation. On 27 January Craig revealed at Stormont that two RUC men had been attacked by a crowd in Clonard and rescued by troops, who told them to stay out of the area. It was proof of what the government had repeatedly denied – that the Catholic ghettos were 'No-Go' areas to the RUC – and very damaging to Clark. So the Army were ordered to raid Clonard in a show of force.

But for the previous fortnight the Army had actually been holding secret talks with the Belfast Provo leaders in an attempt to keep down rioting. When the Army suddenly raided Clonard, and the house of one of the men they'd been talking to, the Provos were angry. There was heavy rioting both in Clonard and in the New Lodge Road. The next day, 4 February, Major-General Farrar Hockley, the British land forces commander, appeared on television and named as IRA leaders the five men the British Army had been talking to: Frank Card, Billy McKee, Leo Martin, and Liam and Kevin Hannaway. Now the Provos were enraged and they stepped up the violence. On 6 February they shot a British soldier dead on the New Lodge Road – the first British soldier to be killed in action in the North for almost fifty years. The same night the Army killed a civilian in Ardoyne and a Provo officer, Jim Saunders, was shot dead in a confused three-way battle between the IRA, Loyalists and the British Army in the Bone area. Chichester-Clark panicked and announced on television: 'Northern Ireland is at war with the IRA Provisionals.' The Provos were to take him at his word.

On 9 February five civilians were killed by what appeared to be an IRA land-mine intended for the British Army on Brougher Mountain in Co.Tyrone. On 15 February a second British soldier died from gunshot wounds he'd got in Ardoyne. On 26 February two RUC men were shot dead in Ardoyne, one of them, Cecil Patterson, a Special Branch inspector detested by Republicans for his part in interrogations in the 1950s. Then on 10 March the bodies of three young Scottish soldiers were found in a ditch on the outskirts of Belfast. They'd been drinking in a city centre pub when they were picked up by a Provo unit from Ardoyne, enticed away, and shot as a reprisal for Army repression in Ardoyne.

In an area not yet used to daily assassinations, the killing of the three soldiers caused considerable shock. It also gave the Unionist hard-liners the issue they wanted. Two days later Billy Hull, a Loyalist trade union boss in the 95 per cent Protestant shipyard, led a march of 4,000 Loyalist workers to Unionist headquarters to demand the introduction of internment. On 16 March Paisley held a service to commemorate the three soldiers at the Belfast City Hall, with Loyalist workers marching from different parts of the city. On 18 March more Loyalists marched to Stormont while it was debating security.

Chichester-Clark had gone to see Heath in February, and the Stormont cabinet had demanded a whole series of repressive measures: more troops, more arrests, a much larger role for the UDR – the local armed force which had replaced the B Specials – total curfews of Catholic areas and massive punitive or reprisal search-and-raid operations in the ghettos. They were rejected. Even General Farrar Hockley opposed such blanket repression.

Maudling had flown to Belfast and addressed both Houses of Parliament at Stormont on 4 March. It was a disastrous anti-climax. He had nothing to say. Clark flew to London again on 16 March in a final attempt to get permission for repression drastic enough to satisfy his critics. Heath refused. Both the British Army and government realised that intensified repression, and especially internment, would only drive the waverers in the Catholic community into the arms of the Provos, and might also shake the uneasy ascendancy of Lynch in Dublin and throw the South into chaos as well. Westminster had all but abandoned the strategy of forcing reform on the Unionists and trying to remedy Catholic grievances; but they hadn't yet decided on the alternative of total suppression which the Unionists demanded.

Chichester-Clark resigned on 20 March. His final statement neatly summarised the dilemma:

'**The situation however is simply this; it is apparent that public and parliamentary opinion in Northern Ireland looks to the Northern Ireland government for measures which can bring the current IRA campaign swiftly to an end. I have expressed to British ministers the full force of this opinion and have pressed upon them my view that some further initiative is needed. While they have agreed to take any feasible steps open to them to intensify the efforts against the IRA, it remains the professional military view – and one which I indeed have often expressed myself – that it would be misleading the Northern Ireland community to suggest that we are faced with anything but a long haul, and that such initiatives as can be taken are unlikely to effect a radical improvement in the short term**'[14].

On 23 March 1971 Brian Faulkner was elected leader of the Unionist Party by twenty six votes to four. (The alternative was William Craig, now the acknowledged spokesman of the extreme right.) There were few moderates left in the Unionist Party. The basic contradictions of the Northern state were becoming sharper. Frustration at the slowness of reform – there had still been no local elections under 'One Man, One Vote' – and anger at the growing repression, was turning the minority to violence. The Unionist backlash was aimed at going back to the pre-1969 position of unbridled Protestant supremacy and para-military repression to back it up. Forced to take sides between majority and minority, between Unionist and Nationalist, there was no longer any doubt which side the British would choose.

All sections of the Unionist Party were now demanding internment. Faulkner, who had operated it himself as Minister of Home Affairs during the 1950s, was a firm believer in it. Westminster was going to have to agree or lose another Northern Ireland Prime Minister. The Army was still dubious, but on 1 April Faulkner saw Heath and shortly afterwards British military intelligence and the RUC Special Branch began drawing up lists and making contingency plans for internment.

Faulkner began with a neat piece of political juggling. He brought Harry West – expelled from the parliamentary party under Chichester-Clark – back into the cabinet, but balanced this with the appointment of David Bleakley, the former NILP MP, as Minister for Community Relations, reviving an obscure clause of the Government of Ireland Act which allowed the appointment of ministers from outside parliament for six months at a time. He'd evidently studied Brooke's wartime appointment of Harry Midgley.

Reactions varied. Anne Dickson MP, an O'Neill supporter, resigned from the parliamentary party in protest at the inclusion of West in the cabinet. Austin Currie of the SDLP and Billy Blease of the Irish Congress of Trade Unions welcomed Faulkner's accession. The bulk of the Catholic population saw it as another lurch to the right and distrusted Faulkner intensely. The few remaining radicals in the NILP left in disgust at Bleakley's joining the government.

Meanwhile the Provos launched their campaign in earnest. Their strategy was ingenious and new to modern IRA thinking, though a similar tactic had been used in the North in the summer of 1922. Instead of concentrating on the obvious and traditional targets of the RUC and British Army, the Provos decided to hit at the soft underbelly of British interests in the North, business and commerce, with a bombing campaign. Their reasoning was that the mounting economic cost would make British and Northern businessmen and the British government, who would have to pay the compensation, ready to concede the Provos' demands – the main one being the abolition of Stormont.

There were 37 serious explosions in April, 47 in May and 50 in June. There was also conventional military action. On 15 May a Provo, Billy Reid, was killed in a gun-battle with British troops near the city centre. His funeral was followed by fierce rioting in the New Lodge Road. On 22 May a soldier was shot dead in the Markets area, and on 25 May a bomb at Springfield Road RUC barracks on the Falls killed a sergeant in the crack Parachute Regiment, and seriously injured an RUC inspector and a two-year-old child.

Faulkner announced a tougher line; troops could now shoot 'with effect' at anyone acting suspiciously. But he also tried to take the Catholic middle class with him. On 22 June he announced a scheme for three parliamentary committees to review policy and advise on legislation in the fields of social, environmental and industrial services. Membership would be in proportion to party strength at Stormont, but the opposition would provide two of the three chairmen who would be paid a special salary.

The SDLP nearly fell over themselves to welcome the scheme. Paddy Devlin described it as Faulkner's 'best hour'. John Hume said 'It should be made clear to all people today who say that no change has taken place, that this is simply not true. There have been changes in this community'[15]. Only the Peoples Democracy was churlish enough to describe Faulkner's proposals as a sham. But on closer examination that is what they turned out to be. The committees might provide two good jobs for opposition MPs but they would only deal with uncontroversial subjects and would have built-in Unionist majorities. They wouldn't give the oppositon any effective share in power. And just in case he might have gone too far with this gesture, on 28 June Faulkner and five of his ministers went to the Royal Black Preceptory Headquarters in Lurgan to meet the leaders of the Orange Order and discuss the coming parades with them. It served as a timely reminder of where power really lay in Northern Ireland.

The parliamentary manoeuvres went on. On 7 July the SDLP attended the first of what was to be a series of all-party discussions at Stormont. They seemed well satisfied with it. That night the British Army shot Seamus Cusack in the Bogside in Derry. He died on the way to hospital. Shooting 'with effect' had claimed its first victim. There had already been rioting in Derry for three days. It intensified and the next day the Army shot Desmond Beattie dead. The Army claimed both youths were gunmen or bombers. They weren't. The Bogside and Creggan seethed with rage.

John Hume, the MP for Foyle, was alarmed. The SDLP had become too closely identified with Faulkner's administration. They were out of touch with the people in the ghettos. Now he could feel the ground going from under his feet. Provisional Sinn Fein were to hold a rally in Derry at the weekend with their president Ruadhri O'Bradaigh and vice-president, Maire Drumm, speaking. Hume summoned his SDLP colleagues to Derry to discuss the situation. Currie, Cooper and O'Hanlon came, together with a Southern Labour TD. Devlin and Fitt wouldn't go.

They met, while an immense crowd attended the Provo rally and young men queued up to join the IRA. The MPs had to do something. They agreed to demand a public enquiry into the Cusack and Beattie shootings and to withdraw from Stormont if it wasn't granted within four days. Fitt, the party leader, and the least militant of the group, heard the news on the radio. He was aghast and flew straight to London to see Maudling and try to do a deal. There was no deal. Maudling was standing by the Army with its new tough line. On 15 July 1971 Fitt had to lead his colleagues out of Stormont. The rest of the opposition except the one NILP member quickly followed suit.

It was a gesture more symbolic than real since Stormont was about to adjourn for the summer recess anyway, but they issued a statement justifying their action. In fact it summarised the dilemma which had faced every anti-partition opposition since the state was established:

'These events [repression and the Derry shootings] **have led to increasing doubts in our minds over a period of time about the usefulness of our role as parliamentary representatives within the present system. We ... have been faced with a clear choice; either to continue to give credibility to the system which in itself is basically unstable and from which derives the unrest that is destroying our community, or take a stand in order to bring home to those in authority the need for strong political action to solve our problems and prevent any further tragic loss of life which derives from the instability of our political institutions'**[16].

The SDLP had been forced into the same path as the Nationalists in 1921, 1932 and 1938, though none of their predecessors had ever somersaulted quite so completely – from fulsome praise of the government to abstention, in three weeks.

The Provos meanwhile stepped up their campaign. Early on the morning of 12 July there were ten explosions in the centre of Belfast along the route of the Orange march, and a soldier was shot dead later in the day. On 16 July they rescued a wounded IRA man who was under armed guard in a Belfast hospital, and the next day they destroyed the *Daily Mirror's* ultra-modern printing plant at Suffolk, causing £2 million of damage. Altogether there were 91 explosions in July.

The Stormont government was no longer interested in wooing the minority. On 18 July John Taylor, Minister of State for Home Affairs, said:

'I would defend without hesitation the action taken by the Army authorities in Derry against subversives during the past week or so when it was necessary in the end to actually shoot to kill. I feel that it may be necessary to shoot even more in the forthcoming months in Northern Ireland'[17].

The next day Faulkner phoned Heath to request the introduction of internment.

On 23 July nearly two thousand troops were used in a series of dawn raids on Republican homes throughout the North. It was a practice-run for internment and it helped to gather further information on suspects. On 5 August Faulkner went to London and met Heath's cabinet. At last they agreed to try internment, and at 4.30am on 9 August the swoops began. By that evening 342 men had been picked up.

The internment operation seemed almost calculated to cause the maximum outrage to the minority population. Despite the substantial Loyalist violence of 1969, which had continued at a lower pitch during 1970 and 1971 and flared up again in internment week, not a single Loyalist was arrested, much less held. Only two internees were Protestants, one a PD member, the other a Republican sympathiser. Relatively few of the Provos were 'lifted' because RUC intelligence about their organisation was poor and anyway they had anticipated the swoop. IRA veterans of the forties and fifties campaign, many of them old men by now and no longer active, were arrested. There was a blind man and a man of 77 who had first been jailed in 1929. In Armagh troops even arrived to arrest a man who had been dead for four years.

Some had been arrested simply because of their political opposition to the regime. The author was among fifteen PD members picked up while a number of others got away. Eight of us were held, together with the secretary of NICRA and a Belfast city councillor.

Of the 342 picked up 116 were released within 48 hours and the rest interned either in the Crumlin Road prison or on the *Maidstone*, a converted troopship moored at Belfast docks. The men released told harrowing tales. Almost every one had been beaten up. Many had been blindfolded and terrified by being thrown out of a moving helicopter which they were told was high in the air but in fact was only a few feet off the ground. More had been forced to run the gauntlet barefoot between lines of troops with batons and across barbed wire and glass-strewn ground.

The reaction was swift and violent. When the swoops began women in the ghettos rattled dustbin lids to alert the inhabitants. Barricades were built and violent rioting broke out across the city. There were gun-battles everywhere, the fiercest at the Henry Taggart Hall, an Army base opposite Ballymurphy, where five civilians including a priest were killed. In Ardoyne there was shooting between the IRA and Loyalists, and Protestant families moved out, burning their houses behind them. Two whole streets were burnt out and two hundred houses destroyed. The death-toll for 9 August was two British soldiers and ten civilians, seven of them Catholics. After four days there were 22 dead, 19 of them civilians.

Belfast, Derry and Newry were in a state of open war. The Provos launched an all-out onslaught and on 13 August Joe Cahill, their Belfast commander, gave a press conference in a Falls Road school, claiming that their organisation was intact, they had lost only two men killed, and had not been badly affected by internment. The Official IRA, whose men had also been interned, took up the fight as well. In Derry the IRA had managed to seal off the Bogside and Creggan, and for the next year both areas effectively seceded from the Northern Ireland state, with British troops and RUC keeping well outside, and with barricades openly manned by armed IRA men. The minority population was in uproar. All anti-Unionist parties and groups united in a call for a rent and rates strike in protest against internment, but they were only ratifying a *fait accompli*, for the strike had already begun in all the working class estates. Soon even government figures confirmed that there were 26,000 families on rent and rates strike.

If there was any tendency for minority indignation to flag, it was rekindled when news began to filter out about eleven of the internees who had been secretly removed from the internment clearing centres to an unknown destination and held there for seven days. They had had hoods over their heads throughout the seven days, had no idea where they were, and were kept completely isolated. They were severely beaten, forced to stand spreadeagled against walls until they collapsed, given hardly any food, subjected to 'white' noise, prevented from sleeping and constantly interrogated. It was a new technique of sensory deprivation designed to disorient the mind and facilitate interrogation in depth. The orders for the removal of the men had been personally signed by Brian Faulkner.

The all-out war of internment week could not be sustained, and violence returned to a lower level; but the mass alienation of the Catholic population continued and grew. On 16 August 8,000 workers staged a one-day protest strike in Derry. Two days later British troops shot dead a deaf-mute after a protest meeting in Strabane, and broke up a demonstration in Derry with water cannon and rubber bullets, arresting John Hume and Ivan Cooper in the process. On 19 August 30 prominent Catholics in Derry announced that they were resigning their positions on public bodies. They included the chairman of the police liaison committee and Stephen McGonagle, the vice-chairman of the Derry Commission. On 22 August 130 anti-Unionist local government councillors decided to withdraw from local councils. Internment was forcing even the Catholic middle class into open opposition to the state. On 19 August as well, Jack Lynch, who had originally criticised only the 'one-sided' application of internment, called for a complete end to it.

The Provos had gained an enormous boost in membership and support, enough to enable them to weather the shock when a premature bomb explosion at the Northern Ireland Electricity Headquarters in Belfast killed a young man and injured a lot of girl typists and clerks. Feeling in the South too was so strong that when a British armoured car crossed the border into Co.Louth local people surrounded and burnt it, and gave cover to IRA men who killed one of the soliders.

A subtle political change had taken place as well. Up to this, mass support in the Northern Catholic population had been for civil rights and for reform within the Northern state, with Irish unity following gradually. Now most Northern Catholics felt that the Northern state was unreformable, and that they would only get civil rights in a united Ireland. Their objective was no longer to reform Northern Ireland but to destroy it.

By the end of August there had been a total of 100 explosions in the month, and 35 people had been killed; one more than in the previous seven months altogether. By any standards internment had been a disaster.

The Day of Reckoning

After August 1971 the fighting continued more intensely than at any time since 1922 – the British Army, having taken the offensive, kept it up with raids, searches, arrests and internments, and a growing tendency to shoot at sight in minority areas. On the other hand the political resistance was being organised. On 5 September the Provos announced five conditions for a truce: a cease-fire by the British Army; the abolition of Stormont; free elections to a nine-county Ulster parliament, to be called Dail Uladh; the release of detainees; and compensation for those who had suffered through British forces' action. Oddly enough they did not include withdrawal of British troops, or a united Ireland.

On 12 September, despite a good deal of military harassment, 15,000 people attended a massive anti-internment rally at Casement Park in Belfast. Smaller rallies were being held all over the North and the SDLP MPs were forced to share platforms with the more radical groups and pledge themselves not to return to Stormont or to co-operate in any way with the Stormont or Westminster governments until internment ended. Civil resistance committees sprang up in nationalist housing estates and areas to organise the rent and rates strike and other forms of protest, and dual power existed again in a lot of areas. On 17 October the Northern Resistance Movement (NRM) was set up at a conference in Omagh to co-ordinate the resistance committees and organise mass demonstrations. It was supported by the Peoples Democracy and the Provos, with Frank McManus the MP for Fermanagh/South Tyrone[1] as chairman, and it differed from NICRA – now controlled by the Official Republicans – because one of its central demands was the abolition of Stormont.

On 26 October the SDLP and the almost defunct Nationalists held the first meeting of an 'Alternative Assembly' in Dungiven. The attendance of about a hundred people was made up of opposition MPs, Senators and local government councillors. No attempt was made to represent the new street committees and resistance councils. John Hume was elected president and Senator Gerry Lennon, a Nationalist, chairman. The 'Dungiven parliament' served to underline the disintegration of any political consensus in the Northern state. It was also a fairly obvious attempt to win back some initiative from the IRA and the politics of the streets. It was as 'parliamentary' as it could be. The session began with prayers and an Order Paper of Bills to be presented. The Catholic middle class were determined to rebel with dignity. However, the Assembly held only one other meeting.

The British Army met the IRA with tougher and tougher measures of repression. The numbers interned increased steadily to nearly 650 by the end of November. On 19 September many of the internees were transferred to a special internment camp built on an old RAF airfield at Long Kesh near Lisburn: with its Nissen huts surrounded by cages of barbed wire and its perimeter fence and watch-towers, it looked remarkably like a German concentration camp, and thus inflamed feeling more than ever.

The Army also began blowing up border roads again, enraging people in the Southern border counties and leading to frequent riots as the NRM organised rallies to fill in the craters. The troops took a harsher and harsher attitude to civilians in Catholic areas. On 23 October soldiers shot dead two women vigilantes who were touring the Lower Falls with a siren, warning about army raids. The same night they killed three unarmed men in Newry as they carried out a petty robbery. Troop strength had been reinforced early in October and there were now 14,000 troops in Northern Ireland compared with 2,500 before August 1969. Concentrated in the Catholic ghettos they appeared a real army of occupation.

Stormont backed up the Army's physical repression by two new punitive measures. One enabled the government to deduct arrears of rent and rates, plus 'collection charges', from the wages or social security benefits of people on rent and rates strike. The other provided for the suspension of local councils where a majority of councillors were refusing to attend in protest at internment. Soon Newry, Strabane, Keady and Warrenpoint were being run by government commissioners just like in 1921-22.

The IRA replied with furious violence. There were constant bombs and ambushes with some spectacular actions. Nine Provos escaped from the top-security Crumlin Road prison on 16 November. At the end of November a bombing blitz of 30 bombs in two days answered the first of many claims that the IRA were beaten. On 2 December three more Provos, including the Ardoyne commander Martin Meehan, escaped from Crumlin Road and on 12 December the Official IRA shot and killed a Unionist Senator Jack Barnhill and blew up his house. The death toll was mounting steadily. On 23 September a teenage boy and girl in the Officials were killed in a premature blast, on 18 December three Provos died in a blast in Co, Derry. Two Protestants, one of them a well-known Loyalist, were killed by a bomb at a Shankill Road pub on 29 September. Fifteen people died in an explosion at a Catholic pub in the New Lodge Road on 4 December, two adults and two children in a blast at a Shankill Road furniture store on 11 December.

In general the Provos had launched an urban guerrilla offensive against government and commercial offices and buildings throughout the North. They gave warnings to try to avert casualties but their home-made bombs packed with unstable explosives took a high toll both of their own volunteers and of civilians. The Official IRA confined themselves to military and political targets. Loyalist gunmen and bombers were also active, though on a smaller scale.

From 1 January to 8 August 1971 34 people had been killed in the North; eleven British soldiers, four RUC men, and nineteen civilians. From 9 August to the end of the year the figure was 139 dead: 32 British soldiers, seven RUC men, five UDR men and 95 civilians. Internment had turned a campaign of pinpricks into an all-out war.

Faulkner made two paltry gestures towards the minority, but they impressed no-one. On 26 October he produced a Green Paper for discussion, which repeated the idea of parliamentary committees, suggested an enlarged Stormont and discussed the possibility of re-introducing PR for elections. The next day he appointed an elderly establishment Catholic, Dr G.B.Newe, to the cabinet, to advise on Catholic attitudes – like a native interpreter, as many Catholics commented wryly. Newe was the first Catholic ever in a Northern Ireland government, but he was not elected, he represented no one and the patronising arrogance revealed by his appointment only enraged the majority of Catholics even more. Anyway things had gone too far for tinkering with Stormont to have any effect.

At Westminster, the Labour Party, which had maintained a bi-partisan approach with the Tories since 1970, criticised internment and on 8 September Wilson outlined a 6 point plan to solve the Irish Problem. It included the appointment of a resident cabinet minister for the North, PR elections, a Council of Ireland between North and South, and consideration of eventual Irish unity. On 22 September, 60 Labour backbenchers voted against the government's policy on Ireland, and in November Wilson spent four days in Ireland, North and South, and visited Long Kesh. He called for a conference of all major parties in Britain and Ireland and said:

'I believe the situation has now gone so far that it is impossible to conceive of an effective long-term solution in which the agenda does not include consideration of and which is not in some way directed to, finding a means of achieving the aspirations, envisaged half a century ago, of progress towards a united Ireland'[2].

He suggested a united Ireland within the Commonwealth within fifteen years.

Wilson's scheme was impractical, and unacceptable to Republicans. There was no prospect of the South's re-entering the Commonwealth. But he had implicitly acknowledged that the revolt of the minority could not be suppressed by military means alone or without progress towards a united Ireland.

The British government too was evidently considering alternatives. After rejecting Lynch's call for an end to internment on 19 August as unwarranted interference in the internal affairs of the United Kingdom, Heath held a two-day meeting with him on 6–7 September. On 27 September Heath, Faulkner and Lynch held a tripartite discussion on the Northern crisis. Then at the end of October Paisley announced that Westminster was going to suspend the Stormont administration and rule Northern Ireland directly from London. It was promptly denied but the suspicion remained. There could be little doubt that this step was being considered. All that was needed was another deterioration in the situation.

All marches and parades had been banned in the North since 9 August 1971, but on Christmas Day, as the culmination of a series of protest rallies, the Northern Resistance Movement held a march from Belfast to Long Kesh. Over a thousand people took part and marched for several miles along the North's main motorway, the M1, until they were stopped by a massive force of troops and RUC. The march was quite illegal and the turnout, including two Westminster MPs Frank McManus and Bernadette Devlin, was an indication of the strength of minority feeling. The Christmas Day march sparked off a new wave of minority defiance, and six more illegal marches were held in rapid succession over the next few weeks, with NICRA and even the SDLP joining in.

A NICRA march was scheduled for Derry on Sunday 30 January 1972, going from Creggan through the Bogside to the Guildhall Square. It was bound to be very big since it was to be the first march in Derry since internment was introduced. Even the local RUC advised that it be allowed to go ahead and the organisers prosecuted afterwards. But the government refused. They were intent on a show of force and had promised the Derry Unionists that the march wouldn't get out of the ghetto. A battalion of the Paras, the shock troops of the British Army, was drafted in and the route blocked at the exit from the ghetto.

There was inevitably a riot. It wasn't even a big one since the bulk of the marchers were listening to an impromptu meeting. Suddenly the Paras opened fire. They fired repeatedly into the crowd, and then at people fleeing and at others trying to reach the wounded. They killed thirteen civilians. Inevitably the Army claimed that someone had fired at them and that the thirteen dead were all terrorists and gunmen, but even the British government enquiry could produce no credible evidence. The commander of the Paras, Lieut-Colonel Derek Wilford, later got an OBE for his day's work.

Nationalist Ireland exploded after Bloody Sunday. Tens of thousands of workers downed tools and marched in protest in Dundalk, Cork, Galway, Limerick and Dublin. Lynch was forced to declare 2 February, the day of the victims' funerals, a day of national mourning. If he hadn't, most of the South would have closed down anyway. After three days of marches and riots a 30,000-strong crowd finally burnt down the British Embassy in Dublin and another crowd tried to burn the British Rail office in Cork.

In the North there was a one-day protest strike across the six counties, and a three day strike in Derry. There was rioting, hijacking and road-blocking in every Catholic area, and immense crowds thronged Derry for the funerals. On 6 February there was another march in Newry. Despite efforts by NICRA, desperately anxious to defuse the explosive situation, to discourage Southerners from taking part, it was the biggest Nationalist demonstration in the North for fifty years. Estimates put the crowd at over fifty thousand. This was banned from the centre of the town as well, and the NICRA organisers made no effort to defy the ban. But it made no difference: the enormous crowd had shown a whole community in revolt.

At Westminster Bernadette Devlin attacked Maudling and punched him in the face. At home Catholic lawyers resigned Crown Prosecutorships and refused Crown briefs. The alienation of the minority was total, with the clergy and the middle class trying desperately to catch up with the masses.

After Bloody Sunday the minority could not be suppressed.

Marches went on in Fermanagh, Derry, Belfast, Armagh, Tyrone. NRM organisers competed with each other to collect six-month jail terms – all marches were still banned and there was a statutory six-month sentence for the leaders. The IRA fought on and casualties were very high. On 21 February four Provos were blown up in East Belfast. On 22 February the Official IRA bombed the Paras' base at Aldershot in England, killing an Army chaplain and six women cleaners. A bomb in the Abercorn restaurant in Belfast on 4 March killed two people and badly injured several more. Both IRAs denied responsibility for it. On 9 March three Provos were blown up in Clonard Street in Belfast and on 20 March a Provo bomb with an inadequate warning killed two RUC men and four civilians in Donegall Street. But nothing short of the fall of Stormont could shake minority support for violence now.

And the campaign was relentlessly effective. 56 British soldiers had been killed by 20 March, and the centres of Belfast and other towns looked as if they had been blitzed. Strabane Town Hall was blown up at the end of February, destroying all the records and crippling local government in the area. John Taylor, the Minister of State for Home Affairs, was shot and badly wounded the day after.

Even the courts were embarrassing the government. In February the Armagh County Court ruled that an internee had been assaulted and maltreated during the original arresting operation and awarded him damages. Eventually the government had to pay compensation to everyone arrested on 9 August. And in February as well the Northern Ireland High Court ruled that all the actions of the British Army in the North since 1969 had been technically illegal. Westminster had hurriedly and shamefacedly to pass an act indemnifying itself retrospectively.

The position was intolerable. Westminster was rapidly sinking into the morass of an unwinnable colonial war. The government had to act to try to extricate itself.

On 22 March Faulkner and his deputy, Senator Jack Andrews, went to Downing Street and met Heath, Maudling, the Defence Secretary Lord Carrington, and the Leader of the House of Commons William Whitelaw. Heath told them that the Westminster government was going to take all security powers away from Stormont. Faulkner was already under heavy pressure from the right; a Unionist Party thirsting for blood and daily demanding more extreme repression would never agree to surrender control of security. Unionist backbenchers at Stormont had voted to oppose any reduction in Stormont's powers only a week before. He threatened to resign. He was told Westminster would then suspend Stormont and bring in direct rule.

Faulkner returned to Belfast to tell his cabinet. There were two anxious days of vacillation. On 24 March Heath announced that Faulkner and his cabinet were resigning, that Westminster was suspending the Stormont government and parliament, and that William Whitelaw was taking over as Secretary of State for Northern Ireland. The move was evidently well prepared. It seems clear that the threat to take over Stormont's security powers was only a way to precipitate the crisis.

The Loyalists were furious. Faulkner had skilfully divided the hard-line West Ulster Unionist Council when he came into office by including Harry West and John Brooke in the government, but even the introduction of internment hadn't satisfied Craig or Paisley. On 6 September 1971 both had spoken at a mass rally of nearly fifteen thousand workers from the shipyard, Short's aircraft factory, and the other East Belfast factories. They had demanded even tougher repressive measures and the formation of a Loyalist militia. On 14 September Desmond Boal and John McQuade resigned from the Unionist Party and joined Paisley and the Rev William Beattie to form the Democratic Unionist Party. Under the influence of Boal the DUP adopted a semi-radical stance. Paisley opposed internment on the far-sighted grounds that it could be used against Loyalists as well as Republicans. He also advocated complete integration with Britain as the best way of preventing a united Ireland if Stormont was suspended. These unorthodox views led to a brief flirtation with the Southern press and television, but in practice the DUP served as a focus for right-wing discontent.

Craig was the spokesman for the more orthodox right. On 23 October 1971 he was elected chairman of a steering committee of hard-line representatives from 43 of the 52 Unionist constituency parties. The strength of the extreme right was shown on 11 November when Callaghan, the former Home Secretary, visited Belfast. Nearly twenty thousand Loyalist workers downed tools and held a protest rally in the centre of Belfast. Protestant industrial workers, especially in the big, almost exclusively Protestant engineering works, were now becoming a significant factor in Loyalist politics. Unemployment was relatively low, and as the 'aristocrats of labour' with secure jobs in heavily subsidised industries dependent on the British markets, they were the staunchest opponents of a united Ireland. It was not for nothing that the Stormont and Westminster governments had pumped money into the Belfast shipyard over the years[3].

The Protestant workers were organised in the factories and the shipyard by a Loyalist Association of Workers (LAW) led by Billy Hull, the right-wing union boss in the shipyard. The LAW, backed by intimidation and the Orange Order network, wielded considerable power. It was very similar to the Unionist Labour Association in the 1920s. The LAW itself was vehemently anti-socialist and closely aligned with Craig.

After internment was introduced Loyalist 'Defence Associations' like McKeague's SDA sprang up in Protestant areas and drew together to form the Ulster Defence Association (UDA), an openly para-military body which made little effort to conceal the fact that it was arming itself. The RUC and British Army persistently turned a blind eye to UDA activities despite considerable Loyalist gun-fire in internment week and after.

Throughout the winter Craig toured the six counties speaking in Orange Halls and building up support. Then on 9 February 1972 he launched a new political organisation – Vanguard. It was described as 'an umbrella for traditional Loyalist groups' and Craig was backed at the launching by Billy Hull of the LAW, and Rev Martin Smyth, a Presbyterian minister and head of the Orange Order in Belfast. Vanguard held its first public rally in Lisburn on 12 February. The occasion had heavy fascist overtones: Craig drove up with a motor-cycle escort and reviewed 500 men drawn up in military formation. During the rally he read out a pledge and asked his hearers to endorse it by raising their arms three times and shouting, 'I do'. He ended with a threat: 'We are determined, ladies and gentlemen, to preserve our British traditions and way of life. And God help those who get in our way'[4].

Vanguard continued with a series of rallies with the same semi-fascist trappings in provincial towns. They were making inroads into the official party. Four Unionist MPs spoke at a Vanguard meeting in Portadown on 11 March. The series of rallies culminated in a mass demonstration in Belfast's Ormeau Park on 18 March, with an estimated 60,000 present. The UDA and LAW were out in strength and thousands marched in formation wearing para-military uniforms. By then it was clear that Westminster would take some initiative in a couple of days. Craig threatened that if it wasn't satisfactory to Vanguard they would set up a provisional government.

When Heath announced the suspension of Stormont, Vanguard

called a two-day protest strike and a rally at Stormont on 28 March to coincide with the old parliament's last sitting. The strike, backed by intimidation, was effective, shutting off power supplies, stopping public transport and closing most of the major industries. The rally at Stormont was very big, roughly the same size as the one in Ormeau Park, but at it Craig was upstaged by Faulkner in a piece of unparalleled political opportunism. The speakers were to address the crowd from the balcony of the parliament buildings. Faulkner had the building closed to non-MPs, meaning only Craig could get in, and in the meantime addressed the crowd himself, strongly attacking the suspension of Stormont but warning against precipitate action. When Craig did speak however he announced no provisional government and didn't advocate any dramatic new course of action. He wasn't prepared to go over the brink yet. For the rest, the bulk of the Protestant population took the end of 50 years of self-government very quietly. There were no riots, no clashes with the British Army.

On the minority side, opinion was sharply divided. The SDLP, the Catholic Church, the Dublin government, all welcomed direct rule and called for a cease-fire. But the suspension of Stormont was only temporary, there was no indication of what would take its place, there were still almost a thousand men interned and British troops were still on the streets. The NRM, PD and NICRA announced that political resistance would continue.

Both wings of the IRA said they would fight on and the Provos underlined their determination by planting a total of 40 bombs on 13 and 14 April, by bombing the big Courtaulds factory at Carrickfergus on 1 May, and by blowing up the Belfast Co-op, the biggest department store in the city, on 10 May. Moreover British peace hopes were set back severely on 15 April when an Army patrol shot dead Joe McCann, a prominent member of the Official IRA, as he walked, unarmed, along a street in the Markets area of Belfast. The result was two days of violent rioting in Belfast, joint action by the Officials and Provos for a time and three soldiers shot dead.

Nonetheless the suspension of Stormont had fragmented the almost total solidarity of the Catholic population produced by internment and reinforced by Bloody Sunday. Whitelaw followed up with an amnesty for the illegal marches, the release of batches of internees, and the closing of Magilligan camp, a second internment camp which had been opened on the North Derry coast. By mid-June he had released 550 internees, more than half the total held. The Catholic middle class, longing for peace and stability, had been the first to clamour for a cease-fire, but now sections of the working class as well were calling for peace.

An incident in Derry brought things to a head. On 19 May the British Army killed a fifteen-year-old boy in the Bogside. The next day the Official IRA killed nineteen-year-old William Best, a soldier in the Royal Irish Rangers, as a reprisal. But Best was a young Creggan Catholic home on leave from his regiment in Germany. He had never served in Northern Ireland – the British Army's three Irish regiments were never used in the North. There was bitter reaction in the Bogside and angry local women took over the headquarters of the Officials and formed a movement for peace. The church, the press and television whipped up a wave of anti-IRA hysteria and on 29 May the Officials succumbed and declared an unconditional cease-fire.

In fact the cease-fire was partly the result of tensions within the Official Republican movement itself. The Officials' leadership was by now completely committed to a strategy of gradualist reform within the six-county state, and had only been forced into a military campaign, with considerable reluctance, by internment and the pressure of their Northern militants. They had taken advantage of the reaction to the Best shooting to call off a campaign they had never wanted. Relations between Official and Provisional Republicans, never friendly, now became extremely bad, with the Officials calling the Provos 'Green Fascists' and denouncing their bombing campaign as sectarian.

Pressure was mounting on the Provos as well. The attrition of urban guerrilla war was making the ghetto population war-weary. The day before the Official cease-fire a premature explosion in Anderson Street in the Short Strand killed four Provos and two local civilians and wrecked half the street. There was also pressure from the South.

The days when the Provos had the ear of Dublin cabinet ministers had long gone and some IRA men had been caught and jailed in the South. However, the emotional reaction to internment and Bloody Sunday had forced the government and Gardai to turn a very short-sighted eye to IRA activities and the South was still a fairly safe haven for them. Politically naive, the Provos seemed to expect this to go on indefinitely.

But the Dublin government was as anxious for stability and as alarmed by the IRA as London was. The suspension of Stormont gave them their opportunity. Southern opinion about the North was volatile and emotional. The Provos had relied solely on emotional appeals and had made no effort to build up a serious political organisation in the South or even to put across an analysis of the Northern situation. It was fairly easy for the Southern establishment to put across the idea that the fall of Stormont was a victory for the Northern minority and the Provos were jeopardising it, especially when the SDLP, the most publicised spokesmen of the minority, were saying the same.

A riot against prison conditions in Dublin's Mountjoy jail gave the government an excuse to act. The political prisoners in Mountjoy were transferred to military custody at the Curragh camp, and a special criminal court was established to try political cases without a jury. A number of prominent Provisionals including Ruadhri O'Bradaigh and Joe Cahill were arrested. O'Bradaigh and Cahill were released after a fortnight, but a steady stream of Provos were now being jailed by the special criminal court. The new aggressive attitude of the Dublin government was shown on 3 June when a PD protest march at the Curragh camp was met by Irish Army troops with fixed bayonets and loaded sub-machine guns.

Caught between war-weariness and a longing for peace in the North, and harassment of their base-areas in the South, the Provos became more amenable. Whitelaw put out feelers to them and negotiations began through the SDLP, whom they had previously reviled. Whitelaw offered, not an immediate end to internment, but political recognition: something dear to the hearts of the Provo leaders.

On 22 June 1972 the Provos announced that they would cease fire at midnight on 26 June if the British would reciprocate. Whitelaw gave a guarded assent and the cease-fire was on. The Provos fought on literally to the last moment – a soldier was killed in Belfast at one minute to midnight – but the cease-fire came into effect. The Provos stopped bombing and attacking Crown forces, the Army and police stopped raiding and searching for them.

On 7 July six Provo leaders were given a safe-conduct, flown to London and met Whitelaw in the private house of one of his junior ministers in Chelsea. The six were Sean McStiofain, the chief of staff, Daithi O'Connaill, the Provos' main politician, Seamus Twomey, the Belfast commander, Martin McGuinness, the Derry commander, and Gerry Adams and Ivor Bell who were later to succeed Twomey in Belfast. What they discussed was never revealed though it obviously included an end to internment. It was an academic question anyway because two days later the truce broke down.

Even before Stormont was suspended a number of Catholics had been shot in Belfast. On 3 February Bernard Rice from Ardoyne was shot dead from a car which drove off into the Protestant Woodvale. On 26 February two more Catholics were shot, one from a car which drove off into the Shankill area, the other by a gang in a Protestant estate, but both survived. On 13 March a nineteen-year-old Catholic, Patrick McCrory, was shot dead at his front door in a Protestant area in East Belfast. A campaign of random assassination of Catholics had begun. The type of reasoning behind it was given in a letter in the UDA paper in February, which criticised existing Loyalist groups and said:

'Why have they not started to hit back in the only way these nationalist bastards understand? That is ruthless indiscriminate killing . . . If I had a flame-thrower I would roast the slimy excreta that pass for human beings'[5].

The murder of uninvolved Catholic civilians was of course well within the tradition of Protestant para-military groups, from the Ulster Protestant Association in the twenties to the UVF in 1966.

Craig was making a series of extraordinarily violent and inflammatory statements at the same time. On 5 March he was interviewed on Radio Eireann about the scale of a Loyalist backlash.

'Interviewer: "Would this mean killing all Catholics in Ulster?"

'Craig: "It might not go so far as that but it could go as far as killing. It would be similar to the situation in the 1920s where Roman Catholics identified in Republican rebellion could find themselves unwelcome in their places of work and under pressure to leave their homes" '[6].

At his Ormeau Park rally on 18 March he said:

'We must build up dossiers on those men and women in this country who are a menace to this country because one of these days, if and when the politicians fail us, it may be our job to liquidate the enemy'[7].

When Stormont fell the assassinations continued. Two more Catholics were killed in April, while Craig made a still more bloodcurdling speech to the right-wing Monday Club in London on 27 April. He said he was prepared to 'shoot and kill' to keep Ulster British and went on, 'When we say force, we mean force. We will only assassinate our enemies as a last desperate resort when we are denied our democratic rights'[8]. He went on to speak at a joint rally of Vanguard and the neo-fascist National Front the next day. The same day Charles Harding Smith, the chairman of the UDA, and four others, including an RUC man, were arrested in London and charged with trying to purchase arms. They eventually got off, but not before a secret RUC Special Branch list of suspects was found in Smith's house. During the trial Smith produced a character reference from the Chief Constable of the RUC, an incident which did little to improve minority confidence in the RUC.

Four Catholics and a Protestant who had a Catholic girlfriend were killed in May, and another five Catholics and a Protestant living with a Catholic woman early in June. In the middle of May a bomb was planted outside a Catholic bar in Ballymurphy, and in the confusion after the explosion Loyalist gunmen opened fire into the estate from the nearby Protestant Springmartin area. A confused three-way gun-battle left one British soldier, one Protestant and four Catholics including a fourteen-year-old girl, dead. The Loyalist backlash had started in earnest.

The most visible aspect of the backlash was the UDA, now organising in all the hard-line Protestant areas and claiming a membership of nearly sixty thousand. The UDA demanded that the British Army smash the 'No-Go' areas in the Catholic ghettos of Belfast and Derry, and on 13 May they barricaded off the Protestant Woodvale district and set up their own 'No-Go' area. They threatened to set up temporary 'No-Go' areas in different Protestant districts for five consecutive weekends and then to make them permanent if the Army didn't act against the Catholics. Behind the UDA barricades there was massive harassment, beating up and intimidation of Catholics, which soon led to an exodus of Catholic families.

On 20 May the Army tried to bulldoze down UDA barricades in East Belfast; but the attempt started a riot and they withdrew. After that they kept out of the Loyalist 'No-Go' areas. On 27 May in a show of strength the UDA held a mass march of hooded and uniformed men through the centre of Belfast. The Army didn't interfere despite the fact that political uniforms were banned under the Public Order Act. In fact the Army and RUC turned a distinctly tolerant eye on the UDA, despite its fairly open involvement in robberies and assassinations and the fact that it was arming itself. UDA leaders were even issued freely with gun licences. Two years later an unnamed junior Army officer who had served in Northern Ireland wrote that the Army was afraid of a war on two fronts:

'In order to combat this threat, the Army chose, quite deliberately, to give the UDA tacit support. The UDA virtually ran East and North Belfast . . . Almost too late, in the winter of 1972 the Army realised that it had assisted in the birth of a monster. It sought to act, but was only able to cage the beast; the secret of its destruction had been lost with its birth"[9].

At the beginning of June Whitelaw met the UDA leaders, uniforms, masks and all, and got them to postpone their imposition of permanent 'No-Go' areas. The truce enraged them however, and on 30 June permanent concrete barricades were set up in Protestant areas of Belfast and Portadown. The fortnight of the truce saw a dramatic increase in assassinations. The Loyalists killed six Catholics and almost certainly killed three Protestants, two of them, Malcolm and Peter Orr, because they had Catholic girlfriends. And for the first time the IRA or other Catholic groups began to retaliate, killing four Protestants in sectarian reprisals while three others were killed by Catholic vigilantes when they crashed check-points. One case was bizarre. The bodies of two Protestants were found in a partly burnt-out car on the Grosvenor Road – a Catholic area. In the boot was the body of a Catholic who had been shot earlier. It looked as if two Loyalist assassins had been caught with the body of their victim and were then killed themselves.

Meanwhile the exodus of Catholic families from the Protestant 'No-Go' areas had become a stampede – yet the Army refused to protect them. There was a tense confrontation in the Springfield Road area when the UDA extended their area to include a mainly Catholic street. The Army negotiated with them and then retreated. Catholics were aghast. It looked as if the Army were going to let the UDA take over Catholic areas with impunity.

The crunch came in Lenadoon, a new mainly Catholic housing estate on the fringe of Andersonstown. The Northern Ireland Housing Executive allocated some empty houses formerly occupied by Protestants to Catholic refugees. The UDA objected, and when the Catholic families tried to move in the Army stopped them. The Army seemed to be doing the UDA's job for them. There were two days of angry riots in Lenadoon and on 9 July 1972 the Provos opened fire again. The fragile truce was over, brought down by the intransigence of the Loyalist right and the British Army's reluctance to confront them.

The IRA hit back very hard. On 13 July five British soldiers were killed, and three soldiers and an RUC man were killed on 16 July. Five days later on Friday 21 July the Provos launched a major bombing blitz with 22 bombs in Belfast. It went disastrously wrong. The Army claimed the warnings were inadequate, the Provos claimed the Army deliberately didn't act on them. Either way, nine civilians and two soldiers were killed and many more injured. It became known as 'Bloody Friday'.

Bloody Friday shocked most of the Catholic population and gave the Whitelaw administration its opportunity. The minority had been divided by direct rule, almost all had welcomed the truce and many had not supported the renewal of the campaign, especially outside Belfast, where the menace of intimidation and assassinations didn't seem so real. Now they were stunned by Bloody Friday.

There was a short propaganda campaign about the 'No-Go' areas. On 27 July 4,000 extra troops and heavy equipment were sent to Northern Ireland. On 31 July in 'Operation Motorman' the Army moved into the 'No-Go' areas, both Catholic and Protestant, at 4.30 in the morning. The IRA didn't resist and there was no opposition in Belfast. In Derry the people fought back and there was some rioting, but the Army shot two men dead and used heavy tanks for the first time in the North. In Catholic West Belfast the inhabitants woke up to find schools, halls, blocks of flats, and the North's main Gaelic football ground, Casement Park, occupied by the Army and being fortified for a long stay. Eventually there were to be sixteen fortified Army posts in the greater Andersonstown area with a garrison of several thousand troops. The Army also built four huge Wild-West style forts with corrugated iron stockades. West Belfast was under military occupation.

There was a lot of indignation and resentment and there was a major riot after a PD meeting outside Casement Park, with the crowd burning a Saracen armoured car; but some of the indignation was blunted by three car-bombs which went off before a warning was received in the village of Claudy in Co.Derry on the day of Operation Motorman. Nine civilians including a small child were killed. Popular support for the Provos suffered another blow on 23 August when a bomb exploded prematurely in a customs station in Newry, killing the two IRA men who were planting it and seven civilians.

The SDLP had also seen their opportunity after the breakdown of the truce and Bloody Friday. The pledge of no talks with the British administration until internment ended sat uneasily on them. With Stormont suspended they were anxious to be involved in the discussions on what would replace it. The Provos, by negotiating through the SDLP, and by talking to Whitelaw themselves, had opened the door for them. On 7 August, after consultation with Dublin, the SDLP held their first meeting with Whitelaw.

On 4 September Lynch met Heath and discussed the Northern situation with him at the Olympic games in Munich. Whitelaw had already announced that he would hold a round-table conference of Northern parties at the end of September. The SDLP were still too embarrassed by internment for them to attend but they saw Heath in London on 11 September and published a policy document on 20 September which called for joint British-Irish sovereignty or condominium over the North and for a British declaration in favour of eventual unity. It was a position somewhere between the all-out struggle for a united Ireland then being waged and their former parliamentary role within the Northern state.

Whitelaw went ahead with his round-table conference at Darlington in England at the end of September, but only three parties turned up, the Unionists, the NILP, and the Alliance Party – a non-sectarian moderate Unionist group formed in April 1970 with substantial backing from the new commercial and industrial interests. Nonetheless the British government went ahead with their plans, announcing that a referendum on the border would be held early in 1973, followed by local elections with PR and 'One Man, One Vote' in the Spring. On 30 October they published a Green Paper or discussion document on the future of Northern Ireland.

The Green Paper gave the usual commitment that there could be no change in the North's position within the UK without majority consent, but went on to say that any new arrangements for government must involve the minority, adding that 'there are strong arguments that the objective of real participation should be achieved by giving minority interests a share in the exercise of executive power. It also stated that,

'A settlement must also recognise Northern Ireland's position within Ireland as a whole . . . It is therefore clearly desirable that any new arrangements for Northern Ireland should, whilst meeting the wishes of Northern Ireland and Great Britain, be so far as possible, acceptable to and accepted by the Republic of Ireland'.

And it gave a couple of good reasons for securing a settlement acceptable to the South: that both Britain and the Republic would become members of the EEC on 1 January 1973; and that such a settlement would:

'provide a firm basis for concerted governmental and community action against those terrorist organisations which represent a threat to free democratic institutions in Ireland as a whole'[10].

Evidently Westminster felt that by threatening the British government's direct control in the North and indirect control in the South, the military and political resistance would eventually threaten the whole capitalist social and economic system in both parts of Ireland.

The direction of British policy was becoming clearer. It would involve a share in power and patronage for the Catholic middle class in the North; it could be represented in the South as a step towards the national objective of re-unification without the problem of having to assimilate a million recalcitrant Northern Protestants. Lynch met Heath in London on 24 November and indicated his agreement with the Green Paper. The next day the SDLP Conference voted overwhelmingly to start negotiations about the future of the North, regardless of internment. The new policy was eminently satisfactory to the SDLP and the Dublin government. It was one they could sell to their supporters. They got new confidence to attack the IRA.

Lynch's government had already stepped up their offensive. On 6 October they had activated an obscure section of the Offences Against the State Act to close up without warning the Provisional Sinn Fein headquarters at Kevin Street in Dublin, and another building used by the Provos at Blessington Street. On 5 November Mrs Maire Drumm, vice-president of Provisional Sinn Fein, was arrested and jailed for a speech she made in the South. On 19 November, Sean McStiofain was arrested and jailed for six months for membership of the IRA, and on 24 November the government dismissed the entire governing body of Radio/Telefis Eireann for broadcasting an interview with McStiofain contrary to a government directive.

McStiofain went on hunger and thirst strike to demand his release and there were big demonstrations in Dublin, but the government dug in its heels and wouldn't give way. They seemed to be challenging the Provos to a head-on confrontation, confident that they had majority support in the South. MacStiofain eventually gave up his strike. The government also introduced a draconian amendment to the Offences Against the State Act, under which the evidence of a Garda Superintendent that he believed someone to be a member of the IRA would be sufficient to convict. The Bill was too much even for the pro-British Fine Gael Party, who threatened to oppose it. Blaney and the Fianna Fail dissidents were sure to vote against it and it began to look as if the government might be defeated.

Two bombs went off without warning in the centre of Dublin on the day of the vote, killing two men and injuring over a hundred. In a wave of anti-IRA hysteria the Bill was passed by 70 votes to 23. The Provos categorically denied responsibility for the bombs and it was widely believed that they were planted by Loyalists or British agents to influence the vote in the Dail. The South now had a system of virtually legalised internment in operation and the jails rapidly filled. Ruadhri O'Bradaigh was arrested and jailed on 28 December and Martin McGuinness, the Derry Provo commander, on 31 December.

Meanwhile the Provisionals, hit hard by harassment, repression and jailings on both sides of the border, and with their popular support undermined by the condemnations of Dublin, the Church and the SDLP, nonetheless survived and recovered. The Catholic population was again divided along clear, largely class, lines. The middle class longed for peace and saw in the British Green Paper the prospect of a place in the sun. They supported the SDLP or even, if they were snobbish, the Alliance Party. The ghetto working class who were at the receiving end of internment and British Army brutality, supported the Provos. They could see no end to discrimination and Protestant supremacy until the Northern state was ended. The collaboration of Lynch's government with the British outraged them and they turned increasingly against Dublin as well. The Catholic working class was moving to the left, and even the Provisionals were forced into closer alliance with marxists such as those in the Peoples Democracy[11].

The Provos had also become a tougher, more efficient and more disciplined guerrilla force, and were spreading their operations out of Belfast and Derry. By October 1972 they had killed 132 British soldiers. They had some notable successes. The day of the Darlington talks they wrecked Belfast's newest luxury hotel, the Russell Court, causing damage worth nearly £2 million. On 2 October they shot dead a British soldier operating as a laundry man in the Twinbrook estate near Andersonstown: they had uncovered a British undercover spy ring, called the Military Reaction Force (MRF), which was using a bogus laundry firm and massage parlours as a front for intelligence work. The exposure of the MRF also shed some light on the operations of the sinister Special Air Service Regiment, a secret elite counter-terrorist group of the British Army. It was revealed that MRF or SAS plain-clothes patrols in unmarked cars had shot dead two Catholic civilians, Paddy McVeigh and Daniel Rooney, on 12 May and 27 September 1972 respectively. They had also wounded four others on 22 June – and these were only the cases which came to light and were admitted. The most charitable explanation seemed to be that the MRF squads aimed unceremoniously to murder wanted IRA men but had made a number of mistakes. Alternatively, they were out to terrorise and demoralise the Catholic population by random killings. The MRF scheme backfired badly early in 1974 when an RUC patrol shot two MRF men dead in an old van in South Armagh because they were acting suspiciously.

The second half of 1972 had been dominated by the Loyalist backlash however. When the truce ended the Loyalists mounted a campaign of absolute terror against the Catholic population, marked by some particularly ghastly murders. On the night of 11 July, traditionally a Loyalist festival, four armed men burst into the home of a 46-year-old Catholic widow in the Oldpark area of Belfast. They raped the woman several times at gun-point, then shot her and her mentally retarded son. The boy was killed but the mother survived. On the 12th itself one of the few remaining Catholic UDR men[12] was kidnapped in Protestant East Belfast, tortured, branded with a red-hot iron, stabbed and eventually shot dead. Ten days later a Catholic girl singer and her boyfriend were stopped at a UDA barricade and shot dead after the girl had been forced to sing for some of the UDA leaders.

On 13 August the body of Thomas Madden, another Catholic, was found in the Oldpark area. He had been hung up by the arms, stabbed about a hundred and fifty times all over the body and eventually strangled. The day before another Catholic had been found tortured to death off the Antrim Road. Sadistic torture was becoming a common feature of Loyalist killings.

There had been 36 murders in July – nineteen Catholics and seventeen Protestants. The numbers had been fairly equal because the Catholics were retaliating. There were fourteen assassinations in August – nine Catholics and five Protestants, two of whom were killed by Loyalists. From August on there were nearly three Catholics killed for every Protestant, with the vast majority of the killings in Belfast where there are three Protestants to every Catholic. Remarkably, hardly any of the Catholics had connections with the Republican movement. The assassination campaign seemed less a simple expression of sectarian hatred than a deliberate attempt to demoralise the minority by creating an atmosphere of random terror.

With Operation Motorman over, the 'No-Go' areas occupied, and the British government trying to create a political settlement acceptable to the Catholic middle class and the South, the Loyalists became a nuisance and a hindrance. The Army began to treat them less politely and on 7 September a clash between the traditionally brutal Paras and civilians on the Shankill Road provoked a gun-battle which killed one civilian and a UDA gunman, who turned out to be a member of the UDR as well – a feature of this period was the increasing identification of the UDR and the Loyalist militants. By now the UDR was almost entirely Protestant (96 per cent in November 1972) and there was a considerable overlap in membership with the UDA and UVF. A new UDR battalion, the 11th, was formed in the Craigavon area in September 1972 and in October all the weapons in its armoury were stolen without resistance by the UVF.

On 16 September when Loyalists besieged the tiny Catholic ghetto in Larne, Co.Antrim, British troops intervened and shot dead a prominent UVF man. The most serious clash came on 16 October when there was serious rioting in East Belfast and troops in Saracen armoured cars ran down and killed two civilians. Tommy Herron, the UDA vice-chairman, declared war on the British Army and there were two nights of heavy gun-fire in Protestant areas leaving two more civilians dead before Herron called it off under local pressure. Fighting with the British Army wasn't popular among the Protestant population.

Both sides avoided a major confrontation for some time after the two-day war, and in the meantime the Loyalists had their own internal problems. The UDA had become a huge ramshackle organisation heavily infiltrated with gangsters and petty criminals, and involved in protection rackets and extortion, backed up by intimidation, on a grand scale. Many mysterious beatings, shootings and bombings in Protestant areas were simply the UDA enforcing their levies. Most of the local leaders were taking a substantial cut out of the proceeds.

At the beginning of December Charles Harding Smith, the original UDA chairman, returned to Belfast after being acquitted of arms smuggling in London. There was an immediate power struggle, with Smith trying to re-assert himself and at the same time clean up some of the most blatant racketeering. On 7 December Ernie Elliott, the UDA commander in Woodvale, was found shot dead in a Protestant area. He had been brutally tortured. A month later on 22 January 1973, David Fogel, Elliott's second-in-command in Woodvale, fled to London denouncing a take-over bid by Smith backed by the UVF. In the meantime Smith had re-established his control in West Belfast. He had a more difficult task in East Belfast where Tommy Herron, the UDA vice-chairman, held sway and had strong support in the local organisation. There was a compromise with each running his own area, but it was purely temporary. In June 1973 Herron's brother-in-law and bodyguard was shot dead in an attempt to get Herron himself, and eventually in September 1973 Herron was kidnapped and killed. There was little change in policy however, and the new leadership was even more ruthless and single-minded than Herron and Elliott had been.

The assassinations had continued throughout the winter. There were 40 sectarian killings in the last four months of 1972, with 31 of the victims Catholics. Again some had been very brutal. Two Catholic farmers had been hacked to death with knives or pitchforks on their farm in Fermanagh on 24 October, and a 23-year-old Catholic had had his hands and feet almost burnt off and his body branded with a blow-lamp in East Belfast on 2 December. A lot more of the killings were outside Belfast now, and many of them were direct reprisals for the killing of UDR men, strengthening the belief that there were close connections between the UDR and the UDA. On 20 December a UDR man was shot outside Derry: that evening gunmen burst into a Catholic bar in Derry and killed five men in reprisal, one of them a Protestant.

Loyalist activities were spreading South of the border as well. There were several bombings in the South during the winter, with two killed in Co.Cavan on 28 December and a teenage couple stabbed and shot dead in Donegal on New Year's Eve.

But the assassins were going too far. At the turn of the year two Catholics were shot dead leaving new prestige factories in East Belfast – Rolls Royce and the American-owned Hughes Tool Company. There were calls for a strike of all Catholic workers. The industrialists were getting alarmed. The *Belfast Telegraph* called for action. The drive to attract new industry might be jeopardised.

The government had to act. At the end of January, after a brief lull, five Catholics were killed in a couple of days. On 3 February 1973 two Loyalists were arrested and interned, the first Loyalist internees for fifty years. The UDA reacted furiously, taking on the Army in a gun-battle in East Belfast. Seven Catholics were assassinated over the weekend and on 7 February the UDA, LAW and Vanguard called a one-day protest strike.

The strike was enforced by massive intimidation, and gangs of Protestant youths – Tartan gangs – went on a rampage of burning, looting and wrecking. There were heavy gun-battles between Loyalists and the Army, leaving a UVF man dead in East Belfast and a Protestant fireman killed by Loyalists in Sandy Row. The result was disastrous for the Loyalist groups.

The vast majority of Protestants were against clashes with the British Army, most of them supported internment even if a couple of Loyalists had to be held as well, and many were appalled at the vandalism and destruction indulged in by the Tartan gangs. Craig, whose Vanguard organisation was heavily backed by the Protestant small and medium business class, sensed the revulsion of his backers and started to dissociate himself from the para-military groups. The government, seizing its opportunity, quickly arrested another seven Loyalist militants including John McKeague. After that the number of Loyalists interned crept up until there were sixty in Long Kesh in mid-1974 – compared with six hundred Republicans[13].

Meanwhile the government was going ahead with its plans. On 8 March 1973 a referendum on the border was held, as a sop to the Loyalists. All anti-Unionist groups, including the SDLP, called for a boycott and it was remarkably effective. In a low poll, 591,820, or 57 per cent of the electorate, voted to remain part of the UK. Only 6,463 voted for the alternative of unity with the South. On 20 March the Westminster government published a White Paper outlining the new arrangements for governing the North[14].

The Stormont parliament and government were to be replaced by a single-chamber Assembly and an executive. The Assembly would have 78 seats and be elected by PR. The executive would be appointed from the Assembly, but it could 'no longer be solely based upon any single party, if that party draws its support and its elected representation virtually entirely from only one section of a divided community'. There would be a Council of Ireland between North and South, and its form and functions would be worked out at a conference between London, Dublin and the Northern parties after the election. There would continue to be a Secretary of State for Northern Ireland at Westminster, and all power over security matters would be reserved to Westminster. There would also be a Charter of Human Rights and measures to outlaw discrimination. They didn't lose sight of their main objective however: two of the three functions of the Council of Ireland would be 'to secure acceptance of the present status of Northern Ireland', and 'the provision of a firm basis for concerted governmental and community action against terrorist organisations'. And the Westminster parliament would bring in laws to provide for special courts and the continuance of internment.

The White Paper was a neat summary of Westminster policy on Northern Ireland: a share in power and patronage for the Catholic middle class and an 'Irish dimension' to satisfy Dublin, in return for support in the campaign against the IRA and acceptance of the North's constitutional position. A classic piece of neo-colonialism. But would it work? Could the SDLP get away with accepting it while internment was still in operation? Would any section of the Unionist party agree to share power even with the Catholic middle class? Would the Loyalists allow it to get off the ground? The White Paper concluded:

'**They** [the government's proposals] **can be frustrated if interests in Northern Ireland refuse to allow them to be tried or if any section of the community is determined to impose its will on another**'.

Only the Alliance Party welcomed the document with enthusiasm. It was obvious that they were to play a central role, acting as a bridge between Unionists and SDLP in the executive. The SDLP accepted the scheme in principle but demanded an end to internment and the early establishment of a powerful Council of Ireland. The Official Unionists equivocated. Faulkner declared 'We neither reject it [the White Paper] totally nor do we accept it totally', and called for renegotiation of its terms. But the division in his camp was clear when the Grand Orange Lodge condemned the White Paper at the end of April. Craig rejected it as well and announced the formation of a new hard-line party backed by the UDA and LAW. It would be called the Vanguard Unionist Progressive Party and would fight the Assembly elections in alliance with Paisley's DUP and in opposition to the White Paper. The Provos naturally rejected the Westminster scheme: it was after all principally aimed at eroding their support.

Local government elections were held on 30 May 1973 under PR – the first local elections for six years. It was mainly a trial run for the Assembly election. The Provos and the PD called for a boycott, seeing the elections as an attempt to rebuild credible political institutions in the North; but the call was effective only in hard-core Republican areas like Andersonstown, the Creggan in Derry and South Armagh. Elsewhere the poll was fairly high. The results were confusing. The SDLP virtually eliminated all other anti-Unionist groups, but anti-Unionists won an outright majority on only one of the 26 new district councils: Newry and Mourne[15]. Two councils, Derry and Fermanagh, were evenly balanced, and Alliance or Independents held the balance in two more, Magherafelt and Omagh. Ironically the anti-Unionists were worse off under the new system.

There was immense confusion in the Unionist camp, with candidates under many different labels, but they had little difficulty in combining to defeat the SDLP when the new councils met. A significant feature of the election was the virtual disappearance of the Northern Ireland Labour Party which won four seats in the whole six counties, and the poor showing of the Alliance Party. The moderate centre around whom the whole power-sharing scheme was to be constructed was painfully weak.

However the local elections had gone smoothly enough, and the Whitelaw administration went ahead with the Assembly elections on 28 June, using the twelve Westminster constituencies with between five and eight seats each. On the minority side the contest was straightforward. The Provos and PD again urged a boycott but it was less effective. Of the parties represented in the old Stormont the Nationalists and Republican Labour put up only four candidates between them and all were defeated. The SDLP had practically a clear field, their only opposition being from the Official Republicans who put up ten candidates, getting 13,064 votes and no seats. The SDLP nominated 28 candidates and got 159,773 votes and nineteen seats. There was no doubt that they had become the official voice of the Northern minority, with the biggest anti-Unionist parliamentary group in the history of the state.

On the Unionist side there was still confusion. Craig's Vanguard and Paisley's DUP stood in alliance, putting up 24 and sixteen candidates respectively. There was a handful of Independent Loyalists, and there were twelve hard-line Unionists led by Harry West and John Taylor and not supported by Faulkner. There were 44 Official Unionists nominally committed to Faulkner and pledged to support the official manifesto, but as in 1969 many of them managed to remain ambiguous.

Vanguard won 69,348 votes and seven seats, the DUP 76,254 votes and eight seats, the West-Taylor group 61,183 votes and ten seats, and other hard-liners 29,088 votes and two seats, a total of 235,873 votes and 27 seats. The Faulkner group got 211,362 votes and 22 seats. The hard-liners o[f] Loyalists had a small but clear majority, while the Faulkner group itself wa[s] anything but homogeneous and dependable.

The centre virtually collapsed. The NILP with 18 candidates go[t] 18,675 votes and one seat. The Alliance Party with 35 candidates and th[e] tacit backing of Westminster got 66,441 votes and eight seats.

The result was stalemate. The White Paper presumed a substanti[al] non-sectarian bloc in the centre to form the basis of the executive. It wasn'[t] there. The Alliance Party had no bargaining power, they weren't large enough to form a majority in alliance with any of the major groups. The Unionists and Loyalists together had an overwhelming majority, but the White Paper had specified that the executive couldn't be formed from one side of the community only. And the Faulkner Unionists, to ward off the Loyalist challenge, had pledged themselves not to share power 'with anyone whose primary object is to break the union with Great Britain', though their leader had been careful to avoid saying whether that included the SDLP.

For the next two months prospects for the White Paper looked grim. On 9 July four of the Faulkner-Unionist Assemblymen attended a meeting of anti-White Paper Unionists called by the Orange Order. Another Faulknerite died in a car crash on 15 July and a sixth, Nat Minford, was appointed Speaker of the Assembly. When the Assembly met for the first time at Stormont on 31 July Faulkner's parliamentary party was down to 20 members, and at least four of them were unreliable. The Assembly itself broke up in chaos with Minford having to adjourn the session because of Loyalist disruptions. The Loyalists then took over the chamber and tried to continue the meeting by themselves.

Meanwhile feeling was rising in the anti-Unionist population as internment neared its second anniversary and the numbers interned climbed back towards the pre-direct rule figure; while there were now nearly a thousand sentenced political prisoners in jail as well. On 6 July two PD members, Tony Canavan and the author, who had been jailed for organising a PD protest march, had gone on hunger strike to demand political prisoner status. After the hunger strike had lasted 34 days, and serious rioting had broken out in the ghettos, Whitelaw was forced to release the strikers and a hundred other short-term prisoners, and to abolish the Criminal Justice Act with its mandatory six-month jail sentences. But this sop didn't prevent the 9 August internment anniversary demonstrations being the biggest for many months. The White Paper solution looked like failing before it had even begun.

At the end of August Heath himself came to Belfast and warned the party leaders to form an executive quickly. At the beginning of September Whitelaw began separate talks with the three parties who at least partly supported the White Paper – Alliance, SDLP and Faulkner Unionists. On 17 September Heath met the Southern Taoiseach Cosgrave, at Baldonnel military aerodrome outside Dublin in the midst of the biggest security operation in the history of the state. He urged Southern government pressure on the SDLP to come to an agreement.

On 5 October 1973 the three Northern parties met and agreed in principle to form an executive. The SDLP also agreed that there could be no change in the status of Northern Ireland until the next border poll – in ten years time. On 6 November the three parties agreed on a joint social and economic programme for the North, and on 22 November Whitelaw was able to announce the formation of an executive-designate with eleven members, six Unionists, four SDLP, one Alliance. Faulkner would be Chief Executive, Gerry Fitt his deputy. There would be a London-Dublin-Belfast conference as soon as possible to settle the details of the Council of Ireland.

It was an extraordinary agreement. The SDLP, who had pledged themselves to no participation in Northern institutions while internment lasted, were to serve in government while internment continued and under the very man who had introduced it. Faulkner, who had come to power in the old Stormont as a hard-liner, and who had fought the Assembly election on a policy of re-negotiating the White Paper and no power-sharing with supporters of a United Ireland, was to share power with the SDLP. Both groups had a lot of explaining to do. Fitt headed off a revolt at the SDLP conference on 2 December by assuring delegates that the executive wouldn't work if internment continued. Faulkner was in more serious trouble. Two of his Assemblymen effectively went over to the West-Taylor camp in November, and on 20 November – before the executive was announced – an anti-power-sharing motion was defeated by only ten votes at the 750-strong Ulster Unionist Council. (After the announcement five of the seven Unionist MPs at Westminster defected to the West-Taylor group.) The Loyalists reacted to the announcement with rage, broke up an Assembly session on 28 November and physically attacked the Faulknerites in the Assembly on 6 December. The same evening a joint conference of Vanguard, DUP, and the West-Taylor Unionists agreed to establish a United Ulster Unionist Council to bring down the executive.

On 6 December as well the London-Dublin-Belfast Conference began at Sunningdale in England. There had been a general election in the South in February 1973, and the Irish Labour Party, in defiance of several conference decisions, had again agreed to form a coalition with the conservative, anti-Republican Fine Gael. The result was a new government with Liam Cosgrave as Taoiseach. Prominent in the government was Dr Conor Cruise O'Brien, the former anti-partition propagandist, now vehement opponent of Republicanism and a supporter of repressive legislation and political censorship in the media. The coalition had continued the Lynch policy of subservience to Britain and suppression of Republicans. They were, if anything, even more amenable to British plans for the North.

The Sunningdale Conference went on for four days, attended by Heath and Cosgrave and their senior ministers and members of the Northern executive. Eventually they reached agreement. There would be a two-tier Council of Ireland: a fourteen-man Council of Ministers, seven from each side, with unspecified executive powers, and a 60-member Consultative Assembly elected half by the Dail and half by the Northern Assembly. The Council's functions would be mainly in the field of economic and social co-operation. All decisions would have to be unanimous. There would be a small permanent secretariat. In an attempt to make the RUC more acceptable to the Northern minority, the Council of Ministers was to be consulted on appointments to the Northern and Southern police authorities. The British government undertook to review internment (again) and to release some detainees before Christmas.

In return the Southern delegates stated that 'the Irish government fully accepted and solemnly declared that there could be no change in the status of Northern Ireland until a majority of the people of Northern Ireland desired a change in that status.' They undertook to step up the offensive against the IRA and increase co-operation between the Gardai and RUC. An Anglo-Irish Law Commission was established to work out ways of dealing with 'fugitive offenders' from the North who took refuge in the South – Southern laws prohibited extradition for political offences. The whole agreement was to be formally ratified and implemented early in the New Year.

Sunningdale was the high point of British strategy in Ireland. It was a masterpiece of balance and ambiguity. The Unionists could sell the Council of Ireland to their followers on the grounds that the North's constitutional position would be strengthened by Southern recognition and co-operation in action against the IRA, and that the Council would have no power anyway. The SDLP and the Dublin government could argue that they were getting a measure of control over the RUC and that the Council of Ireland was a major step towards a united Ireland. But they were contradictory arguments. The success of the agreement depended on neither side listening to what their allies were saying about it.

The new executive took office on 1 January 1974. Its make-up was:

Chief Executive: Brian Faulkner (Unionist)
Deputy Chief Executive: Gerry Fitt (SDLP)
Minister for Finance: Herbert Kirk (Un)
Minister for Commerce: John Hume (SDLP)
Minister for Education: Basil McIvor (Un)
Minister for Housing: Austin Currie (SDLP)
Minister for Agriculture: Leslie Morrell (Un)
Minister for Health & Social Services: Paddy Devlin (SDLP)
Minister for Environment: Roy Bradford (Un)
Minister for Law Reform: Oliver Napier (Alliance)
Minister for Information: John Baxter (Un).

There were also four non-voting members of the administration, two SDLP, one Unionist and one Alliance. Three days before taking office the SDLP had called for an end to the rent and rates strike against internment – they couldn't very well strike against themselves.

The Provos had not been idle during 1973. They had got new and more modern weapons. On 28 March the Southern Gardai had intercepted a freighter called the *Claudia* off the Irish coast, seized five tons of Russian-made arms, and arrested six men including Joe Cahill the Belfast Provo leader. The arms had come from Libya where the Provos had made contact with President Ghaddafi. There were other shipments, and the Provos began to make extensive use of Russian RPG7 rocket launchers. They had also improved their organisation and training. There were fewer premature bombs and fewer casualties among civilians and among their own men – though six civilians died in bomb blasts in Coleraine on 12 June because of inadequate warnings. The overall level of violence was lower than in 1972, but the Provos continued to launch periodic bombing blitzes to show their capabilities, and there were some spectacular incidents. On 31 October a hijacked helicopter landed in the exercise yard of Mountjoy jail in Dublin and rescued three leading Provisionals, Seamus Twomey, J.B.O'Hagan from Lurgan and Kevin Mallon from Coalisland.

The Provos also got a propaganda boost from an unexpected source in July 1973, when two English brothers, Kenneth and Keith Littlejohn, were convicted in Dublin of a major bank robbery. The Littlejohns claimed to be British agents who had infiltrated the IRA and they confessed to various agent-provocateur activities. The British government admitted their connection with British intelligence, and they or other British agents were popularly suspected of the Dublin car-bombings in December 1972. The general effect of the Littlejohn revelations was to discredit both the British government and the Irish administration which had tolerated British intelligence activities in the South. Jack Lynch compounded the effect by first denying all prior knowledge of the case, then admitting it and claiming he had had a lapse of memory.

With the formation of the executive and the consequent threat to their popular support in the North and their safe refuge in the South, the Provos stepped up their campaign, not only in the North but in Britain where they had already begun a small-scale bombing campaign in the autumn of 1973. The first months of the executive's rule were set against a back-cloth of the continuing IRA campaign. At the end of January 1974 an IRA group including Dr Rose Dugdale, daughter of an English millionaire, staged an abortive air-raid on Strabane RUC Station with a hijacked helicopter. In February nine soldiers and three civilians were killed by a bomb on a motor coach on the M62 in England. In March the former Grand Central Hotel in the centre of Belfast – the major Army post in the city – was bombed twice. A whole block of shops and offices in the centre of Armagh, worth over £1 million, was gutted on 8 April. And all the time there was a steady relentless toll of Crown forces. By 31 May 1974 a total of 214 British soldiers had been killed in Northern Ireland – the British Army's highest death-toll since the Korean War. 44 UDR men and 52 members of the RUC and RUC Reserve had been killed as well.

The Loyalists were active too, despite the extension of internment to cover a handful of them as well. Assassinations of Catholics continued and for the first time Loyalist groups began to admit responsibility and attempt to justify their actions. On 14 May 1973 a Catholic was shot dead in the Lower Falls area of Belfast, and a man rang the newspapers to claim responsibility on behalf of 'a very extreme loyalist group'. He said it was in retaliation for the killing of a UDR man and made it clear that it was his group's policy to take reprisals against Catholic civilians: 'We are issuing a warning to the IRA that if they keep on murdering members of the security forces and harassing loyal citizens of Ulster we will take very stern action against Roman Catholics'[16]. A month later a new organisation emerged, called the 'Ulster Freedom Fighters'. On 26 June the bodies of SDLP Senator Paddy Wilson and a Protestant woman friend were found with multiple stab wounds on the outskirts of Belfast. The UFF claimed responsibility.

The UFF gave an interview to two English journalists in July, identifying their cause and their methods with militant Zionism in Israel:

'We are now fighting for our very survival. Our backs are to the wall. We have more in common with the state of Israel . . . like the Jewish people, each time an act of aggression is committed against our people, we shall retaliate in a way that only the animals of the IRA can understand'[17].

In fact however the UFF seems to have been merely an organisation of convenience created so that UDA members could carry out assassinations without endangering the UDA itself. And the UDA was explaining itself as well. In June leaders of the West Belfast UDA had given a long petulant press statement to a Dublin paper. It stressed their plantation origins and loyalty to the Crown, was filled with a bitter sense of betrayal by Britain, and was anti-communist and anti-revolutionary:

'We are a hybrid race descended from men who colonised Scotland from Ireland in the fifth century and who then colonised Northern Ireland from Scotland in the seventeenth century . . . For 400 years we have known nothing but uprising, murder, destruction and repression. We ourselves have repeatedly come to the support of the British Crown only to be betrayed within another 20 years or so by a fresh government of that Crown . . . Second-class Englishmen, half-caste Irishmen . . . How can we be expected to beat the world revolutionary movement?'[18]

It sounded remarkably like the attitudes of OAS members in Algeria during the War of Independence there. Abandoned by France, unsure of their identity, the OAS still hated and feared the Arab population whose degradation had given the poor whites what little social status they had. As the Northern minority had come to identify with blacks in America during the Civil Rights campaign and with the Palestinian Arabs and other liberation movements as the struggle deepened and turned into an anti-imperialist war, so the Loyalists had come to identify with Zionism, colonialism and counter-revolution.

At any rate UFF, UDA or UVF – who had nominally called a cease-fire in November 1973 to get some of their men out of Long Kesh – the Loyalist assassinations and bombings of Catholic churches and pubs continued, and escalated with the establishment of the executive and the approach of the Council of Ireland. Now the Loyalists concentrated on shooting Catholics at work or on their way to work, effectively driving them out of more factories and building sites in Protestant areas. Eight Catholics were killed at work or on their way to work in Newtownabbey alone in the first few months of 1974.

The executive took office under the relentless pressure of the IRA campaign and the gathering backlash in the Unionist Party. Faulkner's following was steadily disintegrating. On 4 January 1974 a motion rejecting the Sunningdale package was carried by a majority of 80 at the Ulster Unionist Council. Faulkner resigned as Unionist leader – to be succeeded by Harry West – but stayed on as head of the Assembly group and moved to a new headquarters, effectively establishing a new party. For the hard-liners it was a major victory. They had the party name, headquarters, and machine. These would be invaluable assets in an election. Meanwhile Faulkner lost another Assembly member at the end of January. He now led a total of seventeen members, two less than the SDLP.

However the executive was determined to keep going. On 1 February they met members of the Dublin government at Hillsborough, Co.Down, to discuss arrangements for the formal ratification of Sunningdale and the establishment of the Council of Ireland. An Anglo-Irish Legal Commission was set up to study the question of fugitive offenders, and there were meetings between the Commissioner of the Gardai and the Chief Constable of the RUC.

But on 28 February there was a Westminster election. It caught the Faulknerites totally unprepared. They had no party, no electoral machine and were able to field only seven candidates, two of them outgoing MPs. The whole executive alliance was in disarray, with all three parties nominating candidates against each other. In contrast the Official Unionists under Harry West made a pact with the DUP and Vanguard to nominate only one candidate in each constituency (the election was under the straight vote system).

The result was a disaster for the Faulknerites and a serious setback for the executive. The United Ulster Unionist Council (UUUC) won 366,703 votes and eleven seats. The Faulknerites got a mere 94,331 votes and no seats. The details were even more humiliating. Paisley defeated a Faulkner Unionist by 41,282 votes to 13,651 in North Antrim, and Roy Bradford, a senior minister in the executive, was defeated by 38,169 votes to 21,943 in the prosperous and trouble-free North Down constituency. The SDLP scored a pyrrhic victory. In their eagerness to eliminate all opposition to themselves in the anti-Unionist population, they put up candidates against Frank McManus and Bernadette Devlin in the marginal constituencies of Fermanagh-South Tyrone and Mid-Ulster. They got rid of the opposition, but the UUUC took both seats on the split anti-Unionist vote. At the end of the day the UUUC had won an overall majority of votes cast and eleven out of the twelve seats at Westminster.

The Loyalists had won a massive majority among the Protestant population, sweeping away the Faulknerites' electoral base. Faulkner's men panicked and started back-pedalling fast. On 4 March they met at Stormont and decided there could be no Council of Ireland unless the South repealed articles two and three of their Constitution – the ones claiming jurisdiction over the North. They began to pressurise Dublin, London and their SDLP allies.

On 13 March Cosgrave declared in the Dail 'The factual position of Northern Ireland is that it is within the United Kingdom and my government accepts this as a fact.' On 3 April Austin Currie, SDLP Housing Minister and one of the men who had called for the rent and rates strike in 1971, announced that there would be no amnesty for those still on strike, increased the amount which could be deducted from strikers' social welfare benefits, and introduced a punitive 25p a week collection charge. The government stepped up repression and in one week in mid-April 30 people were interned, including several girls and a mother of five children whose husband was already in Long Kesh[19]. On 19 April Harold Wilson, now British Premier again, visited Belfast to boost the executive's morale and warned that there could be no alternative to the Sunningdale package. On 25 April the Anglo-Irish Law Commission submitted its report recommending effectively that people wanted for offences in the North could be tried and sentenced in the South.

But it was all to no avail, the Loyalists were on the offensive now and it wasn't only the Council of Ireland they wanted to stop. On 9 March the UUUC held a victory march to Stormont and Craig declared that they were out to bring down the executive. On 23 April they began a three-day conference at Portrush, Co.Antrim, to work out agreed policy and tactics. It was attended by representatives of the UDA and by Enoch Powell, whose presence ensured them the support or sympathy of significant sections of the Conservative establishment in Britain and of the British officer class. The conference called for the scrapping of Sunningdale, the executive and the 1973 Northern Ireland Constitution Act, and demanded an immediate election in the North. It called for a Northern parliament with full security powers, and a greatly increased UDR and RUC, and threatened the use of selective sanctions including industrial action if Westminster didn't agree.

The Loyalist Association of Workers, always a ramshackle group, had collapsed after the disastrous strike over the internment of Loyalists in February 1973 and in the midst of rows about the embezzlement of funds. Like the UDA it was riddled with racketeering and corruption and its leader, the shipyard union boss Billy Hull, had clashed bitterly with William Craig when Hull had toyed with the idea of turning the LAW into a new 'working class' Loyalist party. But some LAW members who had seen the power of industrial action had set up a new body, the Ulster Workers' Council, at the end of 1973. The UWC made no attempt to build up an unwieldy mass membership like the LAW, they concentrated instead on recruiting shop stewards and key workers, especially in the power stations. They had little difficulty, the power stations' work-force was almost exclusively Protestant, and Loyalists already had a firm grip on shop stewards' and works' committees there and throughout the engineering industry – the LAW had been campaigning since 1971 to oust communists, Catholics and even Labour supporters from union positions in the industry.

The Assembly was to vote on 14 May on a Loyalist motion opposing Sunningdale. The UWC announced that if it were defeated they would call an indefinite 'constitutional stoppage' or general strike. The call was backed by the Ulster Army Council, a co-ordinating committee of Loyalist para-military organisations.

The motion was defeated and the stoppage began on the evening of Tuesday 14 May. It was more of a lock-out than a strike. At the beginning there was little popular support, but masked men with clubs took over the town of Larne in Co.Antrim forcing shops and factories to close. The UDA set up road-blocks all over Belfast and attacked workers entering or leaving factories. Armed men invaded Mackie's factory in West Belfast and forced the workers out. The RUC and British Army made no effort to intervene, troops and RUC men chatted with UDA men at the barricades.

But the key weapon of the UWC was electricity. They were in full control of the power stations and had reduced power output to a couple of hours a day. Industry couldn't operate and workers who did turn up were sent away. By Monday 20 May the stoppage was almost complete. On 21 May the Irish Congress of Trade Unions organised two back-to-work marches in Belfast, one of them led by Len Murray, General Secretary of the

British TUC. Less than 150 workers[20] passed the UDA road-blocks to take part, and they were attacked and jeered by Loyalists. The RUC looked on as usual. The next day the UWC banned petrol supplies to all but essential users – they decided who were essential users and issued passes to them – thereby strengthening their control in the Protestant areas. By now the UUUC leaders, who had been hesitant at the start, had thrown their full weight behind the stoppage and a co-ordinating committee had been set up to run it consisting of Craig, Paisley and West, three UWC leaders and representatives of seven Loyalist para-military groups. Craig boasted 'We are in effective control of the country'.

The stoppage was accompanied by unprecedented violence. On 16 May Craig warned that Sunningdale must be scrapped: 'If they [supporters of Sunningdale] don't realise this there will be further actions taken against the Irish Republic and those who attempt to implement the agreement'[21]. The next day three car bombs exploded in Dublin and one in Monaghan. There were no warnings and all were timed to go off at rush-hour. The death toll was 33, the highest figure for any single incident since 1969. The bombs were planted by the UVF. On 20 May a Catholic student hitching back to the university after the weekend was murdered, and on 24 May two Catholic brothers who ran a pub near Ballymena were shot dead by UWC 'flying pickets' who were wrecking pubs in Co.Antrim.

Pressed by the executive, whose survival was in question, Merlyn Rees, the new Labour Northern Ireland Secretary, had stated at the outset that there could be no compromise and no negotiations with the UWC. On 19 May he declared a State of Emergency, taking power to use troops to maintain essential services. But Rees' firm words contrasted sharply with the inactivity of his troops on the ground. Faced with the choice of a head-on clash between the Loyalists and an Army whose allegiance was dubious, or letting the executive topple, Westminster seemed prepared to jettison the executive.

It was a war of nerves and the demoralised Faulknerites broke first. On 19 May Roy Bradford, an executive minister, called for negotiations with the UWC[22]. The next day Peter McLachlan, a prominent Faulknerite backbencher, called for talks as well, and he was followed by the secretary of the Backbench Committee. The executive took fright and on 22 May they announced that they had agreed that the Council of Ireland should be implemented in two stages. Only a purely consultative Council of Ministers should be established immediately, executive powers for the Council and the Consultative Assembly should be postponed until after the next Assembly elections in 1977-78. The SDLP had fully endorsed the decision.

It was no use, the Loyalists had the executive on the run now and would not be satisfied until it fell. The UWC and UUUC rejected the Council of Ireland move contemptuously and the stoppage went on. By now the Protestant middle classes had panicked as well: the economy was in chaos, they had no light or heat in their homes, they had to queue up to plead for UWC passes from UDA boot-boys in Orange Halls, and all-out war was a constant threat as the battle of nerves went on. University professors, the local branch of the Confederation of British Industry, the Irish Council of Churches all pleaded with Rees to give in.

The executive was desperate. On 23 May Faulkner, Fitt, and Napier, the leader of the Alliance Party, flew to London to beg Wilson to use his troops. On the 25th Wilson made a vituperative broadcast on television calling the Loyalists 'spongers' on Britain. But still there was no action. Meanwhile the minority were terrified in their ghettos. The economic power of the Loyalists had been demonstrated as never before. The Catholics were virtually helpless. There were constant rumours that attacks on the ghettos would be the next stage of Loyalist escalation. The minority had no confidence in the protection of the British Army after watching their collusion with UDA road-blocks – and after three years of military terror in the ghettos. They had even less confidence in the RUC and UDR: at least one member of the UWC executive committee was a serving UDR man, while a secret Loyalist group in the RUC and UDR called 'For Ulster' was believed to be planning a mutiny if troops were used to break the stoppage. The SDLP had to do something if they were to retain any credibility with their supporters. They threatened to resign by 27 May if Wilson didn't use the troops.

That morning troops moved in and occupied 27 petrol stations throughout the North, to supply essential workers like doctors and nurses. It was a pathetic gesture. The Loyalists threatened that if troops went near the power stations they would close them down completely, together with the water and sewage plants. The six-county state was on the verge of chaos, civil war seemed just around the corner. The Faulknerites capitulated. They met and called on Rees to talk to the UWC. When he refused they resigned on 28 May, bringing down the executive with them. The UWC called off their stoppage the next day and Westminster prorogued the Assembly for four months and then indefinitely.

The whole elaborate structure had collapsed like a house of cards, brought down by Loyalist intransigence and the refusal of the British government to intervene to save their own creation. The first adminstration in Northern Ireland ever to contain representatives of the Catholic minority and to make the slightest concessions to their political aspirations had lasted exactly five months.

Three months later a British Army officer writing in the Monday Club magazine boasted that the Westminster government had actually decided on 24 May to use troops to end the stoppage, but the Army had refused. He claimed there was a confrontation between the Army and the politicians and 'For the first time, the Army decided that it was right and that it knew best and the politicians had better toe the line'[23]. The Northern Ireland crisis had cracked the facade of liberal democracy in Britain and shown where the real power lay there as well.

The collapse of the executive and of the whole Sunningdale agreement left a vacuum in the North. The reaction of both Dublin and Westminster was to back away from an intractable problem. On 13 June Cosgrave said 'They [the people of the South] are expressing more and more the idea that unity or close association with a people so deeply imbued with violence and its effects is not what they want'[24], and on 26 June he told the Dail, 'it is now up to the people there [in the North] to reach an agreement among themselves which will allow them to live and work together in peace'[25].

On 4 July the Westminster government brought out a White Paper providing for a constitutional convention so that the people of the North could work out their own solution. It was tantamount to an admission of failure. The Sunningdale package had collapsed. There was no likelihood that the convention could produce a workable alternative.

Prospects for the convention became even gloomier in October 1974 when there was another Westminster election. The UUUC stood again on a platform of uncompromising opposition to power-sharing or a Council of Ireland. They won 407,778 votes, an increase of 40,000 on their February total and 58 per cent of the total vote[26]. The Faulknerites could muster only two candidates and got the derisory total of 20,454 votes, while the combined 'moderate' Unionist and Alliance Party vote was only 70,082. Even in the middle-class university constituency of South Belfast an extreme fundamentalist Protestant minister, Rev Bradford, defeated the former Unionist MP by 18,000 votes.

In February the Faulknerites had explained away the UUUC victory as an emotional reaction to the establishment of the executive. There were no excuses this time. The executive had fallen, Sunningdale was buried. It was clear the Protestant masses had swung solidly behind the UUUC. There was no middle-ground left. On the basis of the October result the UUUC would win a clear and effective majority in the convention elections – about 46 seats out of 78.

The situation had reached an impasse. The Loyalists had rejected Sunningdale, the minority could accept nothing less. The basic contradiction underlying the Northern state was out in the open. Established through the fostering of religious bigotry and set up against the wishes both of the majority of the Irish people and of a minority of the people in its own area, the Northern regime had based itself and its state on Protestant supremacy. It could make no concessions to the minority because concessions would weaken its hold on the Protestant masses and undermine the state. But without concessions the minority would be perpetually disaffected and ready to revolt, and the majority in the whole of Ireland would be perpetually hostile to the North and sympathetic to the minority's revolt. The North was unreformable and yet unreformed, it was inherently unstable. It could only be consolidated – at a terrible cost to the minority – or overthrown. The day of reckoning was at hand.

Postscript: June 1975

Since the bulk of this book was completed in the winter of 1974, there have been several important developments in Northern Ireland, the most significant of which are the Provisionals' cease-fire and the elections to the Northern Convention.

By November 1974, hampered by tight security in the North, the Provisionals were concentrating on a bombing campaign in England, attacking commercial targets and soldiers' pubs. Three soldiers, two women soldiers and two civilians were killed in blasts at Guildford and Woolwich; and then on 21 November bombs went off without warning in three city-centre pubs in Birmingham, killing 21 people, all of them civilians and two of them Irish. The Provisionals denied responsibility but they were universally blamed. A wave of anti-Irish hysteria in Britain enabled the government to bring in a draconian 'anti-terrorist' law banning the IRA, giving the police power to detain Irish suspects for five days without charge, and taking powers to prevent Irish people from entering Britain and to deport people of Irish origin to Ireland, even if they had lived in Britain for some years. It was quickly used to deport a number of Irish political activists and by May 1975 exclusion orders had been made against 50 people.

In Ireland the Birmingham bombing had a drastic effect, especially in the South. It alienated masses of people normally sympathetic to the Northern struggle. The Dublin government took the opportunity to introduce a Bill making it possible to try people in the South for 'terrorist' offences committed in the North or in Britain, and increased their harassment of Republicans. But most important was the loss of public support. The Provisionals were subjected to a barrage of pressures, in the shape of hostile propaganda and peace marches. On 10 December, Provo representatives met a group of Protestant clergy at Feakle in Co.Clare. The clergy acted as intermediaries with Merlyn Rees, the British Secretary for Northern Ireland, and on 22 December the Provisionals declared a cease-fire.

The British response was limited. Rees released 45 internees, fewer than the number released the previous Christmas, there was no let-up in

Army activity, and attempts were made to re-introduce the RUC into the Catholic ghettos. The Provos resumed their campaign on 16 January 1975. But secret negotiations continued behind the scenes between Provisional Sinn Fein and Rees' officials, and another indefinite cease-fire began on 11 February.

This time the Provisionals had got slightly better terms. The government and Sinn Fein set up a series of parallel incident centres where complaints about Army and RUC activity could be dealt with, which gave Sinn Fein's prestige a boost. The release of internees speeded up a bit and the last women internees were released at the end of April. However by May there were still 300 Republicans[1] interned, over 800 sentenced political prisoners in jail and the British Army and RUC were still very much in evidence. The truth was that Rees had little room for manoeuvre and there were few further concessions he could make. He was under considerable pressure both from the Loyalists and from the Army itself. On 12 April indeed the British GOC in Northern Ireland, General Sir Frank King, had made an unprecedented public attack on the government's policies, criticising the release of internees and claiming that, given a free hand, the Army could have smashed the IRA in another few months.

The cease-fire didn't change the basic situation. The Provos no longer held the centre of the stage. The initiative lay with the Loyalists, who were organising for the Convention elections while their para-military murder squads continued to terrorise the minority with complete impunity – 35 Catholics were killed in sectarian attacks in the first four months of 1975. The purpose of the Convention was to devise a satisfactory scheme for the government of the North, but it was generally assumed that Westminster would insist on power-sharing and some form of 'Irish dimension' as they had for the Assembly. On 25 March however Harold Wilson flew to Belfast to announce the election date. His speech was significant. He declared that no solution the Convention devised would be excluded, and his nearest reference to power-sharing was coupled with what looked like a clear warning to the SDLP:

'Nor would the government be a party to the exclusion of the minority by the majority, or to a refusal by the minority to work with the majority'[2].

The 'Irish dimension' was not mentioned once, and Wilson later told Harry West, the UUUC leader, that the words 'power-sharing' had been deliberately omitted from his speech[3].

The election was on 1 May. The Provisionals called for a boycott, so did the PD and the newly-formed Irish Republican Socialist Party[4]. The total poll, 64 per cent, was fairly low. The result was a sweeping victory for the UUUC. For the third time in succession they won a small majority of the total vote, with 356,065 first preferences (54·1 per cent), and a resounding majority of the Protestant electorate; while their main rivals, Brian Faulkner's new Unionist Party of Northern Ireland (UPNI), were utterly routed, winning only 50,891 first preferences. The UUUC won 46 of the Convention's 78 seats while an Independent Loyalist associated with the UVF won another one, giving the hard-line Loyalists an overall majority of sixteen. Faulkner's UPNI won a mere five seats, with Faulkner himself scraping in on the ninth count in South Down. The SDLP, who had confidently expected to win three or four extra seats, held their vote fairly steady at 156,001, but the boycott hit them hard in the finely-balanced Armagh and Mid-Ulster constituencies and they lost a seat in each, reducing them to seventeen seats. The Alliance Party won eight seats and the almost defunct Northern Ireland Labour Party one. The Official Republicans, who had based their whole strategy on winning seats in the Convention, fared disastrously. They gained 14,515 first preferences, 2·2 per cent of the total, and none of their candidates came near to winning a seat.

There was no doubt now about what the Convention would recommend. The UUUC had campaigned vehemently against power-sharing, and for a return to majority rule with local control over security. Harry West spelt it out clearly at the opening meeting of the convention on 8 May:

'Whatever others may consent to do we [the UUUC] **are not going to be responsible for allowing the hand of such a person** [someone who believes in a united Ireland] **to be laid on the actual steering wheel of state'**[5].

The SDLP and the Dublin government frantically appealed to Westminster but Wilson had already made his attitude clear: 'No solution is excluded.' A Loyalist take-over was only a matter of time.

Conclusions

The Northern state was established with the help of British troops and British guns. British troops were heavily involved in the bitter fighting in the six counties in 1920-22, and it was British troops who were used to recapture the Belleek-Letter triangle in Co.Fermanagh when it was seized by the IRA in June 1922. It was the British government that set up the Special Constabulary in 1920, and armed, supplied and even paid for the A, B and C Specials until the boundary of the new state was confirmed in 1925.

Westminster had needed little urging to hold on to the North. It was only after a hard-fought and bloody guerrilla war that Britain had grudgingly conceded a measure of independence to the rest of Ireland, and she was all the more anxious to keep the six counties, the most economically developed part of Ireland, with its shipyards, its engineering and textile industries, and its strategic potential – which was to prove of such value during the Second World War.

Under pressure from John Redmond and the Irish Nationalists, in 1911 the British Liberal government had agreed in principle to Home Rule for the whole of Ireland. But, faced with Unionist resistance, and Nationalist demands after the 1916 Rising not simply for limited Home Rule but for political and economic independence, the Liberals changed their attitude. The temporary exclusion of the six counties was proposed by Asquith's government as early as 1914. By May 1916 Lloyd George was assuring Carson that the exclusion would be permanent[1]. The Conservatives needed no persuasion at all on the subject of Ulster. The Conservative Party and the British military establishment had supported the Ulster Unionists from the beginning, and had actually threatened civil war in Britain if Ulster was coerced.

Since 1922 Britain has kept a military garrison in the North and has underwritten the defence of the six-county state. The garrison has served to reinforce the RUC and B Specials whenever necessary: British troops were on stand-by to intervene during the ODR strike in Belfast in 1932, and they did intervene in the riots of 1935. Throughout the Second World War the North was an armed camp, and during the 1950s' IRA campaign British troops backed up RUC and B Special patrols, and the British Army armed and trained the RUC Commando force. Eventually in August 1969 British troops intervened on the streets again 'in aid of the civil power', taking over from the exhausted and overstretched RUC.

The British Army and British guns have thus never been far below the surface of political life in the Orange State throughout the 54 years of its existence. The long and costly[2] campaign, with its high death toll since 1971, is clear evidence that Britain's interest in the North is unabated. And all the time, but especially since the establishment of the welfare state, Westminster has subsidised the running of the Stormont regime.

The reason for this involvement is not hard to find. In 1974, 45 per cent of all firms in Northern Ireland employing 500 or more workers were controlled from Britain, as were 28 out of 51 firms employing between 250 and 500 workers; while Northern Ireland produced one third of the total output of artificial fibres in the United Kingdom[3]. The old traditional industries of shipbuilding and engineering might have declined – but Northern Ireland was still an important centre for British investment.

The six-county state was not an arbitrary creation of British imperialism to enable it to keep a foothold in the most industrialised part of Ireland, however. The state had local roots: in the development of industries geared to serve the imperial market, and in the parallel development of a Unionist movement determined to stay part of the British economy. The Northern state was thus the product of a partnership between British imperialism on the one hand, and on the other the Ulster industrialists, businessmen and landowners united together in the Unionist party.

But the Unionist businessmen won their mass support through the Orange Order and by fostering and exploiting differences between Protestant and Catholic in the North. They consolidated that support by discrimination against Catholics in the industries and local councils which they controlled. Once in power in the new state, they had ample opportunity to step up discrimination and strengthen their position by gerrymandering and wholesale political repression. Britain did not interfere so long as the North remained stable and gave no trouble. And Britain allowed an elaborate sectarian police state to be built up without protest, permitting it to be backed in the last resort by British forces.

The Unionist bosses were eminently successful. They stayed in power for fifty years and they kept their mass support. Dominated as it was by landowners and industrialists, the Unionist Party still beat off with ease any challenge from Labour even in the heavily-industrialised city of Belfast. Only once since the state was established did a working-class revolt seriously threaten to break down the sectarian barriers and unite Protestant and Catholic workers against the regime, and that was the ODR strike in 1932 in the depths of the great depression. Even then the revolt was quickly ended by a combination of concessions, force, and a series of inflammatory speeches by Unionist leaders – notably Sir Basil Brooke – which, at a time of fierce competition for the few jobs available, soon brought sectarian feeling back to fever pitch. The result was the riots of 1935.

Since then every attempt by political groups to unite and mobilise the working class on social and economic issues has foundered, because it has come up against the question of discrimination and Protestant privilege. The Northern Ireland Labour Party tried to ignore the issue, and became a poor man's Unionist Party; other groups opposed the Orange system and lost the support of all but a handful of Protestant workers. In the siege atmosphere of the six counties the Unionist leaders have had no difficulty in representing any challenge to the Unionist party, or any criticism of the regime, as a threat to the existence of the state.

It seemed a foolproof system. But it contained a basic flaw – the Catholic minority. The Northern Catholics shared the nationalist aspirations of the mass of the Irish people. They did not want partition – indeed they had stronger reasons than most for opposing it. They had experience of the Unionist system at local level, even when the North was administered from Dublin Castle[4]. They had no desire to continue the experience under a Unionist government. However they were beaten into submission between 1920 and 1922 and forced to accept the new state.

The minority began life under the Belfast regime bitter and alienated, and they refused to take part in its institutions; but they had been demoralised by continual defeat and Joe Devlin and the Nationalist Party, representing the Catholic commercial class who wanted to get on with making money, soon won support for a policy of working for reform within the Northern parliament. The Unionists could concede nothing however, even if they had wanted to. Their hold on the Protestant masses depended on the Orange Order and discrimination; they were shackled to Protestant supremacy. Devlin and his colleagues were treated with contempt and forced into abstentionism, and the frustration of the minority eventually erupted into an abortive campaign by the IRA. This was the first of several cycles of parliamentary agitation followed by rebuff and abstentionism, then by a military campaign – all strategies proving equally unsuccessful, and only confirming the total alienation of the minority from the state.

There was also the South. Partition had been accepted there only after a bloody civil war, when even the Free State government had accepted it with reluctance. All the major parties in the South were committed to uniting Ireland and the new constitution adopted in 1937 re-asserted that the six counties were part of the national territory. In practice the Southern business class and the major parties quickly lost interest in the North; but the arrogance of the Unionist regime and its treatment of the Northern minority kept public sympathy sufficiently alive in the 26 counties to provide a sound base of support for the IRA and a permanent threat to the Stormont government.

For forty years the North went on unchanged: it remained a rigidly repressive police regime, confronting a hostile minority within and maintaining a permanent state of cold war with the South. But in the early 1960s things began to change. With the repeal of the Control of Manufactures Act in the South in 1958, British investment there increased sharply. 40 per cent of new firms established in Ireland between 1958 and 1965 were British-controlled[5], and by 1971 60 per cent of the total profits of publicly-quoted companies in the South were going to Britain[6]. The Anglo-Irish Free Trade Agreement in 1965 accelerated the process, until by 1971, 55 per cent of the South's imports came from Britain and 66 per cent of its exports went there. The Southern economy was now dominated by Britain, to whom it was becoming as important as the North, so that North-South rapprochement and economic co-operation became British policy. In the longer term the stability of the South became as necessary to Britain as that of the North.

The major obstacle to North-South rapprochement was the treatment of the Catholic minority in the North, and so the Westminster government began nudging Stormont gently towards reform. At the same time there were stirrings among the minority. The first generation to go through university on scholarships under the post-war education scheme emerged. They had no experience of the previous defeats and were not demoralised. They chafed at their own second-class status and began to articulate the grievances of their community. Under direct pressure from Westminster and indirect pressure from the new class of managers of foreign-owned firms who were replacing the old Ulster industrial families, the Unionist government under O'Neill made a few conciliatory gestures.

But the Unionists had relied on discrimination and Orange supremacy for too long to be able to jettison it. The Orange ideology was too deep-rooted to be dispensed with overnight, especially at a time of change and confusion when new industries were replacing old ones, threatening small businessmen and established skilled workers, when new blocks of flats were replacing old slums, new towns replacing old villages. Orangeism provided stability and status in a changing world, and defended jobs and positions. The very suggestion of reform produced a Protestant backlash, long before any reforms were actually introduced: the Malvern Street killing was in 1966, two years before the Civil Rights campaign got under way.

The Stormont government began to retreat. The minority, having had their hopes raised and dashed again, were spurred on by small but significant socialist and Republican groups, and responded with the Civil Rights movement. The movement and the brutal reaction to it by the Loyalists and the state stirred the slumbering population of the South as well.

By this time Britain was getting impatient with her former allies in the North. British interests required a stable peaceful Ireland where production and the rate of profit were not disturbed by political upheavals. That in turn required the dismantling of the Orange system in the North to remove the grievances of the Catholic middle class and provide opportunities for their aspiring young politicians. But at the same time Britain was not prepared to tolerate chaos or the violent overthrow of the state, giving opportunities to the small but growing revolutionary forces in Ireland. So in August 1969, when Stormont's upholding of Orange triumphalism (the Apprentice Boys' march in Derry) provoked a minority revolt and popular feeling almost forced the Southern government to intervene, British troops were used to rescue Stormont but Westminster began to press a series of reforms on the reluctant Unionists.

The effort met with little success. Once the Ulster industrialists had used the Orange ideology and Protestant supremacy to establish the Northern state; now the Ulster-based industries had all but disappeared, and with them most of the economic reasons for the six-county state. But

Orangeism and Protestant supremacy had remained – and now they were themselves virtually the reason for the existence of the state: to dismantle Protestant supremacy would be to dismantle the state itself. The Unionists resisted stubbornly. The British had intervened to defend the state and reform it; but failing to reform it they were forced to concentrate more and more on defending it.

At first the minority had sought only reform within the state, and they had welcomed the British troops as the instruments of change. Now the reforms were blocked and the British Army became an army of occupation. Embittered, the mood of the minority changed: more and more Catholics came to want the destruction of the Northern state and an end to British control. A struggle for civil rights had become a struggle against imperialism, for national liberation.

In August 1971 the British government sanctioned the introduction of internment; the anti-imperialist movement replied with all-out war. From then on the Army was out to smash Republican resistance. Britain might be in favour of North-South co-operation between solid bourgeois governments in Belfast and Dublin, she might be in favour of reforming the Northern Ireland regime, but she could not tolerate the armed overthrow of the state. The Provisional IRA who were doing the bulk of the fighting were no marxists and were not committed to the overthrow of the capitalist system nor even the wholesale expropriation of foreign-owned firms. In fact their political ideology was confused, incoherent and laced with clericalist anti-communism. But even a right-wing nationalist regime in Ireland would be bound to try to assert a measure of economic independence, which could be very damaging to British interests at a time when Britain was already in the throes of a serious economic crisis. And there were more radical, including some marxist, groups involved in the struggle, whose propaganda influenced substantial sections of the nationalist population – in the turmoil produced by the conflict, the anti-imperialist movement might well be forced into much more radical measures.

The revolt was remarkably determined, the minority population remarkably united: there was solid if passive support from the people of the South. The revolt could be crushed only if the minority were divided and the IRA attacked from the rear by the South. The situation was more desperate and the Northern state in more danger than at any time since it was established, so the British took steps that were unprecedented, giving their Unionist allies short shrift in the process. They suspended Stormont, brought in PR for elections to a new Assembly, and negotiated the complex Sunningdale agreement. It was a masterpiece of political juggling. It gave the Catholic middle class, through the SDLP, their much-coveted share in power. It provided for North-South links and enabled the Dublin government to claim that they were moving towards a united Ireland. And it bought the full support of both for all-out war on the IRA. It even won the confidence of about half the Northern minority.

But Sunningdale also brought out the grim reality of the Northern problem. It was the most thoroughgoing effort ever to stabilise the state, yet it was to be brought down – by the Loyalists, who were determined to restore Orange supremacy at all costs. And the collapse of Sunningdale underlined another grim reality: that the British government were not prepared to confront the Loyalists even to enforce their own chosen solution which was backed by both British parties, by the Dublin government, and by the industrialists and managers of the North.

Today the situation has been neatly turned on its head. Britain, once the master in the Northern state, is fast becoming the servant of the Ulster Loyalists. Orangeism, once the mere tool of the Unionist bourgeoisie, has become the dominant force in Northern politics. The Loyalists are intent on restoring the Orange system and returning to the pre-1968 set-up. They even want greater powers than the old Stormont had. They have won a majority of the electorate for this line in three successive elections, and with a solid majority in the constitutional Convention they are demanding power and control of security. The British government is still nominally committed to some form of power-sharing and an 'Irish dimension', but they are back-pedalling fast. They may yet make half-hearted efforts to negotiate a watered-down Sunningdale, but the Loyalists are in no mood to compromise, and though in theory Westminster can always revert to indefinite direct rule, in practice, faced with the escalating cost of a massive military presence in Northern Ireland, plagued with a grave economic crisis at home, and with public demand growing for withdrawal from the North, it is an option they will be very reluctant to take up.

They will still be faced with the Loyalist demand for power. If Britain rejects it, the Loyalists can call another UWC 'strike' backed by the para-military groups and given authority and respectability by their successive election victories. Perhaps such a 'strike' could be broken, but it is unlikely to be. The British Army refused to confront the Loyalists in 1974, and they will hardly do so now. And Westminster will not want to commit its Army to a second front at a time when the public is calling for withdrawal. The Loyalists still have important sentimental and ideological links with sections of the British establishment – links strengthened by the election of Enoch Powell as UUUC MP for South Down – who would violently oppose any action against them. And, after all, if the Loyalists were crushed it would open the way for the anti-imperialist forces to seize power. The UUUC are by definition right-wing and pro-imperialist: far from interfering with British or any other outside economic interests, they would welcome and encourage them. The IRA are anti-imperialist guerrillas with unsavoury left-wing allies. Forced to choose between the UUUC and the IRA, Britain will choose the UUUC.

A Loyalist regime in the North seems more and more likely. And it looks as if the British government, recognising that, has been preparing to install them in power, and to give them arms and equipment enough to consolidate their position. In September 1974, under Loyalist pressure, Rees authorised massive increases in the RUC and RUC Reserve, making the target figures: RUC 7,250 (compared with 3,000 in 1968) and RUC Reserve 1,400 full-time and 5,500 part-time. Taken together with the 8,000 members of the UDR, that makes a total of over 22,000 armed forces or 7,000 more than the number of British troops in the North at the end of 1974.

A Loyalist regime would be violent, brutal and semi-fascist in character. Since the Sunningdale solution was initially backed by big business, the professional classes and much of the traditional Unionist leadership, Loyalist opposition has been in the hands of the Protestant petty bourgeoisie led by the most extreme Protestant supremacists, such as Craig and Paisley, and backed by the storm-troopers and assassins of the UDA, UVF and the other para-military groups, all mobilised and held together by the Orange ideology. Under Loyalist control, party and state would become virtually one as they did under the old regime, and the para-military groups would be absorbed into the forces of the state. Political criticism would be ruthlessly suppressed or beaten off the streets, as it already has been in the Protestant working-class areas. Pogroms would be inevitable and the minority would have to fight for their very survival.

They could not look to the Southern government for aid. After their initial revulsion from Northern affairs following the collapse of Sunningdale, the Dublin government has vacillated between accepting a Loyalist takeover as inevitable and trying to placate the Loyalists or urging the continuance of direct rule. In October 1974 Cosgrave and members of his cabinet actually received two members of the UDA at Leinster House[7]. In May 1975 after the Convention elections Conor Cruise O'Brien, a member of the Dublin government, said that it was now impossible to enforce power-sharing or an 'Irish dimension', and called for the continuance of direct rule by Britain indefinitely. Either way however Dublin has continued its offensive against the IRA. In December 1974 they introduced their Bill for the trial in the South of people charged with 'terrorist' offences in the North and in Britain, and in April 1975 began to debate it in the Seanad. In the meantime they stepped up their harassment of Republicans in the 26 counties.

Even the Provisionals, who grew out of the need to defend the Catholic ghettos in 1969-70, were thrown into confusion by the Loyalist backlash and have failed to see the gravity of the current situation. Underestimating the strength and virulence of Orangeism, they saw the growth of 'working-class' Protestant para-military groups as in some way progressive. Daithi O'Conaill, vice-president of Sinn Fein, praised the 'discipline' of the UWC stoppage, Sinn Fein members were involved in a bizarre trip to Libya with UDA men, and the IRA held abortive negotiations with the UDA and UVF in an attempt to stave off a direct conflict. But the conflict is inevitable now the Loyalists have won a majority in the Convention election. The choice is simple: collision or capitulation.

No compromise is possible in the North any longer. To get power and hold on to it the Loyalists must defeat and destroy minority resistance. To avoid enslavement the minority must destroy Loyalism. No one can be neutral in this struggle.

On the face of it the odds against the minority are formidable. The Loyalists are well-armed and well-prepared. They will have control of the apparatus and funds of government. The RUC and UDR are solidly Loyalist and can be backed up with the UVF and UDA – the monster at whose birth the British Army assisted. A Loyalist government can expect to be supplied and paid by Britain and to have powerful friends in Westminster and Whitehall. It can also confidently expect that the Dublin government will continue to attack their mutual enemy – the anti-imperialist forces – in the rear. And it has a majority in the six-county state.

But the minority have gained a new toughness and self-confidence from six years of struggle, and the threat of a Loyalist take-over may serve to unite them more than any issue since Bloody Sunday; while the Provisionals' military campaign has built up a nucleus of experienced guerrilla fighters to give backbone to the resistance. In Britain the demand is growing in the working-class movement for withdrawal of British troops from the North. If it developed into an embargo on supplies for a Loyalist regime this could be an effective weapon, the more so as the British economic crisis worsens and the British government may have neither the will nor the means to prop up an unsavoury semi-fascist regime in the six counties.

But the deciding factor will be the South. Already there is growing discontent at the Dublin government's collaboration with the British Army and the Loyalists. The government – and the opposition – are unpopular and discredited, the population restless and frustrated. Any Dublin government which jails Republicans or even stands aloof during an all-out struggle in the North will provoke a popular revolt. At the same time the South is also in the throes of a deadly serious economic crisis, as the industries established under economic protection collapse in the free trade conditions of the EEC and nothing replaces them. Unemployment is over 100,000, the highest figure since the disastrous 1950s, and this time the government can't export the problem to Britain through emigration, since Britain is in trouble too. Industrial unrest is spreading rapidly.

The two problems – economic collapse and collaboration with Britain – are connected. They spring from the growing British domination of the South's economy, which has forced the South to follow Britain into the EEC and has turned the Dublin government into little more than a puppet of Westminster. If the connection is grasped by the angry workers of the South, a Loyalist take-over in the North could spark off a revolt which would sweep aside the government in Dublin and bring the mass of the Southern working class into the struggle, finally sounding the death-knell of Orangeism and the six-county state.

But the connection will have to be explained and demonstrated and the Southern masses will have to be organised. The Provisionals have been the major force on the anti-imperialist side in this struggle so far. But by themselves they cannot bring it to its conclusion. They cannot mobilise the Southern workers and small farmers against the Dublin regime, because they lack any clear analysis of imperialism, the economic crisis, or the reasons for Southern collaboration, and they have no clear class basis. In the South they have confined themselves to rallying emotional support for the war in the North and have mounted no serious opposition to the Dublin government. Even in the North their political confusion and lack of direction have prevented their building a mass movement to accompany their military campaign, or even seriously challenging the SDLP.

Yet to succeed, resistance to the Loyalists must be based on a strong, politically-conscious mass movement in the North and on the mobilisation of the Southern masses in opposition both to the collaborationist policy of the government and to the imperialist-dominated economic system. Only the revolutionary left has grasped the connection between the economic crisis and the national struggle, and the crucial importance of mass involvement by the anti-imperialist population on both sides of the border. The revolutionary left in Ireland is small but growing. If a Loyalist take-over in the North is to be averted, this new force must come more and more to the forefront of the struggle. Loyalism can only be defeated by the strength of the Irish working class.

The stakes are high in the Northern conflict. A successful struggle in the North could not only defeat the Loyalists and unite Ireland but it could topple the Southern regime as well and complete the anti-imperialist revolution in the whole country. And a revolution in Ireland could have incalculable consequences in an ailing Britain, and indeed, during the present crisis of Western capitalism, throughout Europe.

The choice in Ireland has become devastatingly simple: between, on the one hand, a semi-fascist Orange statelet in the North matched by a pro-imperialist police state in the South, and, on the other hand, an anti-imperialist and socialist revolution.

Individuals

Note: In general Unionists and Loyalists may be assumed to be Protestants, Republicans and Nationalists to be Catholics. Religion or religious background is only specified where there might be some doubt.

John M. Andrews 1871–1951: Northern Ireland Prime Minister. Director of family linen firm. Chairman, Ulster Unionist Labour Association. MP for Mid-Down at Stormont 1921–49. Minister of Labour 1921–40. Prime Minister 1940–43. Overthrown in internal party revolt. Member of the Orange Order. His son, J.L.O. Andrews, became Deputy Prime Minister 1969–72.

James Baird: Belfast trade unionist. Protestant. Was a member of the Independent Labour Party (ILP) and the Boilermakers' Society. Played an active part in the 1919 engineering strike. Elected as a Labour councillor to Belfast Corporation in 1920. Expelled from the shipyard in July 1920 as a 'rotten Prod' (Protestant). Unsuccessful ILP candidate in South Belfast in first elections to the Northern Ireland parliament in 1921. Opposed partition.

Richard Dawson Bates 1877–1949: Unionist minister. Belfast solicitor. Secretary to the Ulster Unionist Council 1905–21. MP in the Northern Ireland parliament 1921–45. Minister of Home Affairs 1921–43. Member of the Orange Order.

Jack Beattie 1889–1961: Belfast Labour Politician. Protestant shipyard worker. Member of the ILP and organiser of the Associated Blacksmiths' Society, 1919–25. Elected at head of poll as Northern Ireland Labour MP for East Belfast at Stormont in 1925. Re-elected MP for Pottinger 1929–49. Elected MP for West Belfast at Westminster 1943–50 and 1951–55. Strongly anti-partitionist, he was expelled from the Northern Ireland Labour Party in 1934, re-admitted 1942 and expelled again in 1944. One of the founders of the Irish Labour Party (IrLP) in Belfast in 1949. Northern organiser of the Irish National Teachers' Organisation from 1934 on.

Neal Blaney 1922– : Southern politician. TD (Member of the Dail) for Donegal North-East 1948 to present day. Minister in Fianna Fail governments 1957–70. Dismissed from government in May 1970 and charged with smuggling arms for Northern Catholic Defence Committees. Acquitted, but expelled from Fianna Fail. Holds right-wing Nationalist views.

David Bleakley 1925– : Labour politician. Protestant shipyard worker, now a teacher. Northern Ireland Labour Party (NILP) MP for Belfast, Victoria, at Stormont 1958–65. Though no longer an MP, made Minister for Community Relations for six months in Brian Faulkner's Unionist government in 1971. Elected the sole NILP member in the Northern Ireland Assembly in 1973. Pro-Unionist in outlook.

Kevin Boland 1917– : Southern politician. Son of former Fianna Fail Minister Gerry Boland, TD for Dublin South County 1957–70. Minister in Fianna Fail governments 1957–70. Resigned from government in 1970 in protest at the dismissal of Neal Blaney and Charles Haughey. Resigned from Dail as well and founded new party, Aontacht Eireann (Irish Unity). A strong traditional Nationalist.

Desmond Boal 1929– : Unionist politician. Wealthy barrister and MP for Belfast, Shankill, at Stormont 1960–72. Closely associated with Rev Ian Paisley and a constant hard-line critic of successive Unionist governments. First chairman of Paisley's Democratic Unionist Party in 1971. Broke with Paisley early in 1974 and briefly advocated a federated Ireland with autonomy for the six counties. Something of a political eccentric. Member of the Orange Order.

Sir Basil Brooke, Viscount Brookeborough 1888–1974: Prime Minister of Northern Ireland. Fermanagh landowner, and country squire. One of the founders of the B Specials. MP at Stormont for Lisnaskea, 1929–68. Minister of Agriculture 1933–41. Minister of Commerce 1941–43. Prime Minister 1943–63. Traditional Unionist and noted for his anti-Catholic speeches in the 1930s. Member of the Orange Order.

Dr Noel Browne 1915– : Southern politician. Medical doctor. Elected a Clann Na Poblachta TD in 1948 and immediately became Minister for Health in the first inter-party government in the South. Defeated in his attempt to set up a National Health Service by the Catholic hierarchy and the medical profession, he resigned and brought down the government in 1951. Joined Fianna Fail for a few years, then founded his own leftist party, the National Progressive Democrats in 1960. Finally joined the Irish Labour Party 1964, and is currently a Senator in the South.

Joe Cahill: Belfast IRA leader sentenced to death with Tom Williams and four others for killing an RUC man in 1942. Only Williams was hanged. Interned in the 1950s. Leading figure in the establishment of Provisional IRA in Belfast. Commander of Provisionals' Belfast brigade when internment was introduced in 1971. Jailed in the South for smuggling arms from Libya 1973.

T.J. Campbell 1871–1946: Northern Nationalist politician. Barrister and editor of *Irish News,* a Belfast Catholic newspaper. Unsuccessful Home Rule candidate in 1918 general election and close associate of Joe Devlin. Member of Northern Ireland Senate 1929–34. Succeeded Devlin as Nationalist MP for Belfast Central at Stormont 1934–46. Continued to attend Stormont during Second World War despite boycott by Nationalist MPs. Appointed county court judge 1945.

Edward Carson, Lord Carson of Duncairn 1854–1935: Unionist leader. Dublin Protestant. Successful barrister in both Irish and English courts. Elected Unionist MP for Dublin University at Westminster in 1892, he became Solicitor General for Ireland in the Conservative government the same year and Solicitor General for England 1900–05. Elected leader of the Ulster Unionist Council in 1911, he presided over the signing of the Covenant and the formation of the UVF. Guided Unionists through Home Rule crisis of 1911–14 and War of Independence 1919–21, with interlude as British Attorney General 1915–16, First Lord of the Admiralty 1916–17 and a member of Lloyd George's War Cabinet 1917–18. Refused premiership of the new Northern Ireland state and retired from Irish politics in 1921, when he was created Lord Carson of Duncairn. Member of the Orange Order.

Major James Chichester-Clark, Lord Moyola 1923– : Prime Minister of Northern Ireland. A country squire, he succeeded his father and grandfather as MP for South Derry at Stormont in 1960. Cousin of Captain T.O'Neill, also former Prime Minister. Chief Whip of Unionist Party 1963–66. Minister of Agriculture 1967–69. Prime Minister 1969–71. Made Lord Moyola 1972. Member of the Orange Order.

Michael Collins 1890–1922: Head of Southern Provisional government. Born in Cork, worked as a post office clerk in London. Leading figure in the Irish Republican Brotherhood (IRB) secret group behind the IRA. Minister of Finance in Dail Eireann government 1919–22. Director of Intelligence of IRA 1919–22. Negotiated the Treaty with Britain. Chairman of the Provisional government of Irish Free State 1922. Killed in Republican ambush during the civil war, August 1922.

James Connolly 1868–1916: Socialist leader. Born in Edinburgh of poor Irish parents. Founded Irish Socialist Republican Party 1896. Went to America 1903–10 and worked as organiser for Industrial Workers of the World (the Wobblies). Belfast organiser of Irish Transport and General Workers' Union (ITGWU) 1911–13. Deeply involved in the great Dublin lock-out of 1913 and in organising the Irish Citizen Army – a workers' defence force. A convinced marxist revolutionary, was in the forefront of the struggle against British imperialism and allied with the revolutionary nationalists to organise the 1916 Rising and sign the proclamation of the Republic. Wounded in the Rising he was shot by the British authorities on 12 May 1916.

Ivan Cooper 1944– : SDLP leader. Protestant factory manager. Member of Young Unionists. Active in early Civil Rights movement in Derry 1968–69. Elected Independent MP for Mid-Derry at Stormont 1969. Founder member of the SDLP 1970. Member of Northern Ireland Assembly 1973–75. Minister for Community Relations in Northern Ireland Executive, January–May 1974.

Liam Cosgrave 1920– : Southern Taoiseach (Prime Minister). Barrister and son of William T. Cosgrave, first President of the Irish Free State. Fine Gael TD 1943 to present day. Minister for External Affairs in Inter-Party government, 1954–57. Leader of Fine Gael 1965, Taoiseach of Coalition government, March 1973.

Sir James Craig, Lord Craigavon 1871–1940: First Prime Minister of Northern Ireland. Company director and landowner. Unionist MP for East Down at Westminster 1906–21. Treasurer of the Household 1916–18; Parliamentary Secretary to Ministry of Pensions 1919–20, Admiralty 1920–21, all at Westminster. MP at Stormont 1921–40. Prime Minister of Northern Ireland 1921–40. Member of the Orange Order. Made Lord Craigavon 1926. His brother Charles Curtis Craig was also a Unionist MP at Westminster 1903–29 and Parliamentary Secretary to the Ministry of Pensions 1923–24.

William Craig 1924– : Loyalist leader. Solicitor and MP for Larne at Stormont 1960–73. Unionist Chief Whip 1962–63. Held various ministries 1963–68. Dismissed from Ministry of Home Affairs 1968. Set up hard-line Unionist, Ulster Vanguard, later Vanguard Unionist Party, 1972. Member of Northern Ireland Assembly 1973–75. MP for East Belfast at Westminster, 1974 to date. Extreme right-winger, closely associated with Loyalist para-military groups. Member of the Orange Order. Not related to Sir James Craig.

Austin Currie 1939–   : SDLP politician. Teacher. MP for East Tyrone at Stormont 1964–73. Elected as a Nationalist, prominent in early Civil Rights movement 1968–69. Founder member of SDLP 1970. Member of Northern Ireland Assembly 1973–75. Minister for Housing in Northern Ireland Executive, January–May 1974.

Eamon De Valera 1882–1975: Southern Taoiseach and President. Born in New York, of Spanish father and Irish mother, brought up in Ireland. Teacher. Commandant in Irish Volunteers in 1916 Rising and sentenced to death by court martial. Reprieved and became President of Dail government 1919. Opposed the Treaty. Political head of anti-Treaty forces in civil war 1922–23. Founded Fianna Fail Party 1926. President of Executive Council (Prime Minister) and then Taoiseach of Fianna Fail governments 1932–48, 1951–54, 1957–59. President of the Republic of Ireland 1959–73.

Bernadette Devlin: now McAliskey 1947–   : Member of Peoples Democracy 1968–69 and prominent in early Civil Rights movement. MP for Mid-Ulster at Westminster 1969–1974. Elected while still a student. Formerly non-party socialist, now (1975) member of Irish Republican Socialist Party. Not related to Joe or Paddy Devlin.

Joe Devlin 1871–1934: Northern Nationalist leader. Barman and journalist. Home Rule MP at Westminster for North Kilkenny 1902–06, West Belfast 1906–22. General Secretary of United Irish League (UIL), Home Rule party, 1904–20. National President of Ancient Order of Hibernians (AOH) 1905 to his death, and linked AOH to UIL. MP at Stormont 1921–34 and leader of the Nationalists there. Founder and chairman of National League of the North, 1928. MP for Fermanagh and Tyrone at Westminster 1929–34. Not related to Bernadette or Paddy Devlin.

Paddy Devlin 1925–   : SDLP politician. Mill foreman. IRA member, interned in the 1940s. Irish Labour councillor, Belfast Corporation, 1956–58. MP for Belfast Falls at Stormont 1969–73. Elected at NILP, founder member of SDLP, 1970. Member of Northern Ireland Assembly 1973–75. Minister for Health and Social Services in Northern Ireland Executive, January–May 1974. Not related to Bernadette or Joe Devlin.

Harry Diamond 1908–   : Belfast opposition politician. Fitter in an engineering factory. Nationalist member of Belfast Poor Law Guardian Board 1929–36. MP for Belfast Falls at Stormont 1945–69. Elected as Socialist Republican he joined Irish Labour Party 1949 and was expelled 1951. Joined with Gerry Fitt MP, to set up Republican Labour Party 1965.

Maire Drumm: Vice-President of Provisional Sinn Fein. Born in South Armagh. Belfast housewife. Has served a number of jail sentences in both North and South. Her husband was interned for a total of ten years in the 1940s, 1950s and 1971–73.

Brian Faulkner 1921–   : Northern Ireland Prime Minister. Company director in family linen firm. Unionist MP for East Down at Stormont 1949–73. Chief Whip 1956–59, Minister of Home Affairs 1959–63, Minister of Commerce 1963–69, Minister of Development 1969–71, Prime Minister 1971–72, until Stormont was suspended. Member of Northern Ireland Assembly 1973–75. Leader of reformist breakaway Unionist Party of Northern Ireland, set up in 1974. Chief Executive in Northern Ireland Executive, January–May 1974. Member of the Orange Order.

Gerry Fitt 1926–   : SDLP leader. Merchant seaman and unemployed. Elected Independent Irish Labour councillor on Belfast Corporation 1958. MP for Belfast Dock at Stormont 1962–73, MP for West Belfast at Westminster 1966–   . Elected as Independent Irish Labour. Joined with Harry Diamond to set up Republican Labour Party 1965. Founder member and leader of SDLP 1970. Member of Northern Ireland Assembly 1973–75, Deputy Chief Executive in Northern Ireland Executive, January–May 1974.

Tommy Geehan   –1964: Belfast Unemployed leader. Catholic background. Member of Revolutionary Workers' Group 1930–33. Chairman of Belfast Outdoor Relief (ODR) Workers' Committee and organiser of ODR strike 1932. Organiser of Irish Unemployed Workers' Movement 1933–36. 'Unemployed' candidate in Belfast Corporation and Poor Law Guardians' elections 1933. Active in Republican Congress Movement 1934. Member of Communist Party of Ireland from 1933, but later quarrelled with them and left politics.

Cathal Goulding 1922–   : IRA leader. Dublin housepainter. Involved in re-organisation of IRA after 1945. Sentenced, with Sean MacStiofan, to eight years' jail in England for raid on Felstead School OTC Depot. Became Chief of Staff of IRA in 1962. Prominently identified with swing away from violence and national question, and concentration on social issues in 1960s. Chief of Staff of Official IRA after split with Provisionals.

John Graham: Belfast IRA man. Protestant and member of Ulster Union Club, a mainly Protestant constitutional nationalist group. One of a number of Protestants in IRA during the Second World War. Joined IRA about

1938. Member of Special Operations Group, Director of Intelligence for the North and editor of IRA paper *Republican News.* Captured by RUC after gun battle 1942 and jailed.

William Grant 1877–1949: Unionist Minister. Shipyard worker, organiser for the UVF and founder member of the Ulster Unionist Labour Association in 1918. Involved in 1919 engineering strike, Unionist MP at Stormont, North Belfast and Duncairn, 1921–49, Minister of Public Security 1941–43, Minister of Labour 1943–44, Minister of Health and Local Government 1944–49. Member of the Orange Order.

Frank Hanna 1915–   : Belfast Catholic politician. Solicitor. MP for Belfast Central at Stormont 1947–65, elected as NILP 1947, then resigned from NILP. Joined the Irish Labour Party (IrLP) in 1949 and re-elected, then resigned from IrLP. Formed clericalist Independent Labour Group 1958, which ousted IrLP in Catholic areas.

John Hanna: Belfast trade unionist. A Protestant and former Master of an Orange Lodge, he was involved with Jim Larkin in the 1907 carters' and dockers' strike in Belfast. He joined the ILP and was active in the 1919 engineering strike. Expelled from work in 1920 as a 'rotten Prod', he became chairman of the Expelled Workers' Committee. Unsuccessful ILP candidate for West Belfast in 1921 Northern Ireland election. Strongly opposed to partition. Not related to Frank Hanna.

T.J.S.Harbinson 1864–1930: Nationalist politician. Solicitor, member of Home Rule party (UIL) up to 1921, then Nationalist MP at Westminster (East Tyrone, then Fermanagh and Tyrone) 1918–24, 1929–30. MP for Fermanagh and Tyrone at Stormont 1921–29.

Charles Haughey 1925–   : Southern politician. Accountant and businessman, TD for Dublin North-East 1957 to present day. Minister in Fianna Fail governments 1961–70. Dismissed from government May 1970 and charged together with Neal Blaney with smuggling arms for Northern Catholic defence committees. Acquitted and remained in Fianna Fail. Re-appointed to Fianna Fail front bench 1975. Married to daughter of Sean Lemass, former Taoiseach.

Cahir Healy 1877–1970: Nationalist politician. Journalist and insurance official. Originally Sinn Fein supporter, then Nationalist. Interned 1922–24 on prison ship *Argenta* and again 1941–42 in Brixton prison under Defence of the Realm Act. MP for Fermanagh and Tyrone at Westminster 1922–24, 1931–35, 1950–55, MP for Fermanagh and Tyrone, then South Fermanagh, at Stormont 1925–65.

Tommy Henderson 1887–1970: Independent Unionist politician. MP at Stormont for North Belfast, then Belfast Shankill, 1925–53. A Protestant housepainter and founder member of Unionist Labour Association. Stood as Independent Unionist in 1925, when Unionist Party turned him down as an official candidate. Occasionally criticised government on social issues, but ardently Loyalist on the constitution. Member of the Orange Order.

Sir Denis Henry 1864–1925: Unionist politician and judge. Catholic barrister, Unionist MP for South Derry at Westminster 1916–21. Attorney General for Ireland 1919–21, Lord Chief Justice of Northern Ireland 1921–25. The only Catholic Unionist MP ever.

Tommy Herron 1938–73: Loyalist leader. Car salesman, vice-chairman and leading spokesman of the para-military Ulster Defence Association 1972–73. Kidnapped and shot dead, probably in internal feud, September 1973.

Billy Hull 1912– : Loyalist leader. Shipyard worker, convenor of shop stewards in Harland and Wolff's engine shop. Former NILP member, resigned 1969 in protest at Wilson government's attitude to Northern Ireland. Founded Loyalist Association of Workers. Member of inner council of UDA 1972–73. Founder member of Vanguard 1972.

John Hume 1937– : SDLP politician. Derry school-teacher. Active in Civil Rights movement 1968–69, MP for Derry, Foyle, at Stormont 1969–73. Elected as Independent, founder member of SDLP, 1970. Member of Northern Ireland Assembly 1973–75. Minister of Commerce in Northern Ireland Executive, January–May 1974.

Liam Kelly: Northern Republican. Co-operative manager. Expelled from IRA 1951 and formed new armed group Saor Uladh and political group Fianna Uladh. Abstentionist MP for Mid-Tyrone at Stormont 1953–58. Jailed for seditious speech 1953–54. Member of Southern Senate 1954–57. Launched independent military campaign on border November 1955. Went to USA 1959. Currently chairman of Republican clubs there.

Sam Kyle 1884–1962: Labour politician. Protestant trade union official, member of ILP. Unsuccessful Labour candidate for Belfast Shankill in 1918 Westminster election. MP for North Belfast in Northern Ireland parliament 1925–29 and leader of Labour Party. Moved to Dublin as Irish Secretary of ATGWU in 1932. Labour member of Southern Senate 1944–48. President of Irish Trade Union Congress 1940.

Sean F. Lemass 1894–1971: Southern Taoiseach. Businessman and company director. Took part in 1916 Rising, War of Independence and civil war (on Republican side). Interned by both British and Free State governments. Sinn Fein then Fianna Fail TD for Dublin South 1924–71. Minister for Industry and Commerce 1932–39, 1941–48, 1951–54, 1957–59. Minister for Supplies 1939–45. Tanaiste (Deputy Prime Minister) 1945–48, 1951–54, 1957–59. Taoiseach 1959–66, then retired.

Marquis of Londonderry 1878–1949: Unionist minister. Irish landowner and coal-mine owner in Co.Durham, England. Conservative MP for Maidstone at Westminster 1906–15, then in House of Lords. Member of Northern Ireland Senate and Minister of Education 1921–26. Secretary of State for Air in Westminster government 1931–35. Leader of House of Lords 1935–36.

Jack Lynch 1917– : Southern Taoiseach. Civil servant, then barrister. Fianna Fail TD for Cork City 1948 to present day. Minister in Fianna Fail governments 1957–66. Taoiseach 1966–73. Leader of opposition in the Dail 1973 to date. Sacked Neal Blaney and Charles Haughey from his cabinet in 1970 over the arms smuggling affair.

Eddie McAteer 1924– : Nationalist politician. Derry tax consultant. Nationalist MP for Mid-Derry 1945–53, Foyle 1953–69. Leader of Nationalist parliamentary party 1964–69, then president of the Nationalist Party. Unsuccessful candidate in Co.Derry in Northern Ireland Assembly elections 1973. Brother of Hugh McAteer, the Republican leader.

Hugh McAteer –1970: Northern IRA man. Travel agent. A Derry man, he joined the IRA in 1933, became Northern commander and then chief of staff, 1942. Arrested October 1942 and sentenced to 15 years in jail. Escaped January 1943. Re-captured November 1943. Active in formation of the Provisional IRA just before his death. Brother of Eddie McAteer, the Nationalist politician.

Sean McBride 1904– : Southern politician. Barrister, son of Major John McBride, executed for his part in 1916 Rising, and Maud Gonne McBride. Fought on Republican side in civil war. IRA leader throughout 1920s and 1930s. Chief of staff 1936–37. Dropped out during Second World War. Founded Clann na Poblachta Party 1946, which won ten seats in the Dail in 1948 and formed Coalition government with Fine Gael and Labour Party. TD for Dublin South-West 1947–57. Minister for External Affairs 1948–51. Brought down second Coalition government in South in 1957 over Northern and economic policies. General Secretary International Commission of Jurists 1963–70. Currently United Nations Commissioner for Namibia (South West Africa). Winner of Nobel Peace Prize 1974.

John McKeague 1930–   : Loyalist leader. Printer and former hotel manager. Associated with Rev Ian Paisley 1968–69. Charged with involvement in bombings which toppled Terence O'Neill in 1969, but acquitted. Founder and chairman of Shankill Defence Association 1969–72. Editor of *Loyalist News*. Associated with banned para-military group, Red Hand Commandos. Jailed for three years for armed robbery 1973. Released January 1975.

Rev Godfrey McManaway 1898–1951: Unionist politician. Church of Ireland rector. Unionist MP for Derry City at Stormont 1947–51. MP for West Belfast at Westminster February–October 1950. Disqualified from Westminster because he was an Anglican clergyman and then resigned from Stormont. Member of the Orange Order.

William McMullen: Belfast trade unionist. Protestant shipyard worker, Met James Connolly in 1910 and became Belfast chairman of his party, the ILP (Ireland). Full-time official of the Irish Transport and General Workers' Union and Labour MP for West Belfast at Stormont 1925–29. Strongly anti-partitionist. President of Irish TUC 1927–28. Associated with Republican Congress movement 1934. Moved to Dublin and became President of ITGWU. Member of Southern Senate 1951–54.

Sean McStiofain (originally John Stephenson) 1928–   : IRA leader. Born in London but with Irish connections. Served in RAF. Railway shunter. Joined IRA in London 1949. Jailed in England for eight years, together with Cathal Goulding, for raid on Felstead OTC centre. Learnt Irish in jail and adopted Irish form of his name. Moved to Ireland on his release and became organiser for Irish language body. Actively involved in setting up Provisional IRA and became its first chief of staff. Jailed in South for six months for membership of IRA, November 1972. Went on hunger and thirst strike for ten days in protest. No longer active in IRA.

Harry Midgley 1893–1957: Unionist minister. Protestant joiner, then trade union official. Joined ILP in 1910. Served in First World War. Unsuccessful Labour candidate in 1921 election to Northern Ireland parliament, when he took anti-partitionist line. MP for Belfast Dock 1933–38, Belfast Willowfield 1941–57. Left Labour Party 1942 and set up pro-Unionist Commonwealth Labour Party. Brought into Brooke's war time Cabinet as Minister of Public Security 1943–45, then reverted to back benches. Joined Unionist Party 1947, appointed Minister of Labour 1949–52, Minister of Education 1952–57. Member of the Orange Order.

J.W.Nixon 1880–1949: Independent Unionist politician. A District Inspector in the RIC and RUC with a record for toughness 1920–22. Dismissed from RUC in 1924 for making inflammatory speech at an Orange function. Elected as Independent Unionist MP for Belfast Woodvale at Stormont in 1929 and held seat until death in 1949. More loyalist than the official party. Member of the Orange Order.

Ruadhri O'Bradaigh: Republican leader. School-teacher. Joined IRA as student. Active in 1950s campaign, leading raid on Arborfield REME barracks in England 1955, and taking part in attack on Derrylin RUC barracks 1956. Elected as Sinn Fein TD for Longford-Westmeath 1957–61. Interned in the Curragh and escaped 1958. IRA chief of staff 1958–59 and 1961–62. Played leading role in formation of Provisionals and president of Provisional Sinn Fein 1970 to date.

Daithi O'Conaill: IRA leader. Cork school-teacher. Active in 1950s campaign on border. Involved in attack on Brookeborough RUC barracks January 1957, when Sean South and Fergal O'Hanlon were killed. Interned in South and escaped with Ruadhri O'Bradaigh 1958. Wounded and captured in RUC ambush in Tyrone November 1960, and sentenced to eight years in jail. Actively involved in formation of Provisionals. Vice-president of Provisional Sinn Fein 1970 to date.

Eoin O'Duffy 1892–1944: Right-wing Southern politician. Assistant chief of staff of IRA 1921 with rank of general and truce liaison officer in the North. Angered Unionists by belligerent speech in Armagh September 1921. Strong supporter of the Treaty and deputy chief of staff of pro-Treaty forces 1922. First Commissioner of new police force, Civic Guards. Dismissed by Fianna Fail government in 1933 and became head of National Guard, a para-military body wearing blue shirts, and president of United Ireland Party combining Blueshirts and Free State (Fine Gael) party. Deposed by United Ireland Party 1934, founded National Corporate Party on fascist lines 1935. Led Irish Brigade fighting for Franco in Spanish Civil War 1936–37. Then left politics.

Terence O'Neill, Lord O'Neill of the Maine 1914–   : Northern Ireland Prime Minister. County squire and son of a Unionist MP at Westminster, served as captain in Second World War. Unionist MP for Bannside at Stormont 1946–70. Minister of Home Affairs 1953–56, Minister of Finance 1956–63; Prime Minister 1963–69. Resigned under hard-line backbench pressure, 1 May 1969. Made Lord O'Neill of the Maine January 1970. Member of the Orange Order.

Rev Ian Paisley 1926– : Loyalist politician. Protestant fundamentalist minister. Son of a Baptist minister and ordained by his father 1946. Founded breakaway Free Presbyterian Church 1951 and is now perpetual Moderator of it. Founded Ulster Protestant Action in early 1960s, led extra-parliamentary opposition to Terence O'Neill in late 1960s and served two short jail terms. MP for Bannside at Stormont 1970–73. MP for N.Antrim at Westminster 1970 to date. Elected as Protestant Unionist but founded Democratic Unionist Party 1971, and joined with William Craig and Harry West in United Ulster Unionist Coalition 1974. Member of Northern Ireland Assembly 1973–75.

Norman Porter: Loyalist politician. Protestant fundamentalist. Northern Ireland head of National Union of Protestants 1948–53, then founded Evangelical Protestant Society. Editor of *Ulster Protestant* and active on extreme fringes of Unionism in 1950s. Elected as Independent (Protestant) Unionist MP for Belfast Clifton at Stormont 1953. Narrowly defeated 1958.

John Redmond 1856–1918: Home Rule leader. Catholic landowner. MP for Wexford, then Waterford, at Westminster 1881–1918. Leader of Parnellite section of Home Rule Party 1891–1900. Chairman and leader of the re-united Irish Parliamentary Party, 1900 to his death in March 1918. Wielded great influence in Westminster parliament 1910–14 and secured passage of Home Rule Bill. Agreed in 1916 to temporary exclusion of the six counties. Supported British Empire in First World War and urged Irish Volunteers to join the British Army.

Betty Sinclair 1910– : Belfast trade unionist. Protestant mill worker and active in textile trade union in 1930s. Member of the Communist Party 1932 to date and its Northern Ireland secretary 1942–45. Full-time secretary Belfast and District Trades Council, 1947–75. Founder member and chairman 1968–69 of Northern Ireland Civil Rights Association.

Gusty Spence 1933– : Loyalist leader. Shipyard worker, member of a family of Unionist Party activists. Ex-British soldier, served as military policeman in Cyprus. Member of Ulster Protestant Action in early 1960s. Founder of new UVF. Convicted of murder of Catholic barman in early 1966 and sentenced to life imprisonment. Escaped July 1972. Recaptured October 1972.

Joe Stewart 1889–1964: Nationalist politician. Publican and auctioneer. Supporter of old Home Rule Party. Prominent in local government in

Co. Tyrone 1921–64. MP for East Tyrone at Stormont 1929–64. Leader of Nationalist Party 1958–64. Member of AOH.

John Taylor 1937– : Unionist politician. Civil engineer. MP for South Tyrone at Stormont 1965–73. Member of Northern Ireland Assembly 1973–75. Parliamentary Secretary, Ministry of Home Affairs 1969–70, Minister of State, Home Affairs 1970–72. Unionist hard-liner and prominent member of Harry West's official Unionist Party and United Ulster Unionist Coalition. Member of the Orange Order.

Theobald Wolfe Tone 1763–1798: Founder of Irish Republicanism. A Protestant barrister and strong supporter of the American and French revolutions. Founded the Society of United Irishmen in 1791 to unite 'Protestant, Catholic and dissenter' in the cause of Irish independence. Full-time secretary to the Catholic Committee – a body seeking civil rights for Catholics– 1792. Went to United States 1795 and France 1796. Tried to persuade Directory and then Napoleon to invade Ireland. Captured on French ship when trying to land at Lough Swilly October 1798. Court martialled and sentenced to death, but committed suicide before sentence was carried out.

Seamus Twomey 1920– : Belfast IRA leader. Manager of bookmakers' firm. Active in IRA in 1940s, then dropped out. Played leading part in establishing Provisional IRA, and commander of Belfast Brigade 1971–72. Member of IRA delegation which met William Whitelaw July 1972. Jailed for three years in the South 1973. Escaped by helicopter from Mountjoy jail, with two other Provisional leaders, 31 October 1973. Believed to be chief of staff of Provisionals 1974.

Edmond Warnock 1887–1971: Unionist politician. Barrister. Served in First World War. MP for Belfast St Anne's at Stormont 1938–69. A strong right-winger he was active in the revolt which brought down the Andrews government in 1943, and remained a constant critic of O'Neill's policies in the 1960s. Minister of Home Affairs 1944–49, Attorney General 1949–56. Member of the Orange Order.

Harry West 1919– : Unionist politician. Large farmer. MP for Enniskillen at Stormont 1954–73. MP for Fermanagh-South Tyrone at Westminster, February–October 1974. Member of Northern Ireland Assembly 1973–75, Parliamentary Secretary, Ministry of Agriculture 1958–60. Minister of Agriculture 1960–67, then dismissed over land deal. Unionist hard-liner, leader of Official Unionist Party 1974 to date, and leader of United Ulster Unionist Coalition. Member of the Orange Order.

William Whitelaw 1918–   : British politician. Landowner. Conservative MP for Penrith and Border 1955 to date. Held minor government posts 1957–64. Opposition Chief Whip 1964–70. Lord President of the Council 1970–72, Secretary of State for Northern Ireland 1972–73. Unsuccessful candidate for Tory leadership 1975.

Lieut.-Colonel Sir Charles Wickham 1879–1972: Head of the RUC. An Englishman, educated at Harrow and Sandhurst. Joined British Army 1899 and served in Boer War and First World War. Served as Lieutenant Colonel with British Military Mission in Russian civil war 1918–20. Divisional Commissioner for Ulster in Royal Irish Constabulary 1920–22 and responsible for raising Ulster Special Constabulary. Inspector-General RUC 1922–45. Head of British Police and Prisons Mission to Greece 1945–52 during civil war against ELAS communist guerillas.

Tom Williams 1924–42: Belfast IRA man, commander of C Company, Belfast Brigade, Clonard area 1941–42. In charge of diversionary ambush on RUC patrol 5 April 1942, in which one RUC man was shot dead, Williams wounded, with five other IRA men captured. All six were sentenced to death, but five were reprieved and only Williams as officer in charge was executed. Hanged in Crumlin Road jail 2 September 1942.

Sir Henry Wilson 1864–1922: From Southern Protestant landowning family. Army officer. Joined British Army 1884. Served in Boer War. Director of Military Operations 1910. Major General 1913. Member of Allied Supreme War Council 1917. Chief of the Imperial General Staff 1918–22, Field Marshal 1919, military adviser to Northern Ireland government from January 1922. Unionist MP for North Down at Westminster, February–June 1922. Always a strong Unionist supporter and active in securing sympathy of British Army during Home Rule crisis and 1919–22 period. Shot dead in London 22 June 1922 by two IRA men who were later hanged.

Organisations

Alliance Party: A non-sectarian moderate Unionist party. Committed to maintaining the link with Britain but reforming the Northern state. Set up in April 1970 and has substantial Catholic as well as Protestant membership. Its support and membership is overwhelmingly middle-class. Took part in the short-lived power-sharing Executive in Northern Ireland in 1974.

Amalgamated Transport and General Workers' Union (ATGWU): The name used by the British Transport and General Workers' Union in Ireland to distinguish itself from the Irish Transport and General Workers' Union. The ATGWU operates on both sides of the border though the bulk of its membership is in the North, where it is the largest single union. It has both Protestant and Catholic members.

Ancient Order of Hibernians (AOH): Originally an Irish-American benevolent society. Joe Devlin, the Northern Nationalist leader, re-organised it in 1904–05 as a Catholic equivalent of the Orange Order with banners, parades and regalia and tied it closely to the Home Rule party, the United Irish League. Dedicated to 'Faith and Fatherland' it was always extremely conservative, anti-socialist and anti-revolutionary, and intensely Catholic. It has been in decline ever since 1922 and is now virtually defunct.

Anti-Partition League (APL): The main Nationalist party in the North in the decade after the Second World War. Formed in 1945, the League re-united constitutional Nationalists around a policy of attempting to end partition by parliamentary and extra-parliamentary agitation coupled with publicity campaigns in Britain and abroad. The APL also re-organised the Nationalist movement, establishing local branches and holding annual conferences. It gradually disintegrated in the mid-1950s however.

Apprentice Boys: A Protestant and Loyalist organisation similar to the Orange Order. It commemorates thirteen Protestant apprentices who shut the gates of Derry against the forces of the Catholic King James II during the Great Siege in 1688. Apprentice Boys from all over the North parade in Derry on 12 August each year. Membership usually overlaps with the Orange Order.

Black and Tans and the **Auxiliaries:** Special forces recruited in England on a semi-mercenary basis to reinforce the Royal Irish Constabulary – much depleted by deaths and resignations – during the War of Independence. The Black and Tans were recruited largely from unemployed ex-service men and wore khaki uniforms with black police caps and belts – hence the name. The Auxiliaries were recruited from ex-officers, paid £1 a day, and specialised in intelligence work. Both groups were brutal and undisciplined and the Auxiliaries' commanding officer Brigadier F.P. Crozier, resigned in protest at their conduct. They served in Ireland from 1920 to 1922 and at the peak period there were 1,400 Auxiliaries and 7,000 Black and Tans in the country.

Blueshirts: Extreme right-wing semi-fascist body in the South, associated with the Fine Gael party and led by General Eoin O'Duffy, a former IRA officer and Chief of Police under the Cosgrave government 1923–32. The Blueshirts, who were active from 1933 to 1937, wore a uniform modelled on Mussolini's Blackshirts and used the Fascist salute. They engaged in violent clashes with the IRA, left-wing groups and the De Valera government. In 1936 O'Duffy led a contingent of Blueshirts to Spain to fight for Franco in the Civil War. They returned after a year having seen little action apart from an accidental clash with another Fascist unit. After that they disintegrated.

Campaign for Democracy in Ulster (CDU): A group of left-wing British Labour MPs and those with Irish connections, set up in 1965 to campaign against gerrymandering and discrimination in Northern Ireland. One of their main demands was for a Westminster Enquiry into the government of Northern Ireland. They worked closely with Gerry Fitt MP and were active until 1969.

Campaign for Social Justice in Northern Ireland (CSJ): A group of middle-class and professional Catholics set up to collect and publicise facts and figures about religious discrimination and social injustice in the North. Established early in 1964, they worked closely with the CDU and the British National Council for Civil Liberties as well as the opposition parties in the North and helped to found the Northern Ireland Civil Rights Association in 1967.

Central Citizens' Defence Committee (CCDC): Originally a co-ordinating body for local Republican Defence Committees set up in the Catholic ghettos of Belfast after the attacks by Loyalists and B Specials in August 1969, and basically a front for the IRA. It was quickly taken over by the Catholic clergy and their allies and became a mouthpiece for their conservative, anti-Republican politics. Its chairman, Tom Conaty, a wealthy

Catholic businessman, was a member of the British government's Advisory Commission in the North after the suspension of Stormont in 1972.

Clann na Poblachta (CnaP): A populist Republican party in the South. Founded by Sean McBride in 1946 it included many ex-IRA men and took substantial support from Fianna Fail while its radical social programme attracted left-wingers. Clann na Poblachta won 10 seats in the 1948 Southern election and formed a Coalition government with Fine Gael and Labour. The Coalition collapsed in 1951 over a radical health scheme proposed by CnaP Minister Noel Browne. The party won only two seats in the 1951 election. It helped to support another Coalition government in 1954 but never recovered from the 1951 debacle and was finally dissolved in 1965.

Commonwealth Labour Party (CLP): A pro-Unionist breakaway from the Northern Ireland Labour Party. Set up by Harry Midgley MP in December 1942, it strongly supported the war effort and the link with Britain and the Commonwealth and had a right-wing social democratic policy on social and economic issues. The CLP put up six candidates in the 1945 Stormont election but only Midgley got in. In 1947 Midgley joined the Unionist Party without consulting his colleagues and the CLP fell apart.

Communist Party of Ireland (CPI): Founded in 1933 as an all-Ireland marxist party, it took a strong anti-partitionist and pro-Republican stand in the 1930s. The Southern section was dissolved in 1941 due to falling membership and the problems created by their support for Southern neutrality in the war, while the Northern section was enthusiastically backing the war effort. The Northern section continued as the CP (Northern Ireland) and, by moderating its stand on partition, won substantial support among Protestant workers for a time. The Southern section was re-established in 1948 as the Irish Workers' League, later the Irish Workers' Party, and both sections were re-united as the Communist Party of Ireland in 1970.

Dail Eireann (The Parliament of Ireland): The Assembly set up by the Sinn Fein MPs elected to Westminster in 1918 who refused to take their seats. The Parliament in Southern Ireland has also been known as Dail Eireann since 1921 and its upper House is known as Seanad Eireann. Members of the Dail are known as Teachta Dala (TD) which means Parliamentary Deputy.

Democratic Unionist Party (DUP): A Loyalist party of the extreme right founded by Ian Paisley in November 1971. Under the influence of

Desmond Boal MP it initially adopted a semi-radical position on social and economic issues and opposed the use of internment but quickly reverted to orthodox right-wing attitudes. In 1974 it joined with the official Unionist and Vanguard parties to form the United Ulster Unionist Coalition. The DUP is closely associated with the Free Presbyterian Church, a breakaway fundamentalist Protestant church founded by Paisley in 1951 of which he is the permanent Moderator or Head.

Fianna Fail (FF): Political party formed by De Valera in 1926 when he broke away from Sinn Fein in order to enter the Free State Dail. Fianna Fail's policies were ostensibly mildly radical and Republican and most of the former Sinn Fein TDs joined it. De Valera got into power in 1932 and Fianna Fail remained in power from then until 1973 with only two short breaks from 1948 to 1951 and from 1954 to 1957. Today, though currently in opposition, Fianna Fail is the biggest party in the country and in the Dail. It has long since dropped any pretensions to radicalism or Republicanism however. In the EEC it aligns itself with the French Gaullist party.

Fine Gael (FG): Southern political party formed by a merger between Cumann na nGaedheal (the Free State government party in the 1920s), the National Centre Party, led by a son of the last leader of the UIL, and General O'Duffy's Blueshirts. Founded in 1933 with O'Duffy as its first leader, it looked as if Fine Gael would become a semi-Fascist party on the European model. O'Duffy was forced to resign however and it settled down to become an orthodox conservative party, pro-British and anti-Republican. Fine Gael led the two previous Coalition governments in the South and is currently in power there in alliance with the Irish Labour Party.

Friends of Ireland Group: Group of left-wing Labour back-benchers at Westminster who opposed Unionist rule in Northern Ireland. Set up in 1945 they worked closely with the Anti-Partition League and Jack Beattie, the anti-partition Labour MP, in attempts to influence the Attlee government. After 1951 they became inactive. One of the group's leading figures was Geoffrey Bing MP, an Ulster Protestant who was MP for an English constituency.

Garda Siochana or Gardai (Civic Guards): The police force in the South. Established in 1923 as a (normally) unarmed force to replace the old heavily-armed RIC. The Gardai have always had an armed Special Branch however to deal with political dissent.

Independent Labour Party (ILP): The British socialist party founded by Keir Hardie and to the left of the trade union-based Labour Party. There were a number of active ILP branches in the North before partition and even when a Northern Ireland Labour Party was formed in 1924 the ILP existed parallel to it until the 1930s.

Irish Citizen Army: Set up by James Larkin, the Labour leader, as a workers' defence force after a great industrial struggle in Dublin in 1913. James Connolly began to fashion it as a revolutionary socialist force. The Citizen Army took part with the Irish Volunteers in the 1916 Rising but after the death of Connolly it went into decline. It took part in the War of Independence and on the Republican side in the Civil War but then disintegrated. It was briefly revived in 1935-36 by Michael Price, one of the Republican Congress leaders, and some of its members fought with the International Brigade in the Spanish Civil War.

Irish Labour Party (IrLP): The official trade union-based social democratic party in the South. Although it traces its origins to James Connolly and has retained a radical fringe over the years, it has always been solidly respectable and constitutionalist. It provided a 'loyal opposition' in the Dail during the civil war and has formed a Coalition government with the conservative Fine Gael party on three occasions.

In 1948-49 anti-partitionist and left-wing members of the NILP joined with other anti-partition Labour groups to form a Northern section of the IrLP considerably more radical than the parent party. It quickly split into warring factions however and by the 1960s was practically defunct.

Irish Republican Army (IRA): The guerrilla force which fought the War of Independence against the RIC and British Army 1919-21. The IRA split over the Treaty in 1922 with the pro-Treaty group becoming the army of the new Free State and the anti-Treaty group keeping the IRA title. After the civil war the IRA hid their weapons and continued to organise and train. De Valera and his followers split from them to enter the Dail in 1926 and Peadar O'Donnell, Frank Ryan and other left-wingers left in the 1930s.

The result was an underground organisation totally dedicated to ending partition by force and uninterested in 'politics'. The IRA carried out a bombing campaign in England 1939-40 and two campaigns in the North, 1942-44 and 1956-62, all without success. In the mid-1960s they moved to the left and became involved in the Civil Rights movement in the North and social and economic agitation in the South.

Frustration at this 'political' role and at the IRA's failure to defend the Catholic ghettos in Belfast in August 1969 led to a further split, into the Provisional and Official IRA. The Officials favoured political action to reform Northern Ireland, the Provisionals a military campaign to destroy it. The Officials were leftist-oriented and influenced by the Communist Party, the Provisionals an amalgam of right-wing traditionalists and confused left-wing militants. Since 1970 the Provisionals have fought a remarkably effective campaign of combined urban and rural guerrilla war against the British Army, RUC and UDR. The Officials fought a brief campaign after the introduction of internment in August 1971 but called it off early in 1972. They have maintained a cease-fire since.

Irish Republican Brotherhood (IRB): A revolutionary secret society dedicated to the establishment of an Irish Republic by force. It was first known as the Fenians and organised an unsuccessful rising in 1867 and a bombing campaign in England. It was re-organised as the IRB in 1873 and eventually infiltrated the Sinn Fein party and the Irish Volunteers. It was the IRB which planned the 1916 Rising and re-organised the Volunteers into the IRA in 1918-19. Michael Collins was a leading figure in the IRB and under his influence it supported the Treaty and swung much of the IRA behind it. The IRB ceased to have much influence after Collins' death in 1922.

Irish Trade Union Congress (ITUC); known since 1959 as the **Irish Congress of Trade Unions (ICTU):** The co-ordinating body of trade unions in Ireland, set up in 1894. It is an all-Ireland body and almost all unions, North and South, are affiliated to it. However since many unions operating in Ireland are British-based these are affiliated to the British TUC as well. The ICTU has an annual Northern conference and an autonomous Northern Ireland Committee in addition to its national executive.

Irish Transport and General Workers' Union (ITGWU): Founded by James Larkin in 1908 as a militant Irish breakaway from the British National Union of Dock Labourers. Larkin went to America in 1914 and didn't return until 1923. James Connolly ran the union from 1914 to 1916 but after that it was taken over by cautious men who concentrated on rebuilding it after the disruption caused by the Rising and the 'Troubles'. When Larkin returned he clashed violently with the new leaders and was expelled in 1924, going on to set up a new breakaway body, the Workers' Union of Ireland. Since then the ITGWU has grown into the largest union in the country but has lost most of its original militancy. The ITGWU has a substantial membership in the North but it is almost entirely Catholic.

Irish Volunteers: A Nationalist force established – with Sinn Fein and IRB prompting – in November 1913 to counter the UVF already formed in the North. By mid-1914 the Irish Volunteers had almost 100,000 members, but the organisation split when the First World War began and John Redmond, the leader of the Home Rule Party, urged the members to join the British Army. A minority rejected Redmond's leadership and came under tighter IRB control under the influence of Patrick Pearse. It was this group which, together with Connolly's Citizen Army, staged the 1916 Rising. After 1916 the Volunteers were re-organised to become the IRA.

Local Defence Volunteers (LDV), later the **Ulster Home Guard:** A 25-30,000 strong Territorial Army-type force established in the North in 1940 as a defence against invasion during the Second World War. It was attached to and trained by the B Specials and was almost entirely Protestant. It never saw action and was disbanded at the end of 1944.

Mansion House Anti-Partition Committee: A committee established after a conference of all the major parties in the South in the Mansion House in Dublin in January 1949. The Committee organised the 'Chapel Gates' collection to finance anti-partition candidates in the Northern general election of 1949. They also produced a series of pamphlets on gerrymandering and discrimination in the North and on partition itself.

National Democratic Party (NDP): A mildly anti-partitionist party whose immediate aim was to work for reforms within the Northern constitution and who were committed to Irish unity only with the consent of the Northern majority. Established by a group of young Catholic graduates early in 1965 after they had failed to modernise the Nationalist party. Mainly middle-class in appeal it never had much support outside Belfast. The NDP dissolved itself into the SDLP in October 1970.

Nationalist Party: General name for the main constitutional anti-partition party in the North from 1921 on. (From 1928 to the mid-1930s the proper title was the National League of the North, and from 1945 to the mid-1950s it was the Anti-Partition League). The Nationalist Party has been the official title since the mid-1950s. In the 1950s and early 1960s the Nationalists had no party structure and they held their first annual conference only in 1966. Dull, cautious and clergy-dominated, they were quickly by-passed by the civil rights upsurge in 1968-69 and lost half their nine seats at Stormont in the 1969 election and the rest in 1973. They are now practically defunct.

National League of the North: Main party of the Nationalist and Catholic minority in the North in the late 1920s and early 1930s. Set up in 1928 it included former Sinn Fein supporters as well as members of the old Home

Rule Party, the UIL, and had a structure of branches and annual conferences. Led by Joe Devlin MP, it had a fairly radical social programme as well as opposing partition, but it was effectively a Catholic party and was strongly influenced by the Catholic clergy. The League disintegrated when its members withdrew from parliament and Devlin died 1932-34.

Northern Ireland Civil Rights Association (NICRA): Set up in 1967 by the Campaign for Social Justice, the Republicans and other opposition groups as a local equivalent of the British National Council for Civil Liberties – a multi-party lobbying organisation on civil rights issues. The civil rights explosion turned NICRA briefly into the co-ordinating body of a militant extra-parliamentary mass movement (1968-70). Since 1971 it has been dominated by the Official Republicans and the CPI and has reverted to its former role as a lobbying body.

Northern Ireland Labour Party (NILP): Trade union-based Labour Party established in 1924 with both Protestant and Catholic members. Initially neutral on the partition issue though working within the Northern Ireland constitution. Most of its anti-partition members left in 1948-49 and in 1949 the NILP took a strongly Unionist position on partition and became effectively a Protestant party. In the mid-1960s it began to support calls for civil rights and won more Catholic and liberal support, but later lost most of it to the SDLP and the Alliance Party and reverted to a hard-line Unionist stance. On social and economic issues the NILP always took a cautious social-democratic position.

Northern Resistance Movement (NRM): A militant anti-imperialist protest organisation set up after the introduction of internment in August 1971, committed to the abolition of Stormont. Supported by the Peoples Democracy and the Provisionals. The NRM organised a series of major protests in 1971-72 but declined after the Provisionals' truce of July 1972 and the British Army occupation of the ghettos in August 1972.

Orange Order: Politico-religious organisation dedicated to maintaining Protestant supremacy and the link with Britain. No Catholic and no-one whose close relatives are Catholics may be a member. Founded in Co.Armagh in 1795 during Catholic-Protestant clashes over land, it spread quickly, with some government encouragement, throughout Ulster and among Protestants in the rest of Ireland. The Orange Order declined in importance during the nineteenth century but revived in the 1880s when Home Rule became a serious possibility, and many prominent and respectable Unionists joined it. With its banners, sashes and parades and its fiercely anti-Catholic rhetoric it has been very effective in mobilising the Protestant masses in the Unionist cause. It has also frequently been the instrument of discrimination and patronage. The Orange Order is still strongly represented in the official Unionist Party and the UUUC.

Outdoor Relief (ODR) Committee: A committee of the unemployed workers engaged on task schemes to qualify for Outdoor Relief – public assistance granted without having to enter the workhouse – in the 1930s. The Committee was active in 1931–32 and organised a strike by ODR workers for higher rates of relief and less degrading conditions.

Peoples Democracy (PD): Formed in Belfast in October 1968 as a leftist, student-based civil rights organisation and played a leading role in the early Civil Rights campaign. It also played a major part in organising popular resistance in the Northern ghettos after the introduction of internment, and was the only leftist organisation to give support to the Provisionals' military campaign. The PD has been active in the South as well as against both Fianna Fail and Coalition governments. It has now become a much more tightly-organised marxist group.

Poor Law Guardians (PLG): Local Boards set up under the nineteenth century Poor Law to run the workhouses and administer poor relief. The Boards of Guardians were distinct from the local councils, though they covered the same areas and were elected on the same rate-payers franchise. They were financed by a special poor rate. This antiquated system, workhouses and all, was still in operation in Northern Ireland until 1948 when a new Ministry of Health and Local Government took over.

Progressive Unionists: A group which contested the 1938 Stormont election against the official Unionist Party. Strongly in favour of the Union with Britain and led by W.J.Stewart, an official Unionist MP at Westminster, they attacked the government's lack of action over unemployment, bad housing and agriculture. They were easily defeated however and quickly vanished from the scene.

Protestant Unionists: The name used by Paisley and his supporters when contesting local government and parliamentary elections 1964-70.

Provisional Government (of the Irish Free State): The administration, headed by Michael Collins and established in accordance with the Treaty, to which the British handed over responsibility for the 26 counties early in 1922. The Provisional government overlapped with the Dail executive headed by Arthur Griffith, but had been elected in January 1922 by the pro-Treaty members of the Dail meeting together with the four Unionist

MPs for Dublin University to constitute the 'Parliament of Southern Ireland' provided for in the Government of Ireland Act. The Provisional government was replaced by the Executive Council of the Irish Free State headed by W.T.Cosgrave and elected by the Dail – now a purely 26-county affair – in September 1922.

Republican Congress: An attempt in the 1930s to unite Republicans, socialists and trade unionists in both parts of Ireland in an anti-imperialist United Front. The leading figures were Peadar O'Donnell, George Gilmore and Michael Price, who resigned from the IRA early in 1934 when it refused to back the idea. They convened a Congress of the Republican left in Dublin in September 1934 but it split over tactics. The movement continued until 1936 when the bulk of its activists went to Spain to fight with the International Brigade.

Republican Labour Party (RLP): Small splinter group of the Irish Labour Party in Belfast. Led by Harry Diamond 1953-62. Joined by Gerry Fitt MP and another Irish Labour splinter group in 1962 and won several seats on Belfast Corporation. Anti-partition in policy but never very socialist, it was confined to Belfast and had no real party organisation. It disintegrated after Fitt joined the SDLP in 1970.

Revolutionary Workers' Groups (RWG): Local marxist groups in Belfast, Dublin and other centres established in 1930 as a prelude to the formation of a Communist Party. Dedicated to the establishment of an Irish Workers' Republic they were actively involved in trade union and unemployed struggles and played a major part in the 1932 ODR strike in Belfast. The RWG became the Communist Party of Ireland in 1933.

Royal Irish Constabulary (RIC): The centrally-controlled Irish police force established in the 1830s and called the RIC in 1867. It was an armed para-military force stationed in barracks throughout the country, and its function was as much to suppress political discontent as to deal with civil crime. It was almost entirely Irish, mainly Catholic, and about 12,000 strong. It was a major target in the War of Independence and its morale was shattered by constant attacks. The RIC was disbanded in 1922.

Royal Ulster Constabulary (RUC): The new Northern Ireland police force established in 1922. Closely modelled on the RIC, it was also a centrally-controlled, armed, para-military force. It was recruited half from the old RIC, half from the Special Constabulary – themselves recruited from the UVF. It was always strongly Protestant and Unionist with Catholics only about 10 per cent of the total membership. In the unstable conditions of the North a high proportion of its time has always been spent in suppressing the nationalist minority.

Saor Eire (Free Ireland): Radical leftist organisation sponsored by the IRA in a leftward swing 1931-33. Replaced by the Republican Congress in 1934. The name was revived by a small Republican group active in the South 1967-70; their activities were almost entirely military however and the group was broken up by the Gardai after a bank raid in 1970 when a Guard was killed.

Saor Uladh (Free Ulster): Republican military group in the North. Founded by Liam Kelly in 1951, it differed from the IRA in that it recognised the 26-county state. Saor Uladh launched a military campaign in the North in November 1955, a year before the IRA campaign began. They linked up with a dissident IRA group in the South and fought their own campaign from 1955 to 1959. Liam Kelly was elected to Stormont in 1953 and to the Southern Seanad in 1954, but went to America in 1959. Saor Uladh sponsored a political group called Fianna Uladh as well but it was short-lived.

Sinn Fein: Founded in 1907 by Arthur Griffith as a separatist but not a Republican party. It was infiltrated by the IRB and after 1916 became the main voice of militant Republicanism, advocating abstention from the Westminster parliament and supporting the armed resistance of the IRA. Sinn Fein split over the Treaty in 1922, with the anti-Treaty majority keeping the title and adopting an abstentionist policy towards the new Free State parliament as well. De Valera and his supporters left in 1926 to set up Fianna Fail and enter the Dail and a group of left-wingers broke away in the 1930s to set up the Republican Congress.

From the 1930s on Sinn Fein has functioned mainly as the political wing of the IRA, militantly nationalist and abstentionist but with a confused distributist social policy. In the 1960s it swung to the left in line with the IRA and became involved in social and economic agitation. In 1970 it split along the same lines as the IRA into *Sinn Fein, Kevin Street* (Provisional) and *Sinn Fein, Gardiner Place* (Official) – the names come from the streets in Dublin where they have their headquarters. The Provisionals were at once more militant – on the Northern issue – and more traditionalist, opposing the swing to the left and the moves to end abstentionism. Since 1970 the Officials have become steadily more reformist, filling the vacuum left as the Irish Labour Party moves to the right. The Provisionals have expanded and won support on the Northern issue but have remained anti-marxist with a populist social policy.

Social Democratic and Labour Party (SDLP): Set up in August 1970 by 6 opposition MPs at Stormont. 3 of them, Paddy Devlin, Gerry Fitt, and Austin Currie, were members of existing parties. Rapidly ousted the Nationalists as the main opposition party in the North. Highly opportunist in policy the SDLP has swung from outright opposition to the Northern state in 1971 to participation with the Unionist Party in the power-sharing Executive in 1974. Effectively the SDLP has become the voice of the Catholic middle class in the North, though not as clergy-dominated or exclusively Catholic as the old Nationalist Party. It is mildly reformist in social policy.

Socialist Republican Party: Left-wing anti-partition group set up in Belfast in 1945 with support from some Protestant trade unionists. The leading figure was Harry Diamond who was elected Socialist Republican MP for Falls in the same year. The group helped establish the Northern section of the Irish Labour Party in 1949.

Special Air Services Regiment (SAS) and **Military Reaction Force (MRF):** The SAS is a highly-secret crack unit of the British Army. Set up during the Second World War it has been used for plain-clothes, counter-insurgency and special operations work in a number of countries, the most recent being Aden and Muscat and Oman. After many denials Westminster finally admitted that SAS personnel were active in Northern Ireland, though still denying that they operated as SAS units. The MRF consists of armed plain-clothes squads patrolling in unmarked cars or under cover of apparently legitimate businesses. MRF squads admitted responsibility for killing two unarmed Catholic civilians in 1972 and have been accused of killing several more.

Ulster Defence Association (UDA): Hard-line Loyalist para-military group formed at the end of 1971 out of existing 'defence' groups. Staged a series of mass rallies of masked and uniformed men early in 1972. The UDA is heavily armed and has been mainly responsible for the assassination campaign against Catholic civilians 1972-75. It is also heavily involved in gangsterism and protection rackets, and a number of its leaders have been killed or wounded in internecine struggles. The UDA is closely linked with William Craig's Vanguard Party and provided the muscle for the UWC 'strike' in May 1974.

Ulster Defence Regiment (UDR): A local part-time military force established in 1970 to replace the B Specials. Under British Army control, it was intended to be religiously mixed and only lightly armed. It was quickly infiltrated by the Loyalist para-military groups and most of the Catholics left after the introduction of internment. By January 1974 its membership was over 97 per cent Protestant. At the same time Loyalist pressure has ensured that the UDR is now armed with self-loading rifles, sub-machine guns, Bren guns and Browning machine guns mounted on armoured cars. Its strength early in 1975 was about 8,000.

Ulster Freedom Fighters (UFF): An extreme Loyalist murder squad who announced their existence and their intention of killing Catholics in 1973. They claimed responsibility for the murder of an SDLP Senator in June 1973 and subsequently of many other Catholics. It is generally assumed that the UFF is simply a pseudonym for UDA murder gangs.

Ulster Protestant Action (UPA): Group set up by Paisley in 1959 at a time of rising unemployment. One of its objects was to safeguard jobs for Protestants and it also campaigned against any deviation from rigid Orange supremacy by the Unionist Party. The UPA worked for the election of Desmond Boal MP in a Belfast by-election in 1961 and contested local government elections up to 1965. Gusty Spence, later a founder of the new UVF, was one of its activists.

Ulster Protestant Association (UPA): A Loyalist murder squad operating in Belfast 1920-23 and responsible for many murders of Catholics. Like the modern UDA it was also heavily involved in protection rackets and gangsterism.

Ulster Protestant League (UPL): An extreme Loyalist group set up in Belfast in 1931 during the great depression to 'safeguard the employment of Protestants'. The UPL held many inflammatory and provocative rallies and demonstrations in the city over the next few years and played a major part in fomenting the 1935 riots.

Ulster Protestant Volunteers (UPV): Founded by Paisley in 1966 and active up to 1969. Despite its military title and structure and the fact that it was controlled by an 'Ulster Constitution Defence Committee' (UCDC), Paisley maintained that the UPV had no connection with the use of force. Its membership overlapped considerably with the UVF.

Ulster Special Constabulary (USC): The 'Specials' were an auxiliary para-military force raised in 1920 by the British administration. There were three categories: A Specials, who were full-time, lived in barracks and reinforced the dwindling RIC; B Specials, who were part-time and mounted patrols and manned check-points at night; and C Specials who did no regular duties but were armed and could be quickly mobilised. The Specials were entirely Protestant and were recruited from the UVF and the Orange Order.

The A and C Specials were disbanded in 1925 but the 'B men' were retained and frequently mobilised during IRA campaigns or other disturbances. They were disbanded in 1969 as a result of civil rights protests.

Ulster Union Club: An anti-partition propaganda and discussion group formed during the Second World War. Led by Captain Denis Ireland its membership was mainly Protestant and some of its members progressed from it to join the IRA.

Ulster Unionist Labour Association (UULA): Established by Carson in 1918 to counter the influence of Labour on Protestant workers. The UULA was an organisation of working-class Loyalists affiliated to the Unionist Party, who allocated them a handful of seats in the 1918 Westminster election and in the new Northern Ireland parliament. It ceased to have much importance after about 1925.

Ulster Unionist Party: An Ulster Unionist Council separate from the Southern Irish Unionists was established in 1905, committed to opposing Home Rule and to keeping Ireland, and especially Ulster, within the United Kingdom. It had close links with the British Conservative Party and was dominated by industrialists, merchants and landowners. From the beginning the Orange Order was directly represented on the Council, which became the governing body of an Ulster Unionist Party. The party was and has remained the voice of the vast majority of Northern Protestants: it formed the government of the new six-county state in 1921 and remained in power until Stormont was suspended in 1972. It is now alliance with the DUP and the Vanguard Party in the United Ulster Unionist Coalition.

Ulster Volunteer Force (UVF): 1913-23. Established in 1913 by the Ulster Unionist Council as a private army to resist Home Rule, and commanded by a retired Indian Army General. The UVF was armed with 25,000 German rifles smuggled into the North in 1914. On Carson's urging many UVF men joined the British Army when the First World War broke out and were formed into a separate unit, the 36th (Ulster) Division. The UVF was re-formed in 1920 during the War of Independence and was heavily involved in the onslaught on the Catholic population of the North over the next few years.

Ulster Volunteer Force (UVF): 1966-75. The old UVF disappeared after 1922, but in 1966 the name was revived by a small Loyalist group who murdered two Catholics that summer. They re-emerged to plant a series of bombs which toppled the Prime Minister Terence O'Neill in 1969, and since then the UVF has expanded into a large para-military organisation, more disciplined than the UDA but equally involved in sectarian killings. Despite occasional semi-radical utterances the UVF is violently anti-socialist and has connections with the British National Front organisation.

Ulster Workers' Council (UWC) and **Loyalist Association of Workers (LAW):** The LAW was set up at the end of 1971 by Billy Hull, a Loyalist shop steward in the Belfast shipyard. It organised a number of 'strikes' to demand more repression against the minority and the release of Loyalist internees. It was ramshackle and corrupt and collapsed in 1973. It was replaced at the end of the year by the UWC, a smaller, tighter organisation which concentrated on recruiting key workers, especially in the power stations. They used this strength to good effect when they called the 'strike' in May 1974 which brought down the power-sharing Executive. The UWC has close connections with the Loyalist para-military groups which backed their 'strike' with massive intimidation.

Unionist Party of Northern Ireland (UPNI): In January 1974 the Unionist Council rejected Brian Faulkner's policy of participating in the power-sharing Executive. Faulkner, who was leader of the Unionist Party, resigned and after the fall of the Executive he formed the UPNI as a modernising Unionist group prepared to share power with the SDLP but opposed to a Council of Ireland. The UPNI fared disastrously in the 1975 Convention elections, winning only five seats.

United Irish League (UIL): Set up in 1898 as a mass organisation to agitate for land reform, the UIL helped to re-unite the divided Irish Home Rule Party and then provided its constituency organisation and branches. The UIL was effectively the voice of the Irish Catholic middle class and the Church before the First World War. Mildly reformist on social issues, it was solidly constitutionalist and anti-revolutionary. After 1916 it was swept aside by Sinn Fein everywhere except in the North, where Joe Devlin and the AOH held it together a little longer. Some of the Belfast branches were still in existence up to 1925.

United Irishmen: Founded in 1791 in Belfast, the United Irishmen was a revolutionary democratic society inspired by the French Revolution and dedicated to establishing an independent democratic Republic in Ireland. Its founders were Wolfe Tone, a Dublin Protestant, and a group of middle-class Presbyterians in Belfast. It had considerable support among Northern Presbyterian weavers, then the most radical group in Ireland, and aimed to unite them with the discontented masses of the Catholic population.

The United Irishmen were in direct contact with France and hoped to stage a rising with French support. The rising took place in 1798 in Antrim and Down in the North and Wexford in the South but was easily defeated. A French Expedition arrived two months too late, in August 1798, and was defeated as well.

United Ulster Unionist Council (UUUC): A hard-line Loyalist alliance formed in 1974 to bring down the power-sharing Executive and demand a return to the old Stormont system. The UUUC is made up of the official Unionist Party, the Democratic Unionist Party and the Vanguard Party and is jointly led by the three party leaders: Harry West, Ian Paisley and William Craig. It has close links with the Loyalist para-military groups. The UUUC won a large majority in the 1975 Northern Ireland Convention election.

Vanguard Unionist Progressive Party (VUPP): Founded by William Craig in February 1972 as an umbrella organisation for Loyalist parliamentarians and para-military groups, generally called Ulster Vanguard. It held a series of fascist-style rallies early in 1972 with Craig reviewing men in military formation and crowds giving him the Fascist salute. In March 1973 Vanguard became a formal political party with Craig as leader. Since then it has been the furthest right of the three UUUC parties and the one with the closest links with the para-military groups.

Young Socialists: A group of marxist-influenced young left-wingers in Belfast who were active on issues such as the Vietnam war and local civil rights in 1967-68. The Young Socialists helped to found the Peoples Democracy and provided its political hard-core. They finally dissolved into PD in 1969.

References

Introduction

1. Ulster was an ancient provincial division containing nine counties: Antrim, Armagh, Cavan, Derry, Donegal, Down, Fermanagh, Monaghan and Tyrone. The Northern Ireland state now contains six of the nine counties.

2. E.R.R.Green, 'The Beginnings of Industrial Revolution' in J.C.Beckett and T.W.Moody, eds. *Ulster Since 1800*, BBC, London 1955, Vol.1, p.37.

3. David Kennedy, 'Ulster and the Antecedents of Home Rule 1850-86', in Beckett and Moody, *op cit*, BBC, London, 1955, Vol.1, p.91.

4. Patrick Buckland, *Irish Unionism*; Vol.2: *Ulster Unionism and the Origins of Northern Ireland, 1886-1922*, Gill and Macmillan, Dublin 1973, p.39.

5. *Census of Ireland 1911*, Vol.3, Province of Ulster/Belfast. HMSO, London 1912, Cd.6051-I, table 20.

6. Parliament of the United Kingdom (Westminster) *Parliamentary Debates; Official Report* (Hansard). *House of Commons* 5th Series. Vol.26, Col.1458.

7. Sinn Fein was founded by Arthur Griffith in 1905. Griffith himself was a conservative on social and economic issues and supported the idea of a dual monarchy, i.e. the king of England would be king of Ireland but there would be separate and sovereign parliaments. However he advocated the policy of abstention from the Westminster parliament, and setting up an unofficial parliament in Ireland which would take over government functions. This attracted militant nationalists who made Sinn Fein more radical until, after the 1916 Rising, it became clearly Republican.

8. *Census of Ireland, 1911*. General Report, HMSO, London 1913, Cd.6663, tables 19 and 71-2. Also Vol.3, *op cit*, tables 19-22.

9. W.Black, 'Industrial Change in the 20th Century', in J.C.Beckett and R.E.Glasscock, eds. *Belfast, the Origin and Growth of an Industrial City*, BBC, London 1967, p.159.

10. L.M.Cullen, *An Economic History of Ireland Since 1660*, Batsford, London 1972, p.159.

11. *ibid*, pp.160-161.

12. Dorothy McArdle, *The Irish Republic*, Gollancz, London 1937, p.81.

1. A Bloody Beginning: 1918-23

1. These were seats with a small Catholic majority where a split Sinn Fein/UIL vote would let the Unionist win. The UIL, like the Unionists, were adept at calculating the exact religious composition of the electorate.

2. Charles Craig, brother of Sir James, put it like this in 1920:

'The three excluded counties contain some 70,000 Unionists and some 260,000 Sinn Feiners and Nationalists, and the addition of that large bloc of Sinn Feiners and Nationalists would reduce our majority to such a level that

no sane man would undertake to carry on a parliament with it.' Parliament of the United Kingdom, *Parliamentary Debates: Official Report* (Hansard) *House of Commons* Vol.127, Cols.990-1.

3. Joe Devlin was a charismatic figure among the Catholics of Belfast. He was born and reared in a working-class family on the Falls Road, the heart of the Catholic ghetto in West Belfast. Politically something of a populist, he identified closely with his constituents and did a lot of social welfare work, such as organising excursions for mill-girls. Though he represented the interests of the Northern Catholic business class and the Church, he retained strong working-class support through his welfare work and through taking a fairly radical line on social and economic issues. He was a powerful speaker, and as President of the Ancient Order of Hibernians (AOH), a sort of Catholic version of the Orange Order attached to the UIL, he could and did mobilise the forces of Catholic sectarianism when it suited him.

4. An Orange Order-style body commemorating thirteen apprentices who shut the gates of Derry during the Great Siege in 1688.

5. Because of discrimination, the liquor trade was one of the few avenues of advancement open to Catholics and most pubs, spirit groceries (off-licences) and many hotels were Catholic-owned. 80 per cent of publicans and wine and spirit merchants in Belfast in 1911 were Catholics. *Census of Ireland 1911.* Vol.3, Province of Ulster/Belfast. HMSO, London 1912. Cd.6051-I, table 20.

6. The expulsion of the few Catholic workers from the shipyards was something of a Belfast tradition. It had happened in 1886 and 1912. It was to happen again in 1935, 1939, 1969 and 1970.

7. Quoted in J.D.Clarkson, *Labour and Nationalism in Ireland*, Columbia University, New York 1925, p.366.

8. *ibid*, p.367.

9. Because of a series of sectarian riots in the nineteenth century, Catholics, who made up a quarter of Belfast's population, tended to live in tightly-knit ghetto communities. The main Catholic ghettos were: the Falls Road, in West Belfast; Ardoyne and the North Queen Street/Dock area in North Belfast; the Markets area in South Belfast; and the Short Strand area in East Belfast.

10. Prompted by an exaggerated fear that trade unionism and Labour politics might undermine the 'loyalty' of Protestant workers, Carson had established an Ulster Unionist Labour Association (UULA) in 1914 to organise working-class Unionists. It was re-organised in 1918, and three safe Unionist seats were allocated to 'Labour Unionists' in the 1918 election. They were: Thompson Donald, a shipwright; T.H.Burn, a printer; and Sam McGuffin, a Shankill Road draper who was a member of the engineering union. Labour Unionists were also given five seats in the first Northern Ireland parliament and a few in the Senate but they were of little significance after 1925.

The UULA was kept under tight control by the Unionist leaders, and its permanent chairman – and one of its MPs in the Northern parliament – was J.M.Andrews, a County Down mill owner and later Unionist Prime Minister. It was violently anti-socialist, stating 'It is part of the duty of the Unionist Labour Association to expose the real aims and objects of socialism and other anti-British movements'. (J.F.Harbinson, *The Ulster Unionist Party 1882-1973*, Blackstaff Press, Belfast 1973, p.67.) If the UULA differed from the main Unionist Party it was by taking an even more extreme sectarian and Loyalist position. The UULA was actively involved in the expulsions of Catholic workers and in fomenting the subsequent rioting.

11. Spender later became the first Secretary to the Northern Ireland cabinet and head of the Northern Ireland civil service.

12. Patrick Buckland, *Irish Unionism*, Vol.2: *Ulster Unionism and the Origins of Northern Ireland* 1886-1922. Gill and Macmillan, Dublin 1973. pp.160-1.

13. Quoted in G.B.Kenna, *Facts and Figures of the Belfast Pogrom 1920-22*, O'Connell Publishing Co, Dublin 1922, pp.17 and 24.

14. *Daily Mail*, 15 September 1920.

15. The British Transport and General Workers' Union which also operates in Ireland is known there as the Amalgamated Transport and General Workers' Union (ATGWU), to avoid confusion with the ITGWU.

16. The Black and Tans were British ex-soldiers – and sometimes ex-convicts – recruited to reinforce the RIC now heavily depleted by deaths and resignations. They got their name from their mixed khaki and black uniforms and were brutal, undisciplined and thoroughly detested throughout the South and West.

17. The Auxiliaries were similar to the Black and Tans but recruited mainly from ex-British Army officers. They were used a lot in intelligence work and were also brutal and ruthless. It was these two forces which instituted the policy of reprisal killings and shootings.

18. *Northern Whig*, 15 October 1920.

19. Wallace Clark, *Guns in Ulster: a History of the 'B Special' Constabulary in part of Co.Derry*, (RUC) Constabulary Gazette, Belfast 1967, Chapters 2 and 3. See also Mervyn Dane, *The Fermanagh B Specials*, William Trimble Ltd, Enniskillen, 1970, Chapter 1.

20. *Northern Whig*, 18 May 1921.

21. *Newsletter*, 26 May 1921.

22. *Manchester Guardian*, 21 May 1921.

2. Siege or Pogrom: 1921-24

1. Dorothy McArdle, *The Irish Republic*, Gollancz, London 1937, pp.419-20.

2. *ibid.*

3. *ibid*, p.418.

4. *Belfast Newsletter*, 7 June 1921.

5. *ibid.* 'Bolshevism' was a reference to the social radicalism and labour militancy which, though frowned on by the Dail government and IRA leadership, had accompanied the War of Independence. There had been a general strike in Limerick in 1919 against military rule. In May 1920 Knocklong Creamery in Limerick had been taken over and run by the workers and in May 1921 the Arigna coal-mines in Leitrim had been taken over as well. In Mayo and Galway large estates had been seized and sub-divided by the small farmers.

6. The IRA officer in charge was Frank Aiken, later to become Minister for External Affairs in the South.

7. McArdle, *op cit*, p.437.

8. Juries in Belfast were notoriously pro-Unionist.

9. Later first head of the Gardai, the Southern police force, and later still head of a fascist-style organisation called the Blueshirts, linked with the Fine Gael party.

O'Duffy led a party of Blueshirts to Spain to fight for Franco in the Spanish Civil War.

10. In practice all but one of the six Northern Sinn Fein MPs held seats in the Southern parliament as well.

11. Quoted in Kenna, *Facts and Figures of the Belfast Pogrom, 1920-22*, O'Connell Publishing Co, Dublin 1922, pp.42-3.

12. *ibid.*

13. Wickham was an ex-British Army officer who had just returned from service with the British expeditionary force in Russia, fighting the Bolsheviks.

14. Quoted in Kenna, *op cit*, pp.57-8.

15. One of the reasons for the constant attacks on St.Matthew's was that its grounds gave easy access to the whole Short Strand area.

16. 'The Treaty was supported by ex-Unionists and non-Catholics, by the commercial and professional middle classes and the better-off farmers, and by the Catholic Church.' Peter Pyne, 'The Third Sinn Fein Party 1923-6', Part 2, *Economic and Social Review*, Vol.1 no.2, January 1970, p.242.

17. The following month Wilson was elected Unionist MP for North Down at Westminster.

18. Kenna, *op cit*, p.70.

19. Quoted in Kenna, *op cit*, p.72.

20. Kenna, *op cit*, p.142.

21. Sir Arthur Hezlet, *The B Specials*, Tom Stacey Ltd, London 1972, p.82. The RIC was formally disbanded and replaced by the new RUC on 9 June 1922. Prior to that the situation had been confusing. As an all-Ireland force the RIC had been controlled by the British administration in Dublin Castle even after the establishment of the Northern Ireland state. After the establishment of the Provisional government in the South the RIC reverted to control by Westminster. Only after June 1922 did the Belfast government have full control over their own permanent, professional police force.

22. *ibid*, p.76.

23. Quoted in *Irish Independent*, 27 March 1922.

24. Wallace Clark, *Guns in Ulster*, (RUC) Constabulary Gazette, Belfast 1967, p.58.

25. Text given in McArdle, *op cit*, pp.894-6.

26. Collins in fact had no control over the anti-Treaty IRA who had not accepted the Pact.

27. Both letters quoted by Kenna, *op cit*, pp.135-146.

28. Quoted by Kenna, *op cit*, p.97.

29. *The Plain People*, Sinn Fein, Dublin, 17 June 1922.

30. Uncle of Captain Terence O'Neill, future Prime Minister of Northern Ireland.

31. Patrick Buckland, *Irish Unionism*, Gill and Macmillan, Dublin 1973. Vol.2, *Ulster Unionism and the origins of Northern Ireland 1886-1922*, p.171.

32. Later dismissed from the RUC for making a violently inflammatory speech.

33. Parliament of Northern Ireland, *Parliamentary Debates, Official Report* (Hansard) *House of Commons*, Vol.2, Cols.603-4.

34. Letter from Rory O'Connor in Mountjoy jail, 1922. Quoted in McArdle, *op cit*, p.899.

35. The Northern government has since dealt with the problem by building a road across Boa Island and connecting it to the mainland with bridges.

36. The civil war lasted from June 1922 to May 1923. The Republican or anti-Treaty forces in the Four Courts were forced to surrender and the better-armed Free State troops with British-supplied artillery steadily drove them out of the cities and towns in the Southern and Western counties where they had most support. From October 1922 the Republicans were forced to fight a guerrilla campaign which was suppressed with extraordinary ferocity by the Free State government, until the Republicans broke it off and dumped arms in May 1923. De Valera headed a Republican 'Emergency government' during the civil war but it never wielded effective authority.

The civil war claimed the lives of some leading figures on both sides. On the Free State side Michael Collins was killed in an ambush in Co.Cork in August 1922. On the Republican side Cathal Brugha, Minister of Defence in the first Dail government, was killed in the Dublin fighting, and Liam Lynch, chief of staff of the Republican forces was shot dead in the Tipperary mountains in April 1923.

37. Memo by District Inspector Spears to Minister of Home Affairs, 1923. Public Record Office, Northern Ireland. T 2258.

38. Northern Ireland Parliamentary Debates (Hansard) House of Commons, *op cit*, Vol.2, Col. 1020.

3. Consolidation

1. The AOH (Ancient Order of Hibernians) began in America as a benevolent society providing social activities and insurance benefits for Irish immigrants. Devlin re-organised it in Ireland as an exclusively Catholic body, dedicated to 'Faith and Fatherland' – and the success of the United Irish League. It held parades with bands, banners and sashes like the Orangemen but never had the power over the Catholic population the Orange Order had over the Protestants since it had no patronage to distribute or privileged position to defend. Politically the AOH was conservative and constitutionalist and it was cordially detested by Republicans and socialists. It went into decline after 1916 and has wielded little influence since.

The Irish National Foresters (INF) was more strictly a benevolent society with mild nationalist leanings, running social clubs and insurance funds.

2. *Irish News*, 5 April 1921.

3. Baird and Hanna were leading trade unionists in Belfast. Hanna had played an important role in a dockers' and carters' strike in 1907 and had been active in the virtual general strike of engineering workers in January 1919. He was chairman of the expelled workers' committee. Baird was an industrial militant and one of the instigators of the 1919 strike.

4. *Irish News*, 21 May 1921.

5. Joe Devlin was elected for two seats, West Belfast and Co.Antrim. He resigned the Co.Antrim seat and was replaced by another Nationalist, T.S.McAllister.

6. See Chapter 2 above, p. 46.

7. Dorothy McArdle, *The Irish Republic*, Gollancz, London 1937, pp.507-8.

8. *ibid*, p.512.

9. The British proposals and the final Treaty are given in the appendix to McArdle, *op cit.*

10. *ibid.*

11. St.John Ervine, *Craigavon, Ulsterman,* Allen and Unwin, London 1949, p.454.

12. McArdle, *op cit,* pp.550, 552.

13. Parliament of the United Kingdom, *Parliamentary Debates: Official Report* (Hansard) *House of Lords.* 5th series, Vol.48, Col.69.

14. McArdle, *op cit,* p.602.

15. Parliament of the United Kingdom *Parliamentary Debates: Official Report* (Hansard) *House of Commons.* Vol.150, Col.1279.

16. Parliament of Northern Ireland, *Parliamentary Debates, Official Report* (Hansard) *House of Commons,* Vol.2, Col.314.

17. This was De Valera's final attempt to compromise with the pro-Treaty group and avert civil war. The joint panel was to contain pro-and anti-Treaty candidates in the same proportions as in the existing Dail and each side was to campaign for the full panel. After the election a coalition government with a pro-Treaty majority was to be formed which would clarify the Treaty terms with the British. Other pro-Treaty groups were to be allowed to contest the election as well however, and did so, considerably increasing the pro-Treaty majority.

18. They were to continue the boycott until 1927.

19. St.John Ervine, *op cit,* p.5.

20. Quoted in McArdle, *op cit,* pp.796-7.

21. Sir Arthur Hezlet, *The B Specials,* Tom Stacey, London 1972, pp.106 and 108.

22. There was no contest in Co.Down where eight MPs including De Valera and a Nationalist were returned unopposed.

23. United Kingdom Parliamentary Debates (Hansard) House of Commons, *op cit,* Vol.189, Col.361.

24. St.John Ervine, *op cit,* p.507.

25. *ibid.*

4. A Protestant State

1. Parliament of Northern Ireland, *Parliamentary Debates: Official Report* (Hansard) *House of Commons,* Vol.1, Col.400.

2. The urban council elections actually went ahead on the old boundaries but without PR.

3. *Northern Whig* and *Newsletter,* 13 July 1923.

4. *Disturbances in Northern Ireland,* Report of the Commission appointed by the Governor of Northern Ireland (Cameron Report), HMSO, Belfast 1969, Cmd.532, p.59, para.134.

5. Two rural councils which had always been Unionist-controlled became Nationalist after 1945 because of shifts in population. They were Limavady and Ballycastle RDCs.

6. Frank Gallagher, *The Indivisible Island,* Gollancz, London 1957, pp.251-3.

7. Later Attorney General and now a high court judge.

8. *Northern Whig,* 11 January 1946.

9. Gallagher, *op cit,* pp.209-10.

10. Quoted in *Discrimination: a Study in Injustice to a Minority*, Mansion House Anti-Partition Conference, Dublin 1949.

11. Fermanagh Civil Rights Association *Fermanagh Facts*, 1969.

12. *ibid.*

13. Quoted in *One Vote Equals Two*, published by the Mansion House Anti-Partition Conference, Dublin 1949.

14. *Impartial Reporter*, Enniskillen, 14 November 1963.

15. *Irish News*, 13 April 1948.

16. *Londonderry Sentinel*, 19 January 1950.

17. See below, Chapter 10, p.

18. Cameron Report, *op cit*, para.10, p.13.

19. *Northern Whig*, 2 April 1925.

20. Article by G.C.Duggan, former Northern Ireland Comptroller and Auditor General in the *Irish Times*, 4 May 1967.

21. Later Prime Minister from 1943 to 1963.

22. *Fermanagh Times*, 13 July 1933.

23. *Londonderry Sentinel*, 20 March 1934.

24. Northern Ireland Parliamentary Debates (Hansard) House of Commons, *op cit*, Vol.16, Col.618, 21 March 1934.

25. All figures from *The Plain Truth*, Campaign for Social Justice in Northern Ireland, Dungannon, 1969.

26. *Derry People*, 26 September 1946.

27. *The Plain Truth*, Campaign for Social Justice in Northern Ireland, Dungannon, 1969, p.35.

28. By 1975 as a result of intimidation and assassinations the number had been reduced to about a hundred. cf. Paddy Devlin, *The Fall of the Northern Ireland Executive*, P.Devlin, Belfast 1975, p.75.

29. D.P.Barritt and C.F.Carter, *The Northern Ireland Problem*, Oxford University Press 1962, p.54.

30. F.W.Boal, P.Doherty, D.G.Pringle, *The Spatial Distribution of some Social Problems in the Belfast Urban Area*, Northern Ireland Community Relations Commission, Belfast 1974.

31. *The Plain Truth, op cit*, p.4.

32. Northern Ireland Parliamentary Debates (Hansard) House of Commons, *op cit*, Vol.16, Cols.1091, 1095.

33. *ibid*, Vol.2, Col.102.

34. National Council for Civil Liberties, *Report of a Commission of Inquiry appointed to examine the purpose and effect of the Civil Authorities (Special Powers) Acts, 1922 and 1933*, London 1936. Reprinted London 1972, p.11.

35. *Newsletter*, 2 November 1920.

36. Major-General Sir C.E.Calwell, *Field-Marshal Sir Henry Wilson: his Life and Diaries*, Cassell, London 1927, Vol.2, p.340.

37. *Manchester Guardian*, 19 May 1921.

38. Northern Ireland Parliamentary Debates (Hansard) House of Commons, *op cit*, Vol.18, Col.208, 19 February 1936.

39. Report of the Advisory Committee on Police in Northern Ireland (Hunt Report), Cmd.535, HMSO Belfast, October 1969, para. 163.

40. *ibid*, para.120.

41. Wickham retired in 1945 and went to Greece as head of the British Police and

Prisons Mission to organise the right-wing forces of the Greek monarchy in the civil war against the ELAS guerrillas. To re-organise the Greek police Wickham used some of the police who had collaborated with the Nazis during the German occupation; and the subsequent record of his police force under the various Greek dictators has not been impressive. One of his subordinates in the Greek mission was J.B.Flanagan, the current head of the RUC.

42. NCCL, *op cit*, p.27.
43. *ibid*, p.40.

5 The Opposition enters . . . and Leaves 1925-32

1. Devlin stood as an Independent with Labour support in Liverpool Exchange, where he was defeated by 3,000 votes by a Conservative.

2. A similar situation arose after the 1925 election when Eamon Donnelly, MP for Co.Armagh, was banned from the North under an exclusion order.

3. Fermanagh and Tyrone: Sir C.Falls (Un) 44,716; M.McCartan (S.F.) 6,812; J.Pringle (Un) 44,711; T.Corrigan (S.F.) 6,685.
West Belfast: R.J.Lynn (Un) 28,435; H.Midgley (Lab) 21,122; P.Nash (S.F.) 2,688.

4. Midgley at this time was believed to be an anti-partitionist. The *Newsletter* had quoted him as saying at the declaration of the poll in 1921: 'They of the Labour movement did not believe that the partition of the working classes in Ireland would ever solve the problems of the country and for that reason they were going to work for that unity which would bring about political and economic emancipation.' (*Newsletter*, 26 May 1921). But he was already trimming his sails. (See below: Chapter 5, p.107.)

5. *Irish News*, 24 March 1925.

6. The candidates, all Protestants, were: Jack Beattie, former shipyard worker and local organiser of the Associated Blacksmiths' Society; Sam Kyle, local organiser of the Workers' Union, a general union with most of its members in the textile industry; and William McMullen, former shipyard worker and Belfast organiser of the Dublin-based Irish Transport and General Workers' Union. McMullen had worked closely with James Connolly in Belfast and was a strong anti-partitionist; Beattie was also a firm anti-partitionist and became more so later, and Kyle was mildly in favour of a united Ireland. They avoided the partition issue during the election however.

7. *Newsletter*, 8 February 1919.

8. *Newsletter*, 4 February 1919.

9. For a more detailed account of the strike see article by the author in the *Northern Star*, No.3, Peoples Democracy, Belfast 1971.

10. Figures from A.Wilson, *PR Urban Elections in Ulster 1920*, Electoral Reform Society, London 1972. Reprint.

11. *ibid.*

12. William Grant MP: 'The Hon. Member knows very well that I voted against that unofficial strike and that when it took place my trade union asked me, though I was opposed to the strike, to go on the negotiating committee in order to try to secure a return of the men to work.' Parliament of Northern Ireland, *Parliamentary Debates: Official Report* (Hansard) *House of Commons*, Vol.27, Col.955, 30 March 1944.

13. James Baird in a letter to the *Northern Whig*, 6 February 1919.

14. Northern Ireland Parliamentary Debates (Hansard) House of Commons, *op cit*, Vol.6, Col.39.

15. *ibid*, Vol.6, Col.268.

16. *ibid*, Vol.6, Cols.276-7.

17. *ibid*, Vol.7, Col.43.

18. *ibid*, Vol.7, Col.29.

19. *ibid*, Vol.7, Col.534.

20. *ibid*, Vol.7, Col.541.

21. *ibid*, Vol.8, Cols.40-52.

22. *ibid*, Vol.10, Cols.1365-6.

23. *ibid*, Vol.8, Col.4129.

24. *ibid*, Vol.8, Col.2276.

25. Basil McGuckin, MP for Co.Derry and a wealthy barrister, had moved to Dublin and dropped out of politics.

26. *Irish News*, 30 July 1928.

27. *ibid*, 29 May 1928.

28. *ibid*, 30 July 1928.

29. Pottinger had a substantial Catholic minority concentrated in the Short Strand ghetto. Beattie got almost all the Catholic votes plus those of some of the more radical Protestants. The other seats where Labour did well in 1929 were similar: Oldpark contained the Ardoyne and Bone ghettos; Dock contained the Catholic New Lodge Road.

30. Information from a member of the deputation.

31. *Irish News*, 21 May 1929.

32. *ibid*, 13 May 1929.

33. St.John Ervine, *Craigavon, Ulsterman*, Allen & Unwin, London 1949, p.519.

34. Northern Ireland Parliamentary Debates (Hansard) House of Commons, *op cit*, Vol.12, Cols.107-8.

35. *ibid*, Vol.12, Col.71.

36. *ibid*, Vol.14, Col.103.

37. *ibid*, Vol.14, Cols.44-5.

38. *Irish News*, 7 November 1932.

39. *ibid*.

6. The Violent Thirties

1. Parliament of Northern Ireland, *Parliamentary Debates: Official Reports* (Hansard) *House of Commons* Vol.6, Col.1751.

2. *ibid*, Vol.6, Col.1085.

3. *ibid*, Vol.6, Cols.1140-1.

4. *ibid*, Vol.6, Col.1133.

5. *Newsletter*, 26 November 1926.

6. *ibid*, 2 November 1926.

7. Babington (Un), 18,857, Ald.G.Donaldson (Lab), 8,856.

8. The actual number of persons involved was smaller as a person could make more than one application.

9. *Newsletter*, 10 October 1932.

10. 'Tick' was a system of buying by weekly instalments which included high interest rates. Since few working-class families could save on their miserable wages, nearly everything they owned was bought on 'tick' and the 'tick-man' or instalment collector was a constant – and detested – feature of working-class life. The 'tick' business made no allowances for the depression or widespread unemployment.

11. Interview with Murtagh Morgan.

12. *Newsletter*, 5 October 1932.

13. Cage cars were armoured open trucks with wire cages at the back to ward off missiles and grenades.

14. *Newsletter*, 8 October 1932.

15. *ibid*, 11 October 1932.

16. *ibid*.

17. *ibid*, 17 October 1932.

18. When De Valera entered the Dail at the head of his new Fianna Fail party in 1927 the IRA gradually moved to the left. Under the influence of left-wing activists such as Peadar O'Donnell local IRA units became involved in agitation against land annuities in the countryside and in strikes and social agitation in the towns. Eventually in 1931 the IRA leadership launched a new leftist party called Saor Eire with a very radical programme. IRA units and Saor Eire worked closely with the Revolutionary Workers' Groups. The new radicalism sat uneasily on the militarists and 'physical force' men however, and in 1934 O'Donnell and other leftwingers were expelled when they organised a Republican Congress in an attempt to unite all the Republican and radical forces in the country.

19. *Newsletter*, 13 October 1932.

20. *ibid*.

21. *ibid*.

22. *ibid*, 17 October 1932.

23. *ibid*, 15 October 1932.

24. London, Midland and Scottish Railway Company.

25. Great Northern Railway Company. The GNR operated on both sides of the border, running the Belfast-Dublin rail service. It also ran bus services and freight lorries.

26. *Newsletter*, 13 February 1933.

27. *ibid*, 3 March 1933.

28. *ibid*, 21 March 1933.

29. *ibid*, 25 March 1933.

30. The RWG as marxists were strongly against partition as a product of imperialism and were in favour of a united socialist Ireland.

31. *Newsletter*, 5 April 1933.

32. *ibid*, 13 July 1932.

33. *ibid*, 13 July 1933.

34. *Northern Whig*, 28 August 1933.

35. Northern Ireland Parliamentary Debates (Hansard) House of Commons, *op cit*, Vol.16, Col.1095.

36. Fred Heatley, *St Joseph's Centenary 1872-1972: Story of a Dockside Parish*, Irish News Ltd, Belfast 1972, p.28.

37. *Newsletter*, 24 June 1935.

38. 'Ultach', 'The Real Case Against Partition', in *Capuchin Annual 1943*, Dublin 1943, p.298.

39. Detailed figures given in a memorandum concerning the 1935 riots, prepared by a Catholic Committee and privately circulated to British MPs, Belfast 1935.

40. *Capuchin Annual 1943, op cit*, p.299.

41. *ibid*, p.298.

42. Quoted in the Catholic Committee memorandum, *op cit.*

43. *Manchester Guardian*, 13 July 1935.

44. *Newsletter*, 14 July 1936.

45. T.J.Campbell MP, 'Pogroms 1857-1935', in *Capuchin Annual 1943, op cit*, pp.465-7.

46. *ibid.*

47. *Irish News*, 27 November 1933.

48. Northern Ireland Parliamentary Debates (Hansard) House of Commons, *op cit*, Vol.16, Col.1078.

49. Now a resident magistrate in Northern Ireland.

50. Quoted by David Kennedy, 'Catholics in Northern Ireland', in Francis MacManus (ed) *The Years of the Great Test 1926-39*. Mercier Press, Cork 1967, p.145.

51. *Irish News*, 28 January 1938.

52. *ibid.*

53. *ibid*, 10 September 1936.

54. The figures were: G.A.Clark (Un) 3,578, J.Collins (Nat) 2,891 and H.Midgley (Lab) 1,923. Midgley, who was becoming steadily more Unionist in his views, had made no effort to condemn the sectarian activities of the Ulster Protestant League (UPL) and the steady build-up of anti-Catholic attacks in his constituency, which included the York Road/North Queen Street area. He refused pleas to intervene on behalf of Catholic workers intimidated out of factories and at the height of the 1935 riots he conveniently went away on holiday.

55. When Fianna Fail came to power in 1932 they had refused to pay the land annuities, amounting to £4 million, to Britain. These were annual instalments payable by farmers who were buying out their land under the various Land Acts brought in by the British administration before 1922. Britain retaliated by putting special tariffs on Irish produce and an 'economic war' began which was only finally settled by a trade agreement in April 1938.

56. J.F.Harbinson, *The Ulster Unionist Party 1882-1973*, p.221.

7. The War Years: 1939-45

1. Quoted in T.P.Coogan, *The IRA*, Fontana, London 1971, pp.164-5.

2. Joseph T. Carroll, *Ireland in the War Years*, David & Charles, Newton Abbot 1975, pp.96 and 104.

3. *Newsletter*, 22 May 1940.

4. By this time the name had been changed to Ulster Home Guard.

5. Parliament of Northern Ireland, *Parliamentary Debates: Official Report* (Hansard) *House of Commons* Vol.23, Col.1272.

6. *ibid*, Vol.23, Col.2155.

7. St.John Ervine, *Craigavon, Ulsterman*, Allen & Unwin, London 1949, p.562.

8. Northern Ireland Parliamentary Debates (Hansard) House of Commons, *op cit*, Vol.24, Cols.828-9.

9. H.Midgley (Lab) 7,209, T.R.Lavery (Un) 2,435.

10. J.Beattie (Lab) 19,936, Knox Cunningham (Un) 14,426, W.Wilton (Ind Un) 7,551, H.Corvin (Nat) 1,250.

11. *Newsletter*, 13 February 1943.

12. *ibid*, 17 April 1943.

13. *ibid*.

14. Later Lord Chief Justice of Northern Ireland.

15. Sir Arthur Hezlet, *The B Specials*, Tom Stacey, London 1972, p.138.

16. Carroll, *op cit*, p.111.

17. Quoted in *Newsletter*, 3 October 1942.

18. *Newsletter*, 3 September 1942.

19. *Discrimination: a study in Injustice to a Minority* Mansion House Anti-Partition Conference, Dublin 1949. (See below, Chapter 8, 197)

20. Northern Ireland Parliamentary Debates (Hansard) House of Commons, *op cit*, Vol.28, Col.83.

21. *Irish News*, 4 November 1942.

22. E.Donnelly 4,595, Dr G. McGouran 1,971, John Glass (Lab) 1,821.

23. Short and Harland Ltd, a joint enterprise of Harland and Wolff and Short Brothers, an English firm, opened an aircraft factory in Belfast in 1937. During the war they employed some 14,000 workers and specialised in producing Stirling bombers and Sunderland flying boats.

24. *Newsletter*, 15 October 1942.

25. *ibid*, 12 October 1942.

26. Northern Ireland Parliamentary Debates (Hansard) House of Commons, *op cit*, Vol.27, Col.1047.

27. *Newsletter*, 22 March 1944.

28. *ibid*, 4 April 1944.

29. Quoted in F.S.Lyons, *Ireland since the Famine*, Weidenfeld and Nicolson, London 1971, pp.728-9.

30. Quoted in Coogan, *The IRA, op cit*, p.261.

8. The Anti-Partition League: 1945-51

1. H. Diamond (Soc.Rep.) 5,016, Cllr.J.Collins (Lab.) 3,912, J.A.McGlade (Nat.) 2,766. The Socialist Republican Party had been set up in 1944 by a group of ex-Republicans and some Protestant trade unionists. Its leading personality after Diamond was Victor Halley, a Protestant union official. Diamond had been a Nationalist councillor in the 1930s and an engineering shop steward during the war. The party was militantly anti-partitionist but only mildly leftist in policy.

2. M.Conlon (Nat.) 6,720, P.Agnew (Lab.) 4,143.

3. *Irish News*, 9 June 1945.

4. *ibid*, 22 August 1945.

5. *ibid*, 15 November 1945.

6. F.Hanna (Lab.) 5,566, V.Halley (Soc.Rep.) 2,783.

7. Parliament of Northern Ireland, *Parliamentary Debates: Official Report* (Hansard) *House of Commons*, Vol.30, Col.2164.

8. See Chapter 4 above, p.85-86.

9. *Newsletter*, 14 February 1947.

10. Sean T. O'Kelly (Fianna Fail) 537,965, Sean McEoin (Fine Gael) 335,539, Dr P.McCartan (Ind.) 212,834.

11. Parliament of the United Kingdom, *Parliamentary Debates: Official Report* (Hansard) *House of Commons*, Vol.457, Col.239.

12. *Belfast Telegraph*, 21 January 1949.

13. *Belfast Telegraph*, 24 January 1949.

14. *ibid*, 27 January 1949.

15. *Irish Times*, 29 January 1949.

16. *Manchester Guardian*, 30 January 1949.

17. *Irish News*, 8 February 1949.

18. *ibid*, 27 January 1949.

19. *Belfast Telegraph*, 2 February 1949.

20. *ibid*, 8 February 1949.

21. *ibid*, 20 January 1949.

22. Lambeg drums are a traditional Orange instrument. They are enormous tuneless drums beaten with canes rather than drumsticks, and are very noisy.

23. *Belfast Telegraph*, 9 February 1949.

24. *ibid*, 8 February 1949.

25. *ibid*, 26 October 1946.

26. There had been a single all-Ireland Communist Party from 1933 to 1941. When Hitler invaded Russia the Northern section began to support the war effort while the Southern one continued to support Southern neutrality. Because of this and because of declining membership the Southern section disbanded itself. It was reformed as the Irish Workers' League in 1948 and the two sections were not re-united until 1970.

27. Later to become an extreme right-wing Labour MP.

28. *Newsletter*, 27 September 1947.

29. *Belfast Telegraph*, 20 September 1948.

30. *ibid*.

31. *ibid*.

32. A similar move for similar reasons was attempted in 1970.

33. *Belfast Telegraph*, 31 January 1949.

34. *ibid*, 7 February 1949.

35. John F. Harbinson, 'A History of the Northern Ireland Labour Party 1891-1949'. M.Sc. (Econ.) thesis, Queen's University Belfast, 1966, Chapter 8.

36. McManaway (Un) 33,917, Beattie (Lab) 30,539, J. Steele (SF) 1,482.

37. See above, Chapter 4, p.89.

38. Northern Ireland Parliamentary Debates (Hansard) House of Commons, *op cit*, Vol.33, Col.1379.

39. Much of its propaganda was written by a young civil servant in the Department of External Affairs called Conor Cruise O'Brien. He is now a Minister in the Fine Gael/Labour Coalition government and has drastically changed his views. In June 1974 he declared that he was not actively working for Irish unity and said 'I believe that you are not helping the situation by talking about a unity that is so strongly rejected by a majority of people in the North Both persuasion and force are hopeless'. *Irish Times*, 15 June 1974.

40. Northern Ireland Parliamentary Debates (Hansard) House of Commons, *op cit*, Vol.32, Col.488.
41. *ibid*, Vol.32, Col.492.
42. *ibid*, Vol.35, Col.2071.
43. *ibid*, Vol.33, Col.1376.

9. The Fifties Campaign

1. Edward McAteer, *Irish Action*, Derry [c.1950].
2. Parliament of Northern Ireland, *Parliamentary Debates: Official Report* (Hansard) *House of Commons*, Vol.37, Col.1320.
3. *Irish News*, 21 November 1953.
4. *ibid*, 5 December 1953.
5. *ibid*, 7 December 1953.
6. Northern Ireland Parliamentary Debates (Hansard) House of Commons, *op cit*, Vol.36, Col.2251.
7. *Belfast Telegraph*, 16 April 1954.
8. Mid-Ulster: Tom Mitchell (Rep.) 29,737, C. Beattie (Un.) 29,477.
Fermanagh-South Tyrone: Phil Clarke (Rep.) 30,529, Lieut.Col.R.Grosvenor (Un.) 30,268.
9. *Belfast Telegraph*, 8 May 1956.
10. Coogan, *The IRA*, Fontana, London 1971, p.367.
11. *ibid*, p.361.
12. F.S.L.Lyons, *Ireland Since the Famine*, Weidenfeld and Nicolson, London 1971, p.749.
13. *Irish Times*, 14 May 1956.
14. Quoted in Sir Arthur Hezlet, *The B Specials,* Tom Stacey, London 1972, p.162.
15. Parliament of the United Kingdom, *Parliamentary Debates: Official Report* (Hansard) *House of Commons*, Vol.562, Col.1270.
16. Mallon later became a prominent figure in the Provisional IRA, leading their units in the border areas in a very successful campaign in 1972-73 until arrested and jailed in the South. He was one of the three Provisional IRA leaders who escaped from Dublin's Mountjoy jail in a helicopter in November 1973 and again from Portlaois jail in August 1974.
17. Northern Ireland Parliamentary Debates (Hansard) House of Commons, *op cit*, Vol.41, Cols.17-18.
18. Coogan, *op cit*, p.384.
19. J. Bowyer Bell, *The Secret Army: a History of the IRA 1916-70*, Sphere Books, London 1972, pp.394-5.
20. *Portadown Times*, 15 February 1957.
21. *Belfast Telegraph*, 14 March 1958.
22. Clifton: R.Kinahan (Un.) 5,755, N.Porter (Ind.Un.) 5,710.
23. *Irish News*, 10 November 1959.
24. J.F.Harbinson, *The Ulster Unionist Party 1882-1973*, Blackstaff Press, Belfast 1973, p.44.
25. *ibid*, p.76.
26. *Irish News*, 14 October 1953.
27. Mrs P.McLoughlin (Un.) 34,191, Jack Beattie (Irish Lab.) 16,050, Eamon Boyce (Rep.) 8,447.

28. Woodvale: W.Boyd (NILP), 7,529, N.Martin (Un.) 7,449.

Victoria: D.W.Bleakley (NILP) 7,487, Capt.Henderson (Un.) 7,340.

29. Northern Ireland Parliamentary Debates (Hansard) House of Commons, *op cit*, Vol.42, Col.1864.

10. The Rise and Fall of Terence O'Neill: 1960-69

1. Report of the Joint Working Party on the Economy of Northern Ireland (Hall Report), HMSO London, October 1962, Cmnd.1835, Appendix 2.

2. General Register Office, Northern Ireland: Census of Population 1961. *General Report.* HMSO, Belfast 1965, Table 7.

3. Hall Report, *op cit,* p.27.

4. *Newsletter,* 6 March 1961.

5. Oldpark 3404; Woodvale 2157; Pottinger 1852; Victoria 1214.

6. Though the majority of unions in the North were still British-based, almost all were also affiliated to the Dublin-based Irish Congress of Trade Unions. By agreement with the British TUC the Irish Congress co-ordinated union policy and dealt with economic issues in the North.

7. The Control of Manufactures Act was introduced by the first Fianna Fail government in 1932 in an attempt to keep control of the Irish economy in the hands of Irish capitalists. It provided that a majority shareholding in any new company established in the South should be in Irish hands. By 1958 Irish native capitalism's potential for expansion was exhausted and the Act was hindering the drive to attract foreign capital.

8. *Newsletter,* 15 January 1965.

9. Parliament of Northern Ireland, *Parliamentary Debates: Official Report* (Hansard) *House of Commons,* Vol.59, Col.254, 3 February 1965.

10. David Boulton, *The UVF 1966-73,* Gill and Macmillan, Torc Books, Dublin 1973, p.29. Sharp rises in unemployment seriously affecting the Protestant working-class were regularly accompanied by a growth of sectarian organisations. The Ulster Protestant League was founded in 1931 just as the depression was starting to bite home. Norman Porter's National Union of Protestants was very active in 1952-53 when there was a serious recession in the linen industry, and Porter himself was elected to Stormont in 1953.

11. *Newsletter,* 2 October 1964.

12. Kilfedder 21,337, Diamond 14,678, Boyd 12,571, McMillen 3,256.

13. *Newsletter,* 3 October 1964.

14. *ibid,* 16 March 1966.

15. Quoted in Boulton, *op cit,* p.40.

16. *ibid,* p.51.

17. *Newsletter,* 28 September 1966.

18. Terence O'Neill. *Autobiography,* Hart-Davis, London 1972, p.47.

19. *ibid,* p.137.

20. F.W.Boal, P.Doherty, D.G.Pringle, *The Spatial Distribution of Some Social Problems in the Belfast Area,* Northern Ireland Community Relations Commission, Belfast 1974, p.15.

21. See above, Chapter 4, p.92.

22. J.J.Campbell, *Catholic Schools: a Survey of a Northern Ireland Problem,* Fallon's Educational Supply Co, Belfast 1964, p.24.

23. *Belfast Telegraph*, 30 September 1967.

24. A Catholic voluntary hospital in Belfast which got no assistance from the government.

25. *Irish News*, 3 July 1967.

26. G.Fitt (Republican Labour) 26,292, J.Kilfedder (Un.) 24,281.

27. Later Minister of State for Northern Ireland 1974 – when he administered internment which he had denounced as a member of the CDU.

28. From this period on the author was actively involved in many of the events described, first as a member of the Young Socialists, then of the Peoples Democracy, and later as an executive committee member of NICRA and the Northern Resistance Movement. I have been a member of the Peoples Democracy throughout.

29. The Apprentice Boys were particularly strong in Derry since they were named after the thirteen apprentices who shut the city's gates against King James in 1688 and started the Siege of Derry.

30. I was one of them and it helped to shift my politics several degrees further to the left.

31. John Hume was a local school teacher who had been one of the leading figures in the campaign to have the North's second university sited in Derry, and he was actively involved in the local Credit Union and Co-operative movements. Ivan Cooper was a young Protestant factory manager in Derry. He had been a prominent member of Derry Young Unionists but had joined the NILP in 1967.

32. O'Neill, *op cit*, p.148.

33. Sunday Times Insight Team, *Ulster*, Penguin, Harmondsworth 1972, p.66.

34. B.Egan and V.McCormack. *Burntollet*, LRS Publishers, London 1969, p.60.

35. O'Neill, *op cit*, p.151.

36. The twelve were: A.Anderson (Derry City), A.Ardill (C.Fergus), D.Boal (Shankill), J.Brooke (Lisnaskea), J.Burns (N.Derry), J.Dobson (W.Down), W.Craig (Larne), W.Hinds (Willowfield), T.Lyons (N.Tyrone), J.McQuade (Woodvale), J.Taylor (S.Tyrone), H.West (Enniskillen).

37. T.O'Neill (Un.) 7,745, I.Paisley (Prot.Un.) 6,331, M.Farrell (PD) 2,310.

38. B.Devlin (Unity) 33,648, Mrs Anna Forrest (Un) 29,437.

39. *Belfast Telegraph*, 5 May 1969.

11. The Drift to Disaster: 1969-71

1. Quoted in J.F.Harbinson, *The Ulster Unionist Party 1882-1973*, Blackstaff Press, Belfast 1973, p.154.

2. Quoted in *Violence and Civil Disturbances in Northern Ireland in 1969*, Report of the Tribunal of Enquiry (Scarman Report), Cmd.566. HMSO, Belfast 1972. Vol.2, Appendix A(vii).

3. *ibid*, Appendix A(i).

4. *ibid*, Part 12, Chapter 31, Section 6.

5. Haughey was re-appointed to the Fianna Fail front bench early in 1975 and is now a strong contender to succeed Lynch who has been largely discredited by electoral defeats.

6. *An Phoblacht* (Provisional Sinn Fein paper), Dublin, Vol.1, No.1, February 1970.

7. *An Phoblacht*, Vol.1, No.3, April 1970.

8. It led to a further split in the Officials in December 1974 when a large number of members left in protest at the leadership's lack of emphasis on the Northern question, and established the Irish Republican Socialist Party.

9. The group of twelve Unionist backbenchers who met in Portadown in February 1969 to call for O'Neill's resignation.

10. Bannside: Paisley (Prot.Un.) 7,981; Minford (Un.), 6,778; McHugh (NILP) 3,514.

South Antrim: W.Beattie (Prot.Un.) 7,137; W.Morgan (Un.) 6,179; Corkey (Ind.) 5,212; A.Whitby (NILP) 1,773.

11. The 'Little Twelfth' was an annual Orange festival, about a fortnight before 12 July, when local Orange parades were held all over Belfast.

12. *Newsletter*, 13 July 1970.

13. Saor Eire was a small leftist Republican group who had staged a number of bank robberies, in one of which a Garda had been killed.

14. Quoted in Henry Kelly *How Stormont Fell*, Gill and Macmillan, Dublin 1972, p.13.

15. *ibid*, p.40.

16. *ibid*, p.51.

17. Kelly, *op cit*, p.55.

12. The Day of Reckoning: 1971-75

1. After the election of Bernadette Devlin for Mid-Ulster in 1969 a single anti-Unionist candidate had been agreed on for Fermanagh-South Tyrone in the 1970 Westminster election as well, and he too was successful. The new MP was Frank McManus, a Fermanagh school teacher and former chairman of the Fermanagh Civil Rights Association. His brother Pat McManus, who had been the IRA commander in Fermanagh in the fifties campaign, had been killed in an explosion in 1958. McManus was more militant than the SDLP and was sympathetic to the Provos.

2. *Newsletter*, 9 September 1971.

3. And are continuing to do so. Between 1969 and 1974 the Northern Ireland and UK governments paid out a total of £64 million to the shipyard. *Northern Ireland, Finance and the Economy*, Discussion paper, Northern Ireland Office, HMSO, London 1974. In March 1975 the British government decided to take over Harland and Wolff's and pay off prospective losses up to 1978 estimated at £60 million.

4. *Newsletter*, 14 February 1972.

5. Quoted in Martin Dillon and Denis Lehane, *Political Murder in Northern Ireland*, Penguin, Harmondsworth 1973, p.56.

6. Quoted in Kelly, *op cit*, pp.125-6. One of the most extraordinary aspects of this period was the sympathetic interviewing of the most sectarian and bloodthirsty Loyalists on Radio/Telefis Eireann.

7. *Newsletter*, 20 March 1972.

8. *ibid*, 28 April 1972. **9.** 'Andrew Sefton', article in *Monday World*, magazine of the Monday Club. Quoted in *Irish Times*, 4 September 1974.

10. *The Future of Northern Ireland*. Discussion paper, Northern Ireland Office, HMSO, London 1972, pp.33-4.

11. The Peoples Democracy had steadily evolved since 1968 from a loose student

activist group into a disciplined marxist organisation, which almost alone on the
Irish left gave critical support to the Provisionals' campaign.

12. Encouraged by opposition politicians such as Austin Currie, quite a few
Catholics had joined the UDR when it was first established and in 1970 20 per
cent of its members were Catholics. Most of them left when internment was
introduced.

13. They were not held very long however. All Loyalist internees were released
by April 1975, when there were still over 350 Republicans interned, some of
them held since 1971.

14. *Northern Ireland Constitutional Proposals,* Cmnd.5259, HMSO London, March
1973.

15. These had replaced some 72 borough, urban and rural councils under a local
government reform scheme.

16. Quoted in Dillon and Lehane, *op cit,* p.216.

17. *ibid,* p.286.

18. *ibid,* p.281.

19. Internment of women had begun in January 1973 though the number
interned had never been more than twenty. It had been confined to Republican
women. In the summer of 1973 a number of schoolboys, one only 15 years old,
had also been interned.

20. The marches were held in Loyalist East Belfast. The ICTU made no effort to
mobilise the Catholic workers, who were only too willing to work.

21. *Newsletter,* 17 May 1974.

22. By the end of the year (1974) Bradford, a former O'Neillite who had once
flirted with the idea of Irish unity, had joined the UUUC.

23. *Irish Times,* 4 September 1974.

24. *ibid,* 14 June 1974.

25. *ibid,* 27 June 1974.

26. One of the ten UUUC MPs elected was Enoch Powell, a former spokesman of
the extreme rightwing of the British Conservative Party and a strong supporter
of the Loyalist cause.

Postscript: June 1975

1. Rees had released the last Loyalist internees by April despite an escalating
campaign of sectarian murders.

2. *Irish Times,* 26 March 1975.

3. *ibid.*

4. A leftist Republican group made up mainly of former members of the Official
Republicans, who broke away because of the Officials' growing reformism and
neglect of the national question. Its leading members are Seamus Costello, a
former Ard Comhairle (executive committee) member of Official Sinn Fein, and
Bernadette McAliskey (formerly Devlin). The political position of the IRSP is
still unclear as the Officials tried to smash it soon after its formation in December
1974, and both groups have been involved in a bitter internecine feud ever since.
The feud has claimed five lives so far, including that of Liam McMillen, Belfast
commander of the Official IRA.

5. *Irish Times,* 9 May 1975.

Conclusions

1. Dorothy McArdle, *The Irish Republic*, Gollancz, London 1937, p.181.

2. By May 1975 a total of £103,500,000 had been paid by government in compensation claims for bomb damage, injuries, etc, for the period since 1969 and there was another £44 million in the pipeline. (*Sunday Independent*, 11 May 1975.) This was only one item in the bill for the campaign.

3. *Northern Ireland, Finance and the Economy.* Discussion paper. Northern Ireland Office, HMSO, London 1974.

4. Headquarters of the British administration in Ireland before 1921.

5. D.R.Lysaght, *The Republic of Ireland*, Mercier Press, Cork 1970, p.185.

6. John Palmer, 'The Gombeen Republic', in *International Socialism*, No.51, April/June, 1972.

7. The parliament buildings in Dublin.

Bibliography

General

J.C.Beckett, *The Making of Modern Ireland, 1603-1923*, Faber and Faber, London 1969.

J.C.Beckett and R.E.Glasscock, eds. *Belfast: The Origin and Growth of an Industrial City*, BBC, London 1967. Series of talks on BBC Northern Ireland Radio.

J.C.Beckett and T.W.Moody, eds. *Ulster Since 1800*. Vol.1, *A Political and Economic Survey*; Vol.2, *A Social Survey*, BBC, London 1955 and 1957. Series of talks on BBC Northern Ireland Radio.

J. Bowyer Bell, *The Secret Army: A History of the IRA 1916-70*, Sphere, London 1972.

Andrew Boyd, *Holy War in Belfast*, Anvil Books, Tralee, Co.Kerry 1969. Account of sectarian riots in Belfast in nineteenth century.

Andrew Boyd, *The Rise of the Irish Trade Unions 1729-1970*, Anvil Books, Tralee, Co.Kerry 1972.

I.Budge and C.O'Leary, *Belfast, Approach to Crisis: Study of Belfast Politics 1613-1970*, Macmillan, London 1973.

T.J.Campbell, *Fifty Years of Ulster 1890-1940*, *Irish News*, Belfast 1941. Collection of reminiscences and anecdotes by a Northern Nationalist MP.

W.E.Coe, *The Engineering Industry of the North of Ireland*, David and Charles, Newton Abbot 1969.

Communist Party of Ireland, *Outline History*, New Book Publications, Dublin 1975. Overall history of communist movement in the South plus accounts of Belfast ODR strike (1932) and Communist Party in the North in war years and after.

Tim Pat Coogan, *The IRA*, Fontana, London 1971.

Tim Pat Coogan, *Ireland since the Rising*, Pall Mall Press, London 1966.

L.M.Cullen, *An Economic History of Ireland since 1660*, Batsford, London 1972.

Liam de Paor, *Divided Ulster*, Penguin, Harmondsworth 1970. A brief history of the Ulster problem from a radical viewpoint.

Rev M.W.Dewar, Rev John Brown and Rev S.E.Long, *Orangeism: a New Historical Appreciation 1688-1967*, Orange Order, Belfast 1967.

Sydney Elliott, *Northern Ireland Parliamentary Election Results 1921-72*, Political Reference Publications, Chichester 1973.

St.John Ervine, *Craigavon, Ulsterman*, Allen and Unwin, London 1949. Biography of Sir James Craig, Northern Ireland Premier 1921-40. Fiercely partisan on Unionist side.

Frank Gallagher, *The Indivisible Island: The History of the Partition of Ireland*, Gollancz, London 1957. Strongly anti-Unionist.

John Harbinson, 'A History of the Northern Ireland Labour Party 1891-1949', M.Sc(Econ) thesis, Queen's University, Belfast 1966.

John Harbinson, *The Ulster Unionist Party 1882-1973: its Development and Organisation*, Blackstaff Press, Belfast 1973.

Emrys Jones, *A Social Geography of Belfast*, Oxford University Press, 1960.

F.S.L.Lyons, *Ireland Since the Famine: 1850 to the Present*, Weidenfeld and Nicolson, London 1971.

D.R.O'Connor Lysaght, *The Republic of Ireland*, Mercier Press, Cork 1970. Sketch of economic, social and political background of Southern state from marxist viewpoint.

F.J.Whitford, 'Joseph Devlin, Ulsterman and Irishman', MA (external) thesis London University, September 1939. Political biography of the Northern Nationalist leader. Concentrates on the pre-1922 period.

1900-1923.

Piaras Beaslai, *Michael Collins and the Making of a New Ireland*, 2 Vols, Phoenix Publishing Co, Dublin 1926.

John Boyle, ed. *Leaders and Workers*, Mercier Press, Cork 1964. Portraits of Irish labour leaders pre-1916.

Patrick Buckland, *Irish Unionism*, Vol.1: *The Anglo-Irish and the New Ireland 1885-1922*; Vol.2: *Ulster Unionism and the Origins of Northern Ireland, 1886-1922*, Gill and Macmillan, Dublin 1973.

Patrick Buckland, *Irish Unionism 1885-1923: A Documentary History*, Northern Ireland Public Record Office. HMSO, Belfast 1973.

Major-General Sir C.E.Calwell, *Field-Marshall Sir Henry Wilson: His Life and Diaries*, 2 Vols, Cassell, London 1927.

Wallace Clark, *Guns in Ulster: A History of the B Special Constabulary in part of Co.Derry,* (RUC) Constabulary Gazette, Belfast 1967.

J. Dunsmore Clarkson, *Labour and Nationalism in Ireland,* Columbia University Press, New York 1925. Detailed study of Irish trade union and labour movement, eighteenth century to 1925.

Ian Colvin and E.Marjoribanks, *Life of Lord Carson,* 3 Vols, Gollancz, London 1932-36.

James Connolly, *The Workers' Republic,* The Sign of the Three Candles, Dublin 1970. Collection of articles by Irish marxist revolutionary executed after 1916 Rising. Introduction by William McMullen describing his work with Connolly in Belfast pre-First World War.

Mervyn Dane, *The Fermanagh B Specials,* William Trimble Ltd, Enniskillen 1970.

P. Beresford Ellis, *A History of the Irish Working Class,* Gollancz, London 1972. Sketch of Irish history from earliest times to present day from radical viewpoint.

C.D.Greaves, *The Life and Times of James Connolly,* Lawrence and Wishart, London 1961.

Sir Arthur Hezlet, *The B Specials: A History of the Ulster Special Constabulary,* Tom Stacey, London 1972.

H. Montgomery Hyde, *Carson,* Heinemann, London 1953. Biography by former Unionist MP.

Thomas Jones, *Whitehall Diary.* Vol.3: *Ireland 1918–25,* ed. Keith Middlemas, Oxford University Press, 1971. Extracts from diary and letters of deputy secretary to British Cabinet during War of Independence, Treaty negotiations and Boundary Commission crisis.

G.B.Kenna, *Facts and Figures of the Belfast Pogrom 1920-22,* O'Connell Publishing Co, Dublin 1922. Detailed account of the disturbances in Belfast written by Catholic priest under a pseudonym. Contains list of casualties. Printed but never published. Only a few copies still in existence.

Emmet Larkin, *James Larkin, Irish Labour Leader, 1876-1947,* Routledge and Kegan Paul, London 1965.

Dorothy McArdle, *The Irish Republic: A Documented Chronicle of the Anglo-Irish Conflict and the Partitioning of Ireland,* Gollancz, London 1937; Corgi, London 1968. Preface by Eamon De Valera. The most detailed history of the period 1916-23, written from strongly Republican viewpoint.

Eoin Neeson, *The Civil War in Ireland, 1922-23,* Mercier Press, Cork 1966.

A.T.Q.Stewart, *The Ulster Crisis*, Faber and Faber, London 1967. Account of formation of the UVF and of Larne gun-running in 1914.

Carlton Younger, *A State of Disunion*, Fontana, London 1972. Profiles of Sir James Craig, De Valera, Michael Collins and Arthur Griffith.

1923-68

D.P.Barritt and C.F.Carter, *The Northern Ireland Problem: A Study in Group Relations*, Oxford University Press, 1962. Anodyne book by two Quakers.

J.W.Blake, *Northern Ireland in the Second World War*, HMSO, Belfast 1956. Official history.

J.J.Campbell, *Catholic Schools: A Survey of a Northern Ireland Problem*, Fallons Educational Supply Co, Belfast 1964.

Joseph T. Carroll, *Ireland in the War Years*, David and Charles, Newton Abbot 1975.

Rev William Corkey, *Episode in the History of Protestant Ulster 1923-47: The Story of the Struggle of the Protestant Community to Maintain Bible Instruction in their Schools*, Dorman and Sons, Belfast 1965.

G.C.Duggan, *Northern Ireland – Success or Failure?* Irish Times, Dublin 1950. Reprint of articles in *Irish Times* by former Northern Ireland Comptroller and Auditor General.

George Gilmore, *The Republican Congress 1934*, Dochas Co-operative Society, Dublin 1968. Brief account by one of the organisers.

Irish Boundary Commission: Report, Irish Universities Press, Shannon 1969. Hitherto unpublished report of the Commission with introduction by Geoffrey J. Hand.

K.S.Isles and N.Cuthbert, *An Economic Survey of Northern Ireland*, HMSO, Belfast 1957.

R.J.Lawrence, *The Government of Northern Ireland: Public Finance and Public Services 1921-1964*, Oxford University Press, 1965.

Francis MacManus, ed. *The Years of the Great Test, 1926-39*, Mercier Press, Cork 1967. Series of talks on political, social and economic life in Ireland. First broadcast on Radio Eireann, the Southern radio station. Two chapters on the North.

Patrick F. Magill, 'The Senate in Northern Ireland 1921-62', PhD thesis, Queen's University, Belfast 1965. Dull study by former Nationalist Senator.

Maurice Manning, *The Blueshirts*, Gill and Macmillan, Dublin 1970. Study of General O'Duffy's fascist-style movement in the South in the 1930s.

N.S.Mansergh, *The Government of Northern Ireland*, Allen and Unwin, London 1936.

Arthur Mitchell, *Labour in Irish Politics, 1890-1930*, Irish University Press, Shannon 1974.

K.B.Nowlan and T.D.Williams, eds. *Ireland in the War Years and After, 1939-51*, Gill and Macmillan, Dublin 1969. Series of talks on Radio Eireann.

Donal O'Sullivan, *The Irish Free State and its Senate*, Faber and Faber, London 1940. Detailed history of Southern state 1921-37 with special emphasis on Senate. Strongly conservative, anti-Republican, anti-communist.

Enno Stephan, *Spies in Ireland*, MacDonald, London 1963. Account of activities of German spies in Ireland during Second World War.

J.H.Whyte, *Church and State in Modern Ireland, 1923-70*, Gill and Macmillan, Dublin 1971.

T.Wilson, ed. *Ulster Under Home Rule*, Oxford University Press, 1955.

1968-1975

Paul Arthur, *The Peoples Democracy, 1968-73*, Blackstaff Press, Belfast 1974. Somewhat hostile, academic, social science view.

David Bleakley, *Faulkner: Conflict and Consent in Irish Politics*, Mowbray's, London 1974. Sympathetic biography by former Labour MP who joined Faulkner's Cabinet in 1971.

David Boulton, *The UVF 1966-73: An Anatomy of Loyalist Rebellion*, Gill and Macmillan, Torc Books, Dublin 1973.

Andrew Boyd, *Brian Faulkner and the Crisis of Ulster Unionism*, Anvil Books, Tralee, Co.Kerry 1972. Hostile biography.

Richard Deutsch and Vivien Magowan, *Northern Ireland 1968-73: Chronology of Events*, Vol.1, *1968-71*; Vol.2, *1971-73*, Blackstaff Press, Belfast 1973 and 1974.

Bernadette Devlin, *The Price of My Soul*, Pan Books, London 1969. Part autobiography, part highly personal account of early Civil Rights movement.

Paddy Devlin, *The Fall of the Northern Ireland Executive*, the author, Belfast 1975. Scrappy account by one of its members.

Martin Dillon and Denis Lehane, *Political Murder in Northern Ireland*, Penguin, Harmondsworth 1973. Journalistic account of sectarian assassinations in Belfast. Sympathetic to Loyalists.

Owen Dudley Edwards, *The Sins of Our Fathers: Roots of Conflict in Northern Ireland*, Gill and Macmillan, Dublin 1970.

Bowes Egan and Vincent McCormack, *Burntollet*, LRS Publishers, London 1969. Account of Peoples Democracy march to Derry, January 1969.

Desmond Greaves, *The Irish Crisis*, Lawrence and Wishart, London 1972. Origins and background of current crisis from reformist democratic viewpoint.

Henry Kelly, *How Stormont Fell*, Gill and Macmillan, Dublin 1972.

James Kelly, *Orders for the Captain?* the author, Dublin 1971. Background to Southern arms smuggling trial 1970 by defendant, a former Irish Army intelligence officer.

Eamonn McCann, *War and an Irish Town*, Penguin, Harmondsworth 1974. Historical sketch of Northern Ireland problem plus personal account of events since 1968 especially in Derry. By prominent left-wing activist.

John McGuffin, *Internment*, Anvil Books, Tralee, Co.Kerry 1973. Internment in both parts of Ireland 1916-73. By former Peoples Democracy member who was interned himself in 1971.

John McGuffin, *The Guinea Pigs*, Penguin, Harmondsworth 1974. The British Army's use of sensory deprivation torture in Northern Ireland.

Maria Maguire, *To Take Arms: A Year in the Provisional IRA*, Macmillan, London 1973. Sensational account of flirtation with the Provisionals by young Dublin socialite.

Patrick Marrinan, *Paisley, Man of Wrath*, Anvil Books, Tralee, Co.Kerry 1973. Hostile biography.

Conor Cruise O'Brien, *States of Ireland*, Hutchinson, London 1972. Disjointed anecdotal book, part history, part autobiography, part reflections on current situation in North by a minister in the Dublin government. Vehemently anti-Republican and mildly pro-Unionist.

Terence O'Neill, *Autobiography*, Hart-Davis, London 1972. By former Northern Ireland Premier.

Richard Rose, *Government Without Consensus: An Irish Perspective*, Faber and Faber, London 1971. Social science study of Northern Ireland. Draws heavily on an opinion survey of 1967.

Russell Stetler, *The Battle of the Bogside: The Politics of Violence in Northern Ireland*, Sheed and Ward, London 1970.

Sunday Times Insight Team, *Ulster*, Penguin, Harmondsworth 1972.

Government Reports, White Papers, etc.
In chronological order

Census of Ireland 1911. Vol.3, *Province of Ulster and General Report,* HMSO, London 1912 and 1913, Cd.6051-I and Cd.6663.

Report of the Joint Working Party on the Economy of Northern Ireland (Hall Report), HMSO, London October 1962, Cmnd.1835.

Belfast Regional Survey and Plan: Recommendations and Conclusions (Matthew Report), HMSO, Belfast 1965, Cmd.451.

Economic Development in Northern Ireland (Wilson Report), HMSO, Belfast 1965, Cmd.479.

General Register Office, Northern Ireland, *Census of Population 1961: General Report,* HMSO, Belfast 1965.

Disturbances in Northern Ireland: Report of the Commission appointed by the Governor of Northern Ireland (Cameron Report). HMSO, Belfast, September 1969, Cmd.532. Enquiry into cause of civil rights protests, 1968-69.

Report of the Advisory Committee on Police in Northern Ireland (Hunt Report), HMSO, Belfast October 1969, Cmd.535.

Report of the Enquiry into Allegations against the Security Forces of Physical Brutality in Northern Ireland arising out of Events on 9th August 1971 (Compton Report), HMSO, London November 1971, Cmnd.4823. Report on internment arrests in 1971. Describes sensory deprivation torture as 'ill-treatment'.

Violence and Civil Disturbances in Northern Ireland in 1969: Report of Tribunal of Enquiry (Scarman Report), 2 Vols, HMSO, Belfast April 1972, Cmd.566.

The Future of Northern Ireland: A Paper for Discussion, Northern Ireland Office, HMSO, London 1972. British Green Paper. Guidelines for future government of Northern Ireland.

Report of the Commission to consider Legal Procedures to deal with Terrorist Activities in Northern Ireland (Diplock Report), HMSO, London December 1972, Cmnd.5185.

Report of the Tribunal appointed to Enquire into the Events on Sunday 30th January 1972 which led to Loss of Life in connection with the Procession in Londonderry on that day (Widgery Report), HMSO, London 1972, H.L.101/H.C.220. Enquiry into Bloody Sunday massacre.

Northern Ireland Constitutional Proposals, HMSO, London March 1973, Cmnd.5259. White Paper.

Northern Ireland, Finance and the Economy: Discussion Paper, Northern Ireland Office, HMSO, London 1974.

Report of a Committee to consider, in the Context of Civil Liberties and Human Rights, Measures to deal with Terrorism in Northern Ireland (Gardiner Report), HMSO, London January 1975, Cmnd.5847.

Articles and Pamphlets

Geoffrey Bing, *John Bull's Other Ireland*, Tribune Publications, London 1951. Strongly anti-Unionist pamphlet by Labour MP, member of the Friends of Ireland Group.

R.Black, F.Pinter, R.Overy, *Flight: A Report on Population Movement in Belfast, August 1971*, Northern Ireland Community Relations Commission, Belfast 1975.

F.W.Boal, P.Doherty, D.G.Pringle, *The Spatial Distribution of some Social Problems in the Belfast Urban Area*, Northern Ireland Community Relations Commission, Belfast 1974.

The Capuchin Annual 1943, published at 2 Capel Street, Dublin 1943. Annual magazine of Franciscan religious order, 1929 to date. *1943* was a special issue about the North. Strongly anti-Unionist. One article, 'The Real Case Against Partition' by 'Ultach', was reprinted as a pamphlet called *Orange Terror* and banned under the Special Powers Act in the North.

John Darby and Geoffrey Morris, *Intimidation in Housing*, Northern Ireland Community Relations Commission, Belfast 1974. Mainly about Belfast area 1971-72.

Eire Nua (New Ireland): The Social and Economic Programme of Sinn Fein, (Provisional) Sinn Fein, Dublin 1971.

Michael Farrell, *Struggle in the North*, Pluto Press, London 1969; Peoples Democracy, Belfast 1972. Brief socialist analysis of civil rights struggle 1968-69.

Michael Farrell, *Fascism and the Six Counties*, Peoples Democracy, Belfast 1974.

Michael Farrell, 'The Great Belfast Strike of 1919', in *Northern Star*, No.3, Peoples Democracy, Belfast 1971. Occasional PD journal.

Fermanagh Facts, Fermanagh Civil Rights Association, 1969. Details of discrimination against Catholics in Co.Fermanagh.

Gerry Foley, *Ireland in Rebellion and Problems of the Irish Revolution,* Pathfinder Press, New York 1971 and 1972. Essays sympathetic to official Republican movement by American marxist.

Freedom Struggle, Dublin 1973. Account of Northern struggle by Provisional IRA. Banned in the South.

C.D.Greaves, *The Irish Question and the British People,* Connolly Publications, London 1963. Strongly anti-partitionist study of Northern question.

Fred Heatley, *St Joseph's Centenary 1872-1972: Story of a Dockside Parish,* Irish News, Belfast 1972. Brief history of Catholic parish in Belfast much affected by riots and disturbances.

Irish Communist Organisation (later British and Irish Communist Organisation), *The Economics of Partition,* 1969, *The Two Irish Nations,* 1971, and other pamphlets, ICO Belfast. Militantly Republican in 1969, now extreme Unionist (1974). Their publications vary accordingly.

Tom Hadden and P.Hillyard, *Justice in Northern Ireland: A Study in Social Confidence,* Cobden Trust, London 1973.

D.R.O'Connor Lysaght, *The Making of Northern Ireland (and the basis of its undoing),* Citizens Committee, Dublin 1969. Brief historical sketch from marxist viewpoint.

Edward McAteer, *Irish Action,* Derry, [c.1950].

Mansion House Anti-Partition Conference, *One Vote Equals Two, Discrimination: A Study in Injustice to a Minority* and *Ireland's Right to Unity,* Dublin 1949. Pamphlets on gerrymandering, discrimination and partition by joint committee of all major parties in the South.

Catholic Committee Memorandum concerning the 1935 riots, privately circulated to British MPs. Printed but not published, Belfast 1935.

Harry Midgley, *Spain, the Press, the Pulpit and the Truth,* Belfast, September 1936.

National Council for Civil Liberties, *Report of a Commission of Enquiry Appointed to Examine the Purpose and Effect of the Civil Authorities (Special Powers) Acts 1922 and 1933* (Reprint of 1936 pamphlet), NCCL, London 1972.

Sean Og O Fearghail, *Law? and Orders,* Central Citizens' Defence Committee, Belfast 1970. Account of British Army's curfew of Lower Falls area of Belfast, July 1970.

'Peoples Democracy Militants Discuss Strategy' and Peter Gibbon, 'The Dialectic of Religion and Class in Ulster', in *New Left Review,* No.55, May-June 1969.

The Plain Truth, Campaign for Social Justice in Northern Ireland, Dungannon 1969. Outline of civil rights grievances in the North.

Peter Pyne, 'The 3rd Sinn Fein Party 1923-26', Part 2, in *Economic and Social Review*, Irish Institute of Social and Economic Research, Dublin, Vol.1, No.2, January 1970.

Revolutionary Marxist Group, *Irish Nationalism and British Imperialism* and *British Strategy in Northern Ireland*, Revolutionary Marxist Group, Dublin 1974-75.

District Inspector Spears, 'Memorandum to Northern Ireland Minister of Home Affairs, February 1923', Public Record Office, Northern Ireland, T 2258. Account of activities of Ulster Protestant Association – a Loyalist murder gang – in East Belfast 1920-23 and of eventual RUC action against them.

A.Wilson, *PR Urban Elections in Ulster 1920*, Electoral Reform Society, London 1972. Reprint.

Frank Wright, 'Protestant Ideology and Politics in Ulster' in *European Journal of Sociology*, XIV 1973.

Newspapers, Periodicals, etc.

Belfast Telegraph, Belfast. Moderate Unionist evening paper.

Irish News, Belfast. Nationalist and Catholic daily.

Newsletter, Belfast. Strongly Unionist daily.

Northern Whig, Belfast. Unionist daily. Closed down 1964.

Irish Independent, Dublin. Pro-Fine Gael daily.

Irish Press, Dublin. Pro-Fianna Fail daily.

Irish Times, Dublin. Serious daily. Formerly pro-Unionist, now liberal.

Derry Journal, Derry. Nationalist bi-weekly.

Londonderry Sentinel, Derry. Unionist weekly.

There are about 30 other weekly local papers in the North covering the six counties and most towns.

The Bell, Dublin, 1940-55. Liberal literary and political magazine. Edited for a time by Sean O'Faolain, then by Peadar O'Donnell.

Combat, Belfast, 1972 to date. Weekly paper of the UVF.

Fortnight, Belfast. Fortnightly current affairs magazine. Mildly liberal.

Free Citizen Unfree Citizen, Belfast, 1969 to date. Weekly paper of the Peoples Democracy.

Hibernia, Dublin. Fortnightly. Radical current affairs review.

International Socialism, London, 1960 to date. Theoretical journal of the International Socialists. Bi-monthly.

Irish Workers' Voice, Dublin. Revolutionary Workers Groups/Communist Party paper 1930-36. Reappeared as Irish Workers' Weekly 1939-41. Banned under Special Powers Act in the North in 1940 and re-named *Red Hand* but banned again.

Labour Progress, Belfast, 1941-47. Northern Ireland Labour Party paper.

Loyalist News, Belfast, 1969 to date. Weekly paper of Shankill Defence Association, then Red Hand Commandos (both Loyalist groups). Violently sectarian.

Newssheet, Belfast, 1950-53. Monthly paper of Irish Labour Party in North.

An Phoblacht, Dublin. IRA Paper 1925-37. 1970 to date, weekly paper of Provisional Sinn Fein.

The Plain People, Dublin 1922. Anti-Treaty IRA weekly.

Protestant Telegraph, Belfast, 1966 to date. Paisley's weekly paper. Violently sectarian and Loyalist.

Republican War News/Republican News, Belfast, 1970 to date. Weekly Northern paper of Provisional Sinn Fein. Belfast IRA paper 1939-43.

Socialist Forum, Belfast, 1946-48. Paper of left-wing group in Northern Ireland Labour Party.

An Solas/The Workers' Republic, London 1965–68, and *The Irish Militant* London, 1966-68. Papers of the marxist Irish Workers' Group.

The Ulster Protestant, Belfast, circa 1950-68. Paper of Norman Porter MP's Evangelical Protestant Society. Fiercely anti-Catholic.

United Irishman, Dublin. Monthly paper of Sinn Fein/IRA 1948-70. Now official Republican paper, 1970 to date.

Unity, Belfast, 1942-47 and 1962 to date. Communist Party weekly paper in Belfast.

Voice of the North, Belfast, 1969-71. Anti-Unionist weekly financed by Dublin government. Pro-Fianna Fail.

Index

Agnew, Paddy, 146,178
Alliance Party, 307,308,320,324,350;
  formation of, 300; and
  Executive, 310,312
Amalgamated Transport and
  General Workers' Union
  (ATGWU), 146,193,350
Ancient Order of Hibernians,
  66,69,136,350
Andrews, John Millar, 68,133,136,
  175,336; Prime Minister, 159;
  under attack, 160–1; resigns, 162
Anti-Partition League see Nationalist
  Party
Apprentice Boys, 25,199,240,246,
  259,350
Archdale, Edward Mervyn, 53,68,
  90,133
Ardoyne, 128,190,277,282; in 1969,
  258,259,262–3; in 1970, 272–3
Armagh City, 25,43,82–4,262;
  Civil rights demonstrations,
  245,248; South Armagh, 24,59,
  143,146,167,190,198,220,254,307
Assembly, Northern Ireland (1974),
  306,308–9; prorogued, 319
Attlee, Clement, 183,186,187

Babington, A.B. 123,139
Baird, James, 28,37,67,106,336
Baldwin, Stanley, 78,140,142
Ballymurphy see Belfast
Bates, Sir Richard Dawson, 45,50,
  58,68,82–3,93,96,123,336; made
  Minister of Home Affairs, 44;
  prejudiced against Catholics, 90;
  bans Orange parade, 138,140;
  re-introduces internment, 151
Beattie, Charles, 210
Beattie, Jack, 103,107,114,175,178,
  186,188,190,223–4,336; and
  unemployment, 119,122,124,126;
  expelled from Labour Party, 146,
  172; wins West Belfast, 161,171; on
  Midgley's defection, 163; defeated
  in Pottinger, 187; joins IrLP, 195
Belfast, growth of, 14,18; influx of
  Catholics, 16; Chamber of

Commerce, 60,68; Corporation,
  60,87,160,190,195,232
  rioting in, (19th century) 16;
  (1920–22) 29,31,34,41,42,43–4,
  45,49,55; (1932) 126,128–9;
  (1934–35) 137–9,140–2; (1964)
  234; (1966) 235; (1969) 255,258,
  259–60,262–3,265; (1970) 272–4;
  after internment (1971), 282–3
Ballymurphy, 272,275,282
Bone, the, 31,34,55,190
Falls Rd, 24,128,165,233–4,
  262–3; battle of the lower Falls
  (1970), 273–4
Crumlin Rd jail, 58,167,219
Shankill Rd, 128,139,262–3,266
Short Strand, 146,186; in 1920s,
  29,41,43–4,45,47,55; in 1932,
  128–9; in 1935, 139; in 1970, 273
York St, in 1920s, 40,42–3,44,47,
  56; in 1932, 128; in 1934–35,
  137–140; in the Blitz, 159
Belfast, boycott of, 32,48,52,55,61
Belfast constituencies:
  Dock, 114,143,146,190,244
  Falls, 23,99,115–16,178,224,254;
  by-election, 1942, 170–1
  Oldpark, 114,190,224,254
  Pottinger, 114,143,146,190,224,254
  West, 77,89,99,100,101,103,145;
  Beattie elected, 161,171; (1950–
  51) 195–6; (1955) 224; (1964)
  233–4; (1966) 244
Belfast Protestant Association, 28,233
Belleek Triangle, 59
Bing, Geoffrey, 181,195,198
Black and Tans, 34,47,350–1
Blaney, Neal, 231,260,268–9, 301,
  337
Bleakley, David, 194,225,243,337;
  joins Faulkner government, 278–9
Bloody Sunday (1972), 288–9
Blueshirts, 351
Boal, Desmond, 228,231,232,233,
  237–8,271,337; joins DUP, 291
Bogside see Derry City
Boland, Kevin, 260,268–9,337
Bone, the, see Belfast

Border poll, the, 300,306
Boundary Commission, 45,48,52,71, 72–6,102; at work, 76–8; boundary agreement, 78
Boyd, Billy, 225,232,233,243
Boyd, Tom, 237
Bradford, Roy, 312,315,318
British Army, Curragh mutiny, 20; in Derry 1920, 26; and UVF, 30; strength 1922, 49,61,74; and boundary crisis, 77; and strikes, 106,128,173; and 1935 riots, 139; training RUC Commandos, 200; and 1950s IRA campaign, 216; on standby, 1969, 259; intervenes on streets, 261–3; ambiguous role, 265; suppressing Catholics, 272–4; talking to Provos, 276; brutality, 283; strength 1971, 286; and Bloody Sunday, 289; Operation Motorman, 299; SAS and MRF, 302–3,361; clashes with Loyalists, 304, 305–6; and UWC stoppage, 317–20; GOC attacks government policy, 323; overall role, 325–6
Brooke, Sir Basil, see Brookeborough, Lord
Brooke, Captain John, 271,274
Brookeborough, Lord, 337; starts B Specials, 35; and Catholics, 90–1, 136–7,181,223; Craigavon's choice as successor, 159; strengthens position, 161; becomes Prime Minister, 162; and strikes, 174; and 1949 election, 183–4, 187,188; and Longstone Rd, 207,208; and 1950s IRA campaign, 215; opposes planning and economic co-operation, 227, 230; retires, 228
Browne, Noel, 182,183,198,337
B Specials see Ulster Special Constabulary
Bunting, Major Ronald, 248,249, 250,253,255,258
Burntollet ambush see Peoples Democracy
Byrne, Richard, 115–6,144,145,169, 170

Cahill, Joe, 282,295,312,338
Callaghan, James, 259,264,265,291
Cameron Commission, 89,247,252, 265

Campaign for Democracy in Ulster, 244,351
Campaign for Social Justice in Northern Ireland, 243,245,246, 351
Campbell, T.J. 116,142,144,145,169, 338; on abstentionism, 170–1; becomes a judge, 180
Carson, Edward junior, 187,235
Carson, Edward senior, 19,20,27–8, 30,36–7,338
Casualties, Belfast, (1920) 36; (1921) 46; Six counties (1920–22) 62; (1955–62) 221; (1971) 287; (1970–74) 313
Catholics, position in 19th century, 15; percentage in Ulster in 1911, 17; and RUC, 54; employment patterns, 91–2,241; and 2nd world war, 156; high birth-rate, 214,241–2; change from wanting reform of the state to wanting its destruction, 330
expelled from homes or jobs, (1920s) 28,29,31,40,41,44,53,54, 55,56,60,62; (1935) 139–40; (1939) 173; (1969–75) 259,263, 298,315; assassination of, 296–8, 303,305,313–5,323; retaliation for, 298,303
Catholic clergy, 66,100,101,134,267; and civil war, 62; and 1921 election, 67; and Nationalist party, 103,112–13,116,179; and Spanish civil war, 146; condemn IRA, 167,213
Catholic middle class, 60,69,98,102, 112, 120,144,170,223,238,275,302; new assertiveness in 1960s, 328–9
Catholic schools, 101–2,142,144,169, 180
Central Citizens' Defence Committee, 351–2
Chichester-Clark, Major James, 238,250,256,338; becomes Prime Minister, 257–8; and August 1969, 259–60,261,264; and Loyalist backlash, 271–2; declares war on Provos, 276; demands more repression, 277; resigns, 278
Christle, Joe, 214
Churchill, Winston, 39,49,53,59,61, 74,153–4; war-time telegram to De Valera, 164; victory speech, 176

Civil Rights Association, Northern Ireland (NICRA), 245–9,254–5, 258,260,274,282,285,288,289,357
Civil war, 61,75
Clann na Poblachta, 182,183,198, 205,212,217,352
Clonard, 29,128,263,276
Coalition government (Dublin), 1st, 183,198
Coalition government (Dublin), 2nd, 206,216; and 'aid' for North, 268–9; and Direct Rule, 293; acts against Provos, 301–2,322; meets Northern Executive, 315
Collins, Michael, 43,59,69,72,75,338; head of Provisional government, 47; pact with Craig, 47–8,52,53, 55,73; election pact with De Valera, 74
Commonwealth Labour Party, 172, 190,191
Communist Party, (1933–39), 135, 148,163,165,176,352; and 2nd world war, 172; and war-time strikes, 173,175; after 1945, 190, 191,245,254; British party, 182,188
Conlon, Malachy, 178,179,180,197, 198
Connellan, Joe, 198
Connolly, James, 339
Connolly, Roddy, 192–3,194
Conscription, 156–7,160
Conservative Government (1970–74), 273,277; Green paper (1972), 300–1; White paper (1973), 306–7
Conservative Party, 19,325
Constitution, Eire (1937), 147,205, 212
Convention, Northern Ireland (1975), 320,323,324
Cooper, Ivan, 248,254,260,275,339
Corkey, Rev Professor, 162
Cosgrave, Liam, 309–10, 311,339; and Northern constitution, 316; not interested in unity, 320; meets UDA men, 333
Cosgrave, William T. 75,76,78,79
Costello, John A. 183,184,212,215, 216
Council of Ireland, 23,48,78,306,310, 311,316,318
Craig, Charles Curtis, 23,73,75
Craig, Sir James see Craigavon, Lord
Craig, William, 276,278,291,316, 339–340; Minister of Home

Affairs, 243,244–5,246,247; sacked by O'Neill, 248; attacks Chichester-Clark, 271–2; and Vanguard, 292–3; 'liquidating the enemy', 296; and UWC stoppage, 318
Craigavon, Lord (Sir James Craig), 22,30,31,32,50,339; becomes Prime Minister, 37; negotiations with Lloyd George, 40,42,45,69, 70,71,72; pact with Collins, 47–8, 52,53,54,55,73; and arming Loyalists, 58; and Boundary Commission, 74,78; meets Cosgrave, 75,76,79; and discrimination, 90–1,137; and Protestant state, 92,136,141; and Nationalists, 107–8,117; and abolition of PR, 110–1, and strikes, 130,133; and 2nd world war, 157; dies, 159
Crumlin Rd jail see Belfast
Cunningham, Patrick, 145,178
Curfews, (1920–24) 31,57; (1932) 128–9,131; (1935) 138,139; (1942) 167; (1957) 217; (1970) 273–4
Curran, Major L.E. 85–6,181
Currie, Austin, 245,275,279,340; and Executive, 312,316

Dail Eireann, 352; established, 22, 27; 2nd Dail, 42,151; and Treaty, 47; and Boundary agreement, 79; Nationalists seek seats in, 198
Davison, Sir Joseph, 136–7,138,162
Defence of the Realm Act (DORA), 105,169,172–3,174
Democratic Unionist Party, 291,308, 352–3; and UUUC, 310
Demonstrations, anti-internment, 283,288–9,309; civil rights, 245, 246–8; Orange, 138,204,207–8, 213,222,258,259,272; see also Nationalist Party
Derry city, 18,25,78,94,114,181,245; nationalist majority, 24,188; Corporation, 25,84,89,204,248 rioting in (1920) 25–6; (1952) 203; (1969) 251,255,258,259–61 by-passed in development plans, 240–2; 5 October march, 246–7; 248; August 1969, 259–60; Cusack-Beattie shooting, 280 Bogside, 25,203,251,255,259–62; free area, 283

Derry, march to, see Peoples Democracy

De Valera, Eamon, 21,22,23,39–40, 340; negotiations with Lloyd George, 42,69,70,72; and the Treaty, 46,47; and Northern elections 1921, 67; pact with Collins, 74; jailed in North, 100; enters Dail, 110; talks with Devlin, 142; elected to Stormont, 143; and economic war, 147; suppresses IRA, 150,217; and neutrality, 153–4; and conscription, in the North, 160; and Churchill, 164; and partition, 183; President, 230

Devlin, Bernadette, 255,260,271,272, 288,289,340; defeated, 316

Devlin, Joe, 23,30,51,98,99,340; • talks with De Valera, 67,142; and social issues, 101,108,110,117, 120; and abstentionism, 102–3; takes seat, 107; and treatment of minority, 109,111; establishment of National League, 112–13; and Labour, 115; frustration with parliament, 118; dies, 143, policies, 144

Devlin, Paddy, 254,267,275,279,340; and Executive, 312

Diamond, Harry, 126,178,186,204, 233–4, 239, 340–1; elected 190; joins IrLP, 195; splits from IrLP, 223–4

Discrimination, religious, 16,81,86–91,136–7,140,169,227,242,265

Donald, Thompson, 30,34,53,64,103

Donnelly, Alexander, 144

Donnelly, Eamon, 170–1,178

Drumm, Maire, 280,301,341

Dublin, 18,289; bombs in, 301–2,318

Dungiven, 204,222,250,258

Easter Rising, 1916,20

Economy, Northern Ireland, 225, 227,231,326; development schemes, 227–8,229, 240–1; imbalance between East and West, 240

Economy, Southern, 230–1,328

Eden, Sir Anthony, 215,216

Education policy, 101–2,117

Elections:
local government, 85,131–2,190, 195,224; (1920) 24–5,27,105–6;
(1924) 84; (1973) 300,307–8
Northern Ireland parliament, (1921) 37,66–7; (1925) 77,102–3; (1929) 114–6; (1933) 143; (1938) 145–6; (1945) 177–8,190; (1949) 184–8,194; (1953) 205,207,208, 224; (1958) 219,222,224; (1962) 228; (1965) 232; (1969) 253–4
Northern Ireland Assembly, 308
Northern Ireland Convention, 324
Dail Eireann, (1948) 182–3; (1957) 217–8; (1961) 220
Westminster parliament, (1918) 21; (1922–24) 99,100; (1925) 116–7; (1935) 145; (1945) 178; (1955) 209–10; (1959) 220; (1964) 232,233–4; (1974) 315–6,320–1

Engineering industry, 14,18,227

Enniskillen, 25,84,88,199,200

Executions, 75,153,156,164,165–6

Executive, Northern Ireland, 306, 310; members, 312; meets Dublin government, 315; collapses, 319–20

Farrell, Michael, 249,253,282,309

Faulkner, Brian, 188,208,220,222, 228,264,341; rival to O'Neill, 229,230,232,238; resigns from Cabinet (1969), 252; and 1969 election, 253–4,256; defeated for Prime Minister, 257; joins Chichester-Clark's Cabinet, 258; Prime Minister, 278; and committee system, 279–80; and internment, 281,283; appoints Catholic advisor, 287; and tripartite talks, 288; and suspension of Stormont, 290–1; speaks at Vanguard rally, 293; and White paper, 307; and Assembly, 308–9; Chief Executive, 310,312; resigns, 319

Faulkner Unionists see Unionist Party of Northern Ireland

Fermanagh, County, 77,78,87,114; nationalist majority, 24,77,88,188; County Council, 25,82,84,86

Fermanagh/South Tyrone constituency, formerly Fermanagh and Tyrone, 99,100,103,145,197,209–10,220,316

Fianna Fail, 110,119,170,182–3,184, 217,353; and IRA (1969–70), 268–9

Fine Gael, 183,310,353

Fitt, Gerry, 239,244,245,246,267, 280,341; leader of SDLP, 275; deputy Chief Executive, 310,312

Flags and Emblems Act, 95,207

Forrest, George, 210–11

Franchise, for local elections, 84–5, 88,181; 'One Man, One Vote', 243,248,252,253,256,278,300

Freeland, General, 272,273

Free State Army see Irish Army

Friends of Ireland group, 181–2,188, 197,244,353

Gardai, the, 133,134,155,212,353; and RUC, 315

Geehan, Tommy, 125–8,130,131,341

Gerrymandering, 83–6,89,114,181, 265

Getgood, Bob, 193–4

Goulding, Cathal, 209,268,341

Government of Ireland Act, 23,188

Graham, John, 164,167,341–42

Grant, William, 40,95,106,162,342

Griffith, Arthur, 47,53,69,70–1,72,75

Gyle, James, 107,111,114,144

Hall Thompson, Colonel, 187,196–7, 207–8

Hanna, Frank, 180,186,194,195, 223–4,239,342

Hanna, GeorgeB. junior, 208

Hanna, GeorgeB. senior, 94

Hanna, Rev Hugh, 16,233

Hanna, John, 28,37,67,342

Harbinson, T.J.S. 69,99,112,116–7, 342

Haughey, Charles, 260,268–70,342

Healy, Cahir, 99,111,112,118,120, 145,180,198,200,204,209,342; interned, (1922) 58, (1941) 169; and Nationalist frustration, 144, 197

Heath, Edward, 277,278,281; and tripartite meeting, 288; and suspension of Stormont, 290–1; meets Lynch, 300,301; meets Cosgrave, 309–10; and Sunningdale, 311

Henderson, George, 104,107,111

Henderson, Tommy, 108,115,119, 143,160,343

Henry, Sir Denis, 89–90,343

Herron, Tommy, 304–5,343

Hibernians see Ancient Order of Hibernians

Holmes, Harry, 224

Home Rule Bills, (1886) 15–6; (1893) 16; (1911–12) 19,20

Home Secretary, British, 181,186, 195–6,215,244

Housing, 87,159–60,227

Hull, Billy, 277,291,292,317,343

Hume, John, 248,254,260,279,280, 285,343

Hunger strikes, 155,182,301,309

Hunt Committee, 95,96

IRA, (1919–22), 354; formed, 23; in Derry, 25–6,34; and Truce, 41; and attacks on Catholics, 44; and the Treaty, 46,70–1,52; takes Loyalists hostage, 48–9; resumes attacks in the North, 51; Bandon killings, 56; incendiary campaign, 57–60; outlawed in North, 58; and Belleek Triangle, 59; and civil war, 61; and strikes, 129,133; and Republican Congress, 148; back to physical force, 149–51,176; bombing campaign in Britain, (1939–40) 152–3; and Germany, 154; war-time campaign in Ireland, 154–6,164–8,177; Protestant members, 164–5; reorganising, 201; 1950s campaign, 202,209,210,214–15,216–30; reasons for its failure, 231; and August 1969, 262–3,267; splits (1970), 268,270–1; Officials, 270–1, 354–5; defend the lower Falls, 273–4; military campaign (1971–2), 283,286–7, 290,293; cease-fire, 294 Provisionals, 354–5; policy statements, 270–1; defending the ghettos, 272–3; military campaign, 275–6,277,279,281,282–4,286–7, 290; peace conditions, 285; and Direct Rule, 293; cease-fire and negotiations (1972), 295; ceasefire ends, 298; Bloody Friday, 299; resumed campaign, 302,313; and Libya, 312; cease-fire (1975), 322–3

Independent Labour Party (ILP), 353–54

Industry, development of, in the North, 14,18–19; in the South, 18–19

Internment, in the North, 94–5
   (1920–21) 47, (1922–24) 58,61,65;
   (1938–45) 151,155,156,167,168;
   (1956–61) 216,219,220; (1969)
   262,264; (1971–75) 276,278,281,
   286,290,293; Loyalists interned,
   63–4,305,306; Germans and
   Italians interned, 157; Labour
   Party and, 225; women interned,
   316,323; in the South, 154,167,
   168,216,218,220
Ireland, Denis, 164,183
Irish Army, 61,133,155,260,261,295
Irish Citizen Army, 354
Irish Congress of Trade Unions
   (ICTU), formerly ITUC, 33,156,
   165,214,243,279,355; recognised
   by Northern government, 229;
   and UWC stoppage, 317–8
Irish Labour Party (IrLP), 183,184,
   192,354; in the North, 194–5,199,
   223–4,244; and 3rd Coalition
   government in the South, 310
Irish News, the, 112,116,118,179
Irish Republican Army see IRA
Irish Republican Brotherhood, 355
Irish Transport and General
   Workers' Union, 33,166,355
Irish Volunteers, 355–6

Kelly, Liam, 205–6,213,219,220,343
Kilfedder, James, 233–4
Kyle, Sam, 103,106,107,114,123,343

Labour, Anti-Partition, 185–6,187,
   190,193,194
Labour Government, (1945–51)
   99,177,178,181,188,189,200;
   (1964–70) 230,234, puts pressure
   on Stormont, 243,244,247,249,
   264–5; (1974–) and UWC
   stoppage, 318–9; White paper,
   320; 'anti-terrorist' law, 322
Labour Party, British, 76,117,187,
   191,193,194,210,287
Labour Party, Northern Ireland,
   27,28,100,101,105–6,131,160,165,
   357; and 1921 election, 37,66–7;
   and 1925 election, 77,98,103–4;
   and Partition, 106–7,192–4,196,
   225,232; in parliament, 107;
   support PR, 111; and 1929
   election, 114–5; and Nationalists,
   115–6,146,169; and unemployment, 122–3,125,129; and 1933

election, 143; Midgley leaves,
   171–2; and 1945 election, 190;
   and 1949 election, 185,187; splits
   over Partition, 194–5; after 1949,
   224; wins 4 seats in 1958 election,
   225–6; and 1962 election, 228;
   loses 2 seats in 1965 election, 232;
   and civil rights, 242–3,244,245;
   and 1969 election, 254; and
   Bleakley in government, 279; and
   local elections (1973), 308; and
   Convention elections, 324; work-
   ing-class unity frustrated by
   Protestant supremacy, 327; see
   also Commonwealth Labour Party,
   Irish Labour Party and
   Republican Labour Party
Labour Unionists see Unionist
   Labour Association
Law, Bonar, 19,75
Law, Common, enforcement in
   North and South, 311,315,316,322,
   333
Leeke, George, 108,117,145
Lemass, Sean, 230,231,343–44
Liberal Party, British, 16; Northern
   Ireland, 114,116,117
Linen industry, 14,18,225
Lisburn, 30–1
Lloyd George, D. 23,40,42,70–3,75,
   77
Local Defence Volunteers see
   Ulster Special Constabulary
Local government, nationalist
   victories (1920), 25; Councils
   suspended, 82–3,286; boundaries
   re-drawn, 83–4; see also Elections
Londonderry, Marquis of, 51,68,73,
   344
Long, William, 250,274
Longstone Road (Co. Down), 207–8,
   213,222
Lowry, William, 162,166,174
Lynch, Jack, 247,261,268–9,274,313,
   344; and internment, 276,283;
   tripartite talks, 288, meets Heath,
   300–1

McAleer, Hugh K. 144
McAllister, T.S. 107,109,112,113,
   170,180
McAteer, Eddie, 178,180,199,200,
   203–4,234,243,246,344; opposition
   leader, 239; and march to Derry,
   249; defeated, 254

McAteer, Hugh, 164,167,168,178, 234, 344

McBride, Sean, 142,165,184,197, 344; forms Clann na Poblachta, 182; joins 1st Coalition in South, 183; and Saor Uladh, 205–6; brings down government, 216; defeated, 217

McCaughey, Sean, 164,182

McDermott, J.C. 158,162,165

MacDonald, Ramsay, 17,76,117

McGleenan, Charles, 198,205,219

McGuffin, Sam, 40,64

McGurk, Michael, 169–70,179

McKay, Charles, 27,28,106

McKeague, John, 258,265,266–7, 306,345

McKee, Billy, 267,268,273,276

Mackie's engineering firm, 18,29,91, 173, 174

McMahon murders, 51

McManaway, Rev Godfrey, 181, 195–6,199,345

McManus, Frank 285,288,316

McMullen William, 103–4,107, 115–16,122,124,134,345

McNeill, Eoin, 76,78

McQuade, John, 232,271,291

Macready, Sir Neville, 35,39,47

McSparran, James, 179,180,186,219

MacStiofain, Sean, 209,268,270,295, 301,345

Maginess, Brian, 162,207–8,222

Magougan, Jack, 191,192,195,223–4

Mallon, Kevin, 218–9,312

Malvern St shooting, 236–7,244

Mansion House Anti-Partition Committee, 184–6,197,356

Maudling, Reginald, 273,276,277, 280,289,290

Maxwell, Patrick, 144,145,181,196

Midgley, Harry, 37,67,100,107,191, 221,345; elected, 143; and Spain, 146; wins Willowfield by-election, 160; joins Brooke's government, 162; leaves Labour party, 171–2, and strikes, 173; leaves Cabinet, 190; joins Unionist party, 187,192

Mid-Ulster constituency, 197,209–11, 220,255,316

Minford, Nat, 208,309

Mitchell, Tom, 209–11,220

Morgan, William, 238,253

Mulvey, Anthony, 145,178,188,198

NICRA see Civil Rights Association, Northern Ireland

National Council for Civil Liberties (British), 96–7, 140–2

National Democratic Party see Nationalist Party

Nationalist Party, 356; United Irish League and up to 1928, 17, 21,98,99,101,364 and 1921 election, 37,66–7,69; and 1925 election, 77,102–3; enter parliament, 107–10; National League of the North, established, 111–13, 356–7; and 1929 election, 114; and Labour, 115–6; policies, 117; walk-out of parliament, 118–19; return, 142; creeping abstentionism, 144–5; disintegrating, 146, 169; and Tom Williams case, 166; and Falls by-election (1942), 170–1; and 1945 election, 177–8; take their seats again, 178; Anti-Partition League, formed, 179–80; and 1949 election, 185–8; frustration and confusion, 181, 197–8,201; demonstrations, 199–200,203,206,207; challenged by Saor Uladh and Sinn Fein, 205, 209–11; and 1950s IRA campaign, 213,219; and National Unity, 238–9; Nationalist Party, as official opposition, 239–40,243, 246; lose 3 seats in 1969 election, 253–4; and Alternative Assembly, 285, and Assembly election, 308; National Democratic Party, 239, 275,356; all attempts to get reforms within the system frustrated, 327–8; Nationalist policy statements, 113–14, 119–20,185–6, 204,239

Neill, Ivan, 213–4,238

Newry, 24,25,85,188,190,195,206, 217,241,286; civil rights march 1969, 252; march after Bloody Sunday, 289

Nixon, District Inspector, 58,96,115, 119,143,346

Nixon, Robert, 225,232,238

'No-Go' areas, 265,267,276,297,299

Northern Ireland government, appoints military advisor, 54; indemnifies its agents, 58; and Protestant violence, 62–4; composition, (1921) 68, (1941) 159,

(1943) 162, (1949) 196; wants conscription, 156; and family allowances, 213–14

Northern Resistance Movement (NRM), 285,286,288,357

O'Bradaigh Ruadhri, 217,270,280, 295, 301,346

O'Brien, Conor Cruise, 310,333

O'Conaill, Daithi, 295,333,346

O'Duffy, Eoin, 41,43,169,346

Offences Against the State Act, 154, 216; Special Criminal Court, 295; amendment to act, 301

O'Hanlon, Fergal, 216,217

O'Higgins, Kevin, 53,75,78

O'Mahony, Sean, 69,99

O'Neill, Michael, 210–11

O'Neill, Patrick, 108,112

O'Neill, Terence, 346; becomes Prime Minister, 228–9; meets Lemass, 231; and 1965 election, 232; and Divis St riots, 234; plots against, 237–8; and Catholics, 240,256; pressed by Wilson, 247; reform package and TV speech, 248–9; and march to Derry, 251; and Faulkner, 252; and 1969 election, 253–4; announces 'One Man, One Vote', 255; resigns, 256

Orange Order, 92,140,141,144,276, 280,307,357–8; founded, 14; Liberal Unionists join it, 15–16; and 1921 elections, 67, and RUC, 96; and education, 102,117,197; O'Neill and, 228,240; and Vanguard, 292; Orangeism prevents all efforts to reform and stabilise the state, 331; see also Demonstrations, Orange

Outdoor Relief (ODR) strike see Strikes

Paisley, Ian, 232–4,236–7,245,318, 347; jailed, 235,255; and *Protestant Telegraph*, 235,237,255,266; and civil rights marches, 248–50; challenges O'Neill in 1969 election, 253; elected to Stormont and Westminster, 272; warns about Direct Rule, 288; and DUP, 291; and 1974 elections, 315

Parker, Mrs Dehra, 162,257

Parliament, Northern Ireland,

opened, 39,67,69; social composition (1921), 69; opposition suspended, 111; opposition walks out, 119; move to Stormont, 119; life of parliament extended, 177; sit-down protest, 255; opposition boycott (1969), 261,263; (1971), 280–1; parliament suspended, 290–1

Parliamentary abstentions:
Dail Eireann, 98–9,110
Northern Ireland parliament, 67, 98,102–3,118–19,142,143,144–6, 169–71,177,198,205,270,281
Westminster parliament, 145,177, 197–8

Partition, 22,23,47,67,147,170,177, 179,183,185,186,189,197

Peoples Democracy, 255,258,285, 295,358; founded 247; march to Derry, 249–52; and 1969 election, 253–4; and August 1969, 260,263, 269; members interned, 282

Philbin, Dr William, 267,275

Plantation of Ulster, 13

Political prisoners, 47,53,54,55,61, 182,183,323

Poor Law Guardians, 117,124,125, 128,130,358

Porter, Norman, 208,222,232,347

Porter, Robert, 259,264,275

Powell, Enoch, 316,332

Power-sharing, 300,323

Proportional representation, for local elections, 24,83,300; for parliamentary elections, 66,110,111,116

Protestants, percentage in Ulster (1911), 17; in 6 counties, 24; Protestant supremacy, 14,17,54, 81,141,234,256; decline of Protestant liberalism, 15–17; Protestant workers, 16,19,104,121, 130,131,227,230,233,291–2; Protestant churches, 67; and education, 101–2,117,185,196–7; and Tom Williams, 165

Protestant Telegraph see Paisley, Ian

Provisional government (Dublin), 47,52,58–9,358–9; and civil war, 61; supported by business class, 75; suppresses IRA, 150, 154,164, 217,220

Provisionals see IRA and Sinn Fein

Public Order Act (1951), 95,200,203; amendment, 254,271

Queen's University, Belfast see Universities

RUC, 359–60; established, 47,54; character and composition, 96–7; Commando or reserve force, 96, 200,203,213,218,246,251,255; and ODR strike, 126–9,131; and other strikes, 133–4,191; and 1935 riots, 138–40; and Nationalist demonstrations, 199,200,203,206,208; brutality, 218,219; and Dungiven, 222; and Divis St riots, 233–4; and civil rights demonstrations, 246–52,265; and Bogside siege, 259–60,261; in Belfast, August 1969, 262–3; disarmed, 266; 'conspiracy of silence', 271; and Gardai, 315; and UWC stoppage, 317–8; and 'For Ulster' group, 319; strength in 1975, 332
Rebellion, 1798 see United Irishmen
Redmond, John, 17,20,21,347
Rees, Merlyn, 318,319,322
Rent and rates strike, 283,312,316
Reprisals by police and Specials, (1920–22) 34–6,40,51,53,57,59,70; (1970s) 305,313
Republican Congress, 148,359
Republican Labour Party, 359
Republicans see Sinn Fein
Revolutionary Workers' Groups, 125,126,127,128,129,133,134,135, 359
Rising, 1916, 20
Royal Irish Constabulary (RIC), 23,25–6,34,35,47,54,359
Royal Ulster Constabulary see RUC
Russell, Sean, 151

Sandy Row, 27,139,235
Saor Eire, 360
Saor Uladh, 205–6,213,219,360; military campaign, 212,214,217, 219,221
Senate, Northern Ireland, 68–9,109, 118; Southern, 183,206,213
Shankill Rd see Belfast
Shipyards, 18,124,159,173–5,225, 227,237; Catholics in, 16,91; Catholics expelled from, 28,48, 139,173; workers, 26,37,106,124, 277,291; see also Strikes
Short and Harlands aircraft factory, 159,173,174–5,191,291

Sinclair, Betty, 126,172,254,347
Sinn Fein, 17,20,215,360–1; and elections, (1918) 21; (1921) 37,39,66–7,69; (1924) 99–100; (1925) 103; (1929) 114; (1933) 142–3; (1935) 145; (1955) 209–10; (1957) in the South, 216–17; (1958–59) 219–220; (1964) 233–4; and first Dail, 22; and the Treaty, 46,70–1; anti-Treaty wing, 52; banned, 213; swing to social agitation, 244–5; split (1970) 270–1
Officials, 308,324;
Provisionals, 280,285,301; boycott elections, 307,308,324; incident centres, 323; and Loyalist paramilitaries, 333; political confusion, 334–5
Smyth, Colonel, 28
Social Democratic and Labour Party (SDLP), 361; formed, 275; and Faulkner's committees, 279; withdraw from Stormont, 280–1; and Alternative Assembly, 285–6; and Direct Rule, 293; negotiate with Whitelaw, 299; policy statement, 300; and local elections (1973), 307; and Assembly election, 308; and Executive, 310,312; and UWC stoppage, 319; and Convention election, 324
Social services, 177,189,213–14,238; unemployment relief, 121–2; outdoor relief, 122–3,124–5,127, 130
Socialist Republican Party, 178,179, 180,190,195,361
South, Sean, 216
Spanish civil war, 146,148,150
Special Air Services Regiment (SAS) see British Army
Special Powers Act, 57,123,127,142, 172,199,200,213; introduced, 50, 54; provisions, 93–4,156; papers banned, 94,172; exclusion orders, 100,131,135; inquest prohibited, 166; UVF banned, 236; Republican Clubs banned, 244
Spence, Gusty, 236–7,347
Spender, Col. Wilfred, 30
Steele, Jimmy, 149,167–8
Stewart, Joe, 142,145,170,205, 347–48
Strabane, 25,85,241,286

Strikes, (1919) 27,104–6; ODR strike (1932) 125–32, 358; railway strike (1933), 132–5; engineering strikes (1942 and 1944), 173–5; post-war strikes, 191; Loyalist strikes see Workers, Loyalist Association of

Sunningdale Agreement, 310–11,320

Taylor, John, 275,281,289,348
Teevan, Tom, 89,196
Tone, Wolfe, 348
Topping, W.W.B. 222
Trade unions, 17,130; and expulsion of Catholic workers, 33–4; Belfast Trades Council, 122,124, 142,173,175; shop stewards, 173–5
Treaty, the, 45,46,47,69–72
Tricolour, the, 199,200,203,206,207, 233–4,260
Truce, the (1921), 40,41
Twaddell, W.J. 57
Twomey, Seamus, 268,295,312,348
Tyrone, County, 73,78; nationalist majority, 24,77,188; county council, 25,82,84

Ulster Constitution Defence Committee, and Ulster Protestant Volunteers, 235,237,246,266,362
Ulster Defence Association (UDA), 296–8,303,316,361; Shankill Defence Association, 258–9; UDA set up, 292; two-day war with British army, 304; internal feuds, 304–5; and UFF, 313–4, 362; and UWC stoppage, 317–9
Ulster Defence Regiment, 266,277, 304,305,361–2; and UWC stoppage, 319
Ulster Freedom Fighters (UFF) see UDA
Ulster Protestant Action, 233,236,362
Ulster Protestant Association, 63–4, 362
Ulster Protestant League, 131,136, 137,138,140,143,233,362
Ulster Protestant Volunteers (UPV), see Ulster Constitution Defence Committee
Ulster Special Constabulary, 362–3; formed, 31–2,35,36,41; Wickham circular, 44–5; equipped by Britain, 47; Cloncs incident, 49,55;

strength in 1922, 49–50,61; methods, 51; and RUC, 54; and pogroms, 56; and Belleek, 59; Specials interned, 64; and Boundary crisis, 78–9; A Specials disbanded, 80; Specials entirely Protestant, 95–6; and Local Defence Volunteers, 157,168,356; shooting incidents in 1950s, 211; strength in 1958, 218; mobilised 1966, 235; and Burntollet ambush, 251; and 1969 Troubles, 258, 259–60,261,262,264; Cameron Report and disbandment, 265–6
Ulster Union Club, 164,165,179, 183,363
Ulster Unionist Council see Unionist Party
Ulster Volunteer Force (UVF), 363–4; formed, 19; and Derry riots (1920), 25–6; re-organised, 30; and Specials, 35,44–5,95; re-formed 1966, anti-O'Neill bombings, 255–6,266–7; and UDR, 304, 'cease-fire', 314
Ulster Workers' Council see Workers, Loyalist Association of
Unemployment, 29,92,101,115,147, 158,225,228; agitation, 117,121–32; unemployed workers' committee, 122,124
Unemployment relief see Social services
Unionist Labour Association, 68,106,123,363
Unionist Party, formed, 16; and 1912 Home Rule Bill, 19; and 1918 election, 21; abandons three counties, 24; and 1921 election, 37,66–7; and Craig-Collins pact, 53; and 1925 election, 77; and Specials, 95; and 1924 election, 100; Protestant clergy as MPs, 103,162,181; and ODR strike, 129; backbench revolt against Andrews, 158–62; and 1949 election, 185–8; and Catholics, 222–3; revolt against Brookeborough, 228; and changing power-structure, 230; and Lemass-O'Neill talks, 231–2; anti-O'Neill revolts, 237–8; and 'One Man, One Vote', 252,256, 258; and 1969 election, 253–4; and Chichester-Clark, 272,276;

and Vanguard, 292; and White
paper (1973), 307; and Assembly
election, 308; Faulkner ousted,
315; use of sectarianism, 326–7;
shackled by Orange ideology,
329–30
Independent Unionists, 77,104,
107,110,114–5,117,143,144,159,
208,222
Progressive Unionists, 146–7,358
Protestant Unionists, 237,253,358
Unionist Party of Northern Ireland,
and Faulkner Unionists, 309–10,
312,318,364; and 1974 elections,
315–16,320; leave Executive, 319;
and Convention election, 324
United Irish League see Nationalist
Party
United Irishmen, 13–14,148,364–5
United States troops, 163
United Ulster Unionist Coalition,
(UUUC), 365; formed, 310; and
1974 elections, 315–6,320–1; and
UWC stoppage, 317–9; and
Convention election, 324
Universities, Queen's University,
Belfast, 66,132,178,183,245,247;
New University of Ulster,
Coleraine, 229,241

Vanguard, 292–3,296,305–6,365;
becomes a party, 307,308; and
UUUC, 310

Warnock, Edmond, 158,162,199,
230,231,237,348
West, Harry, 231,271,276,318,324,
348; dismissed by O'Neill, 238;
in Faulkner government, 278;
hard-line leader, 308; and UUUC,
310; Unionist leader, 315
Whitelaw, William, 290–1,299,349;
negotiates with Provos, 295; and
Darlington talks, 300
Wickham, Sir Charles, 44, 96, 127,
349
Williams, Tom, 165, 349
Wilson, Harold, 231,235,244,259,
316; pressurises Stormont, 247,
258; summons Chichester-Clark,
264; proposed solution to Northern
problem, 287–8; and UWC
stoppage, 319; and Convention,
323
Wilson, Sir Henry, 20,47,49,60,95,
349
Workers, Loyalist Association of
(LAW), and Ulster Workers'
Council (UWC), 277,291–2,364;
calls strikes, 293,305–6; LAW
collapses, 317; UWC stoppage,
317–19
Workhouse, the, 122,124,125,126–7
World War, Second, effect on North,
157–8,159–60,163

Young, Sir Arthur, 266,267,272
Young Socialists, 245,246,247,365

44-202

TY LIBRARY
C001
ORANGE STATE

AWN

3>C1/

3>C1/

MILLIKIN UNIVER

NORTHERN IRELAND TH

WITHDR

/DA990.U46F